European Transport Economics

European Transport Economics

Edited by
Jacob Polak and Arnold Heertje

BLACKWELL
Oxford UK & Cambridge USA

First published 1993

Blackwell Publishers
108 Cowley Road
Oxford OX4 1JF
UK

238 Main Street,
Cambridge, Massachusetts 02142
USA

British Library Cataloguing in Publication Data

A CIP catalogue record for this book is available from the British Library.

Library of Congress Cataloging-in-Publication Data
European transport economics/edited by Jacob
Polak and Arnold Heertje.
p. cm.
Published to celebrate the 40th anniversary in 1993 of the
European Conference of Ministers of Transport (ECMT).
Includes bibliographical references and index.
ISBN 0-631-19058-9
1. Transportation—Europe. 2. Transportation and State—Europe.
I. Polak, J.B., 1933– . II. Heertje, Arnold
HE242.A2E95 1993
388′. 094—dc20 92–44818
CIP

Typeset in 10 on 12pt Ehrhardt
by Graphicraft Typesetters Ltd., Hong Kong
Printed in Great Britain by T.J. Press (Padstow) Ltd., Padstow, Cornwall

This book is printed on acid-free paper

Contents

List of Figures

List of Tables

List of Contributors

Herbert Baum, Professor of Economics and Director of the Institute for Transport Economics, University of Cologne

Brian Bayliss, Professor of Business Economics and Director of the Centre for European Industrial Studies, University of Bath

A. De Waele, Head of the Economic Research Division of the ECMT

Manfred M. Fischer, Professor of Geography and Head of the Department of Economic and Social Geography, Vienna University of Economics and Business Administration

G.A. Giannopoulos, Professor of Transportation Engineering, University of Thessaloniki

K.M. Gwilliam, Professor of Transportation Economics and Director of the Rotterdam Transport Centre, Erasmus University

Jan Owen Jansson, Research Leader at the Swedish Road and Traffic Research Institute, Linköping, and visiting Professor of Transport Economics at the University of Linköping

Peter Nijkamp, Professor of Regional, Urban and Environmental Economics and Economic Geography, Free University of Amsterdam

E. Quinet, Professor, Ecole Nationale des Ponts et Chaussées, Paris

Piet Rietveld, Professor of Transport Economics, Free University of Amsterdam

Werner Rothengatter, Professor of Economics, University of Karlsruhe and Head of the Institute for Economic Policy Research and the Division of Transport and Communication

Preface

In 1993 the European Conference of Ministers of Transport (ECMT) will celebrate its fortieth anniversary. It came into being on 17 October 1953 when its protocol was signed in Brussels by the Ministers of Transport – or their representatives – of 16 Western European countries, the Conference's founding Members.

At that time Western Europe was still in the process of reconstructing its inland transport system. It was also looking for new forms of co-operation for the shaping of policy. To get a clearer perspective, it should be recalled, for example, that the Treaty of Rome was not to be signed until four years later. It was also a time at which the railways – still largely relying on steam traction – accounted for the bulk of inland transport activity.

In the meantime, of course, the history of the transport sector has changed course radically from the technological, economic and policy standpoints, perhaps the most striking feature being the spectacular growth in the carriage of passengers and goods by road and all the accompanying problems that have in many cases progressively become more and more serious in spheres such as safety, environmental damage, energy consumption, infrastructure congestion, the organization of urban travel and many others.

At the same time, however, in the past 40 years in Europe we have seen the introduction of loading units (and of large containers in particular, heralded as symbols of a third Industrial Revolution in the field of transport), of the pusher technique on waterways and, more recently, of the high-speed train that has given the old wheel-on-rail technique a new lease of life – all of which has been accompanied by a steady increase in automation and in the use of information technology and logistical methods in inland transport.

Much progress has also been made in transport economics and in the knowledge of its mechanisms and particular characteristics. Originally seen more as an ancillary branch of economic research, based to some extent on an empirical approach, transport economics has gradually gained recognition and paved the way towards scientifically sound theoretical work and modelling techniques.

The ECMT very soon realized the importance of economic research as a means of establishing guidelines for the policy decisions that have to be taken in an increasingly complex sphere in which there are severe constraints.

Accordingly, on the advice of Louis Armand of the Académie Française, the Conference set up an Economic Research and Documentation Centre as early as its tenth anniversary celebrated in Brussels in 1963, a Centre that has since done a great deal to promote co-operation within the international research community. By organizing symposia, round tables and seminars, it has not only stimulated the most advanced research but has also provided an appropriate forum for the researchers themselves to get together and further knowledge in specific fields.

Now, looking back after some decades, there is no denying the fact that, within the concert of intergovernmental organizations concerned with transport, the ECMT has clearly been able to make a most significant contribution on the strength of its economic research.

The pattern of development of co-operation in the policy sphere has also been marked by fundamental changes. In the early years some of the ECMT countries formed the core for the Community of Six which step by step became the Community of Twelve, a development that was broadened with the conclusion in 1991 of the Agreement on 'the European Economic Area' and now embraces 17 ECMT member countries.

However, while such co-operation at policy-making level had been conditioned for many years by the East–West split in Europe, it has rapidly assumed a very different pattern in the light of the events of the recent past, more particularly by enabling the Conference to open up towards the countries of central and Eastern Europe. In so doing the ECMT, among other things, increased its member countries by almost one-half in less than three years, a process that has itself been a source of adjustment problems.

After 40 years' activity then, the Conference sees encouraging prospects ahead, but the question of the right course for the future requires pause for thought.

Given that the protocol establishing the ECMT provides for a remarkable degree of flexibility, the Conference will quite clearly be able to cope with the foreseeable changes. It must, however, remain true to its own specific function, that of providing member countries' Ministers responsible for inland transport with a forum for co-operation, consultation and an exchange of views unfettered by unduly formal legal requirements.

It is this particular asset – together with the contribution made in terms of economic research – that secures for the ECMT its own scope for action among the various international bodies concerned with transport.

There are, of course, a number of ways in which an anniversary can be celebrated. Obviously it could be marked by a specific celebratory event and there is of course a tradition of doing this. But we believe that at such a time it is appropriate to associate the celebration proper with an exercise involving a deeper and more analytical approach, an approach that we in the ECMT have here preferred in view of the many matters of major concern now affecting our economies and, indeed, our societies as a whole, and which have a bearing on developments in the transport sector.

The idea of publishing a book in fact originated in a meeting in 1991 between J.C. Terlouw, then Secretary-General of the ECMT, A. Heertje and J.B. Polak (both faculty members at the University of Amsterdam, the latter also at the University of Groningen), the aim being to celebrate the anniversary by compiling articles by selected specialists from a number of different member countries, articles designed to take a comprehensive view of the major problems in the transport sector, of the situation prevailing in this final decade of the twentieth century and, accordingly, of what the future holds in store for us. A total of ten such articles is included in this volume, together with two others which serve to introduce the volume and bring it to a conclusion.

It is my hope that this book, the product of their initiative, will enable readers to get a better understanding of a number of issues representative of matters of current concern from the standpoint of both theory and practice in the transport sector and of their many technical, economic and policy aspects and interrelationships. In summary, I hope that it will help to pave the way towards our mastery of the new situation that now prevails in the transport sector in Europe.

Dr Gerhard Aurbach
Secretary-General of the ECMT

1

Introduction

Jacob Polak

Little doubt exists that transport economics has become an important branch of economics. Its significance manifests itself on a number of levels.

First, in the practical sphere transport is becoming more and more a source of often heated debate. The reason for this is easily understood. The widely experienced advantages of mobility, both of persons and of goods, are continuously at loggerheads with other human values, in particular those concerning the environment.

Second, at the policy level many major decisions have to be taken. These include setting priorities for the improvement of networks for the various forms of transport – and finding solutions for the problem of their finance – and promoting new methods of transport, both of a technical nature and of an organizational nature. At a more general level the decision about whether government should play an active role in transport or should mainly rely on market forces could have a marked impact on society. Of similar strategic importance is whether governments will decide to abandon a narrow sectoral approach and proceed in a more integrated manner, which will also encompass considerations of physical planning, of impacts on the environment and of implications for those working in the transport industry.

Lastly, from the point of view of economic theory many intriguing questions are at issue, such as the nature of cost functions, especially in multi-product firms, conditions for competitive markets (including the 'contestability issue', possibilities for and consequences of differential pricing in non-competitive markets, the influence of imperfect information on the behaviour of both households and firms and the conditions for optimum welfare from the point of view of society, including the difficulty of how to take account of external effects and the validity of traditional trade theory. Taking into account only these few examples it is already clear that, as with economics in general, transport economics in recent years has witnessed a marked revival and is now again in full swing. For many economists, both theoreticians and practicians, the study of the often complex problems of transport economics is a most challenging task. It is fortunate that these challenges are being met at present on a broad front and that excellent results are being obtained.

This book's objective is to report on these results. Its main intention is to provide a state of the art account of recent developments in transport economics. In addition to this the book aims at opening up prospectives for future research and contributing to the improvement of decision making in the political sphere. From this set of goals it follows that the book is specifically directed at university students and at those engaged in the preparation of policy decisions. It is the sincere hope of the editors that also those charged with actual decision making will be able to spare some time to sample the product which they herewith present. They furthermore flatter themselves with the thought that the book will prove to be of use to the research community.

The objectives as just stated are wholly in line with the intentions of the European Conference of Ministers of Transport (ECMT). As already mentioned by the Secretary-General of the ECMT in the preface to the book, this body, celebrating its fortieth anniversary in 1993, has contributed to the diffusion of the knowledge of transport economics during a large part of its existence. At the occasion of its fortieth anniversary the ECMT deemed that it was appropriate to crown its scientific achievements with a publication the contents of which are intended to be of a more lasting nature.

For the realization of this goal it was necessary to meet two requirements. First, the structure of the book would have to be carefully chosen, and the main fields of present-day debate in transport economics would have to be reflected in the book. Second, the book would have to be of high quality, and the editors have been fortunate enough to be able to involve outstanding transport economists from a cross-section of European countries.

The link between theorizing and transport policy is an essential line of approach in our set-up. All contributors are concerned with the relevance of their theoretical underpinnings for policy making and public choice. At the same time, it is intended to show the present position of transport economics as a theoretical melting pot. With this in mind the function of the book is to serve as a source of information for graduate students and for those economists who, being already advanced in their career, wish to update their knowledge. Against this background the structure of the book follows a natural pattern. New developments at the demand and supply sides of transport markets are dealt with in two chapters. First, Fischer follows developments in the analysis of travel demand over the past three decades. These appear to be extremely heterogeneous. The systematic treatment in this chapter will greatly assist in obtaining a clear picture of the three main approaches: aggregate transport models, the microeconomic approach and the approach based on activity analysis. Beyond and above this a path is indicated which may lead to a point where valuable elements of the different approaches will be merged.

Quinet connects the two questions of the supply of transport, in particular as determined by its cost structure, and of the functioning of transport markets. With regard to the latter question, his main concern is with the conditions leading to a particular competitive situation in the markets for transport, i.e. monopoly, oligopoly or competition. In addition to this the less frequently considered question of the stability of transport markets is addressed.

Technical innovation is a driving force in transport, as in many other areas. This is a clear indication of the fact that transport economics necessarily also has to consider problems of dynamics. Giannopoulos, in reviewing the significance of technical innovation in transport, starts by describing the broad range of current and expected developments. Next, the possible impacts of these innovations are discussed. Finally, thought is given to the ways in which the diffusion of innovations takes place through space and time.

Externalities are becoming more and more important every day. Transport in particular is often pointed to as being very detrimental to the environment. An in-depth treatment of the externalities of transport, both from a theoretical and a practical point of view, may be considered an absolute necessity. The chapter by Rothengatter meets this demand. The groundwork for this chapter is laid by a consideration of various views of the theoretical concept of externalities. Then those externalities for which transport may be held responsible are looked at. The core of the treatment here is the complex problem of the economic valuation of externalities, which is dealt with in terms of the important categories of traffic safety and of the environmental impacts of transport. The link with policy is established by reviewing measures for reducing the external costs of transport. Finally, a highly critical appraisal is given of the thesis, newly developed in some quarters, of the existence of external benefits of (road) transport.

The relationship between transport and regional development is another good example of where sophisticated economic analysis and empirical relevance meet. Rietveld and Nijkamp follow a pattern which does full merit to this relationship. First, approaches for tracking down the impact of transport infrastructure on regional productivity are surveyed. Then the less common question of the importance of infrastructure for locational decisions is looked into. Finally, some models in which both types of impacts are integrated are discussed.

The chapters described thus far already present a host of new insights and suggestions for policy making. In the remaining chapters the emphasis shifts towards a more explicit treatment of the role of government in the provision of transport.

It is common knowledge that various levels of government may be distinguished. In chapters 7, 8 and 9 the level of government on the whole plays no particular role, being mostly identified with national government. In contrast, chapters 10 and 11 specifically deal with policy at a higher-than-national, or supranational, level.

In chapters 7–9 the book follows the traditional distinction between government policy with respect to transport markets and government policy towards infrastructure. This distinction is based on the differing economic characteristics of transport services and of infrastructure services respectively. The validity of this distinction, however, becomes a matter for thought when, as is the case at present, competition gradually enters into the provision of railway infrastructure.

Baum, in his chapter on government and transport markets, first discusses the theoretical basis for explaining government action towards transport markets. The main body of the chapter consists of a description and critical evaluation of the two main possible attitudes of government vis-à-vis transport markets. First, there is the policy of intervening in transport markets, which has long been dominant. Second, there is the policy of the withdrawal of government from transport markets – a more recent occurrence. In this second policy, the elements of deregulation and of privatization and the less common element of the introduction of a competition policy come together.

Infrastructure policy figures in two separate but closely related chapters by Jansson. In the first of these chapters (chapter 8) the short-run policy problem of pricing for the use of infrastructure is examined. The second chapter (chapter 9) considers the problem in the long run, where capacity may be varied, which is equivalent to the problem of investment in infrastructure.

The argument about pricing can be unrolled in a small number of clearly distinguishable steps. The basis of chapter 8 is formed by an analysis of the cost of infrastructure. Then, against the background of a social welfare function, pricing principles are derived. Finally, the question of whether the cost of infrastructure can be covered from the revenue obtained through pricing, of interest both for its theoretical and its practical implications, is discussed for a number of specific cases.

Looking at investment in infrastructure it becomes apparent that any treatment needs to be split between investment in non-urban infrastructure and investment in urban infrastructure. The not unconvincing reason given for this is that in an urban context the integration between transport planning and general land-use planning is of particular importance and is too often neglected.

The specific problems connected with transport policy at a supranational level are the theme of the chapter by Gwilliam. The chapter starts with a general description of the ways in which problems of transport policy may be classified, e.g. according to agency or to objective. Then the very fundamental question of what makes a transport policy issue one of supranational concern is addressed. After this clarifying exposition the main issues for supranational transport policy – such as transport sector efficiency, the environment and national economic development – are discussed.

Lastly, the chances for a supranational regime in transport in Europe are assessed.

The chapter by Bayliss cannot be classified as easily as the other chapters in the book. It is characterized by its taking together a number of strands which run through several of the preceding chapters. The main contention in this chapter is that a grave danger exists of a distorted view being formed of future developments in freight transport. This opinion is supported by the argument that transport has been too frequently analysed in an isolated manner. This shortcoming could be remedied by a greater awareness of interrelationships between transport and developments in industry, between transport and the creation of a single European market and between developments in industry and the creation of a single European market.

Lastly, in an epilogue, De Waele – Head of Economic Research of the ECMT – brings the book around full circle by focusing on the main areas of concern to policy makers in transport. By first presenting the facts, i.e. the patterns of development in the various modes of (inland) transport, the problems for transport policy become clear. This is mainly seen as the question whether rail and road will be able to cope with future transport demand. A varied list of solutions concludes the chapter and thereby ends the book on a not unduly pessimistic note.

After this brief sketch of the panorama composed of the various chapters the editors express the wish that the book will find its place in the academic study of transport economics as well as serve as a background for policy making in the years to come. They cannot but be grateful to the ECMT for having taken the initiative for this book and for their Schumpeterian skill in having turned their ideas into practice.

2

Travel Demand

Manfred M. Fischer

2.1 INTRODUCTION

The demand for transport is not merely an area of theoretical analysis. The subject is also of great practical relevance. This will become immediately clear from the following discussion. Transport planning is basically concerned with the establishment of a stable relationship between the demand for and the supply of transport infrastructure and transport services. In the recent past and in the current situation the relationship between supply and demand has been somewhat one-sided in many European countries, in the sense that the demand for transport services has outstripped both investment outlay and institutional ability to deal with the complexity of the problems attached to the renewal and expansion of transport infrastructure. This strong contrast between traffic growth and infrastructure investment since the 1970s has resulted in transport bottlenecks in many countries and regions (see Nijkamp et al., 1990).

As already mentioned in the introduction, in this chapter attention is focused on passenger transport or travel demand. The legacy of more than three decades of travel demand analysis is a large, rather diverse and often disparate body of information. No longer is research into travel demand focused narrowly on the theme of forecasting; the need for understanding travel behaviour itself has become a prominent theme. This broader debate has resulted in a flux of new ideas, methodologies and techniques which have proved stimulating to transport researchers but which might have frustrated transport practitioners seeking to identify the state of the art in the field.

The development of ideas about travel demand over the last few decades has almost exclusively been in terms of models. This contribution, therefore, is primarily concerned with passenger travel models. Various aspects relating to the development of travel demand models are discussed and some views on outstanding research issues are offered. The discussion will be at a relatively general level, and while the material is wide-ranging, it is inevitably selective. In structuring the discussion it is convenient to refer to three broad classes of models which characterize the development and progression in the field:

1 the traditional four-stage transport models associated with the large urban transport studies and characterized by an aggregate and descriptive use of data;
2 the microeconomic approach of travel choice behaviour underpinned with random utility theory and emphasizing the explanation of behaviour at the level of the individual; and
3 the activity-oriented approach based on more holistic research styles and viewing travel behaviour as daily or multi-day patterns of behaviour, related to and derived from differences in life styles and activity participation among the population.

Accordingly, the chapter is divided into three major parts. Section 2.2 considers the more traditional research style of the aggregate four-stage approach, while in section 2.3 more recent theoretical issues and research requirements relating to the microeconomic approach are analysed. Activity-based studies have been emerging in the 1980s as a challenge to the established travel demand techniques. Major aspects of the conceptual foundation and methodological developments of the activity-based approach are discussed in section 2.4. In a final brief section some research and development priorities for the 1990s are sketched.

2.2 THE TRADITIONAL FOUR-STAGE TRANSPORT APPROACH

In this aggregate approach the focus is on zones – or, in more practical terms, specific geographical areas – as generators of travel and as destinations for travel. Such a focus is appropriate for the kind of large-scale, long-range transport planning which has dominated planning in the past.

The demand forecasting process

Most large-scale travel demand studies in an urban context – not only in the 1960s and 1970s but also in current planning practice – are built around the classical four-stage travel demand forecasting process outlined in figure 2.1 (for more details see, for example, Sheppard, 1986). They basically rely on the following passenger demand model approach (see Williams and Ortuzar, 1979):

$$T(k, i, j, m, r) = G_i^k \, T_{ij}^k \, M_{ij}^{km} \, R_{ij}^{kmr} \tag{2.1}$$

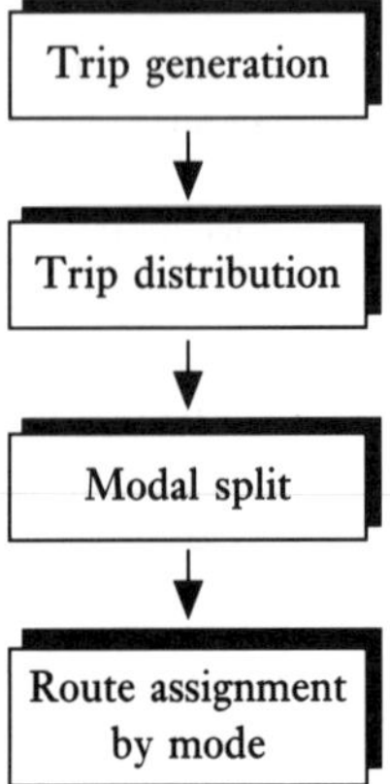

Figure 2.1 The four-stage model of the demand forecasting process.

in which the number of trips $T(k, i, j, m, r)$ by persons of type k between locations (zones) i and j on mode m by route r is expressed in terms of the attributes of the transport system. G_i^k is the total number of trips made by persons of type k generated in zone i, T_{ij}^k is that proportion attracted to zone j, M_{ij}^{km} denotes the proportion of T_{ij}^k associated with mode m (e.g. car, bus or rail), while the route share R_{ij}^{kmr} is similarly defined. The four quantities G_i^k, T_{ij}^k, M_{ij}^{km} and R_{ij}^{kmr} correspond to the four stages of demand forecasting – trip generation, trip distribution, mode choice and network assignment – designed to predict traffic flows on the links of a transport network from knowledge of land-use, car-ownership, economic, population and travel conditions.

Trip Generation

Trip generation is the first submodel of the conventional four-stage model sequence. Trip generation models attempt to predict the total quantity G_i^k of travel measured in terms of the number of trips of a certain kind (usually home-based work trips) leaving a zone i during a fixed period of time (usually peak or off-peak hours) and based upon attributes of that zone. Two types of methodologies – linear regression and category analysis (households with equal characteristics are assumed to produce an equal number of trips) – are generally used for modelling the generation of trips.

Trip generation models may be criticized for several limitations. The most severe is their evident inability to predict the 'hidden demand' which is released by transport improvements. Hidden demand may be defined as trips which may have been considered before the transport improvement (e.g. a shorter route) was made but only became actual trips after the improvement. Also the interrelation between the transport system and land-use patterns is not captured in this type of model.

Trip Distribution

Trip distribution models link the origin and destination ends of the trip produced by the trip generation model. That is, a trip destination model predicts how many trips made by persons of type k and originating in zone $i(i = 1, \ldots, n)$ will terminate in zone $j(j = 1, \ldots, n)$, i.e. T_{ij}^{k}. A variety of trip distribution models have been proposed, including classical gravity models, intervening opportunity models and entropy models (see, for example, Wilson, 1969, 1970). Although these models are very different, they all contain three basic elements to model the distribution of trips: the number of trips generated by a zone i of origin, the degree to which the *in situ* characteristics of a particular zone j of destination attracts trip makers and the inhibiting effect of separation (e.g. distance or generalized costs, i.e. a measure combining money costs, time costs and possible other types of costs to the traveller).

Modal Split

Modal split or mode choice is concerned with the prediction of the number of trips from each origin to each destination which will use each transport mode. Thus, the objective of modal split or mode choice analysis is the prediction of M_{ij}^{km}, the number of trips made by persons of type k from i to j by mode m, given a prediction of the number of trips T_{ij}^{k}. Mode selection is usually seen as a choice between just two broad categories: private cars and public transport. Certain groups of travellers can be virtually eliminated before considering modal split. For example, passengers who cannot afford or cannot drive a car must generally take public transport. Thus, in this case, the first step in modal split analysis is to identify the fraction of the population of each zone who are limited to public transport and to allocate these subpopulations to the one mode which they use.

Two basic model types have been used to predict M_{ij}^{km}: modal split models and mode choice models, where the former term refers to aggregate and the latter to disaggregate model forms. The core of disaggregated logit-type choice models (see section 2.3) in the context of mode choice modelling is accepted practice nowadays. The modal-split stage of the travel forecasting model provides useful information for transport policy in general and in particular for decisions such as whether to invest in a new subway system, to implement an exclusive high-occupancy vehicle lane for buses and/or car pools etc.

Trip assignment

The final step in the conventional four-stage model sequence is generally referred to as trip or traffic assignment (route choice). The rationale behind trip assignment is based on the assumption that all trips between zones follow the 'best' route, 'best' being defined in terms of travel time or generalized cost. It is implicitly assumed that travellers are sufficiently familiar with the travel network to make their optimal route choice, an assumption which is quite reasonable for work and shopping trips but is questionable for recreational trips. Network assignment models (such as all-or-nothing assignment, multipath assignment and constrained assignment models) contain two components: a tree-building process for searching out the 'best' route for each interzonal movement in a network and a procedure for allocating the interzonal modal trip volume among the paths (see Bovy and Stern, 1990).

Criticisms of the approach

Many conceptual, methodological and technical problems have been identified in the aggregate four-stage sequential approach. One is the absence of any feedback between the various stages – e.g. mode choice and trip distribution or route choice and mode choice – of the travel demand forecasting process. The submodels are applied in a unidirectional way and any errors are compounded in any forward linkage.

More significantly, the traditional research style of large-scale modelling has been strongly criticized in academia in the 1970s because it is

1 descriptive rather than explanatory in nature,
2 theoretically deficient and in particular lacking in a behavioural rationale,
3 subject to aggregation biases,
4 policy insensitive and unresponsive to exploratory new policies in the context of transport system management, and
5 expensive to develop and operate.

At the same time aggregate models have been improved considerably by introducing household- and individual-based category analyses for trip generation, incorporating the generalized cost concept(with micro parameters) within the entropy maximizing-based trip distribution stage, integrating disaggregate logit-type models in the context of mode choice and interrelating the stages of the travel demand forecasting process. The SELNEC transport model, developed by Wilson et al. (1969), and its descendants are prominent examples of aggregate models which anticipated elements of the disaggregate modelling philosophy (see section 2.3 below) and are free from some of the abovementioned criticisms. Thus, in many respects the distinction between aggregate and disaggregate models is becoming blurred (see Williams and Ortuzar, 1982).

There is no doubt now that travel demand models, whether aggregate or disaggregate, should be based on a well-specified behavioural representation of the travel decision process. It is possible to develop aggregate travel demand models derived from a realistic representation of travel decision making at the micro level. Thus, the clearest remaining distinctive feature between the two classes of travel demand model is the level of data analysis. Each model type has a distinct role to play in transport planning and policy (see Jones, 1983). Aggregate models provide important insights into the working of the (urban) transport system as a whole and are appropriate for large-scale, long-range transport planning. Disaggregate models can provide insights into the nature of the travel decision process and are more suited for the type of transport planning and policy which has become more important since the late 1970s, the finer scaled, shorter time-frame, low-capital-cost planning epitomized by transport system management (see Hanson and Schwab, 1986).

2.3 THE MICROECONOMIC APPROACH OF TRAVEL CHOICE

The disaggregate approach takes individuals or households rather than zones as the units of observation and analysis. There are three major reasons for shifting the focus of research away from zones to individuals or households. The first is related to theory building and derives from the desire to explain how and why traffic flow patterns emerge. There is now consensus that the decision-making unit is the adequate level at which to build travel choice theory. The second is related to the potential of increased policy sensitivity at a much finer scale of analysis. The third is more technical in nature and relates to the potential for a greater statistical efficiency of data requirements (see Hanson and Schwab, 1986).

The specific focus in this section is on the random utility-based discrete choice approach of travel choice behaviour which has proved a great stimulus to the promotion of disaggregate travel choice models. Its essential conceptual contribution lies in its explicit treatment of the processes making perfect predictions of travel choice behaviour unattainable. Before progressing to the choice-theoretic framework we first introduce some basic notions, such as travel choice behaviour, and characterize the travel decision process in some detail.

The travel decision-making process

The need to travel arises at the level of the individual and at this level choices about travel are important. An individual's travel choices are conceived of as the selection decision between commodities which are discrete in nature, such as, for example, the mode of travel to use, as opposed to quantities that are

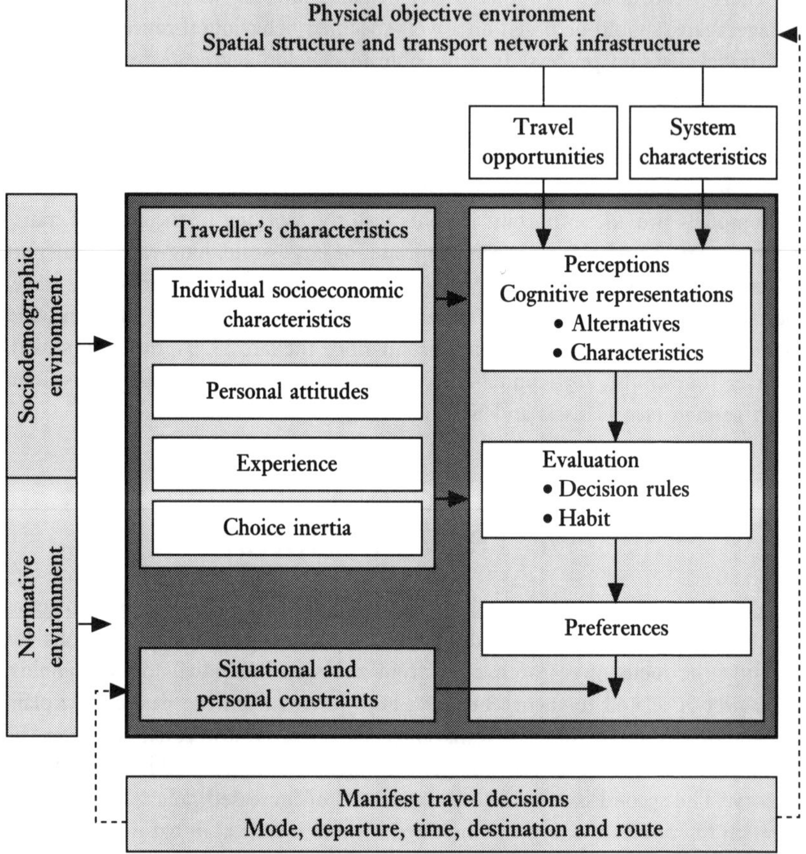

Figure 2.2 The decision-making process: a simplified view.

continuously variable, e.g. amounts of apples or pears. Travel behaviour is reflected, among other things, by pre-trip decisions consisting of destination, mode, route and departure time choices, and *en route* decisions which may consist of decisions such as the diversion of alternative routes or the rescheduling of intended trips (see Khattak, 1991). Figure 2.2 describes in a simplified manner the decision-making problem with which the traveller is faced. According to this framework, travel choice is principally concerned with two points:

1 the individual in question with his or her subjective needs, travel experience, preferences, perceptions and attitudes, influenced by both the sociodemographic environment in which the individual lives (including, for example, his or her household, car ownership, age and other individual

characteristics) and the normative environment including the set of norms and values derived from society; and

2 the physical environment (including the built-up surroundings, the transport network infrastructure etc.) determining the objective travel opportunities and their characteristics.

The decision-making process itself is viewed to consist of the formation of perceptions and cognitive representations of travel opportunities and their characteristics, and attitude formation, i.e. learned predispositions to respond to a situation in a consistent way (see Golledge and Stimson, 1987; Bovy and Stern, 1990). In route choice contexts – quite in contrast to other travel choices – the set of choice opportunities may be quite extensive and complex. The traveller has only limited knowledge (cognition) of all the opportunities available. Cognition is associated with his or her experiences and the system of acquiring information, i.e. the information channels used. There is a growing body of literature confirming the widely held view that in travel choice contexts individuals act under restricted knowledge of their alternatives and of their attribute values. The traveller may have – to a certain degree – a distorted image (cognitive representation) of the actual situation. This often appears to be the case with regard to both costs and qualitative aspects of the private car versus public transport decision. There may be constraints which preclude certain alternatives, especially in the context of route choice and destination choice behaviour (see Bovy and Stern, 1990). An example of the latter may be that there are only a limited number of large specialized stores over the whole area of a particular city.

The perceived choice options are likely to be evaluated consciously in unfamiliar choice contexts and subconsciously in routine contexts. For example, travellers may get into the habit of taking a certain mode and route through a familiar network. Inertia or habits may play a role in so far as certain thresholds in the evaluation need to be crossed before changing (attitudes towards) routine behaviour. Situational and personal constraints along with preferences then determine observable choices.

The decision-making process outlined in figure 2.2 indicates that travel choice is by no means a direct and simple derivative of the observable attributes of the traveller and of the transport network. The black box in figure 2.2, the so-called traveller's world, may be considered as a complicated system of filters through which choice-relevant information is selected and transformed. Two types of filters are of central importance in the choice process: perception/cognition filters and evaluation filters. Through perception filters the universal set of choice options is narrowed into feasible choice sets, i.e. sets of choice alternatives which are known to the individual and are actively considered in the choice process. The individual receives a certain cognition of the existence of choice options and a certain perception of the characteristics of these alternatives while through evaluation filters these perceptions are transformed into a desirability (utility) scale (Bovy and Stern, 1990).

The decision-making problem is also characterized by dynamic components. Perception/cognition filters as well as attitudes are likely to change via learning processes because of discrepancies between anticipated and actual experience. Finally, it is worthwhile to mention that strong individual differences in travel behaviour may occur which cannot easily be derived from observable personal characteristics such as sex or age. This diversity is caused by the filter functions (perception, cognition and evaluation) which differ from individual to individual.

The discrete choice framework and random utility choice models

Classical travel choice theory explains individual behaviour as the outcome of a two-step recursive process. First, exogenous forces pose a travel choice problem, i.e. an individual decision maker and an associated choice set. Then, with the choice set well defined, the decision maker chooses among the available travel options. In general, research on travel choice theory has focused on the second stage of the decision process, the characterization of classes of decision rules, the formalization of choice set structure and the analysis of the attributes of the outcome when decision rules of a given class are applied to choice sets of a specified structure.

Random utility choice theory is based upon the hypothesis of preference (utility) maximization which postulates that the distribution of demands in a population is the result of individual preference (utility) maximization, with preferences influenced by unobservable variables. Utilities are treated as random variables not to reflect a lack of rationality of the decision maker, but to reflect a lack of information concerning the characteristics of alternatives and decision makers on the part of the observer/researcher.

Basic concepts and conceptual considerations

Figure 2.3 illustrates the general strategy adopted by the microeconomic approach to accommodate various aspects of the travel decision-making process characterized by figure 2.2. The approach requires four primary ingredients:

1 a population I of decision makers i which may be partitioned into population segments $s = 1, \ldots, s$ defined by some socioeconomic descriptors;
2 objects of travel choice (such as routes, modes, destinations or times of travel) and a set A_s of travel options available to i (known as a choice set definition);

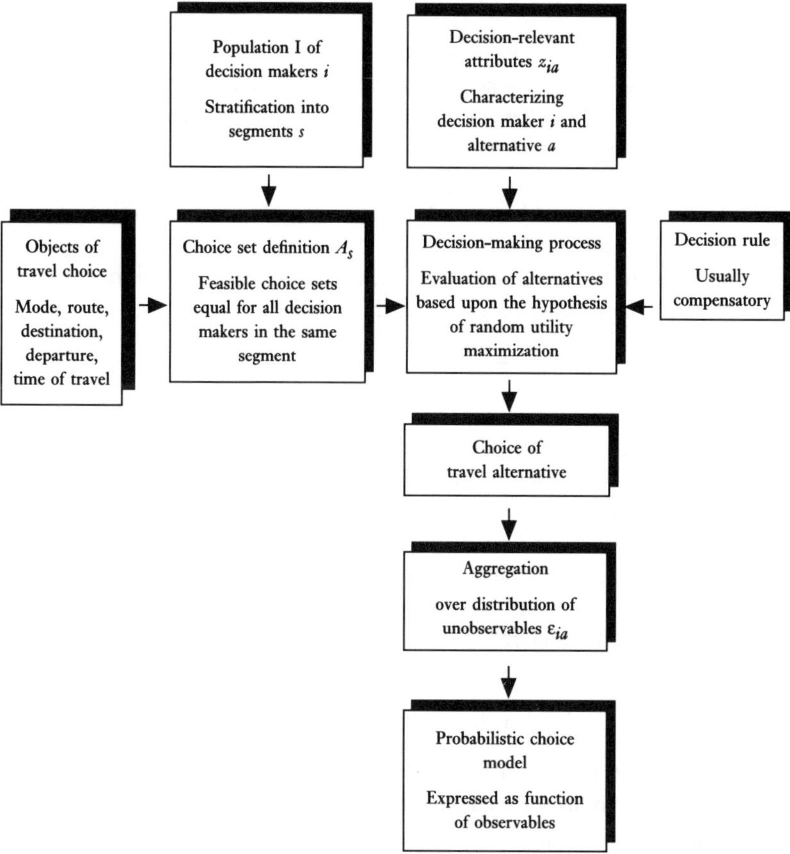

Figure 2.3 Major elements of the microeconomic random utility based approach.

3 decision-relevant characteristics z_{ia} of both the decision maker i and alternative a; and
4 a decision rule for combining them.

The hypothesis of random preference (utility) maximization plays a key role for modelling the travel decision-making process and assumes that there exists a mathematical function U, the (indirect) utility function, such that decision maker i prefers travel option a to option a' if and only if $U(Z_{ia}) = U_{ia}$ (the value of the utility function corresponding to the attributes of the pair (i, a) exceeds $U(z_{ia'}) = U_{ia'}$ (the value of the utility function corresponding to (l, a'). In other words, decision makers are assumed always to choose the utility-maximizing alternatives, i.e.

$$U(z_{ia}) > U(z_{ia'}) \qquad \text{for all } a' \neq a,\ a' \in A_s. \tag{2.2}$$

It is generally recognized that not all the attributes characterizing the decision makers and the alternatives which are relevant to choices among travel alternatives are known to the researcher, and that it is usually not feasible to measure or observe the values of all the known attributes. Moreover, there may be unobserved taste variations in a population (segment) influencing measurement errors (see Ben-Akiva and Lerman, 1985; Fischer and Nijkamp, 1985; Horowitz, 1986).

In random utility travel choice models, these inherent uncertainties are dealt with using random utility functions of the following form:

$$U_{ia} = U\,[f_1(x_{ia}), f_2(x_{ia}), f_3(\varepsilon_{ia})] \tag{2.3}$$

where U_{ia} is the overall utility (or preference) of alternative a, $U(.)$ denotes the utility function (for the sth population segment), $f_1(X_{ia})$ is the function measuring the average (systematic) taste of decision makers within s, $f_2(X_{ia})$ is a random function representing the idiosyncratic variations in taste (random taste variation) and $f_3(\varepsilon_{ia})$ is a random disturbance term capturing the effects of unobserved but decision-relevant attributes of both the decision makers and the alternatives. x_{ia} is a vector of observed characteristics of the pair (i, a). In applications it has generally been assumed that the utility values for, say, alternative a may be expressed as

$$U_{ia} = x_{ia}\beta + (x_{ia}\delta_i + \zeta_{ia}) = v_{ia} + \varepsilon_{ia} \tag{2.4}$$

where the first term, v_{ia}, on the right-hand side of (2.4) is referred to as the systematic (deterministic) component of utility, while the second term, ε_{ia}, denotes the random component. This component consists of two parts. ζ_{ia} is a random disturbance term capturing the effects of unobserved attributes of the decision maker and the choice alternatives, while $x_{ia}\delta_j$ represents the idiosyncratic tastes of i. β is a vector of the deterministic component of utility and δ_i the taste variation parameter vector. This linear-in-the-parameters and additive form is not so restrictive as it might appear at first glance, as non-linearities and non-additivities may be readily accommodated.

In typical travel choice applications, observed attributes of decision makers might include automobile ownership, income and household size. Unobserved attributes of individuals might relate to social status (except income), occupation, health and schedule commitments affecting travel choices. Observed characteristics of alternatives typically involve travel times and costs if the travel options are modes, and employment and population levels if the alternatives are locations. Unobserved attributes of alternatives typically include reliability and comfort if the travel options are modes, and the prices, quality and variety of available goods and services if the alternatives are locations (see Horowitz, 1983).

Random utility travel choice models specify the probability p_{ia} that a randomly selected travel decision maker i chooses alternative $a \in A_s$:

$$p_{ia} = \text{prob}(u_{ia} > u_{ia'}, \text{ for all } a' \neq a,\ a' \in A_s) \qquad (2.5)$$

conditional on the matrix $x_i = (x_{ia}, a \in A_s)$ of observed attributes characterizing i's choice problem and an unknown parameter vector θ including parameters of the utility function U (i.e. b and d_j) and parameters of the distribution F of the random components $\varepsilon_i = (\varepsilon_{ia}, a \in A_s)$. The choice probabilities are assumed to fulfil the conditions that they are non-negative, sum to unity and depend only on the measured attributes of travel options and individual characteristics.

Functional forms

The primary issues in selecting a functional form for the choice probabilities in (2.5) are computational practicability and flexibility in representing patterns of similarity across travel options. Three major classes of concrete functional forms for random utility travel choice models may be distinguished. These are logit models, based on the work of Luce (1959), probit models, based on the work of Thurstone (1927), and elimination models, based on the work of Tversky (1972a, b) (see McFadden, 1981, for more details). Figure 2.4 outlines these classes as well as their most important members.

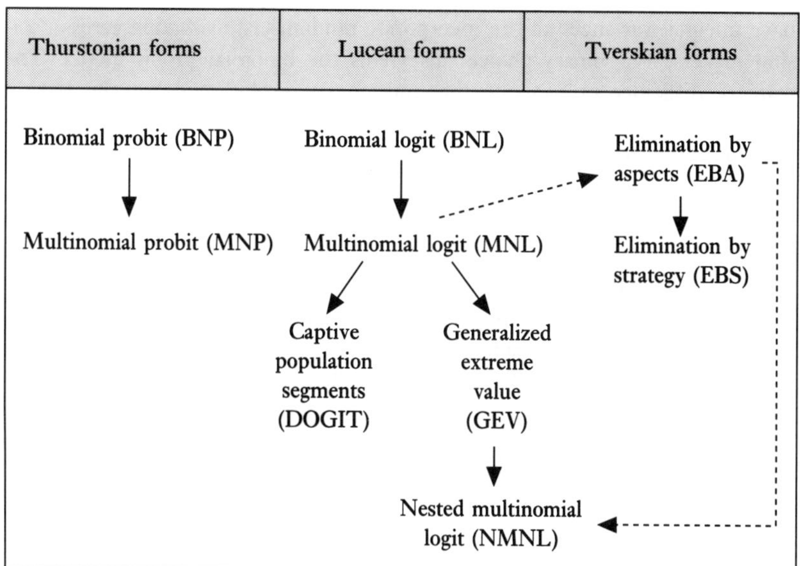

Figure 2.4 Three major classes of functional forms.
Source: McFadden, 1981

By far the best known functional form, the multinomial logit (MNL), allows easy computation and interpretation but has a very restrictive pattern of interalternative substitution:

$$p_{ia} = \frac{\exp(x_{ia}\beta)}{\sum_{a' \in A} \exp(x_{ia'}\beta)} \tag{2.6}$$

derived from the assumption that the random terms ε_i are independently and identically distributed with the Gumbel type I extreme value distribution. In the MNL no allowance is made for random taste variation. The values of the parameter vector must be estimated by fitting the model to data consisting of observations of the choices and measurements of the attributes for a random sample of decision makers. Usually the maximum likelihood procedure is used for this purpose. The most significant feature of MNL is the independence of irrelevant alternatives (IIA) property – a property which implies that the relative choice probability of any two alternatives depends exclusively on their systematic components and can give rise to somewhat odd and erroneous predictions when the travel options are clear substitutes for each other.

Because of its simplicity, the MNL model form has been a primary focus of attention in attempts to use functional generalizations to transcend the limitations inherent in the IIA property of MNL. The most general ones are Thurstonian forms which can be derived by assuming the errors to have a multivariate normal distribution (see Hausman and Wise, 1978). These model forms allow the random components of the travel options to be correlated, to have unequal variances and to incorporate random taste variation across decision makers. For binary choice this yields the binomial probit model. The primary difficulty in applying the multinomial probit model is the lack of practical, accurate procedures for approximating the choice probabilities when the number of alternatives is large, as is usually the case in destination and route choice contexts.

The most promising and widely adopted generalization of the MNL form is the nested multinomial logit (NMNL) model which can be obtained as a special case of the generalized extreme value (GEV) model form by choosing appropriate values of the parameter of the GEV distribution (see, for example, Sobel, 1980; Ben-Akiva and Lerman, 1985).

To illustrate the NMNL model, a simple journey-to-work mode choice context may be considered as displayed in figure 2.5, in which four travel options are distinguished: drive alone, shared ride, metro and bus. Using the MNL model, one would treat the four modes as distinctly independent alternatives and assume that each individual selects one particular mode following a simultaneous evaluation of all four. In contrast, using the NMNL model one would treat the trip decision process as a recursive sequential choice structure where results of the decision on the lower decision level feed into that of the

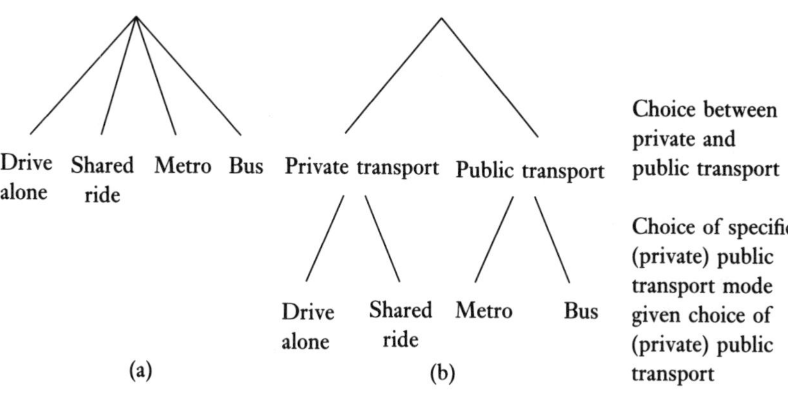

Figure 2.5 Alternative decision structures and model forms for a simple travel-to-work mode choice example: (a) the MNL form; (b) the NMNL form.

higher level. The NMNL form has the advantage of retaining the desirable computational properties and other characteristics of the MNL model and embodying more general properties of cross-substitution, but is less general than Thurstonian forms.

All the functional forms considered so far belong to the family of compensatory choice models, assuming that the travel decision-making process is compensatory in nature, in other words that individuals 'trade off' attributes of the travel options such as time and money costs in the decision process. Non-compensatory models employ other decision rules. The most prominent examples are the elimination-by-aspects models (see figure 2.4) where lexicographic and satisfaction rules are combined (see, for example, Recker and Golob, 1979). Choice is viewed as a process in which the attributes are hierarchically ranked by the importance associated to them and alternatives are eliminated from the choice set until a single alternative remains.

These models, however, are more complicated than the MNL model and require considerable *a priori* information. Thus, empirical practice confines itself to the exclusively used Lucean forms in general and the MNL model in particular. Their domain of applicability has been steadily extended from binary mode choice to simultaneous choices over complex choice sets in a destination or route choice context (see, for example, Kern et al., 1984; Borgers and Timmermans, 1986).

Revealed versus stated choice models

Traditionally travel choice models have been based on data obtained by direct observation of travel behaviour or in surveys asking for actual travel behaviour, i.e. revealed (preference) data. Such data, however, have some limitations which restrict their general suitability. First, it might be difficult to obtain sufficient variation in the revealed preference data to analyse all variables of interest. Second, there may be strong correlations between explanatory variables of interest (especially travel time and cost) which make it difficult to estimate model parameters reflecting the proper trade-off ratios. Third, the revealed preference data approach cannot be used in a direct way to evaluate demand under conditions which do not yet exist (such as new forms of public transport, new regulations affecting the use of cars etc.). In view of these problems the use of stated (preference) or experimental data became an attractive option in travel demand analysis (see Louvière and Hensher, 1982; Kroes and Sheldon, 1988).

Stated (preference) data relate to observations of choices made by individuals in laboratory choice experiments carried out in hypothetical environments. A key feature of the stated data approach is that individuals are exposed to a set of choice experiments generated by some controlled experimental design procedure (e.g. full or fractional factorial design) so that the independent variables can be made truly independent. A crucial issue in the design is the definition of the variables (factors) of interest and the values (levels) of the factors which need to be evaluated by the respondents. The last few years have seen an increasing attention devoted to computer integrative procedures to increase the reliability of the behavioural responses of the respondents.

Choice models based on revealed data are termed revealed choice models, while choice models based on stated data are called stated choice models. Revealed and stated choice models have complementary advantages and disadvantages. Revealed choice models have high external validity in the sense that they are calibrated to real data. This advantage, however, may be considerably diluted by the difficulty of defining the choice set in destination and route choice contexts, and by the concern about the accuracy of the data actually used in making the choice. Stated choice models have several advantages over the revealed choice models in analysing travel behaviour. The most important one refers to the controlled nature of the choice experiments which allows greater freedom in defining travel choice contexts, alternatives and attributes as well as a direct comparison with the responses across individuals. With these advantages comes the liability that the success of the stated preference approach largely depends on the consistency of the hypothetical alternatives and the corresponding sets of attributes with their perception in actual choice situations (see Wardman, 1988). Stated choice models are becoming increasingly employed in academic studies (especially in destination and route choice contexts) and in policy analysis to analyse how people would adjust their behaviour under radically different alternative futures (e.g. new forms of public transport or new regulations affecting the use of cars).

Range of applications of random utility models

Random utility models have found an increasing range of application in travel demand analysis. They have been used simply to replace the forecasting components of aggregate models, but often inflexibility in the large-scale aggregate frameworks has restricted the benefits obtained. Most success has been found in specialized policy analysis. For example, car pooling has been studied by Ben-Akiva and Atherton (1977), the elasticity of gasoline taxes, parking taxes, transit fares and housing taxes to finance public transport has been studied by Anas (1982) and the effectiveness of ride-sharing incentives on work trips to reduce congestion and air pollution has been studied by Brownstone and Golob (1992).

The early applications were confined to mode choice in the urban area for work trips. The choice of mode for travel to work has been analysed extensively using different types of data from widely differing urban areas (see, for example, Domencich and McFadden, 1975; Ben-Akiva and Lerman, 1985). Initially satisfied with identifying those attributes characterizing the system and/or individual which significantly affected the choice decision, transport researchers have since broadened their scope to include virtually every aspect of an individual's choice of travel mode. Consequently, considerable efforts have been devoted to the valuation of traveller's time, to unidimensional and multidimensional procedures for obtaining an index of vehicle safety, comfort and other qualitative aspects, to procedures which attempt to minimize aggregation biases due to spatial or socioeconomic groupings etc. These and other issues have been analysed both in isolation and together with related individual decisions such as trip purpose, time of day of travel, frequency of travel and residential and employment location choice.

Although still dominated by mode choice studies the application of discrete choice models now includes departure time (see, for example, Abkowits, 1981; Brownstone and Small, 1989), route choice (see, for example, Bovy and Stern, 1990), automobile ownership and use (see, for example, Hensher et al., 1989), travel frequency (see, for example, Domencich and McFadden, 1975) and multi-destination travel or 'trip chaining' (see Horowitz, 1979). Most of the studies assume that trip decisions are being made independently. However, some also explore relationships between decisions, such as, for example, between mode, destination and frequency (see Domencich and McFadden, 1975); between mode, destination and trip chaining (see Horowitz, 1980); between frequency, mode and destination; and between time of day of travel (see Charles River Associates, 1967), shopping mode and destination choice (see Ben-Akiva and Lerman, 1985).

Work has also progressed on applying discrete choice models to intercity travel demand situations. Recently, Koppelman and Hirsch (1989) have developed

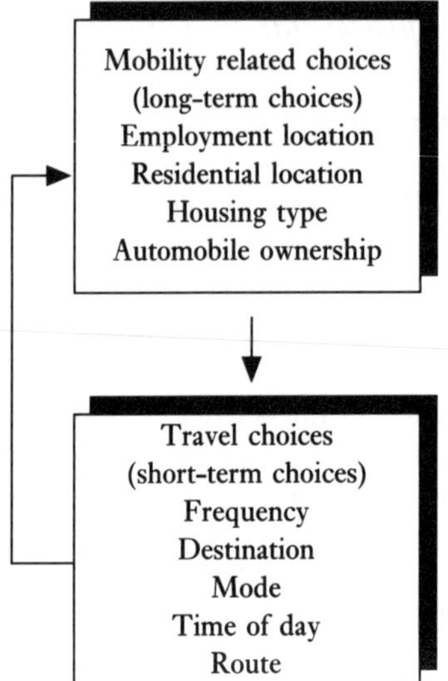

Figure 2.6 A simple hierarchy of travel and travel-related choices.
Source: Ben-Akiva and Lerman, 1979, p. 669

an intercity travel demand model representing trip frequency, trip destination, mode and service class choice in the form of a nested decision structure.

Changes in the transport system are likely to have significant effects not only on travel decisions but also on travel-related choices such as car ownership, employment and residential location. In turn, these decisions may have a significant impact on travel demand, since travel decisions of an individual are constrained by fixed employment and residential location as well as by fixed automobile ownership or availability. Thus, a fully successful travel demand model has to take into account the structural relationships between these decisions which directly or indirectly influence trip making behaviour (see Domencich and McFadden, 1975). There are good reasons why the long-run mobility-related choices are assumed to be intertwined with the short-run travel choices while within each bundle of decisions a simultaneous structure may be assumed. Figure 2.6 illustrates one possible choice hierarchy in a travel and mobility-related context. Until the nature of the interactions between transport services, travel and travel-related decisions is better understood, there is only little hope that travel choice models will provide reliable tools for long-term policy analysis.

With the exception of mode choice modelling, most transport applications of random utility models have been carried out by individuals who are either mainly engaged in or closely associated with travel choice behaviour analysis. The ability of discrete choice models to represent broad ranges of travel choices and policies has not yet been fully exploited in transport planning practice.

Criticisms and limitations of travel choice models

Random utility travel choice models represent an important advance over other operational modelling approaches and reflect an increasing awareness of the need to understand a wide range of travel and travel-related decisions. There has been much research and experience with random utility travel choice models during the last two decades. Strengths and weaknesses of the particular forms of models have been increasingly well understood.

In the past decade various objections and criticisms have been directed at currently implemented probabilistic travel choice models. These have generally focused on limitations of the variants of the MNL model and have generated a whole range of extensions, generalizations and new approaches. More specifically, some of the objects of attention have been related to the incorporation of taste variability in a population, the investigation of alternative individual decision rules, the treatment of similar travel options in choice contexts, the incorporation of time-varying exogenous explanatory variables, unobserved variables with a general serial correlation structure and complex structural interrelationships among decisions taken at different times etc. (see, for example, Fischer and Nijkamp, 1987).

A serious shortcoming of the discrete choice approach is the use of single trips as the basic unit of analysis, despite the widely recognized fact that travel is a derived demand. That is, demand for travel is derived from needs and desires to participate in various activities in space and time. Most operational travel choice models ignore the relationship between activities and travel and thus are unable to provide meaningful information about how changes in the activities themselves may affect individuals' travel behaviour (see Recker et al., 1983). In this context, studies of behaviour within an integrated activity–travel framework are of particular importance (see section 2.4).

A second major problem associated with current travel choice theory is its failure to consider explicitly the mechanism generating choice problems. Little work has been done up to now on relaxing the assumption of homogeneous choice sets, on identifying systematic differences in the choice sets of individuals, on specifying variables which define the individual's choice set and on modelling endogenous choice set formation for appropriate types of individuals. Closely related is the problem of the proper specification of the individual's choice set, a problem far from trivial because meaningful choices can only be made from known and evaluated travel options. Although environmental, informational, personal and situational constraints delineate the set of feasible travel options to an individual, the models fail to identify the options which are perceived and actually considered by the individuals.

Applications of travel choice models have generally assumed that information about travel alternatives available to the decision maker is exogenous and subject to systematic inaccuracies. This classic assumption, however, is unrealistic. Individuals' information is not only imperfect, but is also dependent upon experience with the transport system and upon information-gathering activities (see Manski, 1981). The integration of the dynamic relation between information and travel choice moves one away from the current cross-sectional framework to a dynamic framework where effects of experience, time-discounted preferences, learning processes, habit persistence etc. become central issues.

Finally, it has been argued that the underpinning theory, involving a perfectly discriminating rational man or woman endowed with complete information, is unacceptable for analysing travel behaviour (see, for example, Burnett and Hanson, 1982). Indeed, it is not too difficult to find examples of travel-related situations in which the utility maximization principle does not seem to apply, at least without some substantial conceptual modifications.

2.4 THE ACTIVITY-BASED APPROACH

Activity-based studies have been emerging in the 1980s as a challenge to the established travel demand techniques. The replacement of the trip-based view by a broader, more holistic framework in which travel is analysed as daily or multi-day patterns of behaviour is considered by many scholars to be essential for a deeper understanding of travel behaviour. The growing interest in this approach has been reflected in an increase in the number of studies undertaken in the recent past (see, for example, Jones, 1990) and in the wide range of issues which have been addressed from an activity orientation point of view.

Conceptual foundation and major characteristics

The major conceptual foundations of the activity-based approach can be traced back to two major schools of thought:

1 the time geographic or Lund perspective resulting from attempts to develop a model of society in which constraints can be formulated in physical terms (see Hägerstrand, 1970); and
2 the transductive or Chapel Hill perspective which conceives activities in terms of the individual and his or her physiologically regulated and learned behaviour (see Chapin, 1974).

The two perspectives are complementary in nature. The Lund group paid specific attention to understanding the operation of constraints on travel behaviour in space and time, while the Chapel Hill group primarily focused on individuals' preferences, assessing the relative significance of role and personal factors preconditioning individuals to particular patterns and the relative importance of motivations and other attitudinal factors affecting predisposition to act.

Much of the activity-based work is descriptive rather than theoretical in nature and relates to a wide range of issues including activity patterns and rhythms of individuals and households, the scheduling of activities in time and space, the importance of space–time and other constraints on activity behaviour, interactions among persons (both intra- and inter-household), relationships between activity and travel choices, detailed timing and the duration of activities and travel, routine travel behaviour etc. Despite the wide diversity of the studies, they share a common philosophical ground – not so much a clear common theoretical or methodological orientation – which results from their interest in patterns, linkages, trip timing and constraints.

Although difficult to characterize simply, the following characteristics may be considered to be of central importance (see Jones et al., 1983, 1990; Jones, 1991).

1 The approach emphasizes the need to consider travel within a broader context through the pattern or sequence of activities undertaken by individuals at various locations in space during a period of time (a day, week or month). The way in which the concept of activity patterns has been operationalized differs greatly from study to study.
2 Activities are undertaken to satisfy basic needs (e.g. sleeping, eating), institutional requirements (e.g. school, work), role commitments (e.g. child care, shopping) and personal preferences (e.g. specific leisure activities).
3 There are various degrees of constraint on when activities can be undertaken, for how long, where and with whom. Special emphasis is laid on spatial, temporal and interpersonal constraints and linkages.
4 Emphasis is laid on decision making in a household context, taking into account relationships and interactions among household members.
5 Travel is explicitly treated as a derived demand, representing a space-shifting mechanism by which people move around space to take part in a succession of non-travel activities at different points in time and space. Thus, travel results from activity participation and trip making. Individual trips are manifestations of activity needs and motivations, given perceptions of opportunities and constraints (see Golob, 1985).
6 The observed daily activity and travel patterns are viewed as the outcome of a – widely routinized – activity scheduling and rescheduling process in

which obligatory and discretional activities are fitted into an available period of time, given perceptions of opportunities and subject to various constraints due to physiological factors, institutional requirements, norms and rules of society and family life.

The activity-based approach provides a more realistic but also a more complex view of travel behaviour than the microeconomic approach does. The emphasis on complexity has deepened our qualitative understanding of travel decision processes, options and constraints, but has also inhibited the development of a more comprehensive and rigorous theoretical framework and analytical methodologies up to now.

Methodological developments

Several methodological developments have been motivated by or developed from the activity-based approach which has been fundamental to activity-based research and has made important contributions to other approaches to travel behaviour research, covering aspects of survey data collection, analysis and modelling. The following discussion is largely based on Jones et al. (1990); see also Kitamura (1988) for more details.

Survey data collection

The data requirements of the new approach are very demanding, reflecting the need for more comprehensive data on travel and activity patterns. These requirements have motivated the development of computer-based survey techniques (e.g. the Household Activity and Travel Simulator (HATS) and the IGOR techniques) based on the use of interactive measurement and/or gaming simulations to obtain travel preference and response data in the context of daily or weekly activity patterns and to identify the types of constraints within which travel-activity patterns are formed (see Jones, 1991, for more details).

Analysis of complex travel-activity behaviour

An important issue in the analysis of travel-activity patterns refers to the development of methods which can be used to measure and analyse travel as a complex phenomenon by incorporating relevant linkages and interactions. Two general approaches to measuring travel patterns can be identified. The first – the one usually adopted – decomposes the pattern into dimensions (such as timing, location, mode of travel, activity sequencing) and generates measures for each of the dimensions. The second approach attempts to treat the patterns as a whole in the form of a multidimensional space representation, to analyse the structure of the travel-activity patterns by means of classification procedures and to identify the relationships between travel-activity behaviour and hypothesized determinants of that behaviour. A prominent example is given by the work of Koppelman and Pas (1985). This approach involves defining a set of indicators that adequately characterize the travel patterns; this in itself involves considerable difficulty since activity and travel patterns evolve in a multidimensional space comprising time, location, activity type, duration, trip attributes such as mode of travel, and other factors.

Quantitative modelling of travel behaviour

Research on activity-based travel has made an important contribution to applied travel behaviour modelling in two ways. First, and most successfully, insights obtained by activity-oriented studies have stimulated economists to refine and improve the specifications of existing random utility choice models. Second, but less significant up to now, there have been some first steps towards developing activity-based models (see Jones et al., 1990).

Studies using travel choice models have integrated the results of activity-based work in several ways:

1 by incorporating new types of explanatory variables, e.g. sociodemographic variables representing role, life cycle and life style, which have been identified to be significant determinants of daily travel-activity behaviour;
2 by explicitly treating interdependences (e.g. car availability at the intra-household level or inter-household interdependences through ride sharing) via NMNL model forms;
3 by developing travel choice models with new kinds of dependent variables, such as the duration of travel.

There have been several attempts at modelling activity participation, timing and duration with econometric tools developed for modelling single-trip decisions. Practical illustrations are Van der Hoorn (1983) and Kawakami and Isobe's (1990) one-day travel-activity scheduling model for workers. There have also been efforts to develop more comprehensive activity-based models of activity scheduling based on combinatorial programming or computer simulation. They typically assume that the individual plans beforehand and predetermines his or her entire daily schedule of activities and trips through a simultaneous decision concerned with the daily schedule as a whole. Since the travel activity pattern evolves within a multidimensional space and thus the decision process is characterized by multidimensional aspects, the operational formulation of the decision process is far from easy and involves discrete choices of activities and location as well as continuous allocation of time and financial resources.

Examples include CARLA (Combinatorial Algorithm for Rescheduling Lists of Activities; see Jones et al., 1983) and STARCHILD (Simulation of Travel/Activity Response to Complex Household Interactive Logistics Decisions; see Recker et al., 1983) which capture several important aspects of how people schedule their activities and represent a progression from a less to a more realistic conceptualization (for an overview see Axhausen and Gärling, 1991). The STARCHILD model involves a submodel of individual choice set formulation which includes both the effect of environmental/household constraints and that of individual limitations with respect to information processing and decision making. The model shows great promise as a means of handling complex adaptation processes (Recker et al., 1983).

Shortcomings and Research Problems

The emphasis on patterns, constraints and linkages of activity and travel behaviour provides a more realistic but also more complex view than the trip-based approaches do. Up to now the activity-based approach, however, still lacks a clear methodological orientation and a unified theoretical framework. There is an urgent need to develop a more comprehensive theoretical framework and more adequate analytical techniques.

Development of such a theoretical framework requires the integration of concepts from several disciplines: psychology (perception of constraints, nature of activity participation needs, identification of attitudes, motivation and emotions for activity participation and travel); sociology (life style, life cycle and roles, interdependences in social networks); geography (understanding of spatial aspects of travel and activity participation, nature of spatial cognition and spatial behaviour, acquisition of spatial knowledge, links between travel and residential mobility); and economics (role of time and money in activity participation and travel, utility derived from activity participation) (see also Jones et al., 1990). Equally important is a more explicit treatment of dynamic processes. Up to now activity-based studies take dynamic effects only implicitly into account by looking at life cycle stages and transitions.

2.5 OUTLOOK

The issues addressed in travel demand research have clearly broadened very considerably over the years. At the same time new innovative approaches have emerged. In spite of the progress made, we are still far away from understanding travel behaviour or from the development of a sound theory underpinning travel demand.

Research and development in the 1990s should concentrate on two major priorities. The first is to consolidate and make more widely available existing activity-oriented and choice-theoretic modelling technologies to the practitioner-oriented environment and to demonstrate their usefulness in the policy area. Both the discrete choice and the activity-based approach to travel choice modelling offer a rich potential. The second priority is to improve our theories, refine the methods and integrate different strands of theoretical contributions. One major challenge will be to reconcile the activity-based and the choice-theoretic approaches which widely differ in vocabulary and philosophy. Considering the power of discrete choice models on the one hand and the limited activity modelling work to date on the other, it certainly seems appropriate to devote major future efforts to generalize and refine rather than to discard random utility based travel choice models. One obvious strategy is to define choice sets, constraints and explanatory variables in a more refined way.

Equally important is the need to shift the focus away from the dominating static perspective to a more explicit dynamic perspective, from static cross-section to panel data sources, especially in a rapidly changing policy world. Static methods might provide biased forecasts of, for example, traffic growth, even if the estimates of input variables are correct, and may lead to wrong policy implications (see Goodwin et al., 1990; Meurs, 1991). Methodologies and statistical techniques already exist to cope dynamically with discrete and continuous choices and aggregate and disaggregate data. The emphasis should be on the nature of behavioural adjustment processes inherent in travel choices, leads, lags, thresholds and uncertainties in travel decision making. The further development of dynamic concepts in travel demand analysis is crucial for the derivation of better and more reliable policy instruments.

REFERENCES

Abkowits, M.D. (1981) Understanding the effect of transit service reliability on work-travel behaviour. *Transportation Research Record 794*, 33–41.

Anas, A. (1982) *Residential Location Markets and Urban Transportation. Economic Theory, Econometrics, and Policy Analysis with Discrete Choice Models*. New York: Academic Press.

Axhausen, K.W. and Gärling, T. (1991) *Activity-based approaches to travel analysis: Conceptual frameworks, models and research problems*. TSU 628, Oxford University: Transport Studies Unit.

Ben-Akiva, M. and Atherton, T.J. (1977) Methodology for short-range travel demand predictions: Analysis of car pooling incentives. *Journal of Transport Economics and Policy*, 224–61.

Ben-Akiva, M. and Lerman, S.R. (1979) Disaggregate travel and mobility choice models and measures of accessibility. In D.A. Hensher and P.R. Stopher (eds), *Behavioral Travel Modelling*, London: Croom Helm, 654–79.

—— and —— (1985) *Discrete Choice Analysis: Theory and Application to Travel Demand.* Cambridge, MA: MIT Press.

Borgers, A. and Timmermans, H.J.P. (1986) A model of pedestrian route choice and demand for retail facilities within inner-city shopping areas. *Geographical Analysis*, 115–28.

Bovy, P.H.L. and Stern, E. (1990) *Route Choice: Wayfinding in Transport Networks.* Dordrecht: Kluwer Academic.

Brownstone, D. and Golob, T.F. (1992) The effectiveness of ridesharing incentives. Discrete-choice models of commuting in Southern California. *Regional Science and Urban Economics*, 5–24.

Brownstone, D. and Small, K. (1989) Efficient estimation of nested logit models. *Journal of Business and Economic Statistics*, 67–74.

Burnett, P. and Hanson, S.M. (1982) The analysis of travel as an example of complex human behavior in spatially-constrained situations: Definition and measurement issues. *Transportation Research*, 87–102

Chapin, S.F. Jr. (1974) *Human Activity Patterns in the City. Things People Do in Time and in Space.* New York: Wiley.

Charles River Associates (1967) *Disaggregate Travel Demand Models.* Report prepared for the National Cooperative Highway Research Program, Transportation Research Board. Washington, DC: Charles River Associates.

Domencich, T.A. and McFadden, D. (1975) *Urban Travel Demand: A Behavioral Analysis.* Amsterdam: North-Holland.

Fischer, M.M. and Nijkamp, P. (1985) Developments in explanatory discrete spatial data and choice analysis. *Progress in Human Geography*, 515–51.

—— and —— (1987) From static towards dynamic discrete choice modelling: A state of the art review. *Regional Science and Urban Economics*, 3–27.

Golledge, R.G. and Stimson, R.J. (1987) *Analytical Behaviour Geography.* London: Croom Helm.

Golob, T.F. (1985) Analyzing activity pattern data using qualitative multivariate statistical methods. In P. Nijkamp, H. Leitner and N. Wrigley (eds), *Measuring the Unmeasurable*, Dordrecht: Martinus Nijhoff, 339–56.

Goodwin, P., Kitamura, R. and Meurs, H. (1990) Some principles of dynamic analysis of travel behaviour. In P. Jones (ed.), *Developments in Dynamic and Activity-Based Approaches to Travel Analysis*, Aldershot: Avebury Gower, 56–72.

Hägerstrand, T. (1970) What about people in regional science? *Papers of the Regional Science Association*, 7–21.

Hanson, S. and Schwab, M. (1986) Describing disaggregate flows: Individual and household activity patterns. In S. Hanson (ed.), *The Geography of Urban Transportation*, New York and London: The Guilford Press, 154–78.

Hausman, J.A. and Wise, D.A. (1978) A conditional probit model for qualitative choice: Discrete decisions recognizing interdependence and heterogeneous preferences. *Econometrica*, 403–26.

Hensher, D.A., Barnard, P.O., Smith, N.C. and Milthorpe, F.W. (1989) Modelling the dynamics of car ownership and use: A methodological and empirical synthesis. In The International Association of Travel Behaviour (ed.), *Travel Behaviour Research. Fifth International Conference on Travel Behaviour*, Aldershot: Avebury Gower, 141–73.

van der Hoorn, A.I.J.M. (1983) Experiments with an activity-based travel model. *Transportation*, 61–77.

Horowitz, J.L. (1979) Disaggregate demand models for non-work travel. *Transportation Research Record 673*, 56–71.

—— (1980) A utility maximizing model for the demand for multi-destination non-work travel. *Transportation Research*, 369–86.

—— (1983) Random utility models as practical tools of travel demand analysis: An evaluation. In P.H.L. Bovy (ed.), *Transportation and Stagnation: Challenges for Planning and Research, Proceedings of the 10th Transportation Planning Research Colloquium*, Delft: C.V.S., 386–404.

—— (1986) Modelling choices of residential location and mode of travel to work. In S. Hanson (ed.), *The Geography of Urban Transportation*, New York and London: The Guilford Press, 207–26.

Jones, P.M. (1983) *A new approach to understanding travel behaviour and its implications for transportation planning*. Ph.D. thesis, University of London.

—— (ed.) (1990) *Developments in Dynamic and Activity-Based Approaches to Travel Analysis*. Aldershot: Avebury Gower.

—— (1991) *Some recent methodological developments in our understanding of travel behaviour*. TSU 663, Oxford University: Transport Studies Unit.

Jones, P.M., Dix, M.C., Clarke, M.I. and Heggie, I.G. (1983) *Understanding Travel Behaviour*. Aldershot: Avebury Gower.

Jones, P.M., Koppelman, F. and Orfeuil, J.-P. (1990) Activity analysis: State-of-the-art and future directions. In P. Jones (ed.), *Developments in Dynamic and Activity-Based Approaches to Travel Analysis*, Aldershot: Avebury Gower, 34–55.

Kawakami, S. and Isobe, T. (1990) Development of a one-day travel-activity scheduling model for workers. In P. Jones (ed.), *Developments in Dynamic and Activity-Based Approaches to Travel Analysis*, Aldershot: Avebury Gower, 184–205.

Kern, C.R., Lerman, S.R., Parcells, R.J. and Wolfe, R.A. (1984) *Impact of Transportation Policy on the Spatial Distribution of Retail Activity*. Final report on DOTRC 92024, US Department of Transportation, Washington, DC.

Khattak, A.J. (1991) *Conceptual issues and empirical evidence regarding the effect of information on travel behaviour*. TSU 660, Oxford University: Transport Studies Unit.

Kitamura, R. (1988) An evaluation of activity-based travel analysis. *Transportation*, 9–34.

Koppelman, F.S. and Hirsch, M. (1989) Intercity travel choice behaviour: Theory and empirical analysis. In The International Association for Travel Behaviour (ed.), *Travel Behaviour Research. Fifth International Conference on Travel Behaviour*, Aldershot: Avebury Gower, 227–44.

Koppelman, F.S. and Pas, E.I. (1985) Travel-activity behavior in time and space: Methods for representation and analysis. In P. Nijkamp, H. Leitner and N. Wrigley (eds), *Measuring the Unmeasurable*, Dordrecht: Martinus Nijhoff, 587–627.

Kroes, E.P. and Sheldon, R.J. (1988) Stated preference methods. An introduction. *Journal of Transport Economics and Policy*, 11–25.

Louvière, J.J. and Hensher, D.A. (1982) Design and analysis of simulated choice or allocation experiments in travel choice modeling. *Transportation Research Record 890*, 11–17.

Luce, R.D. (1959) *Individual Choice Behavior: A Theoretical Analysis*. New York: Wiley.

Manski, C.F. (1981) Structural models for discrete data: The analysis of discrete choice. In S. Leinhardt (ed.), *Sociological Methodology 1981*, San Francisco, CA: Jossey-Bass, 58–109.

McFadden, D. (1981) Econometric models of probabilistic choice. In C.F. Manski and D. McFadden (eds), *Structural Analysis of Discrete Data with Econometric Applications*, Cambridge, MA: MIT Press, 198–272.

Meurs, H.J. (1991) *A panel data analysis of travel demand.* Ph.D. thesis, University of Groningen.

Nijkamp, P., Reichman, S. and Wegener, M. (eds) (1990) *Euromobile: Transport, Communications and Mobility in Europe. A Cross-National Comparative Overview.* Aldershot: Avebury Gower in association with the European Science Foundation.

Recker, W.W. and Golob, T.F. (1979) A non-compensatory model of transportation behavior based on sequential consideration of attributes. *Transportation Research*, 269–80.

Recker, W.W., McNally, M.C. and Root, G.S. (1983) A methodology for activity-based travel analysis: The STARCHILD model. In P.H.L. Bovy (ed.), *Transportation and Stagnation: Challenges for Planning and Research, Proceedings of the 10th Transportation Planning Research Colloquium*, Delft: C.V.S., 245–63.

Sheppard, E. (1986) Modeling and predicting aggregate flows. In S. Hanson (ed.), *The Geography of Urban Transportation*, New York and London: The Guilford Press, 91–118.

Sobel, K.L. (1980) Travel demand forecasting by using the nested multinomial logit model. *Transportation Research Record 775*, 48–55.

The International Association of Travel Behaviour (ed.) (1989) *Travel Behaviour Research.* Aldershot: Avebury Gower.

Thurstone, L. (1927) A law of comparative judgement. *Psychological Review*, 273–86.

Tversky, A. (1972a) Elimination-by-aspects: A theory of choice. *Psychological Review*, 281–99.

——(1972b) Choice-by-elimination. *Journal of Mathematical Psychology*, 341–67.

Wardman, M. (1988) A comparison of revealed preference and stated preference models of travel behaviour. *Journal of Transport Economics and Policy*, 71–91.

Williams, H.C.W.L. and Ortuzar, J.D. (1979) *Random utility theory and the structure of travel choice models.* Working Paper No. 261, School of Geography, University of Leeds.

—— and —— (1982) Travel demand and response analysis – some integrating themes. *Transportation Research* A, 345–62.

Wilson, A.G. (1969) The use of entropy-maximising models in the theory of trip distribution, mode split and route split. *Journal of Transportation Economics and Policy*, 108–26.

—— (1970) *Entropy in Urban and Regional Analysis.* London: Pion.

Wilson, A.G., Hawkins, A.F., Hill, G.J. and Wagon, P.J. (1969) Calibrating and testing the SELNEC transport model. *Regional Studies*, 337–50.

3

Transport between Monopoly and Competition: Supply Side and Markets

E. Quinet

3.1 INTRODUCTION

Having discussed transport demand in the previous chapter, it is logical to consider next the supply of transport and the interface between supply and demand, the transport market. In contrast with the previous chapter, the present chapter will cover both passenger and goods transport.

The word 'market' has several meanings. It can be the place where people buy food and other commodities for the home. It can be the business 'marketplace' where goods and services are traded. Or it can be the abstract concept of economists (in the tradition of Walras, 1874) providing the interface between supply of and demand for a particular good where the price and quantities to be bought and sold are determined.

The latter kind of market is known to be no more than a theoretical ideal, and this is perhaps especially true in the field of transport. To begin with, much of the sector's activity lies outside the market and is regulated by government (see chapter 7). Second, even where supply and demand do come into play, the particular characteristics of the sector – especially the fact that, as the saying goes, transport is not something you can stock and carry – give the transport market, or rather markets, the special features examined in section 3.2 below. Third, transport might be defined in terms of the various theoretical market models – more particularly that of pure and perfect competition producing stable long-term equilibrium among many buyers and sellers – but, as will be seen in section 3.3, it is far removed from this archetype.

3.2 SPECIAL FEATURES OF THE TRANSPORT MARKET

That part of the transport industry which is subject to market forces obeys them according to its own inherent character and peculiarities. In classical economic theory, a market consists of a particular good – for which offers of sale and purchase are made – and a price-setting mechanism that establishes the equilibrium between supply and demand. It also has a geographical scope, as determined by the locations of operators, and a dimension in time: the interface between supply and demand usually occurs at intervals between which both are held in abeyance until the next market session.

This is the ideal case. But there is hardly any instance of a market for a perfectly defined and reproducible good with a price-setting mechanism that immediately establishes the equilibrium between supply and demand. Transport, moreover, has its own particularities. Let us first look at those involved in the definition of transport as a good and which result in a profusion of markets in the narrow sense. These markets may, however, be interrelated by similarities in either demand or supply. We shall then examine the way prices are formed and publicized.

The profusion of markets in the narrow sense

Transport, as a marketable good, can be defined as 'the carriage of an object of given specifications, e.g. weight, size, or of a person, from A to B in a given time, under given conditions of safety, reliability or comfort'. It is easy to see that each of these specifications is essential to the definition of transport as a marketable good, since changing any one of them changes the value of transport to the consumer (cf. chapter 2) or its cost to the supplier, which is to say that the market will be different. In the case of home-to-work travel, for example, the time of travel is fundamental to the definition of the good.

Starting-point and destination are other obvious essentials. The offer of transport from Paris to Amsterdam is not much use if you want to go to Milan. In the case of goods, the type of freight carried is crucial. Fresh fruit and vegetables have very different requirements from, say, metal ore.

Taken in this sense, there is a wide range of transport markets, each with its own generally limited supply and demand structure and particular set of features drawn from all those which define transport as a marketable good.

How can order be found in this profusion, and how can we identify market similarities? There are a number of different ways of classifying and interrelating aspects of both demand on the one hand and supply on the other.

Table 3.1 Direct and cross elasticities in interregional passenger traffic (cf. MATISSE)

	Prices for			
	motor fuel	*rail (< 150 km/h)*	*rail (> 150 km/h)*	*air*
Journey of 100–300 km				
Ordinary highway	−1.2	0.1	0.0	0.0
Motorway	−1.3	0.4	0.0	0.0
Rail (< 150 km/h)	1.4	−1.3	0.0	0.0
Rail (> 150 km/h)	0.0	0.0	0.0	0.0
Air	0.3	0.4	0.0	–
Journey of over 700 km				
Ordinary highway	−0.4	0.05	–	0.05
Motorway	−0.6	0.1	0.05	0.1
Rail (< 150 km/h)	0.2	−1.0	−1.4	0.4
Rail (> 150 km/h)	0.2	0.05	0.3	0.4
Air	0.1	0.05	0.3	−1.4

Interrelating markets with reference to demand

Quality of service is one important criterion applying to transport as a good. Clearly, transport services that differ in quality are different. Quality of service[1] may be quantified by reference to the generalized cost of transport: the transport decisions made by users depend on a linear combination of service quality and cost considerations.

Even with identical service quality characteristics, however, different modes of transport are not perfect substitutes. What is the degree of substitution and parallelism between these goods? Some idea may be gained from the MATISSE demand model developed by Julien and Morellet (1990) to analyse interregional passenger traffic. The figures in table 3.1, which refer to long-distance (more than 100 km) travel in Western Europe, reveal the direct and cross-price elasticity of traffic among the different transport modes.

The transport modes considered are air, rail exceeding 150 km/h commercial speed, rail under 150 km/h commercial speed, motorway and ordinary highway. Elasticity is calculated with reference to

1 motor vehicle fuel prices for all road transport,
2 motorway toll charges,
3 rail fares in each category and
4 air fares.

Table 3.1 sets out the findings for journeys over two ranges of distance. These elasticities depend of course on supply in the different modes. The figures here relate to current supply in France which is plentiful in all modes, especially compared, for instance, with rail in North America. The table none the less shows that transport modes are fairly close substitutes. Rail and air are closer over longer distances and rail and road over shorter ones. But where all three modes are available, competition arises and patronage substitution leads to the interlinking, by demand, of the corresponding markets.

Interrelating markets with reference to supply

Interrelating markets with reference to demand can never produce a single market for transport operations which have different origins and destinations, such a difference being categorical. But some links do exist in the latter case, and it is possible to classify together markets where the suppliers are the same, use the same kind of equipment or can move easily from one market to another. It is possible, for example, to speak of an over 100 km goods transport market, to the extent that long-distance carriers can cover a given territory and change routes rapidly at no extra cost. In these circumstances, a rise in transport demand over a route from A to B would begin by pushing up A to B transport prices and would then attract long-distance carriers from other routes, driving up transport prices on those routes, the end result being a uniform long-distance transport price rise over the whole area in question. The scope and speed of the process would depend on whether the transport equipment can be switched easily from one area to another and on the speed with which information on market conditions can be transmitted from place to place.

The above considerations give some indication of patterns of interrelating markets.

In the case of long-distance (greater than 100 km) goods transport, road haulage forms closely interlinked markets, more so than inland waterways – especially in many parts of Europe, where canal systems are inadequately connected – or rail, because of slower transit times due to marshalling problems and rigidities in the management of a centralized pool of rolling stock.

As to regional goods transport, the markets of a single region are interrelated, but interrelating one region with another depends on the intensity of commercial contacts that transport operators in one region may have in another region. The same may be said where countries are concerned.

Turning to passenger transport, similar considerations suggest that urban transport in different towns – to the very limited extent that it obeys market forces – will show little interrelationship. Facilities are usually tailored to each city, and operating staff are settled in the urban areas where they work.

As regards long-distance passenger transport, market interlinking occurs along the same lines as for goods transport.

In all the above situations, however, the speed of adjustments and market linking depend on a factor of vital importance to the transport market, namely the way in which prices are formed and published.

Formation and publication of prices

In the ideal market of economic theory, prices are determined at the point of equilibrium between supply and demand. But this ideal is seldom achieved and hardly ever found in the transport sector where situations are extreme.

The first extreme, which is found in public passenger transport, is that of prices resulting from a published fares structure on display to the public. This would seem to be an ideal instance of publishing prices, but this is only an illusion in cases where the published fares system is very elaborate, because only a handful of initiates are capable of sorting through the maze of information provided. This is the situation wherever yield management, i.e. instant adjustment of prices to demand, and market segmentation are the rule, in other words where there are many complex fares and rates which fluctuate frequently in response to changes in the conditions governing demand. Examples are air passenger and rail freight transport.

The second extreme is found in individual passenger transport, where few people are aware of the real cost of travel. Car-owners, for instance, may not be certain of their petrol consumption and may be even less aware of the cost of vehicle maintenance and depreciation. They may have only a hazy idea of such service quality factors as journey time or safety and are not at all sure about marginal and average costs.

The third case, usually encountered in goods transport, is that of secrecy. Prices are not published. Rival operators learn of them through leaks, by word of mouth or by deduction. Knowledge of market strains travel quickly, however; it is based less on prices than on such other trade criteria as delivery times or the volume of transport services on offer to shippers.

Conclusion

By and large, transport operates in a market system far removed from the ideal market model whereby a well-defined good has its price fixed by the play of supply and demand.

Instead of one single market, there are many. However, these are interlinked on the demand side by the possibility of substitution, e.g. between modes, and on the supply side by the fact that inputs can switch from one market to another. Furthermore, the system by which prices are formed and published is far from being as pure and transparent as it should be under ideal market conditions.

3.3 HOW THE TRANSPORT MARKET OPERATES

We shall now consider how the transport market operates, a subject of vital importance to both government economic policy and the strategies of private companies. Let us try to answer the following three questions.

1 How far away are we from a perfectly competitive market and what we know this can offer in terms of optimum economic efficiency? More particularly, is the situation one of monopoly or oligopoly?
2 Can competition exist in a monopolistic or oligopolistic situation?
3 How stable is the market?

Monopoly or competition?

Whether or not we find on the transport markets a situation that is monopolistic, oligopolistic or providing near perfect competition depends, as it does in all markets, on the conditions governing both demand and supply.

Economists sometimes seek to establish a direct link between cost functions and market structure. In this section, we shall see what cost function analysis tells us about the structure of transport markets. It should first be noted that the 'subadditiveness' of a cost function plays an important role in this regard. The concept of subadditiveness has been defined as follows: 'A cost function is subadditive for a particular output vector y when y can be produced more cheaply by a single firm than by any combination of smaller firms' (Baumol et al., 1982, p. 170).

We cannot enter into a detailed account of this subject here. From the literature the conclusion may be drawn that cost function analysis can tell us only a limited amount about the subadditiveness of a cost function. Econometrics provides only approximate indicators that give some idea of the probable structure of the activity under consideration. To get a clearer picture it is appropriate first to define different categories of economies.

Let the following simple cost function be assumed:

$$C = f(R, Q)$$

where C is the total cost, R is a parameter defining the extensiveness of the network of the transport enterprise and Q is the total quantity transported, expressed for example in passenger-kilometres or in tonne-kilometres.

Then one usually defines the following.

1 Economies of scale:

$$e_e = \frac{f(R, Q)}{Rf'_R + Q f'_Q} = \frac{1}{e_R + e_Q}$$

where e_R and e_Q are the cost elasticities with regard to the size of the network and the total volume of transport respectively.

2 Economies of density, which are connected to the size and the structure of the network and which are calculated from the expression

$$e_D = \frac{f(R, Q)}{Q f'_Q} = \frac{1}{e_Q}$$

Furthermore, one may distinguish economies of scope. These occur when the following condition applies:

$$C(q_1, \ldots, q_n) < C(q_1, \ldots, 00) + \ldots + C(0, \ldots, q_n)$$

where q denotes the quantities of a number of different goods and C is the cost of producing these goods. This condition expresses the fact that the cost of producing two (or more) different goods together is less than the costs of producing these goods separately.

Economies of scale greater than unity show that, traffic density being equal, the more extensive a network is the lower costs will be; such economies favour the extension of transport enterprises. Economies of density greater than unity prove that, in any given network, the unity cost of transport output will be proportionally lower as traffic density is heavier.

There may of course be cases where economies of scale are greater than unity and economies of density less than unity, and vice versa. It is also possible for economies of scale – or of density – to be greater than unity for some variables and less than unity for others. This may be found in particular for economies of density on a given route: when traffic is light, economies of density are greater than unity because, as traffic builds up, a larger and therefore more economical vehicle can be put into service. This advantage ceases to exist when traffic reaches a volume corresponding to the capacity of the largest vehicle, e.g. 40 tonnes for road goods transport or 500 seats for a passenger aircraft.

The value of economies of scale and of density also depends on the degree to which the production system is geared to the volume of output asked of it. A legacy of under-capacity, where capacity falls far short of the optimum, gives rise to economies of density less than unity, which would not be the case if optimal equipment were used. Similarly, inadequate extension of a network may be conducive to economies of scale greater than unity which would not exist if the regulations, or a more intelligent company strategy, had allowed an extension. What can we learn about these matters from statistical analyses?

Most authors focus on hedonic cost functions.[2] The latter are characterized by treating cost as a function not only of quantity of goods produced but also of their qualitative aspects. While there are many such studies they are difficult to analyse and sometimes contradictory. It is not our purpose to examine them exhaustively[3] but simply to set out their main conclusions.

Economies of scale differ appreciably according to the way in which the production function is defined. Twenty or thirty years ago, the only explanatory variable used for production functions was the volume of output in tonne-kilometres or passenger-kilometres; it gave economies of scale much greater than unity. Production function analysis then introduced more parameters relating to the structure of production, such as network features, and modern econometric analyses now show more modest economies of scale. By and large, economies of scale are nearly equal to unity in road transport, are a little more than unity in air transport and are slightly higher in rail transport. Even these results depend on the degree to which the production system is geared to the output needed. In fact, the production system in the transport sector tends to be larger than it needs to be for reasons that will be examined more closely below. Reasoning based on economies of scale tends to favour a monopolistic view, especially where air and rail are concerned.

This predisposition to monopoly is bolstered by the economies of density shown by statistical analysis. These are very often greater than unity, the degree depending on mode but being particularly large in rail and air transport. It is easy to see why.

In the road sector, network size is determined by the routes provided. Economies of density result from the savings achieved on a particular route when the size of the transport vehicles is increased and the cost per tonne, or per passenger, accordingly falls. But such economies of density quickly reach their ceiling. Road transport is therefore characterized by constant density yields.

In the case of air transport, economies of density likewise result from a reduction in the cost per passenger, or a higher load factor when traffic over a given route increases. But the upper limit on aircraft size is greater in comparison with traffic on the route, so that it is possible to achieve economies of density. Seen from this angle, the air transport market is monopolistic or oligopolistic. The same criteria apply to air transport infrastructure, where network size is defined by the number and size of the different terminals making up an airport.

Similar conclusions apply to railways, except that economies of density are of two kinds. One concerns trains – if traffic for a given number of trains increases and leads to increased train capacity, the cost per passenger rises at a slower rate and economies of density do not reach their ceiling until full capacity is reached. The other kind concerns infrastructure, whose cost varies little in relation to the number of trains until full capacity is reached. Since capacity is extremely high

Table 3.2 Transport market structures

	Monopoly	*Oligopoly*	*Competition*
Rail	×		
Road goods transport		×	×
Road passenger transport			
Regular services	×		
Chartered services		×	
Inland waterway transport			
Dumb barge convoys		×	
Powered craft			×
Air			
Intracontinental	×		
Intercontinental		×	
Sea			
Liner traffic	×	×	
Tramp traffic			×

Source: Quinet, 1990

compared with traffic over most routes, rail transport offers the opportunity for achieving large economies of density.

Economies of scope are much more difficult to determine. Little econometric work has been done to draw attention directly to them. One exception is the study by Jara-Diaz (1988) on economies of scope in road haulage in Chile. Other techniques for observing these economies are simulation of a company's operations and observation of its strategy. Regarding the latter, changes in network structure – especially the introduction of hub and spoke networks after deregulation – clearly show that the cost function depends on network structure as well as on total volume carried, so proving that, in relation to pre-deregulation network structures, cost functions offer economies of scope. The borderline between situations where economies of scope exist and those where they do not is not clear. It must be noted, however, that a transport operator's optimum size and structure are not determined solely by the cost function. They depend also on network externalities – the size of the network affects demand by becoming a component of service quality, as expressed by trip frequency, number of destinations and routes covered (Farrell and Saloner, 1987). Such factors produce small economies of scale but large economies of density and real, if hard to determine, economies of scope.

In the light of what was said earlier, namely that market character depends both on demand and on cost structure, we may estimate the results given in table 3.2 – which ought to be valid for territories the size of European countries.

Does competition exist?

The monopolies and oligopolies common in transport do not necessarily rule out the possibility of competition. Even where the number of operators is small, competition can come into play by virtue of potential market entrants, i.e. the concept of the 'contestable' market. Competition may be expressed other than by prices, especially quality of service, e.g. frequency. Let us look at each of these notions in turn.

A contestable market is one where entry and exit are easy, quick and cost-free (Baumol et al., 1982). In such a market, a monopolist or an oligopolist cannot profiteer, as a rival could step in, win customers by offering slightly lower prices and then withdraw if the former counter-attacked.

The contestability of a market depends on several factors, such as client mobility, price flexibility and absence of entry or exit barriers.

Do clients switch easily among suppliers according to the commercial policy of the latter? Passengers certainly do, but goods forwarders tend to be less mobile. This is partly because habits form, but also because transport proper may be only part of the service provided; the carrier may organize his company in such a way that it offers such logistical extras as goods handling and warehousing. A carrier who does this makes his firm more difficult to replace.

Contestability also depends on the flexibility of prices. If these can be adjusted without difficulty, an established firm can easily hold off the trade offensive of a new competitor and the contestability of the market will be correspondingly reduced. Price flexibility varies according to the mode and type of transport – in the case of maritime conferences, tariffs can be changed only with the agreement of all partners to the conference, which can be a cumbersome and slow process. On the other hand, some air carriers continually change their rates in prompt response to steps taken by their competitors.

The absence of entry and exit barriers is the main feature of a contestable market. Where barriers exist, potential competitors either are completely excluded or are discouraged from entering the market.

The chief barrier is non-recoverable outlay, that is, expenditure needed to enter the market but which cannot be recovered on leaving it, a case in point being fixed infrastructure that cannot be re-sold easily. By and large, transport operations involve only a limited amount of non-recoverable outlay. Investment in equipment can mostly be recovered since there are markets for second-hand lorries, aircraft and ships just as for cars. Where the firm entering the market already exists, moreover, or where a firm intends simply to operate a new route, non-recoverable outlay is reduced.

The public authorities may raise artificial barriers of different kinds, mostly to entry:

1 by granting a firm an operating monopoly;
2 by setting quotas or imposing permit requirements on transport.

On the other hand, the authorities may remove barriers to entry or exit by awarding, for example, vessel scrapping grants in waterway transport or investment incentive payments in shipbuilding.

More subtle barriers may exist on the technical and organizational side, such as requirements relating to logistical services, computerized data transmission systems and airport congestion. Logistical services – storage, packing – were introduced in the mid-1970s when a demand economy supplanted the supply economy. Firms which can provide these services have a competitive edge where the shipper is concerned and therefore have an advantage over rivals. Logistical services are of course closely bound up with the introduction of systems for transmitting and processing data regarding goods forwarded. Computerization, which is the backbone of data transmission and processing, is therefore itself a barrier to entry in that it gives rise to discrimination between firms which have access to computer networks and those which do not.

A similar situation is found in air passenger transport as regards computerized booking systems. Only a small number of competing systems exist, and these are controlled by a few large airlines. The systems' value lies in their broad scope, so they form a barrier to entry controlled by the airlines running them.

One final example of a barrier to entry is the natural or organized scarcity of infrastructure such as air terminals. When an airline has its own terminal, competitors may have difficulty in obtaining facilities, thus coming up against a barrier to entry.

A market may be considered contestable where

1 the prices and products offered by competitors are roughly similar and
2 the differential between prices and costs is small.

Accordingly, the goods transport market would seem to be highly contestable, in so far as freight rates for both road and rail are very close to costs. But, where passenger transport is concerned, the diversity of costs and fares, and the wide margins between them, tend to suggest that the market is not contestable.

Having examined contestability, we cannot really draw any precise conclusions, since the characteristics of the markets differ so much. It seems reasonable to assume, however, that markets involving infrastructure – where they exist – are not very contestable owing to the scale of the non-recoverable investment required, whereas markets based on vehicle activity may be highly contestable in view of the low installation costs and the opportunities to re-sell equipment. Their contestability is often eroded, however, either by protective regulations created by the public authorities or by enterprises themselves which seek to raise barriers to entry (control over infrastructure, computerized booking systems), to attract patronage and develop customer loyalty, or to lay stress on quality, a notion we shall now examine.

Competition based on quality may first relate to journey times but, since time is money, this is equivalent to price competition. It may, as in other sectors, be a matter of providing luxury services; if so, the relevant considerations apply fully (Tirole, 1990). We shall focus more especially on the quality aspects of network externalities and their impact on competition and equilibrium. Two points are of particular interest:

1 the size of the network;
2 service frequency and timetables.

The implications of network size have been studied by Encaoua and Perrot (1991) who examine the equilibrium that arises as a result of having two companies which must determine the size of the network they wish to serve before they can establish their timetables and set their prices. The authors find that fairly restrictive assumptions are needed in order to achieve equilibrium; several equilibria are then seen to be possible, but only some of these are optimal from a social standpoint.

Encaoua et al. (1991) have also studied the situation of two enterprises obliged to reach agreement on the compatibility of their respective networks – co-ordination of timetables and interline agreements enabling passengers to use one or the other company's tickets in the event of network externalities. The authors show that the compatibility pact is a dominant strategy for each company. As regards social welfare, the effects are not so clear-cut. The agreement may have the welcome result of improving quality, but it may also reduce the incentives to engage in price competition.

Regarding competition in terms of timetables and frequency of service on given routes, Quinet (1991) has shown that monopoly situations, and to a lesser degree competition, usually lead to less social welfare than exists in a context of co-operation, and that competition can be unstable.

Accordingly, we come to the general question of the conditions governing the stability of transport markets.

Market stability and sustainability

Market stability, defined as the sustainability of a given level of prices, is a major concern for government and the private sector. In the transport sector, however, stability is a matter of particular concern, as may be seen by one of the few series of transport prices for which detailed and reliable statistics are available, namely those of maritime oil freight (Bauchet, 1991) (figure 3.1).

Stability may be analysed by examining in turn both the supply side and the demand side of the transport market.

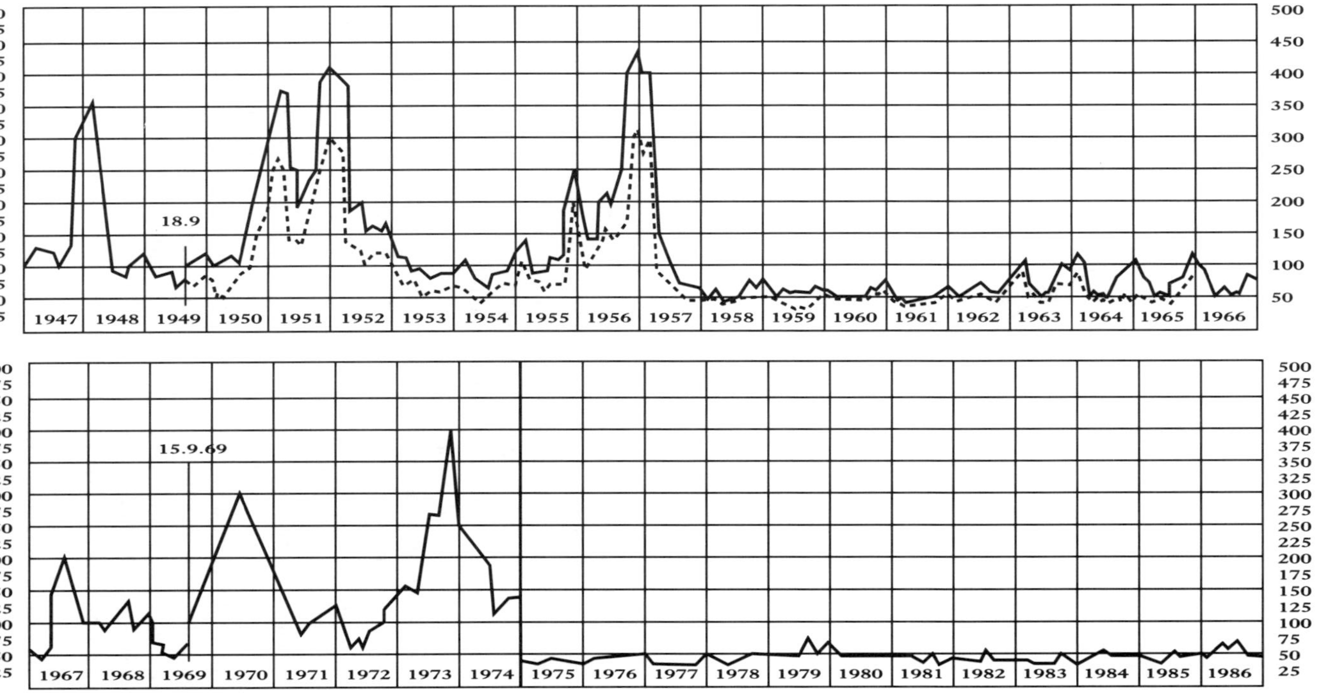

Figure 3.1 Trends in maritime oil freight (tankers).
Source: Bauchet, 1991

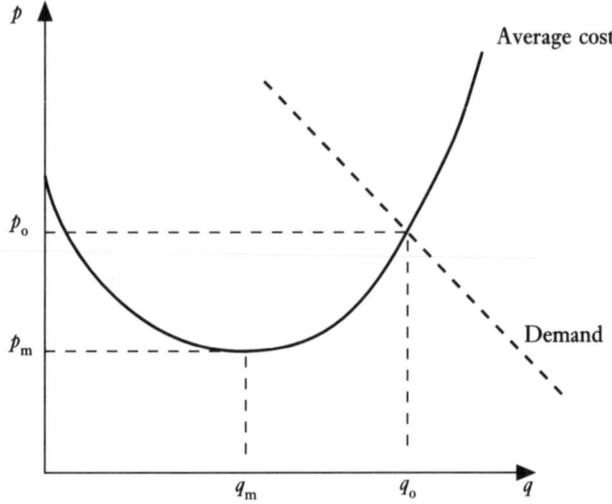

Figure 3.2 Unsustainability.

Expressed simply, an industry – let us say a monopoly – is said to be sustainable if a potential competitor cannot take up some or all of the demand by undercutting the prices set by the monopolist. Broadly speaking, sustainability is equivalent to stability, essentially seen as the maintenance of steady prices. Unsustainability is relatively common. We may take the example of a monopoly which produces a single product. As may be seen from Figure 3.2, unsustainability occurs in the rising part of the average cost curve.

A monopoly is the most advantageous form of organizing production for the community. But the monopolist's market would be broken by a competitor who served only a part of the market at a price lying between p_o and p_m.

The same would apply to oligopolies in the falling or rising segments of the average cost curve for the sector. As with a monopoly, unsustainability occurs when capacity is not, or cannot be, geared to the volume of demand. It is obviously very difficult to determine whether these conclusions are corroborated by any particular real-life situation, especially as figure 3.2 relates to an enterprise producing a single product. In practice, enterprises tend to produce more than one product. This makes analysis more difficult – the calculations for determining a monopoly's sustainability become much more complicated and even harder to verify.

Where there is cross-subsidization, a monopoly is not sustainable. In the transport sector, cross-subsidization is common. It is attributable in particular to the compensatory measures often taken by governments:

1 cross-subsidization in space, as between profitable trunk rail routes and money-losing branch lines or, in the case of urban transport fares, the balance struck between the profits made on central city services and the losses incurred by services in outlying areas;
2 cross-subsidization in time – the difference between peak-hour and off-peak fares, as evidenced by urban or rail passenger ticket prices, is usually much smaller than the corresponding difference in cost.

Cross-subsidization, as mentioned above, is usually practised by the public authorities, who find it a convenient way of financing the public service obligations they impose on carriers: serving sparsely populated areas, ensuring transport regardless of the level of demand, application of uniform prices in time and space. To offset these constraints, the authorities must in all logic protect the monopoly from the weakness induced by the obligations. Otherwise, they expose the monopoly to 'creaming off' by smart competitors who will take the most profitable segment of the clientele by offering lower prices.

The above kinds of unsustainability are static, but there are others of a dynamic nature which may be produced by shifts in demand. In the case of a contestable monopoly, a steady rise in demand may lead to instability. At a given moment the monopoly operates with a certain stock of capital equipment. But, as time goes on, this stock will be inadequate to cope with rising demand. A competitor can then move in with a superior stock of equipment, satisfy the demand at a lower cost and drive out the first monopoly, with a consequent loss of efficiency. The public authorities are obliged therefore to protect the first monopoly.

Technical change may produce the same effect, with demand remaining constant. Changes in technology may render existing equipment obsolete so that the monopoly operating with it is exposed to competition from a new operator using more modern equipment at a lower cost.

But effects like these, linked to increased demand or technical progress, are less common in the transport sector than situations in which the average production cost is higher than the minimum average cost. These, as we have seen, are unsustainable situations in which the monopoly can be bested by new arrivals who serve only part of the market.

What are the cases in which the average production cost can be higher than the minimum average cost? In the transport sector, this situation can arise as a result of a number of factors.

1 Cyclical fluctuations, notably in periods of crisis: Equipment – here meaning vehicles – is geared in size and number to requirements in a 'normal' economic climate. But at a time of crisis, capacity cannot be reduced promptly owing to the long operating life of equipment, ships and aircraft for example, and the surplus capacity entailed can persist for a considerable length of time.

2 Seasonal fluctuations: Transport flows are subject to wide seasonal variations. The amount of equipment needed is calculated to cope with peak periods, but outside of these periods the surplus capacity has the same effects as those described above.
3 Empty return runs: This particular example of imbalances between capacity and demand is very common in road haulage. The road haulier carrying a load from town A to town B will enter the transport market in B to avoid returning empty to A, and will thus increase the total capacity of B's market. Accordingly, B's capacity is clearly determined by chance as a result of a process that is not correlative with the determination of demand. Where there is a great deal of empty return traffic, there is usually a disparity between transport capacity and transport demand which is attributable to chance and will lead to fluctuations in freight rates, keen competition for contracts in the event of surplus capacity, cartel-type agreements and the like.
4 By and large the transport sector suffers from chronic surplus capacity since it is equipped to meet peak traffic needs and is therefore over-equipped at other times. Operators do not seek to reduce capacity for seasonal troughs and, in the event of a crisis, are unable to do so because of the long operating life of their equipment. This inflexibility of supply has its counterpart in inflexibility of demand which is inelastic, at any rate where freight transport is concerned. Quite independently of the theory of sustainability and its applications, here we have conditions whereby equilibrium, though attained at each particular instant, differs considerably from one moment to the next, as may be seen from figure 3.3.

Demand fluctuates around a mean point D_0 owing to seasonal or cyclical variations. Supply is shown in simplified form by the horizontal segment MC, which corresponds to the marginal cost of transport (when demand is inadequate, carriers cover variable costs and write down some of their fixed costs by selling at or slightly above the marginal cost), and by the vertical with capacity on the x axis. In a free market, the mean financial equilibrium of enterprises requires that capacity C be determined in such a way that the break-even price – the point where the supply and demand curves intersect – is equal to the average cost AC.

The structure of the graph shows that slight changes in installed capacity (empty return, runs, breakdowns etc.) or in demand (seasonal variations, crises) will produce far greater changes in the break-even price and be a source of endemic instability in the market, as evidenced by trends in maritime freight. On the whole, transport markets are by no means stable. On many of them the instability of demand in conjunction with the inflexibility of supply and the frequent occurrence of surplus capacity can lead to sharp price fluctuations.

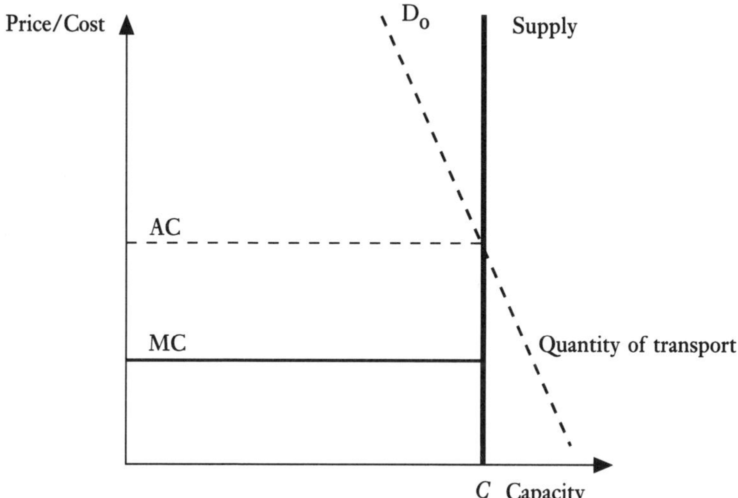

Figure 3.3 Market instability.

Moreover, where certain activities and types of tariff structure, such as those connected with cross-subsidization, are concerned, the market cannot be sustained, i.e. its equilibrium may be upset by an entrant with a 'creaming off' approach.

3.4 CONCLUSION

To sum up, the concept of transport markets would seem to cover a complex set of realities. Much of the transport sector is not subject to regulation by market forces and falls directly or indirectly within the sphere of regulation by the public authorities. There is not one market but a host of rudimentary markets, all interrelated either by virtue of the fact that some of them share a common source of supply, which may therefore switch from one to another within the same category, or by similarities in demand, as for example when the demand may be catered for by interchangeable services offered by different modes of transport.

These markets are far from perfect. Quite aside from methods of determining prices, there are many external factors and strong evidence of monopolistic or oligopolistic tendencies, especially in respect of infrastructure which involves very high fixed costs. Whereas some markets, such as road haulage, are highly contestable, others involving infrastructure are not because the contestability is often eroded by firms seeking to create customer loyalty or set up barriers to entry. Lastly, competition based on quality, e.g. service frequency, number of routes, generates effects that are not easy to analyse and its consequences in terms of social welfare are unclear. There are strong tendencies towards instability.

The market thus operates far from perfectly; it is also a long way from naturally securing optimum economic welfare as understood by Pareto, thus illustrating the generally accepted fact that regulation by market forces is not a law of nature but something to be strived for each day. It is therefore understandable that the public authorities so often try to keep abreast of technological progress, take account of externalities and promote regional development, all topics that will be examined in the following chapters.

NOTES

1 See chapter 2, section 2.3.
2 Among the more important are Keeler, 1974; Spady and Friedlender 1978; Friedlender and Spady, 1981; Harmatuck, 1981; Caves et al., 1984; Bailey et al., 1985; Jara-Diaz, 1988.
3 A detailed survey of the study of cost functions may be found in Winston (1985).

REFERENCES

Bailey, E., Graham, D. and Kaplan, D. (1985) *Deregulating the airlines*. Cambridge, MA: MIT Press.

Bauchet, P. (1991) *Le Transport International dans l'Economie Mondiale*. Paris: Economica.

Baumol, W.J., Panzar, J.C. and Willig, R.D. (1982) *Constestable Markets and the Theory of Industry Structure*. New York: Harcourt Brace Jovanovitch.

Caves, D.W., Christensen, L.R. and Tretheway, M.W. (1984) Economies of density versus economies of scale: why trunk and local service airline costs differ. *Rand Journal of Economics*, 471–89.

Encaoua, D. and Perrot, A. (1991) *Concurrence et coopération dans le Transport Aérien en Europe*. Report for the EC, University of Paris I.

Encaoua, D., Michel, P. and Moreaux, M. (1991) Capacity externalities and compatibility: a game theoretical model. *Transportation Science*, forthcoming.

Farrell, J. and Saloner, G. (1987) Competition, compatibility and standards: the economies of horses, penguins and lemmings. In L. Gabel (ed.), *Product Standardization and Competitive Strategy*, Amsterdam: North-Holland.

Friedlænder, A.F. and Spady, R. (1981) *Freight Transport Regulation: Equity, Efficiency and Competition in the Rail Trucking Industry*. Cambridge, MA: MIT Press.

Harmatuck, D.J. (1981) A motor carrier joint cost function. *Journal of Transport Economics and Policy*, 135–53.

Jara-Diaz, S. (1988) Multi output analysis of trucking operations using spatial disagragates flows. *Transportation Research*, 159–71.

Julien, H. and Morellet, O. (1990) *MATISSE*. Report 129, Paris: INRETS.

Keeler, T.E. (1974) Rail road costs, return to scale and excess capacity. *Review of Economics and Statistics*, 201–8.

Quinet, E. (1990) *Analyse Economique des Transports*. Paris: Presses Universitaires de France.

—— (1991) Organisational structure of public transport and assessment of schedules. *Transport Planning and Technology*, 145–53.

Spady, R. and Friedlænder, A.F. (1978) Hedonic cost functions for the regulated trucking industry. *Bell Journal of Economics*, 159–79.

Tirole, J. (1990) *The Theory of Industrial Organization*. Cambridge, MA: MIT Press.

Walras, L. (1874) *Eléments d'Économie Politique Pure*. Paris: Librairie Générale de Droit et de Jurisprudence, reprinted 1976.

Winston, C. (1985) Conceptual developments in the economics of transportation: an interpretive survey. *Journal of Economic Literature*, 57–94.

4

Technical Innovation in Transport

G.A. Giannopoulos

4.1 INTRODUCTION

If transport economics is the application of economic theory and techniques in the operation of the transport system, including the evaluation and measurement of its economic impacts, then technical innovation in transport is of particular interest to transport economics since it may profoundly affect this operation in many ways.

In very general terms, the benefits of transport services lie in the improvement in economic relations brought about by the spatial transfer of persons, goods and information. Thus, the provision of more effective transport services brought about by technical innovation can be seen as optimizing the use of scarce factors of production. At another level of economic consideration, the explosive expansion of passenger and freight transport has caused high and rising levels of disamenity and environmental pollution wherever there is a substantial volume of transport operations. At the same time, individual and political sensitivity to the nuisance and damage caused by transport is growing. This has led to critical and frequently hostile attitudes to transport and its further growth. In one economic argument this criticism often takes the form of the thesis that transport is simply too cheap, because the provision of transport services by no means takes account of all the costs and the polluter is not made to pay; this is another area where technical innovation, by helping to reduce these external effects, can be of profound interest for the form and method of the theory of transport economics.

In relation to this point is the idea that the effects of technical innovation can reduce the excessive waste of resources often ascribed to transport as a whole. Here, the critical attitude and accusations of waste and uncovered social costs are directed above all at road traffic and the internal combustion engine. Again, in these two areas technical innovation can, and is expected to, play a positive role in the future.

A more evident relationship between technical innovation in transport and transport economics, however, can be obtained when defining 'technical innovation'.

Defining technical innovation

Put simply, 'technical innovation' encompasses the concepts of technological and organizational innovation in the field of transport, and more specifically the infrastructure provision, the vehicles used and the operation of the system.

In a definition given by Schubert (1988) 'innovation' as a concept is defined as encompassing

1 'new alternatives not yet there or not well known';
2 'new ideas set in motion to solve urgent problems'; or
3 'new activities or reorganization of activities such as new services, institutions, rules, policies, planning paradigms etc.'.

Thus, in the field of transport, technical innovation can be related to

1 new types of technology, concerning the means of transport (vehicles);
2 new modes of (private or mass) transport;
3 new means for upgrading the performance and service of existing modes of transport;
4 new types of organization and provision of transport services and/or traffic arrangements; and
5 other changes related to the existing transport system.

An important place in technical innovation and change in the field of transport has been taken recently by the various aspects of information technology and its applications in the management, operation and organization of the transport system. There are two important notions in the term 'information technology'. These are the notions of computing, i.e. creating, handling and storing information, and telecommunications, i.e. transmitting information.

The distinction between computing and telecommunications is increasingly ambiguous and blurred. The ambiguity is expressed in an excellent way by the term 'telematics', which exactly reflects this intermingling of computers and telecommunications in recent years. Over the last few years we have moved from what was a fairly homogeneous technical form of telecommunications to a whole range of heterogeneous technologies, all covered by the term 'telematics' (ECMT, 1983).

It is this wider definition of information technology, i.e. telematics, that we shall be using in this chapter.

In the following we shall be opting for a balanced treatment of telematics and other forms of transport technology.

Contents and structure of the chapter

In treating the subject of technical innovation and innovation in transport, in the context of this book, we shall distinguish between two basic areas of such innovations (see figure 4.1):

1 transport vehicles and infrastructure, i.e. the 'capital goods' used for transport; and
2 the overall operation and management of the system, i.e. the way these 'capital goods' are used.

In the case of (1) the major area of innovation concerns technological breakthroughs and improvements which make the so-called transport 'hardware' more effective, while in the case of (2) the emphasis is on telematics applications that are likely to revolutionize the so-called transport 'software' and 'orgware' in the near future.

A further obvious dimension to consider is the various transport modes (road, rail, air, sea, inland waterways) and combined transport. In most of these the distinction between passenger and freight transport then has to be taken into account (figure 4.1).

To cover the subject of technical innovation in all these aspects in a comprehensive way would require a far lengthier analysis than is possible in the limited space of this chapter. On the other hand, and despite the considerable importance of inland waterways, coastal shipping, pipelines and air transport in certain countries, the relationship between rail and road transport is the crux of the co-ordination problem for transport within Europe. The emphasis is thus put on road and rail (freight and passenger) as well as on combined transport, although some account and reference is made to the other modes of transport.

The material is divided into six sections as follows. After this introduction follows a second section which looks at technical innovations in the field of vehicles and infrastructure construction. The third section concerns technical innovations in the operation and management of the transport system which mainly involve telematics applications in almost all aspects of (road, rail and combined) transport. In the fourth section the discussion focuses on the likely impacts and the processes of innovation diffusion, with a detailed presentation of the latest estimates of the implications of such innovations. Finally, the last section draws some conclusions and policy implications.

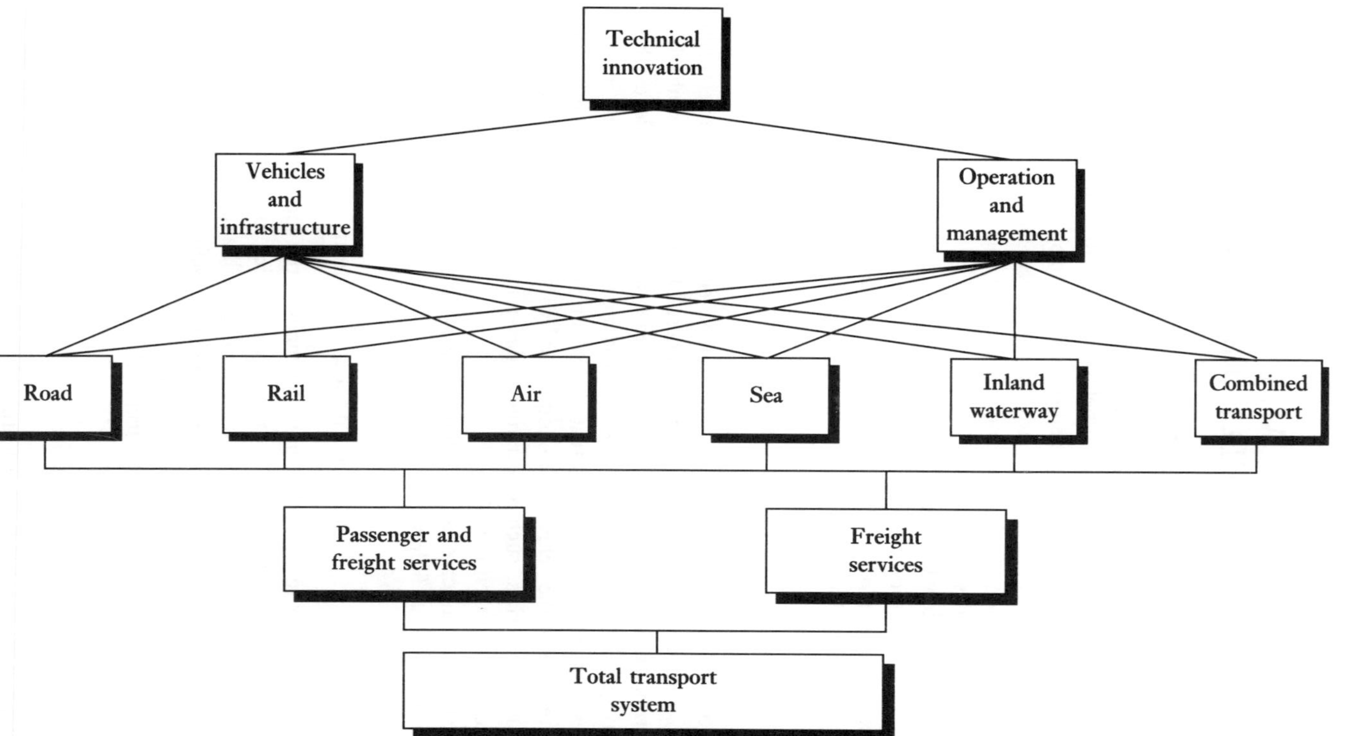

Figure 4.1 Areas of consideration in the study of technical innovation in transport.

4.2 TECHNICAL INNOVATION IN VEHICLES AND INFRASTRUCTURE

Individual road passenger vehicles (cars)

During the last decade several technical problems related to the automobile came to light and new technological fields were developed to solve these problems. Together with the introduction of new technologies in the field, such as chemistry-based technology, great advances were also made in engine combustion and the electronic and mechatronic systems for controlling combustion. As a result, automobiles are increasingly characterized by high reliability, superior performance and low fuel consumption. Furthermore, the industry has begun to accelerate the introduction of communications technology, the development and use of new materials and the utilization of computer-controlled mechanisms.

Technological developments have been aimed further to improve safety and to reduce exhaust pollution and fuel consumption. New safety technology is being introduced to improve the basic functions of automobiles and to increase their operational safety.

To control these and other new systems, new technology began to contribute to the improvement of automobile performance. This included the multiple use of electronic technology and information systems, such as automobile telephones and navigational systems which began to become popular, and equipping automobiles with intelligent systems that enrich automobile life. The performance characteristics of the vehicles were improved by the manufacture of some parts using new materials, such as ceramics, fibre-reinforced plastics (FRPs) and fibre-reinforced metal (FRM).

The trends in automobile technology as seen up to the year 2000 and beyond can be described as follows.

Vehicle control and systems

With the advances in microelectronics technology, the application of electronic control systems is expected to be gradually expanded to engines, driving systems and chassis. Future electronics technology will aim at securing both sophisticated auxiliary driving functions and high safety by providing overall control. This technology will develop further to create automatic driving systems linked with communications technology.

Communications technology

A diagrammatic view of the most probable of these technologies in the cars of the future is shown in figure 4.2. More on this technology is mentioned in the section on telematics applications.

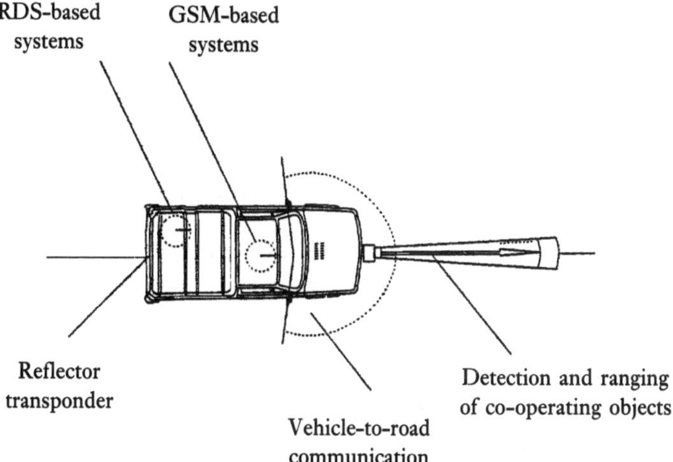

Figure 4.2 The 'communications' innovations in the vehicle of the future.

New materials

New automobile materials that have drawn attention are FRPs and FRM.

Use of next-generation computers for car design

The technology to create fifth-generation and neural computers is being developed progressively. They will have a marked influence on automobile development systems and production technologies.

Use of biotechnology methods and techniques

This technology 'copies' mechanisms and procedures that are available in the organs of living creatures such as bats, dolphins and birds and uses them to detect obstacles and to reduce movement resistance to travel. Therefore, it is very likely that innovations in automotive technology for sensors and actuators will occur as biotechnology progresses.

More environment friendly vehicles

New technology to reduce exhaust pollution such as NO_x and fluorocarbons will continue to be developed, and this has strong potential. The same holds true for noise pollution, especially for heavy vehicles such as trucks and buses.

New energy sources

The number of automobiles using a wide range of new energy sources will also increase, e.g. methanol cars, gas-turbine cars using fine-ceramic materials and hybrid cars that can use different energy sources.

The subject of alternative fuels is inevitably combined with new engine types and merits special attention because of its great importance for energy and environmental conservation.

The most imminent 'new' innovative fuel that will revolutionalize energy sources is electrical energy stored in batteries and used by electrical motors in vehicles.

Bus public transport vehicles

Radical technical innovation in buses (urban or interurban) is already here and is being applied on a limited scale and/or on a trial basis. Other technological advances are still at an experimental stage but may well be applied in the foreseeable future. The major areas of these changes are (Giannopoulos, 1989a)

1 optimization of the diesel engine and the transmission;
2 regeneration of braking energy;
3 alternative fuels, such as methanol, liquified propane gas (LPG), liquified natural gas (LNG);
4 electric buses;
5 automatic guidance systems for buses.

The above advances in technology show that the bus can be much more than just a vehicle 'swimming' along in the general traffic stream and having stops which are nothing more than just a post on the edge of the sidewalk. The developments already on the horizon show that it is well worth exploiting the unused reserves of the bus as a means of mass transport in urban areas. The components of the whole system, i.e. the 'vehicle', the 'roadway/bus stop' and the 'operational control', can be improved so as to form a comprehensive package from which each public transport authority can tailor a system fitting perfectly into its overall transit concept.

Road freight transport

The poor state of many developing countries' roads has led to the need for robust trucks which can deal with severe overloading and poor driving and which are generally less dependent on maintenance.

Perhaps the most important innovation in truck design and construction is the increasing appearance of high-tech equipment on-board the vehicles, as standard or optional, which is intended to enhance operations, improve safety and provide better maintenance. This equipment includes on-board computers which keep track of vital functions of the truck and help the driver in various logistical tasks, mobile data communication equipment for communication with the home base etc.

Rail infrastructure and rolling stock

Rapid technological change to improve performance and increase speed has occurred only in some key areas. Electrification is a first example. Concurrently with electrification other innovations were introduced in many other parts of the system, particularly signalling and signal boxes.

A second main area of innovation is high-speed trains. With the construction of new lines at the end of the 1980s, most notably in France with the TGV, speeds of 400 km/h and then 500 km/h were reached. As very high speeds can be achieved in the classical railway system of wheel–rail contact, speed limits are now being set by economic rather than technological constraints.

Today, in Europe and other parts of the world (EEC, 1990), the technological innovation in very high-speed railways comes under two different technological concepts:

1 the wheel-on-track concept represented by the French TGV; and
2 the magnetic levitation (Mag-lev) concept represented by the German Transrapid project. Transrapid vehicles are designed to cruise at speeds of 300–500 km/h and to transport passengers or express goods. If convenient, passenger and container units can be combined to form mixed train sets of up to ten units.

Road and airport infrastructure construction

Of particular interest are the effects of new materials and methods of construction used in order to make roads, and runways of airports, less costly and faster to build whilst increasing safety. Technical innovation in this field concentrates on new material used for the construction of layers of the roads and airfields and on new equipment and techniques for this construction.

4.3 TECHNICAL INNOVATION IN THE OPERATION AND MANAGEMENT OF THE TRANSPORT SYSTEM

As we move into the twenty-first century, improving the operation and management of the transport system becomes a key policy objective in order to maximize the benefits from the utilization of the available infrastructure and scarce resources in general. Telematics plays a key role in almost all major technical innovations that are currently being tested in this area.

There are several new telematics-based technologies that are in various stages of development and/or implementation. The same technologies may have applications in more than one area of transport operation. For example, the range of new automatic debiting systems may be used for toll collection from private road vehicles or trucks, or for parking payments etc. Similarly, the various route guidance systems may be applicable to private road transport as well as freight transport or public bus transport, and so on.

In this section we have chosen to present first a set of 'generic' technical innovations, i.e. innovations which allow for improvements in several application areas that are likely to appear in the market, say, in the next three to 15 years and which are both well advanced in preparation and form the basis of the majority of possible applications. Next we shall indicate the various application areas where these technologies will be making an impact in the future.

Description of the main technical innovations

Radio data based systems

The radio data system (RDS) is a broadcasting standard established in 1984 by the European Broadcasting Union (EBU). One application of the RDS is its use for navigation purposes, i.e. helping the driver to find his or her way. The autonomous route guidance (ARG) systems currently on the market, e.g. the Bosch Travel-Pilot, contain a digital road map that is based on geographical ('static') data and allow the user to determine the route from the current location to a given destination. These ARG systems cannot take account of changes in traffic conditions which can significantly alter the best routes. With RDS and TMC (traffic message channel) 'dynamic' data become available, and extended ARG systems can be implemented that make use of 'static' and 'dynamic' data when determining the best route.

Intelligent Cruise Control System The attribute 'intelligent' serves to distinguish a future class of cruise control systems which can essentially provide safe distance keeping. For this purpose, vehicles will be equipped to 'sense' other vehicles within their safety zone.

Interactive route guidance systems Interactive route guidance (IRG) systems essentially rely on a two-way communication channel between the vehicle and a control centre.

For IRG the trip destination needs to be delivered to a control centre, which then provides appropriate dynamic routing information back to the equipment in the vehicle.

Automatic debiting systems The technology for automatic vehicle identification and automatic debiting systems provides a technical base for a number of applications such as automated toll collection, parking management and public transport. Automatic debiting can be seen as a convenience for the drivers and travellers, e.g. debiting of parking or toll fees. Alternatively, it offers a more refined way of administering the cash flow.

Clearly, the technical features for automatic debiting should be designed to be flexible, allowing for implementation of various policies. One basic debiting system can then be implemented across Europe for all local road-use pricing variants.

Electronic data interchange for freight management and related activities An electronic data interchange (EDI) system[1] has both physical and logical parts. The physical parts are the data transmission channels, the switching systems and the computers at terminals or nodes in the network. The logical parts are the software, the standards and the protocols for interconnecting and using the physical parts.

In order to use a computer for EDI, it has to be physically adapted to treat the transmission facilities as devices for input and output, and the software must be prepared to permit interaction with the EDI network. Therefore, a crucial prerequisite for the wider adoption and use of EDI is the standardization and normalization of EDI networks.

Notable examples of current European efforts to establish reliable EDI networks are the TRADACOMS and TRADANET systems in the UK (Fenton, 1984, 1985).

Recognizing the uncoordinated development of EDI standards, the United Nations Economic Commission for Europe (UN-ECE) has developed the international standard EDIFACT (Electronic Data Interchange for Administration, Commerce and Transport).

EDI research is vigorously being carried out in Europe and soon the technology is expected to be ready for wide scale application.

Voice and data communications in wired networks Communications innovations fall into two broad categories: mobile networks and fixed networks.

Most of the information handling to prepare and process messages and transactions related to transport takes place in stationary offices. Therefore, mainly wired networks are used for data and voice transmissions.

Mobile voice and data transmissions systems For many years, mobile communications have remained a marginal activity. A breakthrough was achieved about 12 years ago with the adoption of the cellular network concept which, in principle, allows unlimited reuse of the same frequencies. This triggered a renewed interest in terrestrial mobile communications, which is now a very fast growing market almost everywhere in the industrialized countries. Both voice communications and data transmission appear to be essential requirements.

Within the scope of the *Conférence Européenne des Administrations des Postes et des Telecommunications* (CEPT), the PTTs of Western Europe agreed upon the implementation of a new mobile telephone system. In 1987, a decision was taken that similar transmission techniques should be used all over Europe. By February 1988, a sub-group of CEPT named GSM (Groupe Spécial Mobile) specified the technical functions of this cellular radio communication system, which has since been known by the initials GSM. With technological changes from analogue to digital communications and with a pan-European availability for the first time, GSM can be considered a major element in a future communication infrastructure for road transport and traffic in Europe.

The systems available today for mobile voice and data communications are almost entirely based on satellite communications. Well-known examples are INMARSAT (International Maritime Satellite Organization), EUTELSAT (European Mobile Satellite) and OMNITRACS (specifically aimed at the trucking industry).

On-line tracking of shipments and shipment identification The ability to track a shipment all the way through to its final destination has very attractive applications in freight transport. It entails the ability to receive automatically messages from the shipments to appropriate road-side units which will then transmit this information to control centres. The most promising technologies for identifying shipments are bar-codes and electronic tags.

Bar-code reading with laser scanners or cameras for remote reading is a simple method, fast, cheap and relatively reliable. A rapid universal adoption of this technology within the next three to five years can be expected in goods transport for identifying shipments, transport equipment and paper documents. It is already applied in the case of containers. The major disadvantage of bar-codes is the problem of dirt and other obstacles obstructing the reading of the bar-code.

Electronic tags can also be 'read' remotely. Many can store relatively large amounts of data. The relatively high price of about $8 per tag (in 1990) makes them only applicable in situations where they can be reused, e.g. for vehicle or load unit identification.

Vehicle location systems Within the past two years the use of automatic vehicle location has grown exponentially. The main telecommunication technologies used here are satellites, but when the GSM network is in operation it will probably provide better coverage, especially in urban areas.

Main application areas

The aim of this section is to describe the main application areas supported by the technical innovations mentioned above.

Road traffic management and control

The main application areas of interest here are

1 demand management
2 travel information
3 traffic information
4 traffic control
5 vehicle control
6 parking management
7 organization and general management of urban and interurban traffic

Figure 4.3 shows the interrelation of these areas.

In the following each of these application areas is briefly described and functions, or measures, which are of particular importance in the respective field are highlighted. Technologies that constitute 'technical innovation' are described.

Demand management

The management of travel demand includes a number of functions and measures that are needed to preserve the operational capacity of the road network and to avoid uncontrolled increases in traffic. In this context, two main objectives must be addressed:

1 moving the travel demand to more suitable modes; and
2 obtaining a better distribution of traffic both in time (modifying departure times) and space (influencing route choice).

Demand management and user financing for infrastructure are probably due in the near future. These concepts need an early agreement, not only on the principles applied but also on standards for technical systems, e.g. toll collection or automatic debiting. This in fact requires a coherent European transport policy.

Travel information

Travel information can be regarded as the generic term for a number of possibilities to provide the traveller with information relevant to the current situation and with helpful suggestions for a preferred travel choice. The goal is to improve the balance of the distribution of travel demand via optimizing departure times, use of different modes and route choice within the road network.

The communications (networks, user terminal equipment) required for travel information services are available today and will be developed further in the near future, e.g. Minitel, Teletext, ISDN. However, the implementation of viable information-providing services is of particular importance.

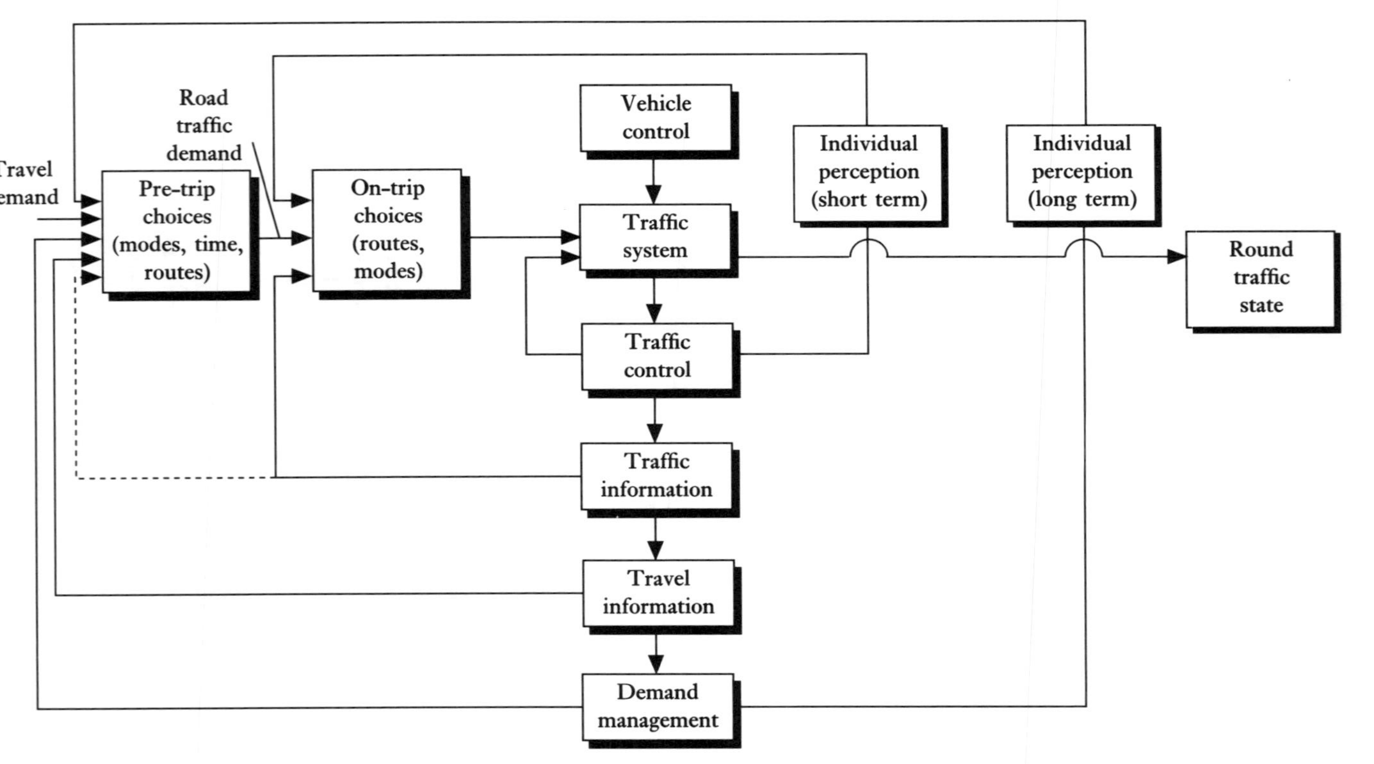

Figure 4.3 Interrelation of main telematics innovation application areas.

Traffic information

This application is specific to road users. While travel information partly affects the 'pre-trip' user choices, traffic information should be considered as relevant mainly to the 'in-trip' decisions.

Two basic classes of traffic information can be distinguished:

1 information describing actual abnormal traffic conditions with short-term forecasts (traffic jams, accidents, road works) – this information could be broadcast by radio channels or displayed via variable message signs; information on traffic events, possibly by on-board navigation systems, will enable the driver to optimize his route planning;
2 specific and individual information, supplied to the driver via suitable channels and on-board equipment, containing direct suggestions on suitable, or best, routes to the destination, e.g. dynamic route guidance.

Traffic control

Traffic control requires collecting huge quantities of data to assess traffic conditions (data are taken by simple sensors), elaborating control algorithms and directing the traffic by different means (traffic lights, signals, variable message signs). In fact, there are no clear separations between traffic information and traffic control since providing the drivers with information is a way of influencing the traffic.

Within traffic control the following functions are of particular importance:

1 flow control, which includes all control measures that can be taken in order to improve the flow within specific links of a network;
2 intersection control, which provides the control of intersections in both an urban and an interurban context;
3 network control, which can comprise environmental monitoring, network surveillance, origin/destination computations, traffic prediction and route optimization.

Vehicle control – co-operative driving

In general the issues in this field cover two major areas: first, how to improve the perception capabilities of the driver and, second, how to improve his or her reaction/driving performance. Despite the complexity of the tasks to be solved, it is realistic to assume that partial solutions will be ready for implementation already in the medium term since the efforts being undertaken in this field are considerable.

Parking management

Two levels of parking management applications can be distinguished. The first (strategic level) is a part of demand management. It consists of a series of parking policies such as restriction or pricing, as a way of affecting the balance of travel within urban areas.

The second (technical level) is a means of managing the stock of available parking spaces. This 'stock' management can be considerably improved using telematics. Parking, booking, park-and-ride and automatic parking debiting are some of the applicable measures.

Organization and general management

The key word for the successful overall outcome of the applications mentioned earlier is integration. Already a substantial part of research work is directed towards the establishment of the so-called integrated road transport environment (IRTE) in both urban and interurban areas. An illustrative sketch of how such an IRTE could look for an urban area is shown in figure 4.4.

Freight logistics and management

Technical innovation in this field is seen to be concentrated in two major areas:

1 implementation of new logistics strategies for the whole transport/delivery operation; and
2 applications of advanced telematics in the road, rail or combined freight transport operation.

New logistic strategies

On the organization structure side, production is no longer considered as a simple transformation process but as a varied and complex activity in which transport plays a key role. Aware of the necessity to manage physical flows in the production process, many firms now consider that processes of production should be controlled in relation to the whole logistics chain.

Demand also drives shifts in organization, such as the increasing need for customized products. The number of transport-related variants is greater when custom-made products are produced directly by the manufacturer.

Many of the largest European carriers have recognized that important changes in demand are taking place among their major customers, especially with respect to the 'regionalization' of their transport and distribution operations. As a consequence, these carriers are repositioning themselves to offer 'one-stop

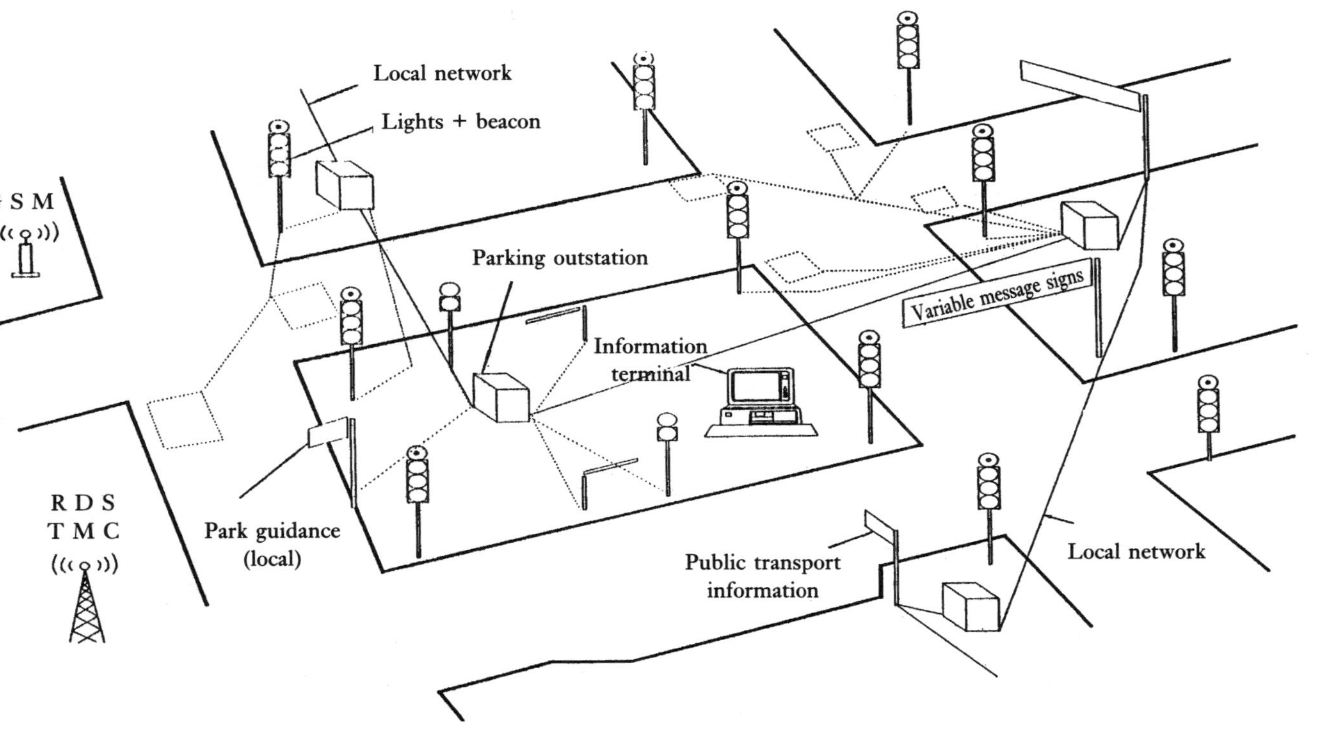

Figure 4.4 An example of an integrated system of applications of telematics innovations in the urban road network.

shopping' to major customers. Many carriers aim to provide some services themselves, e.g. the 'intelligent logistics' such as full transport load (FTL) which any owner-driver can readily perform. In this way, these emerging 'mega-carriers' will be able to offer an appropriate service for any part of the region, according to both the characteristics of transport demand and the cost of providing different types of service.

Thus new informatics applications and their corresponding logistics chains are shaping a new pattern of logistics and distribution 'structures'. Distribution centres and corresponding logistical platforms at various levels (European, national, regional and urban) are now being developed in European countries.

Advanced telematics applications in freight logistics and management

Of the specific applications discussed for freight transport the most preferred today by European operators and forwarders seem to be the following (EUROFRET, 1991; see also table 4.1):

1 one or two standardized and uniform European-wide EDI networks for communication between the various 'actors' of the trade;
2 on-line tracking of shipments;
3 automatic fleet (and driver) identification and monitoring;
4 mobile data communication (two-way); and
5 automatic vehicle positioning systems.

It appears that we are on the verge of a wider market acceptance of many interesting new applications of information technology. Freight transport is probably the first field of transport to benefit from them and make them commercially viable for a wider application.

Public Transport

Applications of technological innovations (telematics) in the field of public transport (bus or rail, urban or interurban) can best be described in terms of seven main functions of such transport as they appear in CASSIOPE (1992), i.e. scheduling, passenger information, fare collection (i.e. establishing, collecting and monitoring the revenue received for public transport services), maintenance (i.e. preparing the fleet of vehicles to the best possible standard for operations and rectifying any faults which may arise, recording and analysing vehicle data, assuring maintenance quality, planning maintenance actions, preparing, performing and controlling maintenance work), strategic planning, management information and operations management.

Table 4.1 Main innovations in freight logistics and management

Innovation	*Functions*	*Use of results*
Automatic vehicle identification	Transmit vehicle information Identification Size and weight Vehicle type or class	Traffic counting and vehicle classification Comply with regulatory requirements Automatic toll collection
Bar coding	Provide product and packing information Identification Size and weight Origin and destination	Sales and inventory Track shipments and check status
Electronic data interchange	Transmit business data and provide electronic business documents Purchase order Bill of lading Packing slip Invoice Electronic funds transfer	Electronic ordering and billing Verify pick-up and delivery
In-vehicle navigation systems	Provide driver information Highway and traffic conditions Location (of vehicle, destination etc.) Alternative routes Automatic vehicle spacing Blind spot warning Crash avoidance	Identify most direct or least time route (avoiding incidents, congestion and delay) Avoid road hazards particularly during bad weather
On-board computer (mobile IT)	Monitor vehicle and driver Vehicle speed Engine rpm Engine idle time Engine oil temperature and pressure Vehicle stop time and distance Driver's braking habits	Decide when normal maintenance needed Diagnose (or prevent) major breakdowns Evaluate driver performance
Two-way communication systems	Exchange messages between dispatcher and driver Trip and shipment information Location (of vehicle, destination etc.) including location of maintenance and repair shops	Manage logistics while in transit Arrange repairs for breakdowns in transit Respond to emergencies

Source: OECD, 1992

Combined Transport

Combined transport operations are of increasing interest because of the increasing concerns about environmental, political and other constraints that are quite often imposed on road freight transport. They mainly involve road–rail and road–sea operations through rail stations or ports.

The technical innovations (mainly telematics) that were mentioned in section 4.1 are also expected to have some extremely useful and beneficial applications in combined transport. Some important applications are as follows:

1 wagon or unit load tracing on international railway networks;
2 automatic capacity booking for unit loads in combined transport (combi) operations (towards the creation of a pan-European booking system);
3 two-way communication of railways and combi companies with road freight operators for administration and financial functions.

In addition, many 'administrative breakthroughs' in the field of combined transport also largely depend on the utilization of these innovations in combi operations or can be facilitated by their utilization. They include

1 the application of tax redemptions or of other incentives for trucks conducting terminal access in transport using combi modes as well as for trucks or unit loads making use of combi operations; and
2 providing trucks using combi links with comparative benefits or other incentives for driving under restrictive traffic conditions.

4.4 DISCUSSION OF THE POSSIBLE IMPACTS AND POLICY IMPLICATIONS

In the preceding sections we gave an account of the main current or expected innovations in a wide range of transport fields and applications.

In this section, a number of fundamental questions are discussed and points are raised in relation to the possible impacts of these innovations, their diffusion process and the likely policy implications that all these considerations imply.

The impacts of technical innovation on the benefits of transport operation

In an equilibrium system with constantly recurring production, exchange and consumption processes that take place in the different locations of an economic space, the transport flows and transport costs are determined by the interdependence of market relations and market forces. Such an equilibrium in an economic space shows a balance between the advantages of the spatial division of labour and the transport costs that have to be accepted. Technical innovation by interfering in this process changes this 'equilibrium' and formulates a new one that hopefully satisfies the needs more. The picture of simultaneous equilibrium in all markets, which explicitly includes spatial distances and transport costs, is of use mainly as a model, but it does show the relationships between the economic space, the transport economy and the associated need to take decisions and introduce innovations as 'technology', in a broad sense, provides them.

In a characteristic example of this model, the impacts of transport-related technical innovations on urban form and development were studied[2] over a 100-year period through case studies on several European cities (Giannopoulos and Curdes, 1992). It was found that, by looking at the urban form at each particular point in time, we look in fact at the result of the 'temporary' equilibrium between the transport system, the accessibility levels and the activities that take place within the spatial structure, and that this equilibrium is 'disturbed' periodically by technical innovations.

It was further noted that innovative events in transport can be identified in almost all the urban areas studied at some point in their development. The most easily identified were those related to the introduction of a new mode of transport and new transport infrastructure.

As regards the other types of innovation, e.g. upgrading of performance or service levels of existing modes or changes in the organization, financing etc., there is evidence that these too have played a traceable role in shaping the transport and spatial equilibrium process. However, their influence is less pronounced than that of the first two types of innovation.

On another level, we observe that today the performance of the different transport modes can be ranked according to certain requirements: they are required to be reliable, safe, rapid and inexpensive. The different modes possess these qualities in varying proportions. The individual modes tend to have a combination of specific aptitude profiles that correspond to the requirement profiles of different buyers of transport services. The types of innovations discussed in earlier chapters are even likely to influence these requirement profiles, thus influencing in a very complex way the acceptance of the whole system.

In the supply of transport services it is not only the technical properties that count but also the organizational possibilities – including transport chains and full service packages – which are playing an increasingly important role. These are the preconditions for the overall logistic planning of the function fields of procurement, production, storage and distribution, and there the new telematic innovations are likely to play a vital role.

For industry and society the economic, technical and organizational variety of transport services and the openness to new services and combinations of services are of the greatest importance. The new telematics-based logistic supply is thus able to meet ever more precisely the demands of shippers for ever better and increasingly integrated solutions to their transport needs.

As regards the share of the impacts of new technology between the various modes we can observe that the particular properties of road haulage permit above all a very high degree of quantitative and qualitative flexibility of supply, making it possible to adjust rapidly to the time, place and quantity requirements of transport demand. This is particularly important in the case of short-term changes in market conditions and patterns of demand. These characteristics also make road transport particularly well able to fit into transport chains and combinations with complementary services (freight forwarding, warehousing, handling etc.). These service activities can be developed and implemented only because the technical potential of the vehicles is exploited by private, profit-oriented enterprises which best exploit the advantages offered by the new technical innovations discussed earlier.

These positive impacts of the new technology for road transport may lead to further co-operation, rather than competition, between the modes and in the longer term also to a more even balance in their market shares. In the immediate future, however, road transport will continue to dominate, and this will lead to increasing volumes of freight running on the roads more regularly between new networks of modal points. This will create the preconditions for grouped consignments and at the same time economic pressure in this direction will increase. Bottlenecks in precisely those parts of the road networks on which long-distance high-volume traffic flows are developing will be considered as some of the negative effects of transport innovation in this field but will at the same time create the conditions for some modal transfer to the railways. To take this negative impact type of argument further it can be said that private road transport can also increase as a result of the increased comfort and safety and this will cause serious strains on the already strained system of road infrastructure. This point raises some obvious policy implications which are taken up in the conclusions.

A final point on the potential of the technical innovations anticipated here is that the improvement in transport links is also likely to induce productivity-enhancing processes or at least to be a necessary precondition for them.

Costs and benefits of specific technical innovations

In this section we give some examples of specific costs and benefits for some of the technical innovations discussed previously. The purpose of this material is to give some first insights on the matter and to highlight the difficulties of obtaining a complete picture of the situation.

Assessing the impact of innovations in vehicle design

Motorized transport for freight or passenger movement stands to profit from safer, more comfortable and more reliable vehicles in the future. Private cars will be more customized for the individual owner, more environmentally friendly and less costly to run.

However, the price per unit is likely to increase for cars, buses and trucks as the amount of 'intelligent' hardware (and software) contained in them increases. This cost increase is likely to be partially offset by the reduction in the cost of manufacturing due to other innovations that will improve and integrate the manufacturing processes.

Perhaps the primary benefits from the application of technical innovation in vehicle design will be the indirect benefits to the environment through the design of more 'ecological' vehicles.

Assessing the impact of telematics-based innovations in the operation and management of the system

Most of the previously discussed innovations in this field will eventually form part of an integrated framework. In an effort to assess the impacts of such an IRTE, the European Community has conducted both an economic/financial analysis and a Delphi study among many experts in the field in Europe (conducted by the special Systems Engineering and Consensus Formulation Office (SECFO) of the EEC's DRIVE (Dedicated Road Infrastructure for Vehicle Safety in Europe) programme).

The IRTE was tested for urban areas under two hypotheses: strategy A, which gives emphasis on the various forms of individual transport and tries to satisfy this type of demand by priority, and strategy B, which is public transport oriented. In both strategies use is made of all, or the most appropriate, telematics innovations that were mentioned in section 4.3.

Understandably the effects resulting from the introduction of telematics innovation applications into the urban traffic environment largely depend on the area characteristics, the transport policy and the type and nature of the applications.

Assessing the impacts of innovations in freight transport operations

The following observations can be made concerning the main applications of innovations mentioned for freight transport.

Some researchers expect EDI to reduce document handling costs by approximately 20 per cent (Wandel, 1989). Research in the USA (Boodman et al., 1989) indicates that the potential for uniform communications standards (UCS), i.e. standardized message functions, in EDI could give direct savings of $67 million per annum in the food industry alone. In addition, further indirect savings could yield a further $256 million per annum in the same industry.

As far as on-line tracking of shipments and vehicle identification is concerned, Boodman and Norris (1989) reported in their survey on the expected use of bar-coding in 'forward-thinking logistically-oriented companies'. They suggested that, by the year 2000, 62 per cent of the inbound and 85 per cent of the outbound shipments in the USA will be bar-coded. Europe will probably opt for electronic tags and so the usage of bar-codes for remote shipment identification may be lower than in the USA. Electronic tags are already being used for container identification. Wandel (1989) reports the results of a Delphi study that showed that 50–80 per cent of all shipments in the USA and Western Europe are expected to have computer-readable addresses by the year 2000.

The potential benefits of this system were assessed on plausible scenarios and assumptions for fleet monitoring, vehicle positioning and mobile data communication applications (Analysys, 1989). The following results were obtained.

1 The unit cost of in-vehicle equipment for fleet monitoring is expected to fall in real terms by about a half over the next six to seven years. The annual demand for in-vehicle units will be around 225,000, with a value of 35–40 million ECU per annum (from 1996 onwards). This will be large enough to sustain a small number of manufacturers.
2 The average annual operating cost of running the fleet monitoring system for France, Germany and Benelux is given by the running costs of the equipment such as the dispatchers' labour, maintenance and so forth, but excluding depreciation. As can be expected, the larger the fleet, the more affordable the fleet monitoring function would be, in relative terms. From 1995 onwards an annual cost of 2800 ECU per fleet per year is estimated giving a total market of 200 million ECU for Europe.
3 The potential revenue for GSM operators from fleet monitoring even assuming a modest penetration rate of 8 per cent of freight vehicles is very significant, growing to 40 per cent of the current total value of the cellular market across the European Community by the year 2000. One European Community statistic suggests that there will be a total of approximately 12 million GSM subscribers by the year 2000; of these the freight vehicles are estimated to be approximately 1 million.

As regards freight vehicle route planning and interactive route guidance applications, Cooper (1989), reporting on a study by the Polytechnic of Central London, estimated a 10 per cent saving in total (multi-drop) vehicle operating costs from daily computer round planning (CRP) as realistically attainable. Given this level of saving, daily CRP is likely to benefit operators with fleets in excess of ten vehicles (per depot). Furthermore, it offers greater control over transport operations, can improve service levels, can reduce the fleet size and the use of hired vehicles and can enhance the ability to ask 'what if' questions.

The market for computerized route planning packages has been estimated by the author to be about 70,000–80,000 medium- and large-sized transport companies in the 12 European Community member countries with an equally large number of private 'producer' companies that operate their own fleets (TRADEMCO/TRUTh, 1992).

Applications of IRG systems in the field of freight transport are foreseen mainly for urban areas and specifically for multi-distribution jobs. No road freight operator at present seems interested in IRG systems for intercity transport as routes seem to be well known and understood.

Expected impacts on logistic costs and combined transport

The implementation of telematics innovations in combi using railway may provide an overall initial savings in logistics costs of 5–7 per cent (Kearney, 1989).

This rather small cost improvement, if seen in association with the fact that combi using railway is in general 15 per cent less costly than combi using all-road transport, may bring forward the net cost advantage of combined transport operations to a desirable threshold.

Diffusion and temporal pattern of technical innovation dissemination

The diffusion of new innovation seems to be particularly slow and usage is unevenly spread in the transport sector. Other industries and professional activities, such as banking and insurance, experience faster service diffusion and successfully use the innovation potential to support their daily operations.

The transport sector as a whole in most European economies contains many small to medium-size companies not 'eager' to adopt innovations that are usually perceived as risky.

Innovation is adopted by the transport industry generally in distinct pragmatic steps (EUROFRET, 1991).

Phase 1: Individual firms 'scramble' to use technology and introduce a particular innovation because they want or need to enhance productivity in the delivery of transport services, or because their customers are asking about it.

Phase 2: Customers require the firm to use a particular technology or innovation as a mandatory service, e.g. just-in-time delivery.

Phase 3: Firms try to differentiate themselves from competitors by promoting their system as better than the other firms' servicing with a view to expanding their market share and/or increasing profitability in their operations.

If one accepts this typology as a valid yardstick, then the motor freight industry is in the later stages of phase 1. In addition, diffusion patterns differ, in fact, by transport mode and product.

Some other general observations are the following.

1 Large transport carriers invest in advanced telematics and other innovations and use the available services much more intensively, and earlier, than small and medium-sized enterprises.
2 Passenger transport uses innovations to a larger extent than freight carriers, with deep linking into related activities including hotel reservations, car rental, entertainment etc.
3 Commercial aviation operators, both for passenger traffic and for air freight, are significantly more advanced in the use of modern telematics equipment and services than land- and water-bound transport operators in most OECD countries.
4 The products currently offered by suppliers appear as technically efficient, but as too expensive and too difficult to integrate within the company and in the transport environment. The companies have to invest in large systems not necessarily adapted to their specific requirements. Additional modules are necessarily purchased from the same supplier. This situation seems prejudicial both to the effectiveness of the operators and to the competitivity of the suppliers.

As regards the timing and time of occurrence of transport innovations it is noted that the life cycle has three distinct stages: introduction, maturity and withdrawal. The length of these stages is not common, nor are the times at which they occur, except in the broadest sense. The pattern observed over a long period of time (see Giannopoulos and Curdes, 1992) is the following.

A sudden burst of growth through drastic technical and organizational innovations and concentrated investment activity can be followed by periods mainly characterized by adjustments that can come close to being a 'steady state'.

As expected, innovations appear earlier in the regions and countries that have been in the forefront of industrialization and modernization. However, there may be exceptions to this mainly when appropriate policies are implemented at a national or international level, e.g. the European Community.

Finally there may be some other reasons why innovation is slow to take place in the transport sector.

The transport sector is far from being a 'homogeneous' sector as first impressions may suggest: it consists of a mix of distinct transport modes, each developed historically around a dominant medium (maritime, road, rail and air) and each operating under distinct market structures including public, private, monopolistic and highly competitive concepts. There are a few huge transport organizations (multimodal) operating on a worldwide basis and a multitude of smaller firms servicing rather local and regional customer needs.

This divergence and segmentation of the transport sector makes it difficult to define 'a market' and thus to develop general purpose systems and applications. Transport innovation and systems, therefore, have to make inroads into each of these distinct market segments in a trial-and-error mode, typical of a market-driven process of diffusion. Examples of this piecemeal approach are inventories, computer-assisted dispatching, mobile guidance and communications etc., each tailored to the particular needs of the transport mode and/or application being considered (OECD, 1992).

The variety of telematics-based systems supplied by the hardware and the associated software industry is quite impressive, and selection in this rapidly changing environment is an extremely difficult task requiring extensive financial resources, technical know-how and expertise. This makes it increasingly difficult for a large number of owner/driver transport operators to keep up with developments.

As a result, there is today a bewildering range of different, stand-alone, firm-specific equipment and proprietary 'solutions' using different operational systems, software and communications back-up facilities, all of which coexist side by side. These systems mostly apply different standards and thus are basically incompatible with each other, which prevents the integration and interconnection needed to allow the real innovation benefits to occur.

4.5 CONCLUSIONS

We are in the midst of new and exciting technological innovations in the field of transport which will mark the whole transport scene in Europe, and elsewhere in the world, for many years to come. As has happened many times in the past, technological innovations come about as a result of certain 'breakthroughs' in our technical knowledge or in our use and method of utilization of known resources. As has also happened in the past we are experiencing now a 'sudden' burst of growth in technical and organizational innovations that affect the transport scene and that once 'established' will be mainly characterized by adjustments that can come close to being a 'steady state'. If we take the average time period for this adjustment to be 30–40 years as in the past (Giannopoulos and Curdes, 1992), then we are at the beginning of a phase of innovation consolidation and diffusion that will extend well into the first two decades of the twenty-first century.

In the field of vehicle construction, advances are being made in engine combustion and the electronic and mechatronic systems for controlling combustion. As a result, automobiles will be increasingly characterized by high reliability, superior performance and low fuel consumption. Furthermore, the industry has begun to accelerate the introduction of communications technology, the development and use of new materials and the utilization of computer-controlled mechanisms.

Following the increased awareness both in the public and the governments of the importance for environmental protection, technological innovations have been aimed further to improve safety and to reduce exhaust pollution and fuel consumption. New safety technology is being introduced to improve the basic functions of automobiles and to increase their operational safety. New fuels and fuel–engine systems are also being developed to make it possible to reduce dependence on hydrocarbon fuels and their harmful effects on the environment.

With regard to the second type of innovations, i.e. those based on telematics and aimed at improving the operation and management of the system of transport, a wide range was described in the preceding sections. As a result of their applications in road and rail passenger transport, as well as on the operation and management of freight transport, considerable improvements are to expected towards reducing the effects on congestion, better utilization of available infrastructure, more reliability of travel of freight deliveries, more journey comfort etc.

However, although technical innovations and changes are already here, even if they are still in an experimental and 'pilot' state, their general application and their acceptance as established elements of everyday transport is a point in question and an area that requires serious and far reaching policy and political decisions that have to be taken at this point in time. The evaluation of the potential effects so far shows that no revolutionary impacts are to be expected, and at least in the case of telematics applications the overall impacts on the various parameters of urban (and interurban) travel will not exceed the level of 10–20 per cent over today's situation.

There are also a large number of scenarios and possibilities as to how these innovations will be organized and managed and how they will be combined to formulate the urban and interurban transport environment of the future. The evaluation, assessment and decision making over these scenarios requires a serious research effort in implementation issues and policies which is not to be seen currently in Europe, with perhaps the only exception being the DRIVE programme of the European Community.

The diffusion of new transport innovation seems to be particularly slow, and usage is unevenly spread in the transport sector. Other industries and professional activities, such as banking and insurance, experience faster service diffusion and successfully use the innovation potential to support their daily operations. There are many reasons for this but perhaps the most notable is that the transport sector is far from being a 'homogeneous' sector as first impressions may suggest.

This divergence and segmentation of the transport sector makes it difficult to define 'a market' and thus to develop general purpose systems and applications. Transport innovation and systems, therefore, have to make inroads into each of these distinct market segments in a trial-and-error mode.

As a final remark, there can be no doubt that transport innovation will have to be blended with an appropriate transport policy.

NOTES

1 EDI is a technology for transferring data between computers.

2 This was part of an international co-operative research effort called URBINNO, funded primarily by the Volkswagen research foundation and other sources.

REFERENCES

Analysys (1989) *Fleet Monitoring: SECFO Scenario*. Working paper for the European Community's DRIVE programme, Systems Engineering and Consensus Formulation Office.

Boodman, D.W. and Norris, R.C. (1989) Progress in distribution: computer to computer ordering. *Handling and Shipping Management*, 33–5.

CASSIOPE (1992) *Computer-Aided System for Scheduling, Information and Operation of Public Transport in Europe*. Final report, DRIVE project V1019.

Cooper, J. (1989) United Kingdom. In Round Table 78, *Telematics in Goods Transport*. European Conference of Ministers of Transport, Paris: OECD, 5–30.

ECMT (1983) *Transport and Telecommunications* (summary of the discussion). Round Table 59. European Conference of Ministers of Transport, Paris: OECD.

EEC (1990) *The European High Speed Train Network*. Report of the high level group, Directorate General VII, Brussels.

EUROFRET (1991) *A European System for International Road Freight Transport Operations*. Final report. Contract V1027, DRIVE I.

Fenton, N. (1984) TRADANET success: trial enters new phase and promise benefits to suppliers and everyone else. *ANAN news*, 101–9.

—— (1985) Articled numbering and data communication. In *Managing PDM to Gain Competitive Advantages*. Conference, London: Institute of Physical Distribution Management.

Giannopoulos, G.A. (1989a) *Bus Planning and Operation in Urban Areas*. Aldershot: Avebury Gower, 201–8.

—— (1989b) The influence of telecommunications on transport operations. *Transport Reviews*, 19–43.

Giannopoulos, G.A. and Curdes, G. (1992) Innovation in urban transport and the influence on urban form: an historical review. *Transport Reviews*, 15–32.

Kearney, A.T. (1989) *Etude prospective d' un réseau européen des transports combinés*. Conference, Brussels: EUROMODAL.

OECD (1992) *Advanced Logistics and Communications in Road Freight Operations*. Final report DSTI/RTR/TA1 (91) 121 REV. 1.

Schubert, V. (1988) *Conceptual Ideas on Innovation*. Conference Proceedings of the URBINNO Conference, Bari. Internal publication.

TRADEMCO/TRUTh (1992) *'Dianomes', a computer based package for routing and scheduling of a fleet of road freight vehicles*. A research and development programme assigned to the above companies by the Mediterranean Integrated Programme for Greece.

Wandel, S. (1989) Sweden. In Round Table 78, *Telematics in Goods Transport*. European Conference of Ministers of Transport, Paris: OECD, 52–96.

5

Externalities of Transport

Werner Rothengatter

5.1 INTRODUCTION

The phenomenon of external effects arising in the production of transport services has already been touched upon in chapter 3.

As the transport sector may be considered an outstanding example of the phenomenon of external effects there is ample reason, as will be the case in the present chapter, for an *in extenso* treatment of this subject.

In general terms it may be stated that economic activities often have accompanying effects which are detrimental not to their initiator but to uninvolved third parties, with the result that they affect the wrong cost centres in private enterprise cost calculations. Pigou (1924) in particular addressed the welfare-related implications of these 'external effects' or 'additional social costs' and indicated the resulting marked disparity between the private and social net products (cf. Pigou, 1924, pp. 172ff.). Externalities can be exchanged between agents within one sector, as in the case of congestion costs ('Pigou's problem'), but they can also occur as an activity's by-products and affect agents who have nothing to do with the activity in question, as with air pollution in agglomerations which can devastate forests and produce erosion damage in remote mountain regions.

Although in the 1950s, starting with the work by Kapp (1950), the economic treatments of external effects were strongly marked by criticism of the economic system and the phenomenon was connected with the capitalist production and distribution system, examination of the facts has shown that externalities are independent of any particular economic system. In neither the market nor the planned economies do suitable signals exist which guarantee that externalities are directly taken into account in economic decision-making.

We shall show that negative and positive externalities are intrinsic elements of modern economies and that, contrasting Pigou, not every externality has to be compensated for by taxes and subsidies. In the case of transport there exist indeed external costs which are detrimental to social welfare if they are not eliminated by public intervention. Positive externalities can also be identified but they are not relevant in the sense that public intervention would become necessary. Furthermore, it would contradict market principles to attempt a global compensation of negative against positive externalities. The market works on the basis of decentral signals and would be distorted by implementing aggregate compensation schemes.

Experience shows that the possibilities of a practical policy to internalize externalities by pricing and regulation in the transport sector are limited. Some historical taboos exist in the European Community member countries that yield a high resistance of the industry and of consumers to any kind of restraining of their private wants in transport. Outstanding examples are the rejection of general speed limits on German Autobahnen or the opposition to charging external costs to the road haulage industry in the Netherlands. Nevertheless, these two countries have the most ambitious objectives in environmental policy.

It is important to note that the following considerations are restricted to the use of the transport infrastructure and do not address the potential externalities which may be generated by the transport network itself and are included in the benefit–cost calculations of the public investor.

The further structure of this chapter is as follows. The next section deals with the concept of externalities. After this, in section 5.3, various levels of interaction between the transport sector and environmental and human resources will be distinguished. Then it will be pointed out under what circumstances government may see cause for action.

Sections 5.4–5.6 consider the sources of transport externalities. Thus, section 5.4 first looks at the effects of transport on quality of life in physical terms. Section 5.5 analyses how two important categories of externalities in transport, namely safety and the environment, may be considered as economic goods. Third, section 5.6 presents some quantitative results of calculations of the external costs of transport. Section 5.7 deals with policy, reviewing measures which may reduce the external costs of transport. In section 5.8 the new proposition that transport – in particular road transport – generates external benefits which may be deducted from its external costs is commented upon. Finally, section 5.9 summarizes the chapter and states its main conclusions.

5.2 THE NATURE OF EXTERNAL ECONOMIES AND DISECONOMIES

General characterization

'Broadly defined, an externality is a relevant cost or benefit that individuals fail to consider when making rational decisions' (DeSerpa, 1988, p. 507). Formally, externalities occur if variables are introduced into the utility function of a consumer or the production function of a producer which are controlled by other actors of the economic and social system rather than by the decision maker himself (see Monissen, 1980, p. 343):

$$u_l = f_l(x_l, x_k)$$
$$y_h = g_h(v_h, v_k) \qquad (5.1)$$

where u_l is the utility level of consumer l, x_l are the factors controlled by consumer l, x_k are the factors controlled by other agents, y_h is the output level of producer h, v_h are the factors controlled by producer h and v_k are the factors controlled by other agents.

Agents who impose externalities on others will not take into account the consequences and impacts on the other parties. This is why a decentralized decision-making of externality-producing and externality-receiving individuals will in general not lead to an overall optimal result. In the context of a Paretian economic framework with atomistic competition (and under a set of very restraining assumptions on technology, preferences and information) externalities lead to a disturbance of market equilibrium. It can be shown using textbook examples (Henderson and Quandt, 1958) or equilibrium modelling that the social optimality of allocation can be restored either by centralization of the interactive decision-making or by internalization of externalities, i.e. making them a decision factor in the planning of decentral decision units. So a general characteristic of externalities is that they do not work through the market mechanism (Scitovsky, 1969, p. 243).

There are a number of classifications which are important when discussing measures to cope with externalities.

Technological externalities

The externality definition given in (5.1) reflects a direct change of the allocation pattern by influencing production technologies or consumers' preference scales. As a consequence every production activity which does not correspond to private costs to the producer will be oversized, while uncompensated cost for a production activity leads to restraining the output level. The same holds for consumption activities.

Pecuniary externalities

In a monetary economy price changes do not always reflect changes of exchange rates between goods. This occurs, for instance, if – as in the case of information – prices can also be an indicator for product quality (Stiglitz, 1987), which means that they will no longer change according to excess demands and thus cannot act as the only adjustment indicator in the market process. As a consequence price changes on one market can induce unexpected quantity reactions on the other which are not a result of a change in excess demand. The existence of pecuniary externalities can be seen as one reason for Keynesian regimes to occur and for multiplier processes to work (Malinvaud, 1977).

Relevant externalities

As, broadly defined, every interaction among different decision units outside the market is called an externality, it is helpful to separate relevant from irrelevant externalities. Buchanan and Stubblebine (1969, p. 201) have suggested a criterion for partitioning externalities which works in a similar way to the Kaldor–Hicks extension of Pareto's criterion of welfare-improving actions:

> An externality is defined to be Pareto-relevant when the extent of the activity may be modified in such a way that the externally affected party, A, can be made better off without the acting party, B, being made worse off. . . . The internal benefits from carrying out the activity, net of costs, may be greater than the external damage that is imposed on other parties (ibid., pp. 202, 208)

In other words, only if the costs of externalities (expressed by the willingness to pay by the disadvantaged party) exceed the internal benefits of the advantaged party are the associated activities relevant in terms of interventions for improving public welfare.

This microeconomic criterion of relevance might give rise to a fundamental macroeconomic misinterpretation (Sälter, 1989): externalities could be regarded as irrelevant as long as the aggregated sum of damages does not exceed the aggregated sum of benefits. Estimating the net effect by a cost–benefit analysis would then result in a binary decision: if the net effect is positive then there is no reason for intervention, or if the net effect is negative then the consequence is to prohibit the activity. A Pigovian allocation of taxes and subsidies would be unnecessary.

Although it can easily be shown by simple counterexamples that this macroeconomic conclusion is wrong (the net benefit can be increased by a change in the allocation) the underlying microeconomic foundation has some appeal. The theory of property rights and the notion of adaptive efficiency confirm the Buchanan–Stubblebine argument that it is not necessary to compensate for every externality that shows up in the economy. But the reasoning behind the definition of relevance is completely different. Externalities in this sense are relevant if they cannot be internalized by contractual arrangements between the involved parties (e.g because of the high transaction costs) or are detrimental to the adaptive efficiency (which also includes a fair income redistribution; see Stiglitz, 1987). Relevant externalities according to this definition are a main cause of market failure and therefore, without a Paretian context, have to be corrected by public intervention.

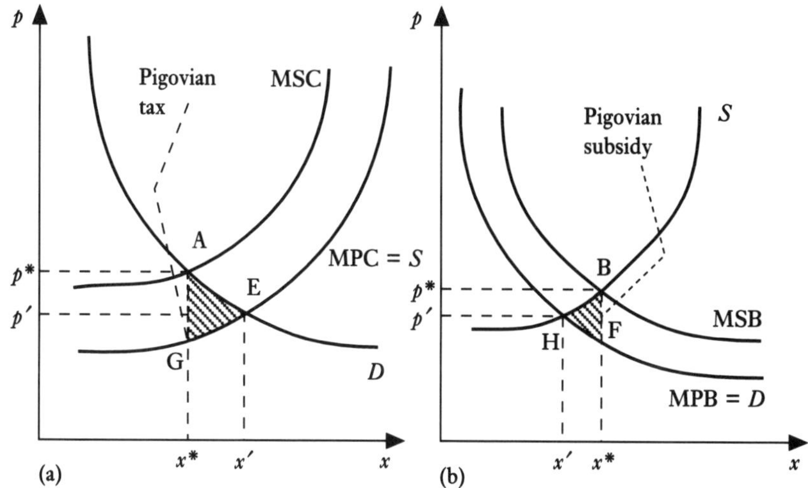

Figure 5.1 Pigovian taxes and subsidies.

Expected/unexpected externalities

There are interactions which are well known by the involved parties such that they can adjust their planning to the externality, although being unable to control it. This is the case for the 'Coase-type' examples (rancher/farmer; bees oakyard; dentist/disturbed neighbour). It also holds for many interaction effects which occur parallel to the market. But other externalities can also occur which cannot be anticipated by the agents concerned because of ignorance or lack of information on the complex feedback mechanisms between activities and their consequences. An example in the second category is soil erosion in the Alp regions which is affected by the dying of woodland which itself is induced by air pollution, whilst this air pollution is produced by a mix of small and large polluters who do not realize any relationship between their individual activity and the consequences in the Alps. The warming up of the atmosphere by the emission of CO_2 also belongs to this category.

The Pigovian concept

In the terms of Pigou (1924), external effects create a divergence between private and social costs. The economic effects are illustrated in figure 5.1. In figure 5.1(a) the market equilibrium quantity *x*' represents the amount that is actually produced and consumed and reflects a balancing of marginal private costs and benefits (corresponding to the intersection of the supply and demand curves). If consumption or production creates external costs, however, the marginal social cost (MSC) curve lies above the market supply curve (equivalent to the marginal private cost (MPC) curve). The socially efficient solution would be found at the intersection between the MSC curve and the demand curve *D*.

To modify private decision-making such that the socially optimal allocation (p^*, x^*) is achieved a tax of amount AG can be introduced for the producers. External benefits create the opposite effect. In figure 5.1(b) they are represented by a shift from the market demand curve *D* which reflects the marginal private benefits (MPB) to the marginal social benefit (MSB) curve. To create private incentives to produce the quantity x^* a subsidy BF has to be offered to the producers. The 'correct' taxes and subsidies are not easy to determine, inasmuch as external costs vary with the rate of output and there is no reason to assume that MSC and MPC or MPB/MSB run parallel.

The Coase theorem

In the case of a small number of parties the problems are less difficult to resolve. As Coase (1960) has shown it is not necessary to establish a complicated system of compensation payments to create private incentives towards socially optimal behaviour. To understand his arguments it is necessary to introduce the concepts of property rights and of reciprocity of externalities. To use a 'Coase-type' example, suppose there are two producers, a rancher raising cattle and a farmer producing wheat. The rancher's cattle might trample the wheat planted on the neighbouring farmland and cause a reduction in the farmer's profits. In the absence of any legal system which prevents the rancher from causing damage to the farmland, the rancher will maximize profits on his own profit curve π_r, resulting in production volume C_1 (figure 5.2). By doing this he reduces the profits of the farmer from position $F_0(\pi_f/C = 0)$ to position $F_1(\pi_f/C = C_1)$. To find the social optimum one can sum up the two profit lines and identify the point of the highest aggregate profit (figure 5.3).

In a consolidated calculus the optimum comes out to be C^* which is lower that C_1, the optimum for the rancher without taking the damage into account. If we introduce a liability rule which says that the rancher has to pay for the losses he has inflicted on the farmer, the rancher will treat these losses as part of his own costs and maximize profits net of liability payments ($\pi_r - L$). Liability payments may be calculated as the difference between the profits that the farmer earns without being influenced by the rancher (F_0) and the actual profits (π_f). In effect the rancher maximizes

$$X - \pi_r L = \pi_r(F_0 - \pi_f) = \pi_r + \pi_f - F_0 \tag{5.2}$$

As F_0 is a constant, maximizing $\pi - L$ is equivalent to maximizing π.

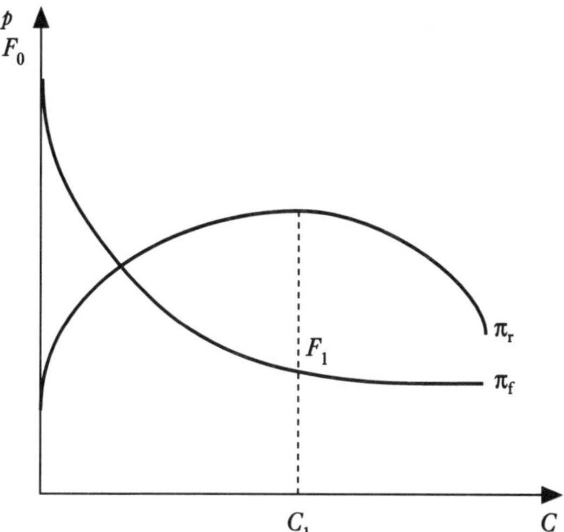

Figure 5.2 Profits of two producers, assuming external diseconomies of producer r.

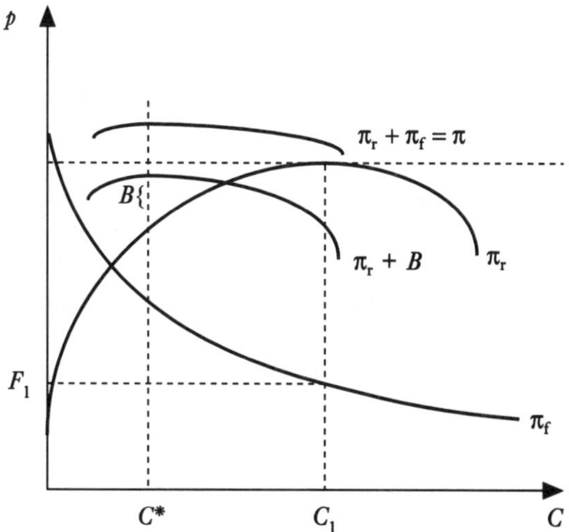

Figure 5.3 Effects of liabilities and bribes.

Suppose on the other hand that the rancher does not have to pay for the damage inflicted on the farmer. If the farmer has the option to bargain with the rancher he can offer a payment ('a bribe') for the reduction of cattle output. The amount of the bribe (*B*) is equal to the difference between the farmer's actual profits (π_f) and the profit (F_1) which the farmer would receive if the rancher did not reduce his production ($B = \pi_f - F_1$). In this case the rancher maximizes

$$\pi_r + B = \pi_r + (\pi_f - F_1) = \pi_r + \pi_f - F_1 \tag{5.3}$$

Again, F_1 is a constant and we obtain the optimal output C^*. This is shown by the maximum of the profit line $\pi_r + B$ in figure 5.3.

The Coase approach to defining the nature of the problem and deriving a solution can be summarized as follows.

1 Externalities arise if the property rights for a jointly used resource are not clearly defined.
2 Externalities are reciprocal, i.e. the production activity of the rancher is harmful for the farmer, but reducing his production activity is harmful to the rancher.
3 If transaction costs are negligible, an efficient allocation of resources will be obtained as long as property rights are clearly defined, regardless of how the property right is assigned (in this example, whether or not the rancher is liable for damages).
4 If effects of income redistribution are negligible, reassigning property rights (shifting liabilities) does not affect resource allocation (the production levels of cattle and wheat in this example).

The important consequence of the Coase argument given in (1)–(4) is that it is not so important to diagnose and estimate the amount of an externality. The most crucial issue is to find subtle forms of exchange and contractual agreements. Many externality problems can then be solved by contracts between the affected agents. If they cannot be solved because of transaction costs or problems of redistribution of income, public assistance is needed. This intervention can consist of defining property rights (legal changes) or helping to find contractual arrangements in the case of crisis situations.

In particular the following argument of Coase (1960, p. 27) has influenced the debate on monetary compensation of externalities:

> The problem which we face in dealing with actions which have harmful effects is not simply one of restraining those responsible for them. What has to be decided is whether the gain from preventing the harm is greater than the loss which would be suffered elsewhere as a result of stopping the action which produces the harm.

As this has been wrongly interpreted as a postulation of public inactivity with respect to environmentally costly productions as long as their social benefits exceed their social costs we shall come back to this argument later.

A broader view of externalities

The Pigovian view of externalities seems to be too narrow. What Pigou had in mind were effects which appear as troublemakers in the equilibrium paradise. Externalities are seen as exceptions from the ideal market pattern of the Pareto world which otherwise would achieve its equilibrium position ('competitive equilibrium' (CE)) by an atomistically decentralized decision-making.

As is well known such a world does not create strong incentives for dynamic changes because the agents act as price takers and stress is placed on internal adjustments to exogenously given price signals. Therefore the concept of CE is equivalent to short-run static efficiency of the economy. In a dynamic world the CE can no longer serve as a reference point (this also holds for its dynamic version, the contingent claims equilibrium (CCE)) because it abstracts from the driving forces of competition, which are

1. progressive innovative strategies to achieve monopoly power in order to yield supernormal profits;
2. conservation strategies to make a profit situation sustainable over time; and
3. catch-up strategies to achieve market leadership using product or process innovation and imitation policies.

In the dynamic context only the notions of 'workable competition' and 'adaptive efficiency' (see Stiglitz, 1990) are appropriate to describe the extraordinary power of a market system.

It is just in the context of these dynamic market phenomena that externalities play an important productive role. In a world of uncertainty agents try to manage their risks by face-to-face contacts and by constructing networks of individual or institutional relationships. With increasing complexity and risk the market mechanism changes from the 'invisible hand' of Adam Smith to 'visible and invisible handshakes' (see Rosen, 1985). For example, implicit contracting substitutes explicit contracts because of the high transaction costs of explicit contracting in a dynamically changing environment. Stiglitz (1987) has shown, taking the examples of the labour and credit markets, that implicit contracts are an efficient way to insure risks if there is enough trust in the reliability of partners in the network. For instance, firms and workers may prefer not to contract explicitly on wages on the basis of the marginal revenue product of labour but to contract on fixed wages for a longer time period such that they implicitly include an insurance premium/indemnity to compensate for the fluctuations of the marginal productivity of labour. Following Rosen

(1985) such markets look partly 'more akin to the marriage market rather than to the bourse'.

A second example is the strategic alliance. Such an alliance might only be informal, e.g. an informal agreement of firm A not to compete with the product of firm B in country X, while firm B does not attack the market of firm A in country Y. In both cases advantages for the parties occur which are not derived from market processes such that they are externalities in the sense of Scitovsky. But obviously the profits are internalized if the external advantages and the external disadvantages equalize in the long run.

While implicit contracts and strategic alliances are examples for voluntary expected externalities there are a number of involuntary (unexpected) externalities. An outstanding prototype for these externalities is the diffusion of information about innovations. Although innovations can be privatized by patent rights, licences or secret research and development, it is almost impossible to keep them perfectly private. A part of the know-how is spread by selling the products which embody the innovative technical progress. A firm cannot prevent its competitors from buying its products on the market and therefore from learning about the technology applied.

The form and the speed of technical progress in a market economy under uncertainty is crucially dependent on the possibility of creating externalities of this kind. This is because the diffusion process is stimulated so that the interdependence between innovation and imitation becomes more intensive. Thus, without trying to be complete in elaborating the role of externalities in a dynamic environment under uncertainty one can summarize as follows.

1 Externalities occur in a world of social and economic interactions if different agents use a resource jointly without explicitly contracting on price and quantity.
2 Externalities may stimulate the market dynamics by enforcing innovations and imitations.
3 Externalities may reduce the risk of agents in an uncertain world in which high transaction costs of explicit contracts or spot market mechanisms exist because of the rapidly changing environment.
4 If externalities are normal events in a system of dynamic adaptive economic interactions there is little need for public intervention. Many of the externalities are mutual and help the affected parties to reduce transaction costs. If they are not mutual the parties involved will be interested in explicit contractual arrangements, which internalize the externalities.

Externalities yielding public interventions

While the Pigovian view implies that every externality that occurs should be compensated for by taxation or subsidization the Coase theorem reduces interventions to externalities in which a large number of parties is involved (transaction costs) or which are associated with redistributional (equity) problems. Introducing a broader view of externalities leads to a further reduction in interventions because many of the externalities stemming from dynamic interactions are not detrimental to market efficiency and should not be compensated for.

What is left is the set of externalities which

1 is improving the adaptive efficiency of the market economy but is not supplied by the private sector because of the public good characteristics (e.g. establishment of a legal system, diplomatic services, health care, education, basic research, basic infrastructure etc.);
2 is detrimental to the adaptive efficiency of the market economy (e.g. exhaustion of non-renewable resources, environmental damage); and
3 cannot be internalized by private arrangements (because of transaction costs, income redistribution problems, problems of asymmetric economic power or ethical problems such as risk of survival).

5.3 EXTERNAL ECONOMIES AND DISECONOMIES OF THE TRANSPORT SECTOR

Three levels of interaction

According to our conclusion in section 5.1, externalities arise if different agents jointly use a resource the property rights of which are not clearly defined. In many cases the market works well despite (or sometimes even because of) the externalities, in others contractual arrangements may solve the problem whilst in the remainder it is only possible to resolve the problem by public intervention. To work out these different types of externalities let us subdivide the interactions in which the transport sector is involved outside the market into three regimes:

1 interactions between the transport sector and the stock of non-renewable resources (environmental and human non-producible capital) – level 1 externalities;
2 interactions within the transport sector – level 2 externalities;
3 interactions between the transport sector and the regime of public and private production and consumption – level 3 externalities.

External diseconomies between the transport sector and the environment (level 1) occur because environmental resources are used without compensation to produce transport services. Therefore a conflict arises between those who use the environment to live in and to enjoy the landscape, flora and fauna, and those who use the environment as a disposal for the waste of their consumption and production.

Externalities within the transport sector (level 2) mainly occur because of the interactions of users of the transport network. One of the most popular Pigou examples deals with congestion on roads where the ignorance of external diseconomies which each user entering the system imposes on the existing users causes a suboptimal user pattern of the network. Wardrop (1952) has put this idea into a precise scheme by which the difference between the 'user optimal' and the 'systems optimal' load pattern of a network can be calculated. This difference corresponds to Pigou's notion of the gap between private and social net product.

Externalities between the public regime and the transport sector (level 3(a)) are exchanged in so far as transport networks are partly regarded as public goods. They provide a base for communication and accessibility which is necessary for establishing the regime of public power and supplying public services (emergency service, minimum level of communication). Externalities between the private and the transport sector (level 3(b)) may follow from three sources.

First, the transport sector is often a part of the public sector such that private users get extra benefits if the public sector does not charge the full costs of the infrastructure and operation. Or they experience losses if the public sector extracts an income from the private sector by particular taxes and user charges that are higher than the costs of the infrastructure and operation.

Second, there are multiple interactions between transport and economic activities which are not directly compensated by the market mechanism. These interactions may induce new forms of operations and distributions logistics and contribute to technical progress.

Third, transport is a part of every exchange activity. Extending and improving networks opens access to regions which are not linked to the non-produced natural transport infrastructure (e.g. waterways). This may contribute to the exploration of new market potentials and create productive interactions which are not completely operative through the market mechanism.

Externalities of the transport sector relevant for public intervention

When elaborating on the Coase approach and the broader view of externalities it was pointed out that many externalities do not call for public intervention because they can be internalized by contractual arrangements (in the case of low transaction costs) or because they are not relevant for the agents, as the transaction costs to remove them are higher than the costs which they induce. In a dynamic world many of these effects are regarded as temporary so that explicit contracts to remove them are too time consuming and costly, and the agents rely on their experience that external advantages and disadvantages will balance over time.

These characteristics hold for the majority of externalities between the transport and the private sector. It will therefore be hard to find good reasons why private industry or private consumption should be taxed in order to compensate the transport sector because of its external benefits and vice versa (level 3 externalities).

In contrast the interactions between environmental and human resources and the transport sector (level 1 externalities) can only be dealt with by public intervention. The reasons for this are as follows.

1 There is no price mechanism for the use of these non-renewable resources. The property rights are not defined and so agents regard the resources as free of charge. Private agents therefore extract too much from these inputs for their production/consumption activities (over-exploitation by under-pricing).
2 While the agents on the side of private production/consumption form powerful economic syndicates, the protectors of the environment lack economic power. Therefore fair contractual arrangements between the private protectors of the environment and the users of environmental resources are impossible.
3 Usually the number of involved parties is very large, and so the transaction costs of contracting on environmental resources are too high to achieve an arrangement.
4 If a risk of life or health is involved neither a bargaining scheme nor a spot market mechanism is an appropriate instrument to generate fair and efficient solutions. Such risks are accidents, the health impacts of professional truck driving and exhaust emissions, as well as extreme noise emissions (aircraft, trucks).

For these reasons it is essential to notice once again the difference between the levels of externalities (figure 5.4). It is obvious that externalities of level 3 (between transport and the private sector) cannot compensate for externalities of level 1 (between transport and the environment). Clearly such a compensation would produce a completely false signalling in the sense that the payments are allocated to the wrong activities, so that a false incentive scheme shifts the economic system in the wrong direction. No clear advice can be made as to the treatment of externalities within the transport sector (level 2). If private management is involved there are sufficient incentives to reduce these congestion externalities without government intervention. So a private road network operation and a financing company would differentiate user charges according to the congestion level and therefore tend to reduce congestion externalities. If the public sector manages the network, congestion usually occurs because of the inflexible

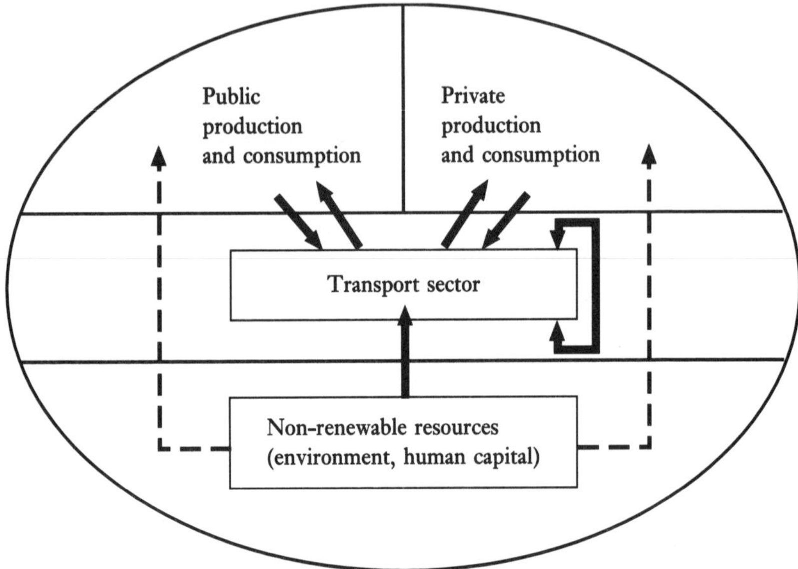

Figure 5.4 Interactions between three regimes.

and incomplete pricing scheme. Being indirectly subsidized the customers do not adjust to the infrastructure supply and induce an overflow of capacity. So the natural solution to the problem of congestion in a mainly privately used network is to manage the network according to private business rules.

After having worked out the relevant externalities it is justifiable to stress interactions between the transport sector and environmental and human resources (level 1). The sources of these externalities and the solution concepts will be described. After this discussion we shall return to the problem of external benefits of transport which has been stressed in recent studies and plays an important role in the transport policy of some European Community countries. According to the discussion above, we shall finally come to the question of whether it is justified to compensate external costs for external benefits of transport.

5.4 DETRIMENTAL EFFECTS OF TRANSPORT ON QUALITY OF LIFE

Accident and environmental costs are in the forefront of the additional social costs associated with the 'social sustainability' of transport. The following

Table 5.1 Incidence of accidents in Europe, 1967–86

	Accidents causing death or injury	*Number of injured*	*Number of deaths*
Belgium	1,284,749	1,752,708	49,214
Denmark	310,267	395,402	17,698
France	4,682,556	6,546,812	265,912
Federal Republic of Germany	7,149,218	9,617,939	285,364
UK	5,140,376	6,652,383	131,008
Greece	390,251	543,196	26,961
Ireland	117,678	172,356	10,569
Italy	3,361,920	4,594,801	177,258
Luxembourg	31,711	42,440	1,923
Netherlands	1,093,404	1,207,178	47,585
Total	23,562,130	31,525,215	1,031,492

considerations are confined to these effects. As a consequence of the above discussion of the different levels of externalities, public infrastructure costs and privately exchanged congestion costs are set aside.

Consequences of accidents

From 1967 to 1986 a total of over 1 million individuals were killed and nearly 32 million were injured on the roads of European Community countries, excluding Spain and Portugal (table 5.1). In peacetime there is no parallel for this enormous toll of lives, and the advocates of the 'Law of Conservation of Disaster' are provided with an impressive confirmation that the risks generated by the human failings of recklessness, aggression and dominance in the course of time produce a more or less constant incidence of victims.

The new resurgence of serious traffic accidents in the Federal Republic of Germany after the unification in 1990 has created a new challenge for traffic safety policy. A doubling of the yearly number of fatalities in East Germany shows clearly that better cars are only a small part of the solution and that stronger interventions are inevitable. Growing numbers of fatalities in conjunction with the observed increased carelessness and aggressiveness on the part of drivers can be viewed as symptoms calling for immediate political intervention, as a solution by private adjustments and arrangements is impossible.

But there are also popular arguments which try to present the traffic behaviour conducive to accidents as economically quite rational and which endeavour to belittle the risk, i.e. to minimize the numerical aspect notwithstanding the total accident figures in table 5.1 which are intended to shock and provoke thought. 'It is possible to drive a private car 13,000 km a year for fifty years with more than a 99 per cent chance of survival', or

> anyone who since the birth of Christ had driven an annual 13 000 km on a road network like that in the Federal Republic of Germany in 1982 would – disregarding other causes of death – have about a 70 per cent chance of still being alive today.
>
> (von Suntum, 1984)

The author quoted also states that the vast majority of endangered third parties are also road users, so that in the final analysis the external effects are exchanged between road users and give no grounds for any further compensation.

These counter-arguments show how the emotional feelings of car drivers can be transformed into rational looking arguments. But they cannot get away from the two main characteristics of the traffic safety problem.

1 The driving mechanisms behind human behaviour in road traffic are highly situation related, instinctive and spontaneous. Research on behavioural psychology (see Nowak, 1987) and observations of traffic behaviour (see Marburger, 1985) show clearly that in many cases drivers do not behave like sovereign agents, and so the public authorities have to set strict rules on people's behaviour.
2 Although immediate material damage is covered by insurance, a large measure of consequential effects remain which the state must cater for by substantial intervention into individual decisions. A self-organizing process cannot work because risks are not equally distributed and the creator of the risk does not take into account the consequences for the risk taker (comparable with Pigou's problem of congestion).

Therefore, all costs imposed on the society by traffic accidents which are not covered privately or by insurance are external and relevant for compensation. They contribute to the reduction in human capital which in the case of fatalities or invalidity is non-renewable. Without stressing the *pretium vivendi* argument it can be argued also that persons who are not immediate factors of the production process (housewives, children, the retired, handicapped) are of a certain value to it, for with indirect contributions and positive externalities they provide for the production sector.

Detriments to the environment

By producing energy to propel motor vehicles internal combustion engines pollute the environment with noise and exhaust gases. In addition, the transport infrastructure occupies space (in the Federal Republic of Germany public highways occupy approximately 3000 km^2 or 1.23 per cent of the country's area).

Table 5.2 Pollutant emissions in the Federal Republic of Germany by groups of emission sources, 1990

	Emission sources				
	CO	*SO_2*	*NO_x*	*CH*	*Dust*
Power stations/ heating stations (%)	1	38	14	1	10
Industry (%)	16	40	11	5	53
Households and small consumers (%)	8	14	4	3	10
Transport (%)	75	8	71	51[a]	27
Total (million tonnes)	8.4	1.0	2.7	2.6	0.3

[a] The remaining 40 per cent stems from solvents.
Source: DIW, 1991

Covered over with asphalt or concrete, this area is lost to nature, affects the levels and flows of groundwater and breaks down ecological relationships with a resulting impact on fauna and flora. In a study of the environmental impacts of transport the Prognos AG (1986) has prepared a detailed survey of the nature and interconnections of the environmental impacts of transport and other emission sources.

The chain of effects begins with the emission of pollutants, which are transmitted to humans by air, land and water in the environment, perhaps undergoing transformation by synergetic processes at the same time, and occur as immissions at the ultimate pollution site. The following by-products of transport are classed as environmental pollutants:

1 waste gases in the form of sulphur dioxide, carbon monoxide, nitrogen oxides, hydrocarbons, soot and dust or heavy metals;
2 solids and liquids in the form of rubber and plastics, metals, petrol and oil or acids;
3 areal pollutants which seal off surfaces, affect the water circuit, cut through settlement/colony structures or interrupt ecological relationships;
4 noise due to internal combustion engines, tyre contact with road surfaces, braking and hooting.

As table 5.2 shows, the transport sector is one of a number of groups of emission sources. Transport is the largest emission source of carbon monoxide, nitrogen oxides and hydrocarbons, although its contributions to sulphur dioxide and dust emissions are comparatively minor. It is true, however, that the generation of dust shows a marked increase over time owing to the growing use of soot-emitting diesel engines.

Transport, and road traffic especially, is held to be the main source of noise pollution. In a random sample of households in 1987, 42 per cent of the total stated 'that the noise of road traffic caused constant or intermittent severe disturbance of their immediate living environment' (DIW, 1991).

In the other areas there is to date little reliable information on the proportional contribution of transport to total emissions. It is even more difficult to find out how much it contributes to immissions, which are the basis for determining the causes and magnitude of damage. The environmental media not only carry the emitted pollutants over short and long distances (e.g. noise and nitric oxides respectively) but also provide the means for their storage and accumulation (e.g. by soil acidification or by the carbon dioxide enrichment of the atmosphere) and for their conversion either by natural action (e.g. photo-oxidation) or by the combination of different pollutants (synergetic effects of nitric oxide/sulphur dioxide and ozone). A direct relation between emission and immission, as in the case of traffic noise, is the exception rather than the rule.

Much more typical are the features characterizing the action of the pollutants:

(a) the location, time and intensity of the pollutant emission do not match those of the environmental impact;
(b) the marginal contributions of certain emission sources to local immissions are not identifiable.

A combination of emission sources, contributing differently to total emission according to their group, is matched by a combination of recipients that are differently affected by immissions according to their group. In this kind of action partnership (of pollutants and polluted) the principle that the polluter should pay must fail despite its convincing appeal on the grounds of equity and fairness, as it is only in isolated instances (e.g. the killing of fish by accidents in the carriage of hazardous goods) that the damage can be traced back to the emissions causing the problem.

In considering pollution impacts a distinction is normally made between human beings, the ecosystem and material goods. As in the case of accidents, first there are items of loss which can be compensated in material terms (e.g. the destruction of building frontages and damage caused by landslips in devastated mountain forests) and second there are losses which are irreversible (e.g. the destruction of historic monuments and works of art, the killing of animals or humans). Here too it might be argued that these sacrifices are the price of technical progress which society is clearly willing to pay as it would otherwise have opted for different technologies.

This again can be opposed by the argument of market failure, which imputes a serious control error to incorrect signals. In matters of the environment as elsewhere, there are innumerable examples of ignorance, playing down of problems and sidestepping of responsibilities, with the result that there is now virtually no disagreement in regarding the environment as a relevant externality which has to be controlled by public intervention.

5.5 SAFETY AND THE ENVIRONMENT AS ECONOMIC GOODS

A central problem in transport economics is the identification of suitable transmission mechanisms enabling the merit and external elements of safety and environmental protection to influence individual decisions relating to traffic behaviour, infrastructure planning and transport policy. In an economic system based on the idea of decentralized market control this could be achieved by government intervention into pricing policy aimed at transforming goods previously regarded as free into scarce goods.

Such a transformation of the merit and external elements into economic cost concepts would have the advantage that it would provide comparability with other economic effects, would enable policy adjustments to be measured and might allow the discussion to be rationalized by treating safety and environmental protection within the reference frame of a specialized discipline. Four alternative approaches are presented below based respectively on resources, utility, prevention and risk.

The resource approach

In the resource approach, all cases of loss caused by accidents and environmental impacts are regarded as depletions of resources which are evaluated by reference either to the costs of replacement or to the lowering of future returns. Human beings, animals and plants are here treated in the same way as material objects, i.e. they are conceptually equated with capital goods so that their cost values (purchase or manufacturing costs) or income values (cash values of future returns) can be determined. For instance, where an accident results in a death, application of the cost value principle involves calculation of the costs incurred in raising human beings of predetermined age levels (less depreciation), whereas the income value principle requires calculation of all the productive contributions over the expected remaining life of the victim. Calculations of losses which have occurred or are expected to occur have to be performed on a 'net' basis, i.e. the consumption of the accident victims has to be deducted as it no longer takes place in the society concerned, considered as the totality of the individuals constituting the economy less the accident victims. However, when evaluating accident prevention, e.g. in the cost–benefit analysis of traffic safety precautions, the consumption of those whose lives have been saved by safety precautions must be included as the society now comprises the individuals in an economy which includes the spared accident victims.

The resource approach is a direct method of evaluation, as it is directly linked to the loss. It is also often described as 'objective', because it measures all the effects relevant to the evaluation using an indicator similar to the 'national product' as a value criterion for the economy as a whole. However, a direct projection into the national product is precluded by the fact that the national product is often shifted upwards by increasing losses, i.e. in the wrong direction in relation to welfare. This indicator is therefore a national product modified by welfare-related hypotheses which identifies loss reductions as welfare enhancing. But as the necessary hypotheses still lack conventionally established general acceptance, unlike the statistically measured national product, it is misleading to apply the term 'objective' to this method of evaluation.

The resource approach can quickly impinge on ethical problem areas, as is frequently demonstrated by the example of accident deaths. In principle, cost value determinations imply that lost capital goods, i.e. human beings, can be reproduced, while calculations of income value on the basis of age level and social position can also generate negative results. For this reason the debate on accident costs has been accompanied by constant efforts to blunt the sensitive points by the use of suitable average concepts and reference quantities. The standardized evaluation techniques for transport projects in the Federal Republic of Germany (1986, 1992) employ average quantities of this kind. Attempts are also made to raise resource values by allowances for human suffering. In roadbuilding cost–benefit analyses in Sweden, for instance, these allowances are derived from previously implemented accident prevention measures, so that the cost value of the human consequences of accidents is made up of a resource component and an indirect component related to the social willingness to pay for accident prevention.

With regard to environmental damage, the resource approach leads to the loss function formulated by Ridker (1967; quoted in Marburger, 1977):

$$D_i = f_i(\text{CO, CH, NO}_x, \ldots) \tag{5.4}$$

where i is the nature of the damage and D_i is a quantitative expression of the physical damage. The term f_i represents the quantitative association of the pollutants and the damage and also contains the assumed synergetic effects.

If the magnitude of type i damage is represented by C_i, then the total costs of the damage to the environment can be written

$$K = \sum_{i=l}^{n} D_i C_i. \tag{5.5}$$

In evaluating the magnitude of the damage C_i it is feasible in principle to substitute the cost of eliminating the damage (damage elimination cost). This presupposes that the destroyed resources are reproducible, and this clearly applies only to the destruction of material goods and minor injuries to health or to repairable environmental impacts. A cost evaluation of the cash value of expected losses of returns seems at first glance hardly practicable as environmental goods do not normally represent resources whose contribution to production appears in the profit and loss accounts of individual enterprises. An attempt must therefore be made to use model simulation to describe the environment's contribution to total economic production, as is shown below (the welfare maximization approach).

The utility approach

Whereas the resource approach attempts the substantial evaluation of loss on the basis of a generally accepted indicator (modified national product), the utility approach is founded on the individual value estimates of those concerned. The theory is based on the hypotheses of individual behaviour of the type used in general equilibrium theory. The most important '*homo oeconomicus* hypothesis' consists of two elements: the information premise assumes that all agents are fully aware of the economically relevant data or can completely safeguard themselves in uncertainty by contingent claims, and the judgement premise postulates that an individual is capable of consistent evaluation (order of preferences, utility function) in all possible economic circumstances. Individuals' notions of utility are expressed in their demand behaviour, so that this behaviour also provides the basis for measuring changes in utility. As demand functions normally contain prices as independent variables, utility quanta defined in money units are obtained. This form of monetarized utility measurement has been familiar since Marshall, who introduced the consumer's surplus concept, and it has undergone further theoretical development in the form of compensating variations (e.g. by Hicks, 1940–1, and Henderson, 1940–1). The decisive element is that individuals respond to changes in their economic situation by a willingness to pay or to sell. This form of evaluation is also 'direct', i.e. related to the loss or profit expected from the change.

The public nature or externality of goods is of itself no reason for rejecting this subjective approach. If the consumers are sovereign, they could by means of Lindahl's voluntary contributions (Lindahl, 1919) determine both the desired provision of the good and the allocation of the costs provided that a mechanism could be found to prevent cheating, as the Lindahl principle no longer operates if individuals can also enjoy a public good as free riders. In practical applications the important point is therefore to establish willingness to pay in such a way that strategic distortions are excluded as far as possible.

If evaluations based on willingness to pay are attempted in the field of accident consequences, it is the willingness to pay of society not founded on individual assessments which must be invoked, as in the case of accident prevention costs arising from safety measures instituted by the government.

In the environmental field the chances for the successful application of the utility approach are better in those problem areas where there are few merit distortions, or in other words where there is a high awareness of the environment. This applies both to local environmental impacts (by smog or water contamination) and to environmental damage with a high publicity status such as the devastation of forests. The issue here is to define the principle of who should pay for what, i.e. the property rights in the environment have to be assigned to one party – the polluters or the polluted. If the property rights in the environment are held by the originator of the pollution, the polluted party is under an obligation to offer the former payment to refrain from disturbing the environment. In these circumstances the willingness to pay approach has to be applied. If on the other hand the property rights are held by the polluted party, then it is the originator of the pollution who must purchase readiness to accept disturbance of the environment, and in this case the willingness to sell approach applies. The results of these two principles may diverge widely from each other, especially when the information about the effects of the pollution is incomplete. The amount of money which must be paid to an individual to obtain his agreement to a deterioration of the environment may then be much greater than the maximum sum he would be prepared to pay to avert an equal deterioration of his environmental conditions.

Willingness to pay or to sell can be measured either by opinion polls or by the observation and evaluation of optional behaviour patterns. Opinion polls have to be very carefully planned to overcome the central problems of the utility approach, i.e. the sovereignty problem, and the free rider problem and to establish for those questioned the concept of a private market for environmental goods. To date the most comprehensive survey in this area has been carried out by Schulz (1985), who asked a total of 4500 Berliners the maximum monthly sum they would be prepared to pay for different air qualities. The result in relation to net monthly income is shown in figure 5.5. If this result is extrapolated for the population of the Federal Republic of Germany, the costs of air pollution (equal to the utility of improving air quality to 'holiday air level') are close to DM50 billion (25 billion ECU) or 3 per cent of gross national product in 1985. The willingness to sell would have to be put at a still higher figure.

The alternative measure is to attempt to approach genuine willingness to pay by the observation of optional behaviour patterns. For instance, the individual can avoid environmental disturbances by selecting other living areas. The additional costs incurred in changing living areas indicate the lower limit of the valuation of an improved quality environment. Connections between income

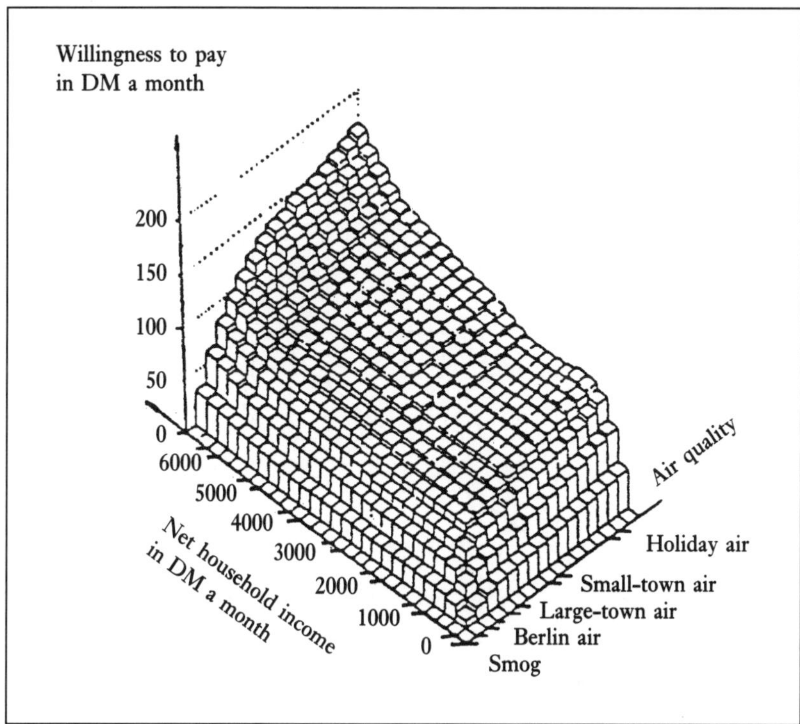

Figure 5.5 Air quality, willingness to pay and income.
Source: Schulz and Wicke, 1987

level and quality of environment in selected living areas are clearly discernible at the empirical level, and this implies that households opt for a higher quality of environment as their income grows. Figure 5.6 shows the percentage decline in rents due to road noise as measured by Pommerehne in Basel (quoted by Wicke, 1986). The function is clearly non-linear, i.e. the rent drops by 1 per cent with a growth in road noise from 30 to 31 dB(A) but by 1.4 per cent with an increase from 70 to 71 dB(A).

The problems of measurement based on avoidance costs lie in separating the environment from other factors and in the behavioural inertia of households, which is much more marked in Europe than in the USA. This manifests itself in the relative unwillingness of Europeans to quit bought or rented living accommodation.

With regard to the problem of value distortion in measuring willingness to sell, the example of the new international airport at Osaka may be mentioned.

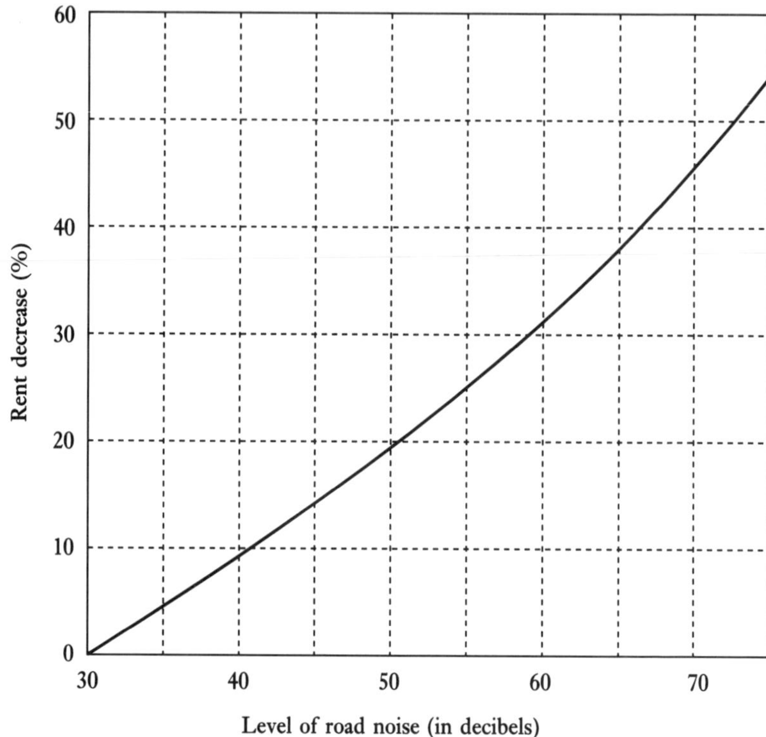

Figure 5.6 Rent decrease by noise: the example of Basel.
Sources: Wicke, 1986; Pommerehne, 1986, p. 205.

Sakakibara (1987) reports that the fishermen of Osaka Bay were also included as an affected group in the negotiations on compensation payments, although there was no evidence to show that the catches were diminished by the take-off or landing of aircraft. However, compensation was negotiated, and the result was that the number of professional fishermen in the Osaka region grew sharply, so that eventually US$147 million had to be paid out.

The welfare maximization approach

The resource (cost) and utility approaches are normally treated as mutually independent alternatives for the direct evaluation of accident consequences and environmental impacts. A brief excursus into welfare theory will show that both cost and utility approaches coincide in a complete formulation of the welfare maximization problem (see Kotz et al., 1984). Let us assume that society values material consumption C and limited resources S (human and environmental capital) and assesses these by means of a utility function which for simplicity is assumed to be the same for every consumer:

$$u = u(C, S) \tag{5.6}$$

where $u_c > 0$ and $u_s > 0$. This expression differs from the textbook formulation by the inclusion of the available natural resources S. If a prolonged period is considered, each year t of this period will be characterized by a consumption volume C_t with a resource stock S_t. If the annual utility values are integrated by addition into the society's overall assessment and society places a higher value on 'today's' than on 'tomorrow's' unit of utility, we obtain the 'utilitarian' form of the welfare function:

$$W = \int_0^\infty u(C_t, S_t) \exp(-\delta t) \, \mathrm{d}t \tag{5.7}$$

where $\delta > 0$ is the social rate of impatience.

For the production of consumption goods a technology is available which converts labour L, capital K and natural resources R into national product Y:

$$Y_t = F(K_t, L_t, R_t) \tag{5.8}$$

$$\frac{\delta F}{\delta v} > 0 \qquad v \in \{K_t, L_t, R_t\}$$

In contrast with the textbook model, the consumption of natural resources appears as an argument of the production function F.

If the stock of natural resources is limited and written as S_0, then the current natural resource stock S_t is given by the expression

$$S_t = S_0 - \int_0^t R_t \, \mathrm{d}t \tag{5.9}$$

i.e. over time S_t is steadily depleted. By definition

$$R_t = \frac{-\mathrm{d}S_t}{\mathrm{d}t} \tag{5.10}$$

From the maximization of equation (5.7) under the further conditions contained in (5.8)–(5.10) and given an income disposal equation it is now possible to derive not only the usual optimum consumption plan but also an optimum plan for resource depletion.

The optimality condition which is important for our reasoning (derived from the Hamiltonian of the system) is

$$\frac{\partial F}{\partial R_t} = \frac{1}{\partial F / \partial K_t} \left(\frac{\partial \dot{F}}{\partial R_t} + \frac{\partial U / \partial S_t}{\partial U / \partial C_t} \right) \tag{5.11}$$

The left-hand side denotes the marginal productivity of the natural resource which equals its price in equilibrium. It can be derived by solving the differential equation (5.11) together with the other optimality conditions. Obviously the price of the natural resource is inversely dependent on the marginal productivity of capital (because of the substitutive relationship between produced capital and non-produced resource). Furthermore the price of the resource is directly dependent on the marginal utility of the resource and inversely dependent on the marginal utility of material consumption. So the (shadow) price of the natural resource increases *ceteris paribus* with the preference for the resource. The important insight of this exercise is that the natural resource has a price although it is not traded on the market.

Although there is difficulty in putting such a global model to empirical use, particularly when individual accidents or environmental impacts have to be evaluated, it none the less provides a conceptual framework for resource and utility evaluation. An attempt can also be made, using a definition of proxy variables for the natural resources, to arrive at a quantitative notion of the economic contribution of environmental resources. Econometric investigations by Müller and Rothengatter (1987) have produced production elasticities of between 0.08 and 0.2, which indicates that the environment's contribution to production can be much higher than the 6 per cent estimated by Wicke (1986).

The prevention approach

The prevention approach is used to determine the costs incurred in preventing a loss, and the economic principle requires selection of the most cost-effective preventive measure. Prevention costs should on no account be regarded as approximations to the direct costs.

As they are related not to the loss but to measures designed to prevent loss, they constitute their own cost category which cannot be compared or grouped with the direct costs. Their magnitude depends on

1 the level of prevention defined by specified limit values and
2 the preventive technology used.

'Objective' and 'subjective' techniques also affect the determination of levels of prevention. For example, medical research can give a guide to the limit values beyond which hygienic consequences are likely to arise. As this information involves probabilities, the setting of limit values necessarily imposes further value judgements which can be based on a survey of subjective attitudes to the tolerability of environmental nuisances or on observation of evasive behaviour. However, unlike the willingness to pay principle, the subjective method does not result in the quantification of monetary value equivalents but in the establishment of tolerance limits.

The setting of rules for limit value measurements is crucial to the formulation of possible preventive technologies. For instance, it is important for noise emission limits to define the point at which these are to be measured, e.g. the boundary of the land plot or an inside wall of the house or flat of the affected individual. Another inhibition of possible preventive measures is the rationality criterion, which means that one nuisance should not be reduced at the cost of increasing another. For instance, the cheapest way of excluding noise is certainly to obstruct its access to the auditory canal (by ear covers or shields), but this measure so reduces the sensation of personal well-being that its use as a means of prevention has not so far been discussed. It is generally assumed that traffic noise can be reduced to the limit value by fitting the affected buildings with soundproof windows. This assumption is not without problems, as the desired effect is achieved only when the windows are closed, and apart from providing visual contact with the outside world windows are also used for ventilation so that either this function or noise reduction cannot be fully achieved.

In the same way that the coincidence of more than one emission source can produce mutually reinforcing or synergetic effects in creating pollution, so preventive measures may be specific or wider in their action. In diesel vehicles, for instance, engine modifications or changes in the fuel composition can reduce noise emission ('knocking' when starting cold) and the formation of soot. An even broader spectrum of effects including safety, noise emission and the formation of exhaust gases is produced by measures affecting behaviour (e.g. speed limits).

If the prevention approach is used to evaluate safety measures and environmental impacts as individual components, there is a danger of duplicating the count if measures have overlapping effects. If, in the choice of measures, an attempt is made to avoid such duplication by limiting the field of consideration to specific preventive measures, this may act against the demand for cost-effectiveness, as the desired limit values might be attainable by cheaper combinations of measures. This point is intended to indicate that the quantification of prevention costs can pose just as many problems as the projection of potential pollutions in the direct approaches. It should also be remembered that this approach is concerned with notional measures which may be taken in the future, so that here the evaluation also contains a speculative element.

In judging the direct and indirect approaches the predominant view is that direct monetary assessments are the desirable solution, although they are for the time being not practicable in all areas because of gaps in our objective knowledge, unsubstantiated hypotheses and simplifying consequences of pollution. The result is that the indirect approach based on prevention costs is used as a back-up to provide some quantitative idea of the money values applicable to various areas of environmental pollution. This is acceptable as long as it can be assumed that the prevention costs are greater than the direct pollution costs. However, if this is not the case and if it can be plausibly argued that the costs of prevention are lower than the discounted future pollution costs, then there is an economic imperative. In cost calculations underpinning future transport plans and policies the prevention approach is then the correct theoretical solution. In this case the prevention costs, for instance when calculating total transport costs, can be compared with and set against direct pollution costs since, once the notional preventive measures have materialized into real actions, they constitute a real consumption of the resources of transport activity.

The risk approach

The relationship between transport activities and accidents or environmental pollution is stochastic in character as every trip is not linked to the certainty of loss but 'merely' increases the risk that a loss may occur. The recognition of risk categories and the possibilities of risk management at the individual and collective levels is another means of approaching the problem of the related additional social costs.

Of course a risk approach is concerned with the future. The resulting action does not rest on a retrospective view of past losses but addresses future risks to which specific probabilities can be assigned and which can be managed with strategy mixes comprising diversification, insurance and prevention.

Diversification

The diversification strategy is of specially close concern to the theory of business finance as investors are inclined to opt not for bonds or equities carrying the maximum expected yield but for a portfolio embracing a range of risk categories so that their risks are spread. Society may adopt a similar strategy for transport by not exclusively backing one type of vehicle such as the car, notwithstanding the preference of individuals for the car now and in the foreseeable future, but instead catering for the parallel development of alternative, e.g. public transport, modes in order to reduce human and environmental risks and provide other options in the event of acute threats to safety or to the environment. This is exemplified by the smog alarms by which people are obliged to use public transport if the immission levels for defined exhausts exceed critical limits.

The reason why countries provide ample and high standard loss-making public transport facilities may be explained as an attempt to spread risks. Therefore the losses of public passenger services may be seen as the price of risk diversification (they are indeed often referred to as 'survival precautions').

Insurance

In the area of safety and the environment under consideration, insurance contracts could be a suitable means of placing future risks into economic categories. For analytical purposes it is for the moment expedient to disregard the existence of insurance companies and to look at insurance contracts as a reciprocal obligation.

Where two individuals are exposed to a risk which may materialize for one or the other of them, the risk can be covered by a reciprocal insurance in which each partner pays a premium measured in such a way that the ratio of the premiums equals that of the respective probabilities of loss. The reciprocal insurance of a pool comprising many insured individuals functions in a similar manner as long as the risks are not mutually correlated (see Markowitz, 1959). However, as soon as the risks borne by individuals are correlated, they can no longer be allocated with actuarial fairness on the principle of the probabilities of loss. The issue then becomes one of social risks, which in an unsafe world are the counterpart to external effects.

Accident and environmental risks bear a heavy social imprint, and private sector willingness to insure these risks is therefore too weak to provide full cover from the premium payments. In these circumstances the state may react by imposing mandatory insurance, and we do indeed find that many countries lay down compulsory third-party insurance. Such insurance covers both material and intangible losses by lump-sum payments (damages, compensation for loss of limbs), although the amounts in Europe are very modest.

It would be conceivable in principle to extend the insurance premiums to the still uncovered additional social costs. If the probabilities and magnitude of monetary losses were known, it would be possible to calculate premiums which

1 would cover future losses in the aggregate and
2 could to a large extent be charged to the individual transport user.

Suppose there is a risk-averse road haulage firm behaving according to the utility function

$$u(X) = \frac{1}{a}[1 - \exp(-ax)] \tag{5.12}$$

where u is the utility level, x is the realization of random income X, and a is the (constant) parameter of risk aversion.

If the random income is defined to be

$$x_i = X_0 - k_i \tag{5.13}$$

where X_0 is the income without external costs of road accidents caused by trucking and k_i is the external costs caused by trucking in a future state of the environment i, the behaviour of the firm depends on the external costs and the probability distribution for their values. In the discrete case we get

$$E(X) = \sum_{i=l}^{n} x_i w_i \tag{5.14}$$

where w_i is the probability for state i to occur.

As the firm is risk averse Jensen's inequality holds:

$$E[u(X)] < u[E(X)]. \tag{5.15}$$

This means that the firm is willing to insure for the risk. For utility function (5.11) the risk premium π can be calculated as (see Heilmann, 1990)

$$\begin{aligned} \pi &= E(X) + \frac{1}{a}\ln[1 - aEu(X)] \\ &= [uE(X) - Eu(X)]\exp[aE(X)] \end{aligned} \tag{5.16}$$

To take a simple example let us assume that the firm has the risk parameter $1/a$, an expected return of 100,000 without paying for external costs and the uncertain payments 20,000 DM/a with probability 0.4, 40,000 DM/a with probability 0.4 and 60,000 DM/a with probability 0.2. The yearly number of ton-kilometres travelled is 1 million. Under these assumptions the expected value of payments for external costs is DM36,000 and the risk premium which the firm is willing to pay is about DM4000, such that the insurance premium would sum to DM40,000 (or 20,000 ECU) per year (equal to 0.04 DM/ton-kilometre).

Prevention

Before the significance of risk-reducing measures is discussed, we shall first consider the problem of 'state-related utility' which leads to the treatment of effects which are difficult to gauge in monetary terms.

The utility of the individual is normally regarded as dependent on his or her consumption or, taking the case of an indirect utility function, as income dependent. It is quite possible, however, that utility also depends on the nature of objects which cannot simply be described by reference to income equivalents. This would be true, for instance, of an irreplaceable heirloom, the individual's own life or that of his or her child (Hirshleifer and Riley, 1979). Besides income c, these authors introduce an heirloom variable h to clarify the relationship. $h = 1$ signifies 'state without loss' and $h = 0$ signifies 'state with loss'. The utility situation can then be represented as shown in figure 5.7. When heirloom loss occurs ($h = 0$), the utility curve drops to a lower level.

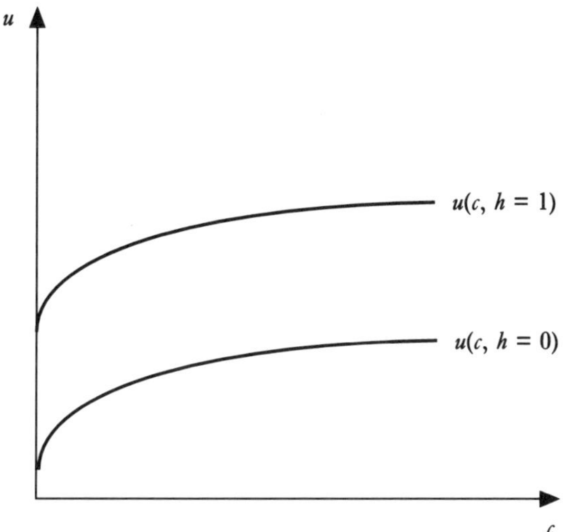

Figure 5.7 State-related utility.

The question of whether or not the individual wishes to be insured against such loss depends on the extent to which income and the heirloom variable are substitutes, i.e. are mutually exchangeable in terms of utility compensation. With heirlooms such as old paintings it is impossible to make a general prediction, some will regard their loss as being capable of compensation: others will not. If $h = 0$ represents a traffic accident in which the claimant is himself at fault and which results in material or slight personal injury, the individuals concerned will require more money than if $h = 1$ and, assuming a desire to cover the risk, the individuals will insure themselves so that the payment received includes this additional sum.

As Hirshleifer and Riley observe, the situation is quite different in the case where h represents the life of the individual's child. Here it seems reasonable to regard h and c as complementary; if the child dies ($h = 0$) the family concerned needs less income as part of the income would have had to be spent on the child. Taking out an insurance policy on the life of the child would therefore be economically irrational. In a case like this it is reasonable to transfer income from the 'state with loss' to the 'state without loss', i.e. to practise a kind of reverse insurance by doing everything to prevent the occurrence of the loss. Where preferences are distorted (merit quality) or where social risks occur, it is up to the state to make the optimum provision for loss. To take a concrete example, a family has very limited possibilities of taking individual measures to protect their child's life against traffic accidents. The family has to rely on the state shouldering the social portion of this task.

The same arguments hold for the environmental risks which are threatening lives of individuals or the existence of mankind. An example is the greenhouse effect which is caused by a warming up of the atmosphere. The emissions of CO_2 and methane play an important role in this context, with transport contributing about 20 per cent of the total.

Assessment

The welfare and risk approaches supply the theoretical foundations for handling the subject but are too abstract for immediate practical application. The resource and individual utility approaches rest on a problematic theoretical foundation. Their use in association with terms such as 'internalization of external effects' or 'socially optimal factor allocation' seems hazardous. On the other hand they do offer the advantage that monetary denotation enables effects to be brought to the foreground which are otherwise treated only peripherally as a result of the tendency already mentioned to suppress the negative.

The indicative action of a monetary denotation should not be underestimated, although it may be objected that figures with little theoretical or empirical back-up can be easily detected, so that the attention gained is thereby converted into rejection. In many cases it can be conclusively argued that a direct evaluation of the consequences of accidents and environmental pollution supplies a bottom limit while the true magnitude may be assumed to be far greater. The determination of bottom cost limits and the assurance that safety and environmental impacts are not neglected in an economic world otherwise anchored in monetary comparisons appear to be the sole plausible arguments for a direct evaluation of 'critical effects' influencing human life and ecological relationships.

The prevention approach, on the other hand, has a theoretical basis rooted in such critical effects. First, it imposes an economic obligation when the prevention costs are lower than the costs of the damage. It may be argued that this condition is fulfilled in the case of the effects mentioned. Second, it is compatible with the implication of risk theory that in a situation of state-related utility and complementary relations between income and the state-altering event the only logical consequence is a reversal of the insurance principle – it is not mastering the consequences of loss but preventing the occurrence of loss which must then be at the centre of economic considerations.

The prevention approach is admittedly not a valid technique for *ex post* cost calculations, as it is based on notions of future effects and measures and not on past resource consumptions. Its usefulness is therefore confined to considerations of the future, e.g. cost–benefit analyses and standard cost calculations.

5.6 SOME RESULTS FOR CALCULATING THE EXTERNAL COSTS OF TRANSPORT

The Bundesanstalt für Straβenwesen (Federal Institute for Road Technology) has calculated the overall economic costs of accidents for 1984 at a total of DM37.1 billion (19 billion ECU). As table 5.3 shows, material damage accounted for a total of about DM17 billion and personal injuries for close to DM20 billion.

The evaluations were carried out using the resource approach, and in the case of personal injuries were based on the gross income value. In 1984 prices an accident resulting in severe injury was evaluated at DM50,000 and an accident resulting only in slight injuries at DM4000. The costs arising from cases of material damage vary with the severity of the accident and the class of road. These cost figures contain no element for the evaluation of subjective consequences.

Grupp (1986) has added to this calculation by computing the income losses as a function of age at death and has arrived at annual accident costs ranging from DM39.7 billion to DM46.2 billion for the mid-1980s.

Using the resource approach, Marburger has estimated the economic costs due to illnesses caused by air pollution. The database here was provided by the statistics on diseases of the respiratory organs and the associated periods off work, hospitalizations and numbers of illnesses and deaths. According to his calculations, the total economic costs due to diseases of the respiratory organs amounted to about DM12 billion based on 1985 data, the share due to air pollution being between DM2.3 billion and DM5.8 billion according to the hypothesis of cause and effect applied. These hypotheses were derived from the relative noxiousness levels of the emitted substances (toxicity factors based on CO equivalents) and from empirically determined relationships between the incidence of illnesses and certain pollutant emissions. Use was again made here of older studies carried out in the USA by Ridker and Lave and Seskin which attributed 20 per cent (Ridker) or 50 per cent (Lave and Seskin) of diseases of the respiratory organs to air pollution (quoted by Marburger, 1977). The share which should be attributed to transport can be determined by assuming that transport's contribution to the total loss due to illnesses is proportional to transport-related emissions. With transport accounting for 27 per cent (weighted with toxicity factors) of emissions, Grupp calculates an annual loss of DM4.6 billion with an uncertainty margin of ±60 per cent, or DM2.7 billion.

It is primarily the prevention cost approach which is applicable to quantifying the consequences of traffic noise. This is particularly true for cost–benefit analyses like those carried out for the Federal German Transport Plan

Table 5.3 Accident costs in the Federal Republic of Germany 1984

		Estimate of the overall economic costs of accidents in 1984						
						Costs of accidents with only material damage		
		Costs for deaths	*Costs for severely injured*	*Costs for slightly injured*	*Costs of material damage from accidents with injury*	*DM3,000 or more for one of those involved*	*Under DM3,000 for each person involved*	*Total*
Cost rate	In town				11,700	19,300	5,600	
in DM	Out of town	1,130,000	51,000	4,000	23,000	21,400	5,100 } 5,500	
per accident	Motorway				51,900	30,400	5,200	
Accident costs in towns in million DM		4,217	3,842	912	2,909	3,206	5,324	20,231
Accidents costs outside towns, not on motorways, in million DM		6,508	2,608	350	2,189	1,130	917	13,700
Accident costs on motorways in million DM		800	308	73	816	870	270	3,137
Sub-total of accident costs outside towns in million DM		7,308	2,916	423	3,005	1,999	1,187	16,837
Total accident costs in and outside towns in million DM		11,525	6,758	1,334	5,913	5,026	6,512	37,868
Total accident costs		Personal injuries and deaths DM19.617 billion			Material damage DM17.451 billion			DM37.1 billion

Source: Froböse, 1986

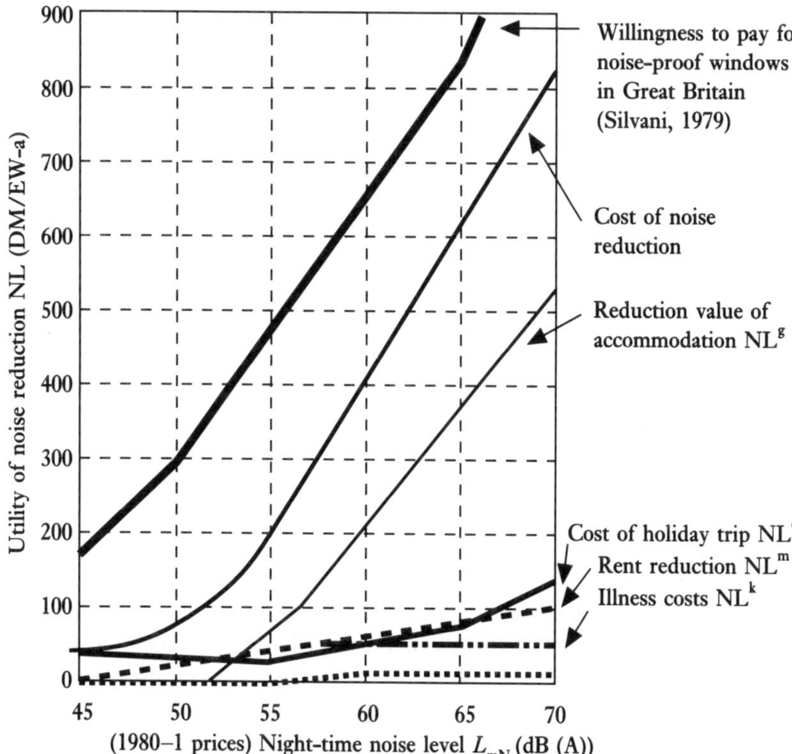

Figure 5.8 Cost estimations for traffic noise.

(Bundesverkehrswegeplanung), in which the monetary values of traffic noise are calculated according to the number of individuals affected in certain noise level areas on the basis of a target level of 45 dB (A) for night-time noise which is attainable by the projected soundproofing of buildings. If the limit values were used to formulate a traffic noise protection law for the existing roads of the Federal Republic of Germany, the cost would be DM5.6 billion.

Grupp quotes noise costs of between DM0.7 billion and DM2 billion per annum obtained by extrapolating the results of a noise study carried out on a section of a motorway. Formulations exist for a resource-related evaluation and these have been assembled by Glück (1986) to provide a comparative survey. The graph also includes a utility estimate from a British study which shows a higher level of noise reduction utility but sets the limit utility of noise reductions in the upper range lower than the resource-related estimates (figure 5.8).

If a reduction of the noise level to 30 dB (A) were targeted, a total value for the nuisance due to road noise of DM29.3 billion would be obtained on the basis of Pommerehne's rent model. This shows that the specification of a limit value (e.g. no noise, tolerable noise, medically acceptable noise) is crucial to the determination of noise costs (figure 5.6).

In a calculation of total transport costs encompassing the environment (air and noise pollution and land consumption), construction and maintenance as well as accidents, Grupp arrives at a sum of DM85–95 billion a year, of which DM68–77 billion are due to road transport and approximately DM14 billion are attributable to the railways. If the view is restricted to accidents and environmental impacts, the total figure is DM50–60 billion including DM48–57 billion for road transport and about DM1 billion for the railways.

There is an urge to compare figures of this kind with economic indicators. For example, Wicke (1986) writes: 'With the aforementioned limitations due to serious underestimates arising from gaps in knowledge and highly conservative damage assessments, it may be assumed that current environmental impacts in the Federal Republic of Germany cause annual losses amounting to at least DM103.5 billion'. That is around 6 per cent of the Federal Republic's GNP in West Germany. Again, Grupp states, 'the social costs of transport account for about 5 per cent, and motor vehicle traffic for about 4 per cent of GNP as usually calculated'.

The latest estimates have been presented by PLANCO Consult (charged by the Deutsche Bundesbahn, 1990) and the UPI-Institute which is known to support the arguments of the Green Party. While PLANCO's estimates are very conservative, resulting in an overall external cost of transport in West Germany of DM60 billion (base: 1987), the UPI investigations result in much higher figures. Altogether this institute estimates the volume of external costs of the transport sector to reach about DM200 billion (base: middle of the 1980s; these are about 10 per cent of the gross national product). It should be noted that the costs of CO_2 are not included in any of the studies quoted. PLANCO (1990) and UPI (1989) estimate the external monetary impacts of freight transport by road at 0.12 DM/ton-kilometre and 0.30 DM/ton-kilometre respectively.

These estimates are about 1.8–4.6 times the allocated expenditures for the infrastructure. The Swedish estimates end up with the factor 2.7 and lie in the range of the German studies as presented by Hansson (1992).

5.7 TRANSPORT POLICY MEASURES TO REDUCE EXTERNAL COSTS

A considerable number of scenarios have been developed in the past years to describe the public possibilities to cope with external costs of transport. The following categories of measures may be distinguished:

1 improving the infrastructure and transport management;
2 applying price policies; and
3 intervening by regulatory actions.

In this chapter we shall restrict our attention to economic incentives to reduce relevant externalities.

Certification

The system of certification employed in the interests of the USA's clean air policy is an extremely economic method of promoting environmental protection by the stimulation of private interest. It has its origin in the 'pollution rights' idea according to which individuals and institutions who contaminate the environment without infringing laws implicitly hold pollution rights. As the use of these rights is not linked to private costs, there is in principle no incentive to economize on their use.

Under the certification system pollution rights actually have to be bought. They are treated as instruments of entitlement and, if not used, they can be disposed of or assigned to an 'environment bank' against payment of the purchase price. In this way the environment is turned into a negotiable commodity and the 'consumers of the environment' can be stimulated by the price of the commodity to adopt environmentally more acceptable technologies in order to capitalize expensive certificates. If provision is also made to reduce over time the pollution entitlement carried by the certificates, there is a permanent stimulus to develop better technologies for environmental protection.

In practice this might work as follows: on type approval a motor vehicle would be allocated to an emission class and the manufacturer would purchase an emission certificate for each vehicle which he would then sell on to the vehicle's buyer. If the manufacturer makes his vehicles environmentally more acceptable, the certificates to be bought become cheaper. On the other hand, if a purchaser retro-fits environmentally beneficial technologies he can exchange an expensive certificate for a cheaper one.

The advantage over fixed limit value specifications lies in the fact that an incentive can also be given to do better than the limit values. For this purpose a corresponding adjustment must be made to the certificate prices. The prevention costs (cf. section 5.4) can provide reference points for the pricing policy. If the price is higher than the prevention costs, prevention and the capitalization of certificates becomes a cost-effective strategy. A further advantage lies in the in-built buoyancy of the system if the pollution entitlement carried by the certificates is periodically lowered.

There are also potential disadvantages (see Walter, 1987):

1 stagnation of the emission market if the downgrading of the pollution rights is absent or insufficient;
2 a danger of technological imbalances due to concentration on the emission limits of 'fashionable pollutants';
3 lack of incentives to invest sunk costs in environmental protection;
4 competitive and bureaucratic problems.

A combination of workable policies

The internalization of external effects in the form of costs and charging these together with the infrastructure costs has been a subject of debate by transport economists since Pigou. Road pricing literature has produced an abundance of proposals (see, for instance, the Smeed Report, 1964). The Scientific Advisory Council (1991) of the German Ministry of Transport has suggested a comprehensive set of workable policy measures:

1 raising fuel taxes
2 relating vehicle taxes to emissions and mileage
3 road pricing and economic parking management
4 removal subsidization for environmentally problematic transport modes
5 dynamic setting of emission standards
6 stricter control of behaviour
7 improvement of the infrastructure
8 professional transport management

A good part of this list consists of price policy, which is regarded as more flexible and efficient because incentive-compatible price settings can stimulate millions of decentral decision makers to improve the environmental quality by simultaneously increasing their utility or profits. It would be necessary, however, to agree on a common European Community standard for a road pricing system to avoid discrimination against foreign drivers. Improving the infrastructure and transport management is regarded to be a necessary but not sufficient condition for reducing external costs. In the first instance an upgrading of the quality of public transport is necessary. The improvement of the road network should be more oriented to saving external costs than to creating new capacities.

While some scientists regard an integrative and co-operative transport management to play a key role in future transport policy using the technical progress of information, communication and electronic control, others are more sceptical. Topp and Rothengatter (1991) for instance argue that co-operative transport management by park-and-ride in agglomerations is most expensive for the public and does not solve the congestion problems as the congestion simply shifts from downtown areas to the park-and-ride areas.

An important aspect is a dynamic approach to limit values (including traffic accident figures) and a sliding budgeting schedule for prevention costs so that the technological state of the art at specific intervals in time can be converted into an updated cost calculation. The sliding investment planning scheme must be paralleled by

1 long-term, graduated specification of emission and immission limits;
2 medium-term provisions for preventive measures and tax rates, or rules for tax exemption; and
3 the revision at medium-term intervals of limit values and inventories of measures.

Short-term policies to adjust the demand to the capacity should be left to the market which means that infrastructure parts with high traffic demand should be managed and operated on the basis of private business rules.

5.8 EXTERNAL BENEFITS OF ROAD TRANSPORT

While it is generally accepted that external diseconomies of road transport exist and have to be compensated for by means of taxes or user charges, there is an upcoming discussion about the deduction of external benefits from the external costs of transport. In particular the road lobby is promoting this argument. The International Road Transport Union (IRU) has enlisted an international group of transport scientists to analyse the social benefits of goods transport on roads, and the General German Automobile Club (ADAC) has initiated a study to calculate the social benefits of car driving. Although quoted in different journals of the road lobby it was not possible to obtain these studies for a scientific evaluation. Therefore the arguments in favour of compensation of social benefits listed in the following may be incomplete. Nevertheless, it seems to be worthwhile to evaluate the propositions – as far as they are known – by the conceptual framework which has been developed in the first sections of this chapter.

Arguments in favour of compensation of external benefits of transport

There is no doubt that there is a social benefit of road transport in the sense that private benefits arise from transport activities and these are of course part of social benefits. But, as Willeke (1991, 1992) argues, further external benefits could be taken into account because of

1 the extension of consumption patterns and improvement in living standards;
2 the development of new structures of spatial patterns, decentralization of production locations, separation of the locations of housing and of employment, specialization of land use or extension of labour markets;
3 the induction of growth and structural effects, individualization and flexibility of freight transport logistics to create new paths for industrial labour division and interaction and the setting of new quality standards such as 'just-in-time' transport;
4 innovations by use of road vehicles, synergetic processes between industry, spatial economy and transport.

The Deutsche Straβenliga (1992) refers to the IRU study when listing the following external benefits of freight transport on roads:

5 a remarkable increase in flexibility and innovation which creates a new quality of service in transport and strengthens the economy for international competition;
6 cost reductions for packing, processing and logistics;
7 the high quality of regional distribution of consumption goods;
8 improvement of location quality, which seems to be extremely important for a country with high production quality and costs;
9 positive employment effects in peripheral regions which have no access to rail.

Following first rough estimates the authors of the study conclude that these external benefits almost equal the external costs so that additional charges on trucking motivated by the internalization of social costs are not justified.

The German Automobile Club ADAC has tried to quantify the external benefits of road transport and presented the following results (in billion Deutschmarks) (ADAC Motorwelt, 6/92, p. 39):

Difference between taxes and fees paid by road users and expenditures for the road network in West Germany	15.2
Public tax income from activities related to road transport	100.0
Benefits from providing access to more than 28 million jobs and distributing 80–90 per cent of goods and services	115–335
	225–450

Comparing this figure with the estimation of external diseconomies of transport which sum to DM46–64 billion according to the calculations of this institute, ADAC concludes that the social benefits of car driving exceed the social costs by five to ten times.

Critical questions

Regarding this reasoning two questions arise:

1 Which of the effects mentioned by Willeke, the Deutsche Straßenliga or the ADAC are really external in the sense that they are exchanged outside the market?
2 Suppose for defining a clear starting base that the external diseconomies of road transport are negligible. Would it under this assumption be justified to subsidize road transport to compensate for the external economies?

Let us start by analysing the first question. Surprisingly enough neither scientists nor consultants who advocate for subtracting external benefits from the external costs of the road users present a clear definition of externalities. What they list is a mixture of

1 consumer/producer surpluses,
2 direct and indirect cost savings,
3 multiplier effects,
4 input–output effects,
5 innovation/technological/structural effects, and
6 direct and indirect involvement of transport activities in production and trade of goods and services.

Most of these effects are not at all external. For instance a difference between the willingness to pay of consumers and the price actually paid (equal to the consumer's surplus) is an absolutely normal and (from the technical point of view) internal result of market processing. If no consumer's surplus occurred this would mean that a perfect monopolist provides for the market supply and extracts the whole willingness to pay of consumers by individual bargaining. This would result in a poor welfare position. So, contrary to the argument that the producer would have to be compensated for the consumer's surplus, it is socially optimal to increase the consumer's surplus as long as the sum of consumer's and producer's surpluses is maximized.

An analogous argumentation can be given with respect to the producer's surplus. If a producer receives low-cost inputs or if he can improve his production technology by using road transport he has an individual advantage and can increase his individual profit. There is no need to compensate the transport sector for providing the possibility to the producer to improve his production efficiency. It is just the function of firms in market economies to buy input factors and combine them efficiently to produce a value added. There is no reason for reimbursement of the input factors if their combination has yielded a profit.

If road transport helps to increase the regional product and employment in less developed regions the externality is incorporated in the infrastructure which has been provided by the public authorities although the costs are not fully paid back by the users. There is no additional contribution stemming from the use of this subsidized infrastructure by the transport sector. As long as the road haulage industry does not cross-subsidize the less developed countryside to assist the public sector there is no reason for an additional compensation for their services beyond the market transport prices.

It is correct that technological progress occurs in which transport activities are involved which is diffused through a branch or even through the whole economy, effecting technological, spatial and structural changes. It is indeed hard in these cases to separate internal from external economies. This is because one would have to observe carefully which of the multiple interactions occur inside or outside the market in the short run and the long run. But regarding the 'broader view' of externalities which we have introduced in section 5.1 we can state that it is not necessary to identify the size of these external benefits of road transport exactly. This is because they are not relevant with respect to public intervention. If external benefits occurred which exceeded the costs of transactions for contractual arrangements rational individuals would try to internalize these effects by private actions. For example, a firm is free to make up a road haulage division of its own if it experiences high benefits from most flexible freight transport logistics. Or alternatively it might make a medium- or long-term contract with a road haulage company to ensure that it received the service it needed just on time.

Therefore we can conclude that the long list of external benefits of private use of the road network which appear in the recent literature is dramatically reduced if we rule out consumer/producer surpluses and all kinds of interactions which are beneficial for the parties involved and internalized in the long run, although not running through the market process. So the theoretical base, which Aberle and Engel (1992) try to construct to define positive externalities of road transport and to derive ways of measurement, collapses. What might be left is the social benefit of emergency services, fire, police and other social services. But a part of this benefit is already considered by subtracting the road track costs of these users from the total bill. Furthermore, that part of social benefits of emergency services would have to be cancelled which is supplied for road accidents. Therefore we end with the proposition that *cum grano salis* there is no economic foundation for subtracting external benefits from the external costs of road use.

Although it is academic after this reasoning to examine how to proceed if there were relevant external benefits of road transport, we shall add some remarks on this problem. From figure 5.4 the external costs of transport predominantly occur by interactions on the first level, i.e. by the uncompensated use of non-renewable resources. External benefits, however, could occur by interactions between transport and the public/private production/consumption sector (level 3). If the private production sector, for instance, benefits more from road transport than it would benefit had all transactions been operated through the market mechanism, then it could be welfare improving if the private production sector compensated the transport sector. In the case that no private solution can be found because of the large number of parties the public could help by raising taxes to the producers and paying subsidies to the transport companies. But it would not be enough to subsidize the transport sector only and leave the position of the sectors benefiting from transport unchanged (which would be the consequence if the external benefits of transport were subtracted from its external costs). So the correct scheme to solve the externality problems occurring on different decision levels would be to let the transport sector pay fully for the external costs of using non-renewable resources and establish a transfer payment from the private production/consumption sector to the transport sector for compensating for external benefits. It is essential that such a scheme allocates the costs and benefits individually, at the location where they occur and to the agents which are concerned. A global macroeconomic benefit/cost calculation with a subsequent allocation of the net benefits or costs would be a wrong measure in a market economy which works on the basis of decentralized decisions.

To underline the argument of subsidizing road transport because of external benefits (which would be justified if the external benefits are relevant and the external costs are zero), three examples are added. The first example is the supply and use of dishwashing machines. A housewife using a dishwasher has more time for her family and can provide a better education to the children so that they can expect a higher future income which is also beneficial for society. Should the producers of dishwashers be paid a subsidy because they have induced activities outside the market (education in the family) which are beneficial for society?

The second example is electricity. Electrical power is the most important input for the modern consumption world. The use of electricity has had enormous consequences for technology, induced numerous interactions even outside the market and has changed our lives. Suppose a CO_2 tax is introduced for the emissions of exhausts. Should electrical power plants using coal, oil or gas be excluded from the tax?

The third example is a communication network which has many parallels to a road network. The benefits which are generated by the use of a data network are also advantageous for people who have no access to this network. High valued services cannot be produced without this technology. Suppose the electronics industry is obliged by environmental considerations to take back and recycle their products after use. Should the computer industry be excluded from this rule?

In all cases a large number of parties is involved in an interaction process in which externalities occur which in our view are not relevant for public compensation. Probably most of the scientists advocating for a compensation of external benefits of road transport will share this opinion and refuse to subsidize dishwashers, electrical power supply or data communication. But why subsidize the most energy consuming and pollution producing forms of transport (which would turn out to be necessary if the external costs are zero, as assumed above, and the external benefits would be defined as relevant)? Maybe the magic of individual mobility helps to crowd out negative and to reinforce positive associations in the human mind. The scientific arguments prominent until now seem to aim at rationalizing this emotional thinking. After a critical methodological analysis they appear to be nothing but a veil lacking real economic substance.

5.9 SUMMARY AND CONCLUSION

1 External economies occur if the production (consumption) function of an economic agent contains independent variables which he cannot control. Such effects do not operate through the market mechanism. In terms of property rights theory their generation is caused by a common use of a single resource by different agents when the property rights of the resource are not well defined.

2 In a Pareto world external economies/diseconomies disturb the equilibrium paradise. It is therefore necessary to remove all externalities by Pigovian subsidies or taxes. It is not easy to determine the correct amount of subsidization/taxation as it is dependent on the activity level of the agents involved.

3 According to the Coase theorem externalities can be internalized by private contracts if the transaction costs are very low and there are no problems of redistribution of income. As these assumptions usually are not given, a broader view of externalities is necessary to show that most externalities are normal interaction effects parallel to the market mechanism which by no means need to be removed by public intervention.

4 In the case of the transport sector the externalities which only public intervention can deal with are associated with the (cost free) consumption of non-renewable resources. In the first instance these are the environment and human capital. The transport sector exhausts these non-renewable resources by pollution, accidents and exploiting manpower for trucking in the sense that truck drivers are not paid the social costs of the inputs which they provide.

5 Congestion costs which are often denoted to be one of the most challenging externalities of the transport sector intrinsically indicate that the organization

of transport infrastructure management is wrong. So instead of trying to find the correct Pigovian taxes the best solution would be to manage road capacities by private companies monitored by public fund agencies.

6 The essential elements of external costs consist of risks which in some cases cannot be described exactly or in terms of monetary equivalents. Unlike other risks in the economic world, complete insurance is not possible, so that risk management has to concentrate on diversification and prevention strategies.

7 The calculation of external costs is associated with a high level of uncertainty because the functional relationships between transport activities and resulting damage are not precisely known. Cost calculations relating to future prevention can provide a sound foundation for economically valid strategies to enhance safety and the protection of the environment.

8 The fuzziness of social cost calculations is an argument to reject public intervention for reducing disamenities of transport. Alternative approaches such as the definition of environmental standards and emission certificates can also help to find the appropriate economic values of the environmental resources because they represent the dual approach to the social cost calculation.

9 Unlike rigid regulatory provisions, pricing strategies have the advantage that they are flexible and perceptible and can provide measured incentives for behaviour consistent with the aims pursued.

10 It is not justified to subtract external benefits of transport from external costs. From the list of external benefits of road transport mentioned in the literature most items are basically not external, for instance externalities are mixed up with consumers' and producers' surpluses. The remaining part is related to normal market interactions and does not give rise to compensating policies.

REFERENCES

Aberle, G. and Engel, M. (1992) Theoretische Grundlagen zur Erfassung und Bewertung des volkswirtschaftlichen Nutzens. *Internationales Verkehrswesen*, 169–75.

Bonus, H. (1983) Ökologische Marktwirtschaft. In H. Markl (ed.), *Natur und Geschichte*, Munich, 289–327.

Bös, D. (1986) *Public Enterprise Economics*. Amsterdam: North-Holland.

Buchanan, J.M. and Stubblebine, W.C. (1969) Externality. In K.J. Arrow and T. Scitovsky (eds), *Readings in Welfare Economics*. London: Allen and Unwin.

BVWP (1986) *Gesamtwirtschaftliche Bewertung von Verkehrsinvestitionen. Bewertungsverfahren für den Bundesverkehrswegeplan 1985*. Documentary series issued by the Federal Minister for Transport, vol. 69, Bonn.

Coase, R.H. (1960) The problem of social cost. *Journal of Law and Economics*, 1–44.

—— (1988) *The Firm, the Market and the Law*. Chicago.

DeSerpa, A.C. (1988) *Microeconomic Theory. Issues and Applications.* Boston, MA: Allyn and Bacon.

Deutsche Straßenliga (1992) Straße, Verkehr und Wirtschaft. *SVW-Info-Dienst* 2/7/92.

DFVLR (Deutsche Forschungs- und Versuchsanstalt für Luft- und Raumfahrt), NVI (The Netherlands Institute of Transport) and IRT (Institut de Recherche des Transports) (1985) *A Study on the Development of a High-Speed Rail Network in the European Community*. Cologne.

DIW (1987a) *Erweiterung methodischer Ansätze zur Wegekostenrechnung und Erarbeitung eines Konzeptes für eine Gesamtkostenrechnung des Verkehrs*. Expert report commissioned by the Federal Minister for Transport, prepared by J. Niklas, H. Rieke, W. Rothengatter, and U. Voigt. Berlin.

—— (1987b) *BVG-Konzept: Arbeitspaket 120, Veränderung der Verkehrsnachfrage*. Expert report commissioned by Berlin Transport Enterprises, prepared by J. Kloas, H. Kuhfeld and U. Kunert, with the collaboration of U. Müller and I. Pfeifer. Berlin.

—— (1991) *Verkehr in Zahlen*. Issued by the Federal Minister for Transport, prepared by H. Enderlein with the collaboration of B. Schrader. Bonn.

Emde, W., Ernst, R., Frerich, J., Huber, H.-J., Hundhausen, S., Krupp, R., Meewes, R. and Schilberg, F. (1985) Einheitliche Kostensätze für die volkswirtschaftliche Bewertung von Straßenverkehrsunfällen – Preisstand 1985. *Straße und Autobahn*, 159–62.

Ewers, H.-J. (1986) Kosten der Umweltverschmutzung – Probleme ihrer Erfassung, Quantifizierung und Bewertung. In Umweltbundesamt (ed.), *Kosten der Umweltverschmutzung*. Berlin, 9–20.

Frerich, J. (1974) *Straßenart und Straßenqualität in ihrer Berechnung zu Unfallhäufigkeit und Unfallstruktur auf den Bundesfernstraßen*. Forschungsbericht Cologne.

Froböse, H.-J. (1986) Straßenverkehrssicherheit und Unfallentwicklung in der Bundesrepublik Deutschland 1970–1984. *Internationales Verkehrswesen*, 19–22.

Glück, K. (1986) Zur monetären Bewertung volkswirtschaftlicher Kosten durch Lärm. In Umweltbundesamt (ed.), *Kosten der Umweltverschmutzung*, Berlin, 187–97.

Group of 12 Railways of the EC (1987) *Charging surface transport operators for the use of the infrastructure. Marginal social costs as a basis for calculation.* Paris.

Grupp, H. (1986) Die sozialen Kosten des Verkehrs. *Verkehr und Technik*, 359–66, 403–7.

Hansson, L. (1992) The environment mobility dilemma. A solution based on market pinciples. In UIC (ed.), *EURAILSPEED 92*, 152–9.

Heilmann, W.-R. (1990) Risk management and insurance. *Forensic Engineering*, 119–34.

Heinemann, K. (1966) *Externe Effekte der Produktion und ihre Bedeutung für die Wirtschaftspolitik*. Berlin: Duncker and Humblot.

Henderson, J.M. (1940–1) Consumer's surplus and the compensating variation. *Review of Economic Studies*, 117–21.

Henderson, J.M. and Quandt, R.E. (1958) *Microeconomic Theory.* New York: McGraw-Hill.

Hicks, J.R. (1940–1) The rehabilitation of consumer's surplus. *Review of Economic Studies*, 108–16.

Hirshleifer, J. and Riley, J.G. (1979) The analytics of uncertainty and information – an expository survey. *Journal of Economic Literature*, 1375–421.

International Road Federation (1990) *World Road Statistics*. Geneva.

Jäger, W. and Lindenlaub, K.H. (1977) *Nutzen-Kosten Untersuchungen von Verkehrssicherheitsmaßnahmen*. In a documentary series published by the Forschungsvereinigung Automobiltechnik e.V., Frankfurt.

Kapp, W.K. (1950) *The Social Costs of Private Enterprise*. Cambridge, MA: Harvard University Press.

Kessel, P., Müller, P. and Rothengatter, W. (1987) *Prioritätenbildung für ausgewählte Projekte der Bundesverkehrswegeplanung*. Expert report commissioned from Ulm University by the Federal Minister for Transport, Ulm.

Kotz, R. and Spremann, K. (1983) Risk aversion and mixing. *Journal of Economics*, 307–28.

Kotz, R., Müller, P. and Rothengatter, W. (1984) *Entwicklung eines Verfahrens für dynamische Investitionsplanung und Ermittlung des bei der Fortschreibung der BVWP anzuwendenden Zinssatzes*. Expert report commissoned from Ulm University by the Federal Minister of Transport, Ulm.

Lindahl, E. (1919) *Die Gerechtigkeit der Besteuerung*. Lund.

Malinvaud, E. (1977) *The Theory of Unemployment Reconsidered*. Oxford: Blackwell.

Marburger, E.-A. (1977) Zur direkten Bewertung volkswirtschaftlicher Zusatzkosten in Form gesundheitlicher Schäden durch Abgasemissionen des Straßenverkehrs. *Zeitschrift für Verkehrswissenschaft*, 195–212.

——(1979) Ein monetärer Bewertungsfaktor für die Beurteilung von Luftverunreinigungen des Straßenverkehrs in den RAS-W. *Zeitschrift für Verkehrswissenschaft*, 234–44.

——(1984) Wirtschaftlichkeit – auch bei der Beurteilung der Straßenverkehrssicherheit? *Zeitschrift für Verkehrswissenschaft*, 125–33.

—— (1985) Gesunder Menschenverstand – Eine Replik auf von Suntum. *Zeitschrift für Verkehrswissenschaft*, 119–22.

—— (1986) Zur ökonomischen Bewertung gesundheitlicher Schäden durch Luftverschmutzung. In Umweltbundesamt (ed.) *Kosten der Umweltverschmutzung*, 51–62, Berlin.

Marburger, E.-A. and Friedel, B. (1987) Seat belt legislation and Seat belt effectiveness in the Federal Republic of Germany. *Journal of Trauma*, 27–36.

Markowitz, H.M. (1959) *Portfolio Selection: Efficient Diversification of Investments*. Cowles Foundation for Research in Economics, Yale University, Monograph 16, New York.

Marshall, A. (1920) *Principles of Economics*, 8th edn. London: Macmillan.

Michalski, W. (1965) *Grundlegung eines operationalen Konzepts der Social Costs*. Tübingen: Mohr.

Ministry of Transport (1964) *Road Pricing: The Economic and Technical Possibilities* (Smeed Report). London: HMSO.

Monissen, H.G. (1980) Externalitäten und ökonomische Analyse. In E. Streissler and C. Watrin (eds), *Zur Theorie marktwirtschaftlicher Ordnungen*. Tübingen: Mohr.

Müller, P. and Rothengatter, W. (1987) Measuring the relevance of natural resources for production. *Zeitschrift für Nationalökonomie und Statistik*, 99–119.

Musgrave, R.A. (1974) *Finanztheorie*. Tübingen: Mohr.

Negishi, T. (1972) *General Equilibrium Theory and International Trade*. Amsterdam: North-Holland.

Nowak, H. (1987) Phänomen Mobilität. *VDA series* 53, 10–18. Frankfurt.

Pigou, A.C. (1924) *The Economics of Welfare*. 2nd edn. London: AMS Press.

Pilot Study on Road Track Cost (1971) *Proposal for a Council Decision Concerning the Introduction of a Common Payment System for the use of Traffic Routes. Memorandum on Payment for the use of Traffic Routes in the Framework of Common Transport Policy*. Commission of the European Communities. Com. (71) 268 fin. Brussels.

PLANCO-Consult (1990) *Externe Kosten des Verkehrs: Schiene, Straße, Binnenschiffahrt*. Report for the Deutsche Bundesbahn, Essen.

Pommerehne, W. (1986) Der monetäre Wert einer Flug- und Straßenlärmreduktion: Eine empirische Analyse auf der Grundlage individueller Präferenzen. In Umweltbundesamt (ed.), *Kosten der Umweltverschmutzung*. Berlin, 199–224.

Prognos AG (1986) *Szenarien zur Entwicklung der Umweltbelastungen durch den Verkehr*. Untersuchung im Auftrag der Deutschen Bundesbahn. Prepared by S. Rommerskirche, H. Arras, P. Cerwenka, B. Greuter, U. Matthes, and H. Meckel, Basel.

—— (1991) *Wirksamkeit verschiedener Maßnahmen zur Reduktion der verkehrlichen CO_2-Emissionen bis zum Jahr 2005*. Report for the Ministry of Transport, Basel.

RAS-W (1986) *Richtlinien für die Anlage von Straßen. Teil: Wirtschaftlichkeitsuntersuchungen*. Forschungsgesellschaft für Straßen- und Verkehrswesen, Cologne.

Rosen, S. (1985) Implicit contracts: a survey. *Journal of Economic Literature*, 1144–75.

Sälter, P.M. (1989) *Externe Effekte: 'Marktversagen' oder Systemmerkmal*? Heidelberg: Physica-Verlag.

Sakakibara, Y. (1987) *Building an Airport in a Crowded Country*. Paper A-112 of the Doshisha University, Kyoto.

Schulz, W. (1985) *Der monetäre Wert besserer Luft*. Frankfurt: Peter Lang.

——(1986) Die Kosten der Luftverschmutzung aus der Sicht der betroffenen Bevölkerung. In Umweltbundesamt (ed.), *Kosten der Umweltverschmutzung*. Berlin, 145–56.

Schulz, W. and Wicke, L. (1987) Der ökonomische Wert der Umwelt. *Zeitschrift für Umweltpolitik & Umweltrecht*, 109–55.

Scitovsky, T. (1969) Two concepts of external economies. *Journal of Political Economy*, 143–51.

Simons, J.G.W. (1992) In Round Table 92, *Benefits of Different Transport Modes*, European Conference of Ministers of Transport, Paris: OECD.

Stiglitz, J.E. (1987) The causes and consequences of the dependence of quality on price. *Journal of Economic Literature*, 1–47.

—— (1990) On the economic role of the state. In A. Heertje (ed.), *The Economic Role of the State*. Oxford: Blackwell.

von Suntum, U. (1984) Methodische Probleme der volkswirtschaftlichen Bewertung von Verkehrsunfällen. *Zeitschrift für Verkehrswissenschaft*, 153–67.

—— (1985) Auf dem Weg in den technokratischen Uberwachungsstaat – Eine Antwort auf Marburgers Kritik. *Zeitschrift für Verkehrswissenschaft*, 123–5.

Topp, H. and Rothengatter, W. (1991) *Verkehrsmanagement-Strategien*. Report for the Ministry of Transport and Technologie Hessen, Kaiserslautern.

UPI Umwelt- und Prognoseinstitut Heidelberg (1989) *Gesellschaftliche Kosten des Straßengüterverkehrs*, Heidelberg.

Waldeyer, H. (1987) Automobil und Umweltrisiken und Handlungserfordernisse. *VDA series* 53, 70–82. Frankfurt.

Walter, J. (1987) Ein (erneuter) Vergleich von Abgaben- und Zertifikatelösungen im Umweltschutz. *Zeitschrift fur Umweltpolitik & Umweltrecht*, 197–205.

Wardrop, J.G. (1952) Some theoretical aspects of road traffic research. Road Paper 36, *Proceedings of the Institution of Civil Engineers*, 325–78.

Wicke, L. (1986) *Die ökologischen Milliarden*. Munich: Kösel-Verlag.

Willeke, R. (1984) Soziale Kosten und Nutzen der Siedlungsballung und des Ballungsverkehrs. *VDA series* 41. Frankfurt.

—— (1991) Soziale Nutzen des Kraftfahrzeugverkehrs. *Schriftenreihe der DVWG* B 136, 49–60.

—— (1992) In Round Table 92, *Benefits of Different Transport Modes*, European Conference of Ministers of Transport, Paris: OECD.

Wissenschaftlicher Beirat beim Bundesminister für Verkehr (1991) *Maßnahmen zur Reduktion der Luftschadstoffemissionen des Verkehrs*. Bericht für den Minister für Verkehr. Bonn.

Wolf, W. (1987) *Eisenbahn und Autowahn*. Personen- und Gütertransport auf Schiene und Straße. Geschichte, Bilanz, Perspektiven. Hamburg: Rasch und Röhring.

6

Transport and Regional Development

Piet Rietveld and Peter Nijkamp

6.1 INTRODUCTION

Transport often gives rise to effects which are not limited to the transport sector itself. An outstanding example is that transport infrastructure is an important factor in the spatial and economic development of cities, regions and countries. The attractiveness of locations for situating economic activities depends, among other things, on their relative accessibility and, with that, on the quality and the amount of transport infrastructure.

The completion of the internal European market has given a new relevance to the relationship between transport and regional development. The single European market has transformed the European regions and nations into a network economy with open access to, but also a strong competition between, major areas in this network. As a result of this competitive process, some regions will become losers and others will become winners. Thus, the regional development issue is going to be a factor of critical importance in Europe. This is also witnessed by the new national and supranational plans in Europe to invest in sophisticated infrastructure in backward regions in order to ensure relatively equal competitive advantages for all regions. Thus transport infrastructure is a critical success factor for competitive performance and internationalization of regional economies. Missing links – or even missing networks as a whole – mean a significant reduction in the potential productivity of a region or nation.

Regional development is the result not only of a proper combination of private production factors such as labour and capital, but also of infrastructure in general and transport infrastructure in particular. Improving infrastructure leads to a higher productivity of private production factors. Conversely, a neglect of infrastructure leads to a lower productivity of the other production factors.

The desired balance between private and public infrastructure in regional development has been the subject of much theoretical and ideological debate. Hirschman (1958) has pointed out, however, that it is illusory to think that a balanced development is possible. Given the lumpiness of transport infrastructure projects, one will often have relatively long periods of excess supply or demand.

Governments have different options with respect to transport infrastructure. First, they may invest in infrastructure as a response to serious bottlenecks taking place due to an expansion of the private sector. This leads to a passive strategy: transport infrastructure is following private investment. Another option is that governments use transport infrastructure as an engine for national or regional development. This implies an active strategy where transport infrastructure is leading and inducing private investment. The latter strategy has a risky element, however, because the response of the private sector to infrastructure improvement can be disappointing. In many countries one will find examples of infrastructure projects which failed because of an insufficient response from the private sector.

The purpose of this chapter is to review the results that have been obtained so far in assessing the response of the private sector to transport infrastructure improvement.

It is important to note that in general the concept of infrastructure is used in a rather loose way in the literature. Most definitions include one or both of the following elements. First, infrastructure is mostly a capital good for which users do not pay a full market price: infrastructure is perceived as a source of external economies (cf. Youngson, 1967; Lakshmanan, 1989). Second, provision of infrastructure to an area leads to a very high cost for the first user and a small marginal cost for an extra user (cf. Diewert, 1986). In this chapter we shall be using both viewpoints in the definition of infrastructure.

The impact of infrastructure on the private sector consists of various elements. In the short run, direct effects will occur in the construction sector and indirect effects in all other sectors via intermediate deliveries. A negative effect, which is often overlooked, is the crowding-out effect: infrastructure must be financed, e.g. by means of government bonds, which may lead to higher interest rates and lower investments. In the long run one has operations and maintenance effects. In the present chapter attention will mainly be focused on still another type of long-run effect: the programme (or spin-off) effects.

Programme effects refer to long-term indirect changes in income, employment or investment in the private sector which are induced by the new opportunities offered by the improvement or extension of infrastructure.

The organization of the chapter is as follows. Some theoretical notions on infrastructure and regional development are discussed in section 6.2. Section

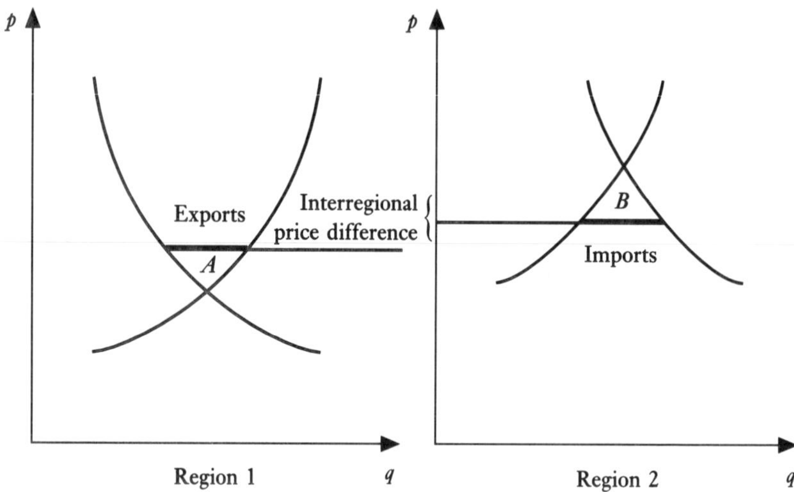

Figure 6.1 Supply and demand in two regions.

6.3 is devoted to studies which focus on the impact of transport infrastructure on productivity in regions. In section 6.4 studies are reviewed which focus on the role of transport infrastructure as a location factor, influencing the location of private investment or employment. In section 6.5 approaches are discussed where an integrated analysis is given of productivity and relocation effects of transport infrastructure on regional development. Section 6.6 offers concluding remarks.

6.2 TRANSPORT INFRASTRUCTURE AND REGIONAL DEVELOPMENT: THEORY

Improvement of transport infrastructure influences both production and household consumption. It leads to a reduction of transport costs and/or travel times. This may give rise to substantial redistribution effects among economic groups and also among regions. In order to analyse the differential effects of improvements of transport infrastructure on regional development, we shall discuss the relationship between transport and interregional trade.

The standard model of interregional trade is illustrated in figure 6.1. Export takes place from region 1 to region 2 when the transport cost is less than the difference in equilibrium price for a certain good in the two regions. Compared with the situation without trade an additional surplus is created consisting of area *A* (accruing to producers in region 1) and area *B* (accruing to consumers in region 2). Thus, both regions benefit from trade according to the model.

Improvement of infrastructure leads to a decrease in transport costs and hence to an increase in transport volumes. The equilibrium price in region 1 will increase, and the price in region 2 will decrease. Thus, in region 2, consumers benefit from the improvement of infrastructure, whereas producers are negatively affected. In region 1 it is the other way around. In employment terms, region 1 benefits, but region 2 is hurt by the improvement of transport infrastructure.

The model sketched above is a partial equilibrium model. It deals with the market for only one good. General equilibrium models are better suited to analysing the effects of changes in infrastructure, but they are of course more complex (see, for instance, Tinbergen, 1957; Takayama and Judge, 1971; Takayama and Labys, 1986). Figure 6.2 (which has been taken in adjusted form from Pluym and Roosma (1984)) presents some of the main effects when more than one sector is considered. In this case the net effects are difficult to predict. Intermediate deliveries play a complicating role. In addition, there may be compensating forces in the regions in which employment is negatively affected by increased competition. Prices of the products concerned will decrease, so that consumers can spend more on other products, part of which will be produced in the same region.

Processes in the long term (relocation of capital and persons) caused by changes in transport infrastructure are even more difficult to predict. Thus, operational models have to be developed to trace the effects of changes in (transport) infrastructure on regional development. This will be the subject of the next sections.

6.3 TRANSPORT INFRASTRUCTURE AND REGIONAL PRODUCTIVITY

In addition to production factors such as labour and private capital, transport infrastructure plays a role as an input in production processes. An improvement of transport infrastructure services implies that a regional economy can make use of its private production factors in a more productive way. Better transport infrastructure means that less capital and labour are needed to reach the same production level.

There are essentially two ways for analysing the productivity gains induced by transport infrastructure improvements. The first takes place at the firm level by measuring carefully the reductions in (transport) costs which can be achieved by infrastructure improvements. The second occurs at the aggregate regional level by investigating the contribution of the production factor infrastructure to regional production, taking into account the contribution of other production factors. This entails the use of regional production functions.

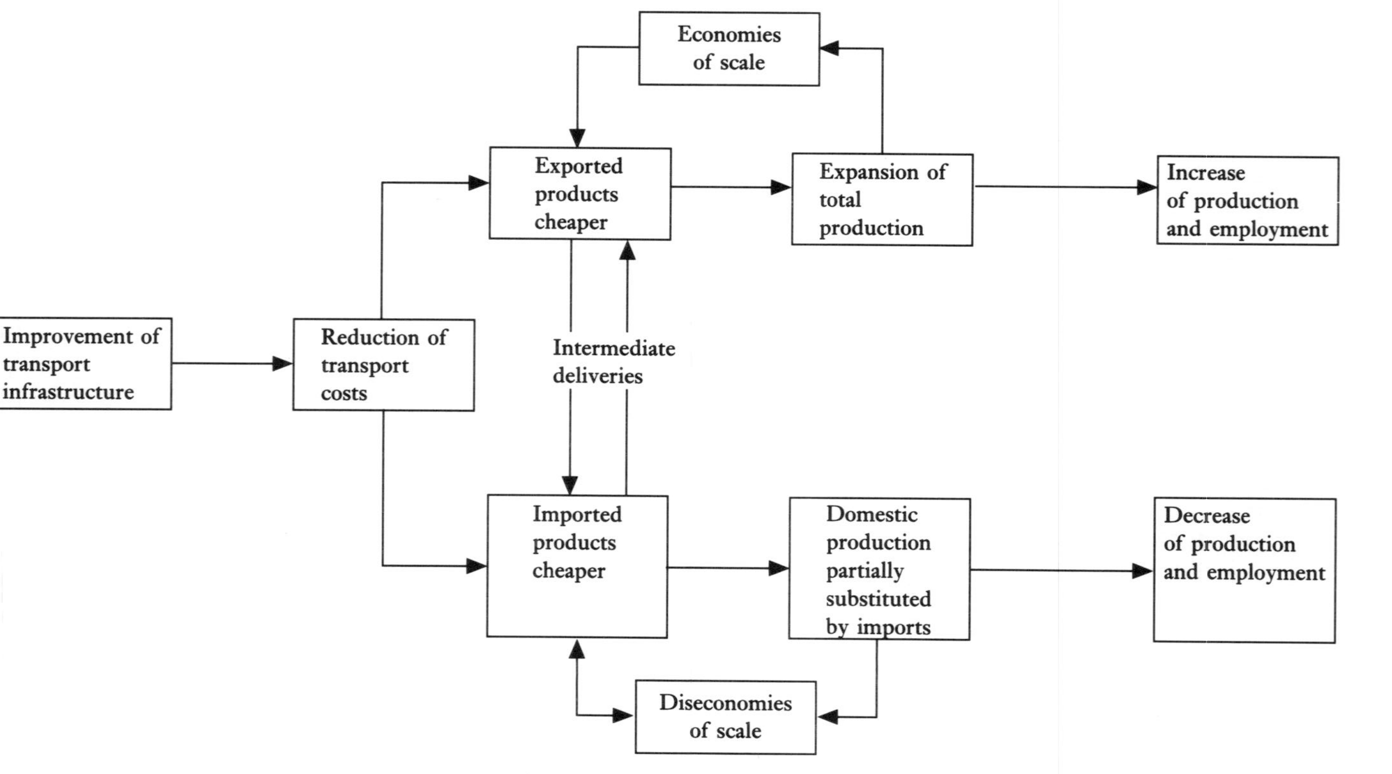

Figure 6.2 Effects of improvement of transport infrastructure.

Analysis at firm level

Microanalysis can be helpful in tracing behavioural determinants and responses of individual firms as a result of new infrastructure. An interesting example of this can be found in Forkenbrock and Foster (1990) who describe the results of various studies concerning the impact of infrastructure on regional development, all using quasi-experimental control group analysis and macroeconomic indicators (e.g. population, employment, income per capita etc.). It is remarkable that the results of these studies appear to be different: some authors find a positive relationship and others a negative or inconclusive one. Thus controlled micro experimentation does not necessarily guarantee satisfactory outcomes. We shall present two examples of a micro approach, taken from Dutch research in this field.

A study by NEA (1990a) addresses the economic costs of inadequate infrastructure in the province of Noord-Brabant on the regional economy. The study focuses on the congested S20 connection between the cities of Nijmegen and Eindhoven. Firms in the region were reported to suffer from excessive transport costs. A careful series of interviews with these firms led to the conclusion that firms with a regional orientation experience an increase in total transport costs of about 1.6 per cent including both capital and labour costs. For firms with an international orientation this figure is 0.7 per cent. For most firms the transport costs do not exceed 30 per cent of total costs (except for transport firms, of course).

Therefore the impact of the delays on productivity of firms is low, except for transport firms themselves. Thus the overall effect of inadequate transport infrastructure on regional productivity must be low in this case. Of course, the impact on the profit rate of individual firms will be higher, even much higher in certain individual cases. An interesting further result of the study is that the actual time losses for firms are much smaller than the time losses as perceived by the firms themselves. This is also an important point for the impact of infrastructure on location decisions of firms. Perceptions deserve more attention in studies of firms' behaviour than they usually receive.

A second case study was carried out by NEA (1990b) in the province of Zuid-Holland. A difference with the former study is that the latter is an *ex post* study: it deals with a realized infrastructure improvement. In the 1980s an industrial area near The Hague received a much better connection with the national highway system. The time gains per car or truck operated by firms in this particular area varied from 2 to 10 per cent. For firms located elsewhere the average time gains were of course much smaller. It appeared from the interviews that firms made little systematic effort to make use of the time gains. A rescheduling of trips did not take place, for example, so that part of the time gains were absorbed by an increase of slack in firms. The overall reduction in transport costs and the related productivity increase due to the transport infrastructure improvement were relatively small in this case study.

A disadvantage of micro case studies of this type is that they only focus on productivity improvements for firms directly affected by infrastructure improvements. Indirect effects, i.e. effects on other firms, are usually not taken into account. Another disadvantage of the case studies is that only one type of infrastructure is taken into account. It is therefore interesting to combine these case studies with modelling approaches using aggregate production functions where such elements can be taken into account. This will be the subject of the next section.

Production function approach

A general formulation of a production function for sector i in region r, with various types of infrastructure, is

$$Q_{ir} = f_{ir}(L_{ir}, K_{ir}; \mathrm{IA}_r, \ldots, \mathrm{IN}_r)$$

where Q_{ir} is the value added in sector i, region r; L_{ir} is the employment in sector i, region r; K_{ir} is the private capital in sector i, region r; and $\mathrm{IA}_r, \ldots, \mathrm{IN}_r$ is the infrastructure of various types in region r.

As far as transport infrastructure is concerned, it is not easy to take into account its network properties in the production function approach. A solution is to distinguish various types of transport infrastructure according to their spatial range: intraregional, interregional and possibly international.

Another problem related to infrastructure is that its impact may transcend the boundaries of regions. A certain region may not have its own airport but can still benefit from an airport nearby. This may be solved by using the concept of accessibility of certain types of infrastructure in the production function.

A summary of models using the production function approach is given in table 6.1. It appears that in most of the models a simplified version of the above production function approach is used. The most complete ones are those developed by Mera (1973) and Fukuchi (1978) for Japan, and Snickars and Granholm (1981) for Sweden.

Sectoral detail is important in these kinds of studies. This is shown by Fukuchi (1978) and Blum (1982), who found that the productivity increase due to infrastructure may by quite different among different economic sectors. This is also confirmed by Biehl (1986), who found that an index of sectoral composition of regional economies explains much more of the variance in regional per capita income than infrastructure does.

The most detailed treatments of infrastructure are given by Blum (1982) and Andersson et al. (1989). As far as transport infrastructure is concerned, Blum distinguished (in a regional study of the Federal Republic of Germany)

Table 6.1 Examples of the production function approach to infrastructure modelling

Author	*Country*	*Number of sectors*	*Number of types of infrastructure*	*Presence of*		*Form of production function*
				labour	*private capital*	
Biehl	EC	1	1	Yes	No	Cobb–Douglas
Blum	FRG	3	8	No	No	Cobb–Douglas
Andersson et al.	Sweden	1	7	Yes	Yes	Cobb–Douglas (with modification)
Snickars and Granholm	Sweden	21	5	Yes	Yes	Leontief
Nijkamp	The Netherlands	1	3	Yes	No	Cobb–Douglas
Fukuchi	Japan	3	3	Yes	Yes	Cobb–Douglas
Kawashima	Japan	8	1	Yes	No	Linear
Mera	Japan	3	4	Yes	Yes	Cobb–Douglas

1 long distance roads
2 all other roads
3 railways
4 ports

For both types of roads and for ports, significant results were obtained. For railways, Blum found zero and even negative effects.

Andersson et al. distinguished the following aspects of transport infrastructure for the Swedish regions:

1 main roads
2 railways
3 airport capacity
4 travel time to major metropolitan areas
5 interregional travel time

For 1970, Andersson et al. found that the impact of railways on regional production was stronger than that of main roads. In 1980 this situation had reversed. According to the estimates, airport capacity itself does not have an influence on regional production. However, if taken in conjunction with research and development, it can be shown to have a positive effect.

The form of the production function chosen is in most cases a Cobb–Douglas function. This implies a considerable degree of substitutability among production factors, e.g. between private and public capital. By investing in private infrastructure, regions can extend their production capacity even when infrastructure is fixed at a low level. An interesting modification of the Cobb–Douglas function is used by Anderson et al. (1989) in order to allow for zones of increasing and of decreasing returns to scale. An entirely different approach is followed by Snickars and Granholm (1981). The Leontief structure they use implies that infrastructure imposes a limit on the extension of employment and private capital in a region.

6.4 INFRASTRUCTURE AND FACTOR MOBILITY

Provision of infrastructure in a certain region leads to an increase in productivity of private production factors such as labour and capital (see section 6.3). This may in turn lead to expansion and relocation of these production factors in the region. This effect is the subject of the present section.

The response of labour and capital to changes in regional infrastructure could be studied by means of the production functions discussed in section 6.3.

These production functions can be used to derive demand functions for labour or capital with relative prices and infrastructure endowment as explanatory variables. In most empirical studies, however, this approach is not followed. Rather, the levels of employment and capital are studied in the context of a rather loose location theory in which relative prices and infrastructure play a role next to a series of other location factors. Among these factors are urbanization economies, sectoral structure, quality of labour, accessibility of markets and particular regional policies.

Four approaches can be observed towards analysing the influence of infrastructure on employment and private capital:

1 the role of transport infrastructure is modelled via its influence on accessibility;
2 the role of transport infrastructure is modelled via its influence on marginal transport costs, which are computed by means of a linear programming transport model;
3 investments in infrastructure are directly linked to private investments in regional economic models;
4 the role of transport infrastructure is analysed by means of surveys among entrepreneurs on the importance of infrastructure relative to other location factors.

Infrastructure and accessibility

Improvement of transport infrastructure leads to a reduction of travel time or cost and hence to an improvement of accessibility of markets or inputs. This may in turn lead to a relocation of labour and capital. Accessibility of a certain variable Z in regions can be defined as

$$\mathrm{ACC}_r(Z) = \sum_{r'} Z_{r'} f(c_{r'r})$$

where $c_{r'r}$ is an index of travel costs between regions r' and r and $f(c_{r'r})$ is a distance decay function. The variable Z may refer to employment, production, inputs etc. Botham (1983) uses the following relationship between regional employment and accessibility:

$$\Delta E_r = a_1 \mathrm{ED}_r + a_2 W_r + a_3 \mathrm{LAPE}_r + a_4 \mathrm{ACC}_r(Z)$$

where ED, w and LAPE denote employment density, wage rate and an index of labour availability. For Z, several of the variables mentioned above have been tried. Finally, ΔE is the differential shift in employment, as defined by shift share analysis.

The above equation has been estimated for 28 regions in the UK for the years 1961–6, the period just before the construction of the UK national highway system. The equation was used for simulating the impact of the highway system as it developed on the distribution of regional employment. The reduction of transport costs induced by the highway system leads to an increase in the accessibilities of the regions. The effects on employment shifts have been computed by means of this equation. The general conclusion is that the impact of the highway system on the regional distribution of employment is rather small. A similar conclusion is also reached by Dodgson (1974), who used the same approach for the effects of the M62 in the UK. However, a similar study carried out by Kau (1976) in the USA gave rise to the conclusion that some regions experienced substantial positive impacts from an extension of the highway system.

Another application of the accessibility concept is given by Evers et al. (1987) in an *ex ante* study on high-speed rail connections in central and northern Europe. The study is more refined than the ones by Botham and Kau, in that some attention is paid to the problem of multiple modes of transport: focus on only one mode of transport may give a distorted view on accessibility as a location factor. It can be shown that the approach adopted by Evers et al. is (under certain conditions) consistent with a utility-based theory of the location of the firm (cf. Rietveld, 1990). The result of the study was that employment relocation induced by the high-speed rail connection would be quite modest.

Illeris and Jakobsen (1991) used the accessibility concept to study the effects of a fixed link across the Great Belt in Denmark. Their conclusion is that the competitive position of the regions concerned will not change much by the fixed link so that relocation will remain of limited importance.

In other studies, accessibility is also included but in a much simpler way, i.e. by using travel time from a specific region to the economic core region in a country. This approach is a feasible option for countries dominated by a single centre (see, for example, Folmer and Nijkamp, 1987; Florax and Folmer, 1988).

Still another approach to accessibility is followed by Mills and Carlino (1989). They measure accessibility by means of the density of the interstate highway network and find that it has a clearly positive impact on employment growth in US counties.

In the studies cited in this section, a positive relationship is found between accessibility and total employment. As discussed in section 6.2, this result is by no means guaranteed by theory. In terms of figure 6.2 it means that the balance between the sectors benefiting from a reduction in transport costs and the sectors hurt by a reduction is positive for the regions. At the level of specific sectors, on might still have negative effects on employment, but this is not reflected by the models discussed here because a sectoral subdivision is not used.

Infrastructure and marginal transport costs

The accessibility concept used in the previous section is closely linked to the gravity model (i.e. the well-known model in which the number of trips between two zones is proportional to some measure of the level of activity in the zones and inversely proportional to some measure of the cost of travel between the zones). It allows for cross-hauling and it yields spatial interaction matrices with a small number of zero interactions. An alternative approach to transport modelling is the linear programming model, which does not allow for cross-hauling and which entails many zeros in the spatial interaction matrix (see Nijkamp and Reggiani, 1992). The model deals with the minimization of total transport costs among a set of regions under constraints concerning total supply and demand. The dual variables of total supply and demand per region represent the marginal costs of receiving inputs and shipping outputs. As indicated by Stevens (1961), the dual variables can be interpreted as location rents.

Harris (1973, 1980) has developed a model of industry location in which the dual variables play a central role. Investments in infrastructure leading to changes in transport costs give rise to changes in the dual variables. The dual variables in turn are determinants of industrial location. In this model, other factors influencing industrial location are the cost of labour, the value of land, prior investments and agglomeration variables. The model has been developed for the USA. It allows for a high degree of spatial detail (approximately 3000 counties), with the sectoral detail also being substantial (up to 100 sectors).

An interesting application of the model is discussed in Harris (1980). According to the model, investments in road and rail infrastructure in a rural county in the USA gave rise to substantial and positive direct effects on employment during the first two years. However, the structural spin-off effects of the infrastructure are negative. After the fourth year, a negative, though modest, effect takes place on regional employment. This is an illustration of the lower part of figure 6.2: regions may be negatively affected by an improvement in transport infrastructure.

Direct links between investments in infrastructure and private investments

The effects of government investments on the national economy and especially on private investments can be studied by means of standard macroeconomic models. Several types of effects have to be taken into account. Multiplier effects of public investments have a positive influence on private investments. In contrast, crowding-out effects may occur which have a negative influence on private investments. Crowding-out occurs because financing infrastructure investments leads to higher interest rates for projects that are financed by means of government bonds. This implies a disincentive for private investors. Another type of effect is spin-off effects. These, on which the present chapter is focused, are usually not taken into account in macroeconomic models, however (cf. Houweling, 1987).

A possible approach to detect spin-off effects of infrastructure investments is the use of causality analysis. For example, in the approach of Pierce and Haugh (1977), statistical tests are developed for correlations between time series with different lag intervals. Using this approach, Den Hartog et al. (1986) found for the Netherlands that there is indeed a causal relationship between public and private investments, taking place within an interval of three or four years. For the reverse relationship (i.e. public investments are caused by private investments), no statistical confirmation could be found.

This result is important in the context of Hirschman's (1958) notion of unbalanced growth. Unbalanced growth means that private and public investments do not follow parallel paths. Periods with a strong emphasis on public investments alternate with periods with a strong emphasis on private investments. The result for the Netherlands suggests that public investments are the leading variable in this process.

A disadvantage of the above approach is that it is not possible to separate indirect, crowding-out and spin-off effects. Since the lag interval is rather short (three or four years), it is not clear whether the causal relationship refers to short-run (indirect or crowding-out) effects or long-run spin-offs. In order to overcome this difficulty, one may change the spatial level of analysis. An important part of the short-term effects of an infrastructure project will occur outside the region in which the project takes place. Long-run spin-off effects are likely to be concentrated in the project region, however. Therefore, Den Hartog et al. (1986) also carried out an analysis at the provincial level. In each region, private investment IP as a share of the gross domestic product Q is explained by government investment IG as a share of the gross domestic product:

$$\Delta\left(\frac{IP}{Q}\right)_{r,t} = \sum_{i=0}^{k}\alpha_i\Delta\left(\frac{IG}{Q}\right)_{N,t-1} + \sum_{i=0}^{k}\beta_i\left\{\Delta\left(\frac{IG}{Q}\right)_{r,t-i} - \Delta\left(\frac{IG}{Q}\right)_{N,t-i}\right\}$$

where the subscripts t and r refer to time and region. The national level is represented by N. Thus, in the above equation, for each region private investments are explained by government investments at both the national and the regional level with certain lags (see also Nijkamp and Blaas, 1992).

Spin-off effects can be detected by means of the β_i coefficients in a cumulative way ($\sum_{i=0}\beta_i$). Empirical results show that spin-off effects are indeed significant for an interval of zero to five years. However, Den Hartog et al. (1986) indicate that this positive result depends strongly on one particular province (Zeeland), which happened to attract high levels of government investment during the period considered. If this province is deleted, spin-off effects are no longer statistically significant. Thus, with the given approach, only when infrastructure investments are large is it possible to show that significant spin-offs take place in the regions.

Entrepreneurial statements about the importance of infrastructure as a location factor

As a complement to the above modelling approaches, one may also make use of direct interviews among entrepreneurs in order to study the relative importance of infrastructure. An example of such an approach is given by Bruinsma (1990), who studied the impact of infrastructure improvements in three Dutch regions. About 15 per cent of the entrepreneurs state that improved or new infrastructure has played a very important role in the development of employment in the firm. One should not exaggerate the importance of infrastructure, however, since market developments and the availability of space for expansion played a more important role according to the entrepreneurs. A special category concerns firms which relocated recently: in about 35 per cent of these cases, infrastructure is mentioned as an important or very important location factor. In each of the regions concerned there has been a major improvement of an existing highway or the construction of a new one. The average share of firms which reported that these activities had a positive impact on the firm's employment varied among the regions from 14 per cent to 26 per cent. In one of the regions the data available allow one to make an estimate of the (minimum) number of jobs created by a new highway per amount of investment. The outcome is that an investment of about Dfl650,000 (or 295,000 ECU) in highways leads to the creation of one permanent job. As a contrast one may use the amount of investment which is needed to generate one man-year of work in the construction sector and related sectors: taking into account the multiplier chain, a Dfl100,000 investment in highways generates work for one person during one year. The difference between the two figures is of course that the first impact has a permanent character whereas the second impact only takes place in the short run.

An obvious disadvantage of the approach described here is that there is no guarantee that actual behaviour of the entrepreneur has been in agreement with his statements. Another disadvantage is that such an interview-based analysis does not take into account indirect effects on other entrepreneurs, possibly located in entirely different regions (see also Vleugel et al., 1991). This raises the issue of generative versus distributive effects which will be discussed in the next section since it is of particular importance for our discussion.

Distributive versus generative growth

Improvement of infrastructure may lead to both distributive and generative effects. Distributive effects relate to a redistribution of economic activity among regions, the national total remaining constant. On the other hand, generative effects occur when the national total (or more generally the total in a system of regions) changes.

A difficulty is that the balance between distributive and generative effects depends on the demarcation of the system of regions. For example, improvement of a national airport in a country may (apart from an interregional redistribution in the country) induce larger flows of air traffic in the country concerned. This might be interpreted as a generative growth effect, but it may also be the consequence of a redistribution of air traffic at a higher international level. In the latter case, the share of other countries would show a decline.

Thus, generative growth effects may simply be an illusion caused by a delimitation of a study area which is too narrowly defined. This does not mean to say, of course, that all generative growth effects are illusory. But one will often observe the tendency that generative growth effects will be smaller the larger the system of regions studied.

In terms of the production function approach (section 6.3), an increase in infrastructure leads to a higher productivity of private production factors. This will lead to lower prices of outputs and/or higher levels of value added. Both will have a generative growth effect on the regions concerned. In the case of footloose industries, distributive effects will be considerable. For these industries, the approach of section 6.4 may be more relevant. Improvement of infrastructure in a region may lead to redistribution of labour or capital from one region to the other.

6.5 AN INTEGRATED ANALYSIS OF PRODUCTIVITY AND RELOCATION EFFECTS OF INFRASTRUCTURE

In the preceding sections we discussed the productivity and relocation effects of transport infrastructure separately. Of course, it would be preferable to use models where the two effects are treated in an integrated way. We shall discuss some interregional models which are suitable for this purpose.

Figure 6.3 gives a schematic example of a model of this type (derived from Amano and Fujita, 1970). For an appropriate analysis of transport costs one needs a detailed treatment of transport networks, route choice and modal choice. This leads to a degree of spatial detail which is difficult to meet in other parts of the model. Los (1980) proposed solving this problem by linking models with different degrees of detail, i.e. by using a transport model with high sectoral and spatial detail. Most operational models in this field give a rather crude treatment of networks, route choice and modal choice.

In this chapter we shall focus on the relationship between transport costs and trade flows.

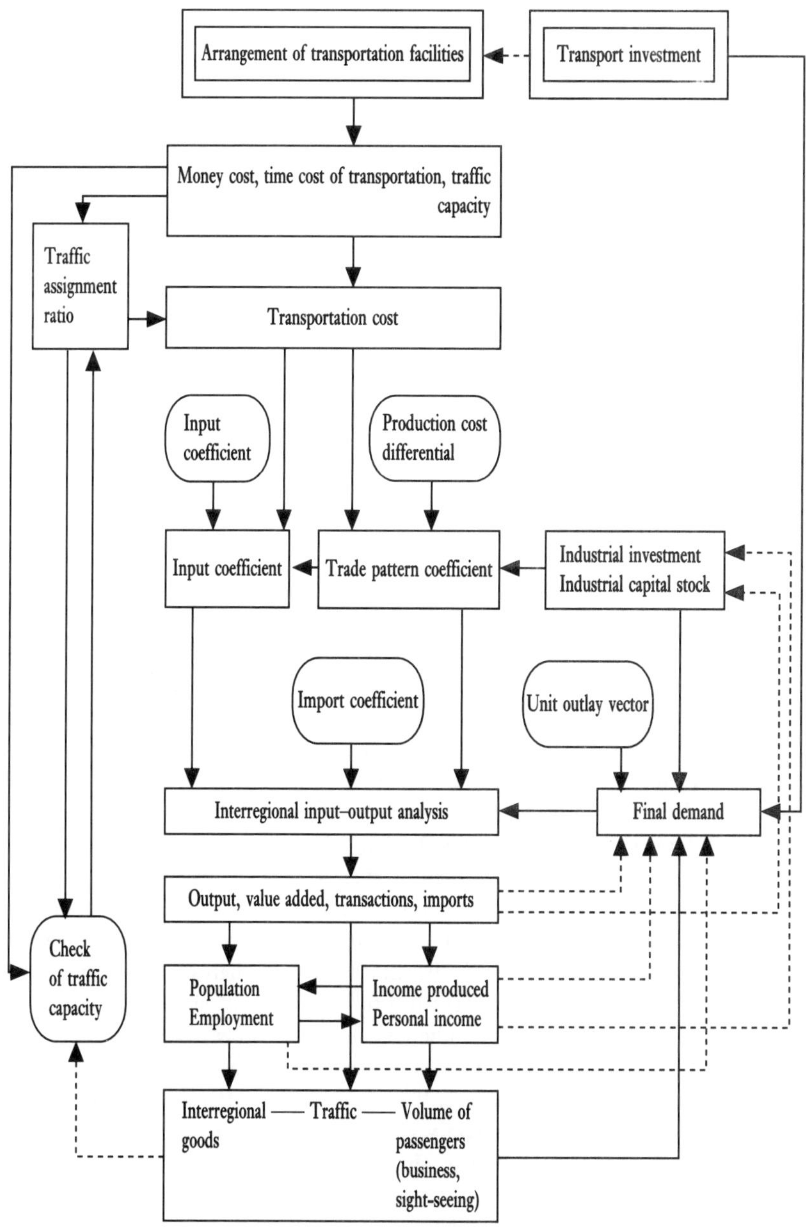

Figure 6.3 System chart of the Amano–Fujita interregional model (a dotted line denotes a time lag of one year).

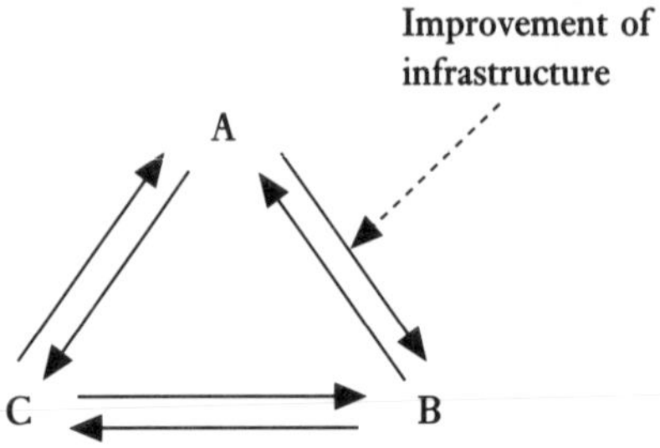

Improvement of infrastructure

A

C B

Origin	Destination A	B	C
A	–	+	O
B	+	–	O
C	–	–	O

Figure 6.4 Response of trade flows to transport costs cost reduction in a three-region framework.

Amano and Fujita (1970) put forth the following formulation for a Japanese interregional model:

$$t_{irs} = \frac{K_{\text{ir}} \exp[-\beta_i(p_{iv} + v_{ivs})]}{\sum_q K_{iq} \exp[-\beta_i(p_{iq} + v_{iqs})]}$$

where the subscripts q, r and s refers to regions and i refers to sectors. K_{ir} and p_{ir} denote capacity and price level in sector i of region r. Furthermore, v_{ir} is transport cost per unit of i between r and s and t_{irs} is the share of regions r in the deliveries to region s for goods produced in sector i. As indicated by Bröcker (1984), this formulation can be based on theories of stochastic choice.

A simple illustration of this equation on the sensitivity of interregional trade flows for changes in transport costs is given in figure 6.4.

In a system consisting of regions A, B and C, infrastructure between A and B is improved, leading to a decrease in transport costs between A and B for all goods in both directions. The effect on the trade share of region C (the region not directly involved) is unambiguously negative according to this equation. For the regions directly involved, the effect on trade shares is not clear, however. The loss on the home market has to be traded off against an increased penetration on the market of the other regions. One thing is clear, namely that the sum of trade shares for A and B together will increase as a consequence of the improvement of infrastructure. The conclusion is that although it is not obvious which of the regions directly involved in the improvement of transport (infrastructure) will be the winner, the regions not involved will certainly be losers.

According to the formulation above, improvements of infrastructure lead to a zero-sum game: ($\Sigma_r t_{irs} = 1$ for all i and s. However, as can be seen from figure 6.1, it is not only trade shares which change but also total trade volumes. Improvement of infrastructure does not only redistribute existing trade flows but may also generate larger trade volumes. Taking into account this generation effect and other indirect effects it is no longer obvious that a zero-sum result will arise. In the Amano–Fujita model, generation effects occur among others because the reduction in transport costs leads to an increase in value added which leads in turn to an increase in labour supply and investments.

Liew and Liew (1985) propose another modelling procedure. Their point of departure is a Cobb–Douglas production function with capital, labour and intermediate purchases for each sector and each region. Liew and Liew assume that consumers fully absorb the advantage of a decrease in transport costs: the equilibrium purchase price in region s is the sum of the equilibrium price of the good in region r plus the cost of shipping it from region r to region s. Another assumption is that in equilibrium transport costs are a constant fraction of the equilibrium price. Using a profit-maximizing approach, Liew and Liew derive a linear logarithmic system of price frontiers. Changes in transport costs give rise to changes in equilibrium prices in the various regions. These in turn give rise to substitution effects in the production process. Thus, it is not only interregional trade shares which change as a consequence of changes in transport costs, but all input–output coefficients may also change. In this respect, the model of Liew and Liew is more general than the model of Amano and Fujita, where input–output coefficients are assumed to be constant.

6.6 CONCLUDING REMARKS

A wide variety of approaches towards analysing infrastructure can be observed. The main findings of this chapter can be summarized as follows (cf. Evers-Koelman et al., 1987; for another recent review of studies see Vickerman, 1991).

1 It should be noted that transport infrastructure is a generic term which deserves much more detailed qualification in order to render itself appropriate for focused policy analysis. It is noteworthy, for instance, that the impact of infrastructure on locational decisions of firms depends also on its uniqueness. An increase in a ubiquitous infrastructure category does not exert a major additional influence on a region. For example, road expansion in an industrial area with a highly developed infrastructure network will have a lower effect than that in an underdeveloped area. Thus, infrastructure is a *sine qua non*, but not a panacea for growth. Besides, infrastructure will only have a positive impact if the region at hand has already a favourable potential for new development.
2 Another basic and often neglected transport policy question concerns the relationship between transport infrastructure and land-use patterns: are

large-scale geographical concentrations of public and/or private activities (e.g. offices, warehouses, facilities) a response to existing transport infrastructure, or have transport developments merely helped what would have occurred anyway? Thus, the assessment of the economic impact of infrastructure requires a clear specification of causality mechanisms.

3 Infrastructure is subject to decreasing marginal productivities. When a region is already well provided with infrastructure, adding infrastructure of the same type is of little value (cf. section 6.3). The provision of an extensive network of highways makes more and more industries footloose. As a result, the importance of road infrastructure as a location factor decreases (cf. Wilson et al., 1982). It is in developing countries with low infrastructure qualities that one expects the highest impacts of infrastructure investments on regional development.

4 As a corollary to the above, it is important to assess the potential effects of new types of infrastructure versus existing types (e.g. telecommunications versus roads). Infrastructure types clearly have their life cycles. Life cycles must not be used in a simplistic way, however. For example, rail traffic is regaining momentum after a long period of decline in Europe by the introduction of high-speed trains.

5 Consider an improvement of a link in a transport network. The programme effects tend to be largest in the regions connected by the link concerned (and other regions for which the link is important). The effect is not necessarily positive for all these regions. Some of them may be negatively influenced by, for example, the loss of markets due to increasing competition. The effect on the other regions, for which the improved link is not important, is much smaller, but it tends to be negative (cf. section 6.5).

6 Improvement of infrastructure is not a sufficient condition for regional development. Many other intermediary factors play a role. The interplay between infrastructure and other relevant factors is often only formulated in a superficial way in the studies surveyed. Especially for studies on specific infrastructure improvements, it is advisable that model-based studies be complemented with micro studies based on interviews with actual and potential users of infrastructure.

7 Improvement of infrastructure gives rise to both distributive and generative effects (section 6.4). Distributive effects tend to be small when in all regions improvements of infrastructure take place at the same speed. Generative effects of infrastructure can easily be over-estimated when the spatial delimitation of the area of study is too narrow. Part of the effects may simply result from an unobserved redistribution at a higher spatial level (section 6.4).

8 Improvement of transport infrastructure leads to a decrease in transport cost. This advantage may be absorbed by entrepreneurs or land owners

in the form of profit or rents; it may also be absorbed by employees (via wages). Another possibility is that the advantage is passed over to consumers in the form of lower prices. This distribution issue receives little systematic attention in the models surveyed, which is regrettable since the regional incidence of infrastructure improvements depends strongly on it.

9 Infrastructure is a multidimensional phenomenon. The importance of synergetic effects between various types of infrastructure has been recognized at the theoretical level. In the present generation of operational multiregional economic models, however, the occurrence of such synergetic effects is usually neglected.

10 Models on infrastructure tend to focus on its use for firms. The use for households must not be neglected, however. Infrastructure is an important location factor for households when relocating. In the long run this will also have implications for the location behaviour of firms.

11 Most of the models have been formulated as tools for impact studies: a change in infrastructure is supposed to lead to a change in the private sector. Infrastructure is an exogenous variable in the models. This is not necessarily an adequate way of modelling infrastructure. As indicated in section 6.1, infrastructure may not only lead the private sector, it may also follow. It is challenging to broaden the scope of models by introducing the possibility of this two-sided relationship.

REFERENCES

Amano, K. and Fujita, M. (1970) A long run economic effect analysis of alternative transportation facility plans – regional and national. *Journal of Regional Science*, 297–323.

Andersson, A.E., Anderstig, C. and Harsman, B. (1989) *Knowledge and Communications Infrastructure and Regional Economic Change*. Umea: University of Umea.

Biehl, D. (1986) *The Contribution of Infrastructure to Regional Development*. Brussels: European Community, regional policy division.

Blum, U. (1982) Effects of transportation investments on regional growth. *Papers of the Regional Science Association*, 151–68.

Botham, R. (1983) The road programme and regional development: the problem of the counterfactual. In K.J. Button and D. Gillingwater (eds), *Transport, location and Spatial Policy*, Aldershot: Avebury Gower, 23–56.

Bröcker, J. (1984) How do international trade barriers affect interregional trade? In A.E. Andersson, W. Isard and T. Puu (eds), *Regional and Industrial Development Theories, Models and Empirical Evidence*, Amsterdam: North Holland, 219–39.

Bruinsma, F. (1990) *Infrastructuur en Werkgelegenheid*. The Hague: Organisatie voor Strategisch Arbeidsmarktonderzoek.

Diewert, W.E. (1986) The measurenent of the economic benefits of infrastructure services. In *Lecture Notes in Economics* 278. Berlin: Springer.

Dodgson, J.S. (1974) Motorway investment, industrial transport costs and sub-regional growth, a case study of the M62. *Regional Studies*, 75–80.

Evers, G.H.M., Meer, P.H. van der, Oosterhaven, J. and Polak, J.B. (1987) Regional impacts of new transport infrastructure: a multisectoral potentials approach. *Transportation*, 113–26.

Evers-Koelman, I., Gent, H.A. van and Nijkamp, P. (1987) Effecten van de aanleg of verbetering van verkeersinfrastructuur op de regionaal-economische ontwikkeling. *Tijdschrift voor Vervoerswetenschap*, 33–60.

Florax, R. and Folmer, H. (1988) *Regional Economic Effects of Universities*. Enschedé: Twente University.

Folmer, H. and Nijkamp, P. (1987) Investment premiums: expensive but hardly effective. *Kyklos*, 43–72.

Forkenbrock, D.J. and Foster, N.S.J. (1990) Economic benefits of a corridor highway investment. *Transportation Research*, 303–12.

Fukuchi, T. (1978) Analyse Economie-Politique d'un Développement Régional Harmonisé. *Collection INSEE*, 227–53.

Harris, C.C. (1973) *The Urban Economies 1985*. Lexington, MA: Heath.

Harris, C.C. (1980) New developments and extensions of the multiregional multi-industry forecasting model. *Journal of Regional Science*, 159–71.

Hartog, H. den, Heineken, K.A., Minne, B., Roemers, R.J.J. and Roodenburg, H.J. (1986) *Investeren in Nederland*. Onderzoeksmemorandum 17, The Hague: Centraal Planbureau.

Hirschman, A.O. (1958) *The Strategy of Economic Development*. New Haven: Yale University Press.

Houweling, A. (1987) *Bereken zelf de Macro-economische Effecten van een Investeringsprogramma*. Onderzoeksmemorandum 33, The Hague: Centraal Planbureau.

Illeris, S. and Jakobsen, L. (1991) The effects of the Fixed Link across the Great Belt. In R.W. Vickerman (ed.), *Infrastructure and Regional Development*. London: Pion, 75–85.

Kau, J.B. (1976) The interaction of transportation and land use. In P.F. Wendt (ed.), *Forecasting Transportation Impacts upon Land Use*, Leiden: Martinus Nijhoff, 112–34.

Kawashima, T. (1978) Regional impact simulation model BALAMO. In H. Straszak and B. Wagle (eds), *Models for Regional Planning and Policy Making. Proceedings of the Joint IBM/IIASA Conference*, Vienna.

Lakshmanan, T.R. (1989) Infrastructure and economic transformation. In A.E. Andersson, D. Batten, B. Johansson and P. Nijkamp (eds), *Advances in Spatial Theory and Dynamics*, Amsterdam: North Holland, 241–61.

Liew, C.K. and Liew, C.J. (1985) Measuring the development impact of a transportation system: a simplified approach. *Journal of Regional Science*, 241–57.

Los, M. (1980) *A Transportation Oriented Multiregional Economic Model for Canada*. Publication 178, Centre of Transport Research, Université de Montréal, Montréal.

Mera, K. (1973) Regional production functions and social overhead capital. *Regional and Urban Economics*, 157–86.

Mills, E.S. and Carlino, G. (1989) Dynamics of county growth. In A.E. Andersson, D. Batten, B. Johansson and P. Nijkamp (eds), *Advances in Spatial Theory and Dynamics*, Amsterdam: North Holland, 195–205.

NEA (1990a) *Congestie en het functioneren van bedrijven, een case-study rondom de S20 in Noord-Brabant*. Rijswijk: NEA.

—— (1990b) *Plaspoelpolder Bedrijfsonderzoek*, Rijswijk: NEA.

Nijkamp, P. (1986) Infrastructure and regional development; a multidimensional policy analysis. *Empirical Economics*, 1–21.

Nijkamp, P. and Blaas, E. (1992) *Impact Assessment and Decision Support in Transportation Planning*. Boston: Kluwer.

Nijkamp, P. and Reggiani, A. (1992) *Interaction, Evolution and Chaos in Space*. Berlin: Springer.

Pierce, D.A. and Haugh, L.D. (1977) Causality in temporal system, characterizations and a survey. *Journal of Economics*, 265–93.

Pitfield, D. (1983) The useful interpretation of freight transport models for regional investment policy. In K.J. Button and D. Gillingwater (eds), *Transport, Location and Spatial Policy*, Aldershot: Avebury Gower, 122–53.

Pluym, W.K. and Roosma, S.Y. (1984) *Economische Betekenis van Transportinfrastructuur*. Groningen: Federatie van Noordelijke Economische Instituten.

Rietveld, P. (1990) Employment effects of changes in transport infrastructure: methodological aspects of the gravity model. *Papers of the Regional Science Association*, 19–30.

Snickars, F. and Granholm, A. (1981) *A Multiregional Planning and Forecasting Model with Special Regard to the Public Sector*. Laxenburg: International Institute for Applied Systems Analysis.

Stevens, B. (1961) Linear programming and location rent. *Journal of Regional Science*, 15–26.

Takayama, T. and Judge, G.C. (1971) *Spatial and Temporal Price and Equilibrium Models*. Amsterdam: North-Holland.

Takayama, T. and Labys, W.C. (1986) Spatial equilibrium analysis. In P. Nijkamp (ed.), *Handbook of Regional Economics*, Amsterdam: Elsevier, 171–99.

Tinbergen, J. (1957) The appraisal of road construction, *Review of Economics and Statistics*, 241–9.

Vickerman, R.W. (1991) *Infrastructure and Regional Development*, London: Pion.

Vleugel, J., Nijkamp, P. and Rietveld, P. (1991) Network infrastructure and regional development. In M. de Smidt, A. Granberg and E. Wever (eds), *Regional Development Strategies and Territorial Production Complexes*, Netherlands Geographical Studies 130, Amsterdam: Royal Netherlands Geographical Society, 189–208.

Wilson, F.R., Stevens, A.M. and Holyoke, T.R. (1982) Impact of transportation on regional development. *Transportation Research Record 851*, 13–16.

Youngson, A.J. (1967) *Overhead Capital*. Edinburgh: Edinburgh University Press.

7

Government and Transport Markets

Herbert Baum

7.1 REGULATORY POLICY IN THE TRANSPORT SECTOR AS A STATE TASK

In earlier chapters it has already been stated that governments may hold explicit views with regard to the provision of transport services – and consequently may develop a transport policy. In this and the following three chapters transport policy will figure as the central theme. While chapters 8 and 9 look at government and transport infrastructure and chapter 10 analyses transport policy in an international setting, the first step, discussed in the present chapter, is to consider the relationship between government and transport markets.

In order to organize the division of labour between economic agents in a given economic area, it is necessary to create an economic order to govern economic activity. The system adopted must decide three basic questions (Giersch, 1960).

1 Who shall have powers of decision over the shaping of the economic tasks of production and distribution?
2 What standards should the decision makers aim at?
3 How should the decisions of the economic agents, who reciprocally influence one another, be co-ordinated?

The answers to these fundamental questions turn out to vary considerably in political practice, but the most efficient system has proved to be the market economy system with decentralized free demand and supply decisions within a competition framework established by the state.

Within the general market economy system there are certain activities that constitute exception areas, in which regulation is partly or totally taken away from market mechanisms and replaced by allocation through regulation, intervention and control.[1] This is the case with 'difficult' markets, where, because of the market structure and market behaviour, economically or politically undesirable effects might appear.

One highly regulated field with a long tradition of intervention is the transport sector.

1 On the transport service production markets – in both freight and passenger transport – the state deliberately exercises control over both suppliers and users in order to achieve market results different from those which would be achieved through free competition.
2 In the field of transport infrastructures the state is both owner and investor. The supply of infrastructure capacity and the conditions for its use influence the succeeding market for transport services. This 'regulatory combination' is created above all through the choice of the investment projects to be implemented and the imputation of infrastructural and external costs.
3 Because of the foreign trade links with ever-increasing frontier-crossing traffic flows, different transport policy regulation systems come into contact with one another. European economic and political integration is going to progress further. In order to ensure that the development of the transport sector is free of discrimination and favours integration, it is essential to harmonize international market policy.

Transport policy is characterized by a high degree of intervention in market events, going far beyond the establishment of framework conditions. The main policy considerations here are not exclusively directed at economic objectives either, but through their influence on the system the political actors try to achieve the primary political goals of retaining or achieving power. Such political instrumentalizing of the transport sector undoubtedly meets with a good public response. The large target audience and the high degree of personal involvement on the part of the public mean that government decisions have considerable political value. The relationship between politics and the market in the transport sector has up to now been of a very dualistic nature: on the one side the demands of economic rationality, on the other the political background.

This chapter seeks to determine the state of the art concerning state market policy in the transport sector. The intention is to bring the descriptions of the lines of development together into an economically rational concept for the future shaping of market policy.

First the historical solutions to the problem of organizing transport markets will be briefly outlined (section 7.2). Which direction is taken obviously depends not only on the economic conditions but also on the degree of political instrumentalizing of market events. The next step is to try to interpret transport market policy on the basis of public choice theory (section 7.3). This is intended to bring about greater rationality of decision making through better knowledge of the market policy conditions, shaping possibilities and obstacles. The starting-point for such a concept is the analysis and evaluation of present market policy and its foreseeable development (section 7.4). Theoretical and practical criticisms lead to the conclusion that the state should withdraw from transport markets ('liberalization'), the components of this retreat being deregulation, privatization and competition rules (sections 7.5–7.7). This concept calls for supportive political accompaniment, the possible forms of which are discussed both for the three fields of liberalization and for the future distribution of transport system roles between market and state.

7.2 TYPES OF MARKET POLICY IN THE TRANSPORT SECTOR

The basic transport sector regulation policy questions have been answered in different ways over the course of time. The main factors that have determined these answers have been the general economic situation, the basic economic policy orientation, the geographical pattern of transport and the resulting differences in the relative importance of the different modes, and the degree of political instrumentalizing of the transport sector for other societal objectives.

1 The beginnings of market policy in the transport sector lay in monopoly control of the railways. The major concern here was protection of the consumer against 'exploitation' by the market-dominant supplier.
2 The transition to transport market protectionism came about during the world economic crisis of the late 1920s. In order to avoid the threat to the very existence of an operational transport system posed by the collapse of the economy, most governments decided on dirigiste market intervention through emergency regulations. These *ad hoc* interventions, which were conceived at first simply as crisis measures to protect transport suppliers, were subsequently expanded into all-embracing systems with price regulation, restrictions on market access and compulsory cartels. The transport sector was thus established as a field of exception from the normal rules of competition.
3 In the post-war period the intervention and control system was retained at first, even in the countries that introduced a market economy system. The pattern of 'controlled competition' was established. A major consideration here was scepticism concerning the capability of competition to give the correct signals in the transport sector, but also of increasing importance

were attempts to achieve other economic and societal goals, e.g. in the fields of environmental protection, energy conservation, land use and social policy, through the administration of the transport markets. The transport sector became an eldorado for political stop and go actions.

4 In the countries belonging to the Council for Mutual Economic Assistance (Comecon), transport was to a very large extent included in the central planning system. Transport enterprises were virtually entirely taken over by the state and organize into combines. The Ministry of Transport was responsible for planning and controlling the entire transport system. Transport tasks were allocated to enterprises and the remuneration was in the form of 'clearing prices' set by the state. The modal split was determined by the state plan. In order to save foreign currencies through energy conservation, the railway share was fixed in some cases, e.g. in freight traffic, at over 70 per cent.

5 The deregulation breakthrough in transport markets came in the late 1970s. After a whole series of minor reforms over many years, the idea of deregulation received a strong economic shot in the arm with the rise of supply side economics. At the centre of this macroeconomic concept stood the elimination of the bureaucratic obstacles that hampered economic activity and employment. Regulation in fields excluded from the normal rules of competition leads to rents which are a burden on the branches of the economy demanding their products. Deregulation reduces the costs of production and expands supply, leading to increased production and employment. In the formerly regulated fields liberalization favours the dynamic enterprises and strengthens innovation competition.

6 After the initial liberalizations in the UK (Transport Act of 1968) and Sweden (1968), the step that really showed the path to take was the deregulation of the USA air transport market (1978). This was followed by the Motor Carrier Act of 1985 in the USA and the Transport Act of 1985 in the UK. With the judgement of the European Court in 1985 and the European Community decision on the single European market, deregulation of frontier-crossing traffic as from 1993 was decided upon. Many national deregulation measures in European Community countries have been or are being introduced in the meantime.

7 The removal of the transport sector from state control and its integration in the market economy is being pursued through the privatization of transport undertakings and transport infrastructures. This trend was triggered above all by financing problems. Transport policy deciders hope that through the privatization of the railways in particular, *inter alia* following the Japanese model, the efficiency of the undertakings will be enhanced and the need for subsidies will be reduced. The UK is leading the way here.

7.3 PUBLIC CHOICE THEORY AS AN EXPLANATORY HYPOTHESIS

As shown by the history of the transport sector, there are obviously various alternative solutions for basic regulatory questions. Which transport policy direction will be chosen depends not only on the problems associated with the economic situation, but also on the preferences and attitudes of the policy actors. Analysis of these attitudes, motivations and decision structures is not only useful for the interpretation of historical development, but also makes a contribution towards the shaping of a future transport policy that is effective and free of contradictions.

The aim and standard in economic theory is the idea that through their decisions governments strive, or should strive, for a socioeconomic optimum. The welfare optimum (Pareto efficiency) is reached when no measure can make the position of any economic subject better without making that of another worse. Quite apart from the fact that individual preferences cannot be aggregated into a social welfare function (Arrow paradox), policy decisions virtually always have advantages for some and disadvantages for others in a complex decision structure. The welfare yardstick of Pareto efficiency has never been and is not now the determining factor for the state's market policy. It has nevertheless acquired a certain importance as a reference standard as an aid to economic decision making and in the evaluation of the effects of concrete policy decisions. Transport market policy in particular has always attached importance to the fact that not only allocative criteria but also complex target functions, with sub-objectives in the fields of social, economic stabilization, land-use and environmental policies, should be taken into account, in the knowledge that a certain allocative inefficiency would have to be accepted as a result.

The behaviour of policy deciders and governments cannot therefore be understood in terms of welfare maximization. Public choice theory, as the 'economic theory of policy', seeks to explain these departures from the welfare economics ideal:[2]

1 the behaviour of politicians and competition between parties is explained by the vote-maximizing hypothesis, by analogy with the profit maximization objective of private entrepreneurs (Downs);
2 the political decision-making process is largely determined by interest groups whose emergence, influence and possibilities of achieving results are demonstrated (Olson);
3 the economic theory of the bureaucracy examines the operation and behaviour of hierarchically structured organizations, notably in the state administration (Tullock).

The use of this body of theory for the field of market policy in the transport sector leads to a whole series of findings regarding past and prospective policy preferences and decisions. These findings, given below, also provide starting-points and recommendations for the shaping of decision processes in order to achieve a higher degree of rationality in transport policy.

1 It can be assumed that, under the influence of politicians, the allocative goal is pushed into the background in favour of distributive goals.
2 Politicians have a strong preference for regulation. They thus assure themselves a body of voters, looked after at the expense of the population as a whole.
3 In a liberalized market it is still not possible to be sure that the politicians will abstain from intervention. Theoretically sounder solutions, e.g. the competition model, will not be accepted by the politicians.
4 Political solutions are unstable. When other public sector problems come to have greater weight, necessary financial resources are no longer forthcoming.
5 The politicians do not want any kind of monitoring of economic success. Since politicians have other criteria for success than those examined in effectiveness analysis, revealing economic failure would interfere with the pursuit of their preferences.
6 In order to implement rational solutions, the possibilities for political influence on market processes should be reduced. An alternative to this is the transfer of transport policy decisions to supranational authorities.
7 The economic consequences of transport policy measures should be monitored (cost–benefit analysis), even though this evaluation principle is not very popular in political circles. In the process, conflicting goals should be made explicit and the costs of political compromises should be shown.
8 If rational objectives are to be set in transport policy, it may be appropriate to narrow the scope for discretionary action and ensure policy continuity through legal commitments.

Using the economic theory of politics to try to forecast future concrete policy decisions and derive recommendations for action nevertheless comes up against the following serious difficulties.

1 The future problems and bases for decisions must be known. It should be possible to estimate these sufficiently well.
2 The problems arising then have to be ranked for solution according to the political preferences of the parties.
3 The selection of transport policy instruments then has to be derived from this political weighting. There are areas of uncertainty here, as the objectives can be achieved through different measures.

4 In forecasting the solution concepts and measures, reaction hypotheses from the political rivals (coalition partners, opposition) should be taken into account.
5 To make the need for protection against political solutions recognizable, it would be necessary to examine the extent to which the political solution deviates from the economically rational solution. On this basis it would be possible to determine the possibilities for an institutional change to reduce the discrepancy between rational and political decisions.

These aspects of the economic theory of politics are taken into account in what follows. In the foreground, however, is the analysis of the material content of an economically soundly based transport market policy. This serves as a reference model for determining the politically induced deviations, estimating the possible efficiency losses and identifying the risks arising from the political instrumentalizing of market events in the transport sector.

7.4 MARKET INTERVENTION IN THE TRANSPORT SECTOR

Objectives and concepts

The regulation of the transport sector is to be put down to the economic policy of 'interventionism'. Interventionism means adhocratic economic policy with state administrative action to 'correct' the functioning and results of a branch of the economy within what is in principle a decentralized economic system with private ownership.[3] It is characteristic of the transport sector that market co-ordination and state control frequently flow into one another and the boundaries between market control and controlled markets are fuzzy. Intervention in the transport sector takes place in both transport service production and infrastructures. The scope for intervention in the sector is particularly great, because through the regulation of transport service production the infrastructure needs can be controlled, while through the infrastructure supply transport service production can be controlled.

Market intervention in the transport sector takes place at several levels:

1 market regulation of the transport industry as an exception from the normal competition rules;
2 supply regulations for transport enterprises;
3 public property rights for transport modes;
4 state investment in transport infrastructures.

The reasons for state intervention in the transport market are of several types (Stigler, 1970–1; von Weizsäcker, 1982), as follows.

1 The market failure thesis argues that market allocation determined by competition would lead to wrong developments and undesirable market results, including cut-throat competition and adjustment difficulties for transport enterprises, because of 'special features' on both the supply and demand sides.
2 Attempts are made to reduce the external effects of certain transport modes, e.g. road traffic, by limiting their market share. To this extent the regulation of markets replaces their internalization.
3 Market intervention is intended to serve the public interest, above all through aiming at social and distribution policy goals and considerations concerning land use, the promotion of small and medium enterprises, environmental protection and general stabilization of the economy.
4 Lastly, state intervention is justified on the grounds that it avoids distortions of competition on the international level. So long as harmonization is not achieved, corrective equalization measures, e.g. through indirect taxes, will be taken.

These various reasons put forward to justify state intervention are formulated as 'aggregate targets', which then serve as standards for state administrative action. It is characteristic that market policy is not subject to any rules to ensure consistency. Instead, *ad hoc* decisions are taken according to the target ranking of the moment, so that over time absolutely no consistent transport policy behaviour pattern is to be seen. The market intervention target package is a combination of several sub-targets.

1 Allocative goals: the optimal division of labour between the transport modes; higher transport service quality; inexpensive supply of transport services.
2 Growth policy goals: enhanced production potential through the optimal use and extension of resources, including the removal of transport infrastructure bottlenecks; reduction of factor losses due to energy consumption, accidents and environmental pollution; promotion of technical progress.
3 Regional economic policy goals: reduction of spatial discrepancies in living condition; development of economically weak regions.
4 Social policy goals: equalization of the mobility opportunities for groups of different social levels; provision of inexpensive transport services.
5 Public finance goals: preservation of the economic conditions of transport enterprises (ability to pay for themselves); coverage of transport infrastructure costs.

These economic policy goals are in transport policy practice often set off against 'social policy' goals, the argument being that the social policy goals should be given priority. These goals are based for the most part on the avoidance, reduction and redistribution of traffic, with a clear preference for public rather than private transport.

The ideas behind social-policy-oriented transport policy are undoubtedly perfectly justifiable. Environmental protection, energy conservation, road safety and the quality of life are all of great importance. What makes them suspect as transport policy goals, however, is the lack of clarity in the objectives and the lack of monitoring of results or of any weighing up of the costs and benefits of transport controlling measures. It is also wrong to claim that there is an unresolvable contradiction between social policy requirements and an economically rational transport policy. The fact is that it is entirely possible within economically sound decisions to take account of the negative effects of transport through internalizing the external costs. In so doing, policy and policy evaluation should continue to be based on economic criteria.

Market intervention instruments

In order to achieve its goals, state transport policy uses a number of regulatory, investment and financial policy instruments. The type and intensity of the measures differ according to the transport markets concerned, e.g. passenger or freight, local or long distance, scheduled or charter, domestic or international, Economic Community or non-Economic Community.[4] In the course of time, with a greater tendency to market economy principles, the type and mix of instruments have changed.

Transport services are subject to price regulation, with forked tariffs, minimum prices and fixed prices all being used. In freight transport, the tariff structure varies according to the value of the goods, distance and weight, in passenger transport according to comfort and travel time.

In both freight and passenger transport there are market entry conditions for transport service suppliers. In some cases state concessions are necessary, these being granted only when there is a sufficient transport need. The granting of concessions is subject to subjective entry requirements (professional and personal suitability, economically viable conditions). Because of their relatively low demands, these entry conditions do not constitute a real barrier. Much more important on the other hand are maximum numbers (quotas) for the concessions to be granted on certain markets, e.g. long-distance road haulage and taxis. In addition there are bans on cabotage (e.g. in road haulage, inland waterway transport and air transport), i.e. foreign carriers are not allowed to operate over purely domestic links.

Some of the transport undertakings are owned by the state, e.g. railways and airlines. Market events can be influenced by the activities of these undertakings. Property rights over undertakings together with market regulation open up possibilities for the state to have a twofold transport strategy.

To a large extent, market control is achieved through state investment in transport infrastructures. Since the competitiveness of transport service suppliers depends on the infrastructure provision, preferential or discriminatory investment policy can influence the market shares of the different transport modes.

Also among the transport market intervention instruments are taxes and subsidies. These do not directly manipulate market results, but they alter the market data from which market results derive. Their interventionist character is particularly marked when these instruments are used selectively, e.g. a specially heavy tax burden on road transport or coverage of the losses of public transport undertakings.

The last type of market intervention instrument comprises supply obligations and operating directions, including obligations to operate and to carry, working conditions and social provision, and monitoring regulations. These influence the costs of the transport service suppliers and thus alter their degree of competitiveness. Here the degree of control exercised to ensure compliance with this type of regulation is important.

Evaluation of transport market interventionism

Theoretical analysis of economic regulation and practical political discussion of the further development of the market economy have for some time been concerned with the weaknesses and shortcomings of market interventionism in fields that form exceptions to the normal competition rules.[5] The overall negative balance provided the basis for the departure from market interventionism and more competition in the transport sector.

Critique of the legitimacy of intervention

In order to justify market intervention in the transport sector, the argument was that there were particular market characteristics that would not permit efficient regulation through normal competitive market mechanisms. Analysis of these market characteristics led to the finding that the thesis of 'market failure' on transport markets does not hold water, however.

1 There are certainly 'special features' of production conditions in the transport sector, such as high fixed costs, long life of the means of production, lower limits to and limited divisibility of investment and the impossibility of storing production, but these characteristics are – even compared with industrial production and the service sector – nothing extraordinary. They do give rise to certain adjustment problems for enterprises, but it is still entirely possible to resolve these problems under market conditions.
2 Because of the low elasticity of demand – or so the argument goes – a vital entrepreneurial action parameter is unable to fulfil its guiding function. In fact the phenomenon of inelastic demand applies only to overall demand for

transport ('total elasticity'). The reason for this is that transport demand is determined by the production activity of the economy as a whole (it is 'derived demand') and there are limited substitution possibilities for transport services. Of decisive importance for the effectiveness of competition, however, are the 'partial elasticities' for the various competitive relationships. Empirical market analyses have shown (Baum et al., 1990) that the cross-price elasticities are far from zero and in some cases allow considerable room for competition between the different modes. What is more, relatively high values were determined for 'quality elasticities', so that non-price competition is able to operate fully on transport markets.

3 The coming into contact of different types of market structure (monopoly in rail transport, many suppliers in road haulage and partial oligopoly in inland waterway transport) is no obstacle to competition either. The decisive factor is that suppliers from the different groups should come into competition with one another on the individual transport markets. It has not been possible to demonstrate empirically that, because of the particular type of market form within a given transport mode, the competitiveness of the supplier is influenced by such things as significant cost advantages for monopolistic or oligopolistic suppliers. In so far as the market power of the supplier might play a role in competitiveness – e.g. through cross-subsidies within the production unit – this should be prevented by the competition authorities.

4 Even the 'natural monopoly' of the railways is no argument against competition. There are economies of scale with sub-additivity of the cost functions in network or grid monopolies. If there is a railway undertaking with a rail network on the market, it would not make economic sense to admit a second railway company with its own, additional network. In principle, however, this does not exclude competition. First, because of the unit cost degression undesirable 'competition on the network' could be replaced by 'competition for the network', with a public call for tenders for the concession. It would be more effective and more practicable, however, to make a separation between the network and railway operations, so that the degressive effects of network costs did not have any effect on the operating costs of service production. This is the path now being taken in the European railway system.

5 Obstacles to market exit in the transport industry, resulting in an 'inverse supply reaction', are also no very decisive criticism of market allocation. The fear is often expressed that small transport businesses, and above all owner-operators, will not react to falling prices and profits by exiting from the market, but will on the contrary further increase their supply in order to make up the lost income, so that the excess capacity is not reduced. The practical importance of such abnormal behaviour is doubtful, however, since

it is possible only if production is associated with costs that do not involve expenditure. The scope for this is limited, e.g. renunciation of profits and no pay for members of the family working in the business. Whether the tendency for 'self-exploitation' can last very long is very doubtful, especially in view of the social insurance system and alternative employment possibilities. Past experience shows that market exit does operate in the transport industry, since appropriate market signals have led many small enterprises to leave the industry.

6 The attempt to reduce the external costs of transport through market regulation with supply restrictions for emission-intensive modes, notably road and air transport, must be regarded as inappropriate. This is one variant of the prohibition solutions, which have no proper relationship with the cause, provide no incentive for emission reduction and do not take account of the capacity limits of the more environmentally friendly modes or of the costs to the economy as a whole of mobility restrictions. A more appropriate solution that could be applied within the market economy framework would be to internalize the external costs.

7 Lastly, the public interest requires no exceptions to the normal competition rules, since it can be served through state tasks for transport undertakings with a specific compensation by the originator. This would have the advantage that the costs of fulfilling particular political desires would be made more transparent so that a more rational shaping of the central government budget could be achieved.

The upshot of all this is that it is just not possible to support the claim of market failure in the transport sector. There are admittedly certain difficulties in regulation through market forces alone, and possible weaknesses in competition, but they constitute no exceptional degree of risk. They can be taken into account in supporting policy measures.

Critique of the efficiency of intervention

Quite apart from the lack of adequate reasons for market regulation, it is above all the concrete effects of state intervention that have shown that it has not been possible to achieve the goals aimed at in many areas and that sometimes development has taken quite the wrong turn.

The effects have in some cases been examined using cost–benefit analysis, which has revealed excessively high costs, over-capitalization, departures from the cost-optimal modal split and excess capacities as the main individual effects. Estimates of the order of magnitude of the losses to the economy as a whole in the USA range from US$4 billion to US$10 billion a year.[6]

The following findings of impact analyses for the European area show the weaknesses of market regulation.[7]

1 Tariff parity between the different modes in freight transport, imposed by regulation, has prevented prices from developing in different directions. This 'over-coordination' has meant that relative prices have not developed according to the respective service and cost characteristics of the different modes, so that certain modes have remained in market segments from which they should have withdrawn, while others have not been as active in certain markets as they should have been given their service advantages. In other words, the inter-modal division of labour has been made less than efficient.

2 As a result of the limited competition on regulated markets, the price for transport services is higher than it should be. Estimates resulting from comparative market analyses for liberalized frontier-crossing freight traffic with Germany have put the regulation-induced surcharge at as much as 30–40 per cent.[8] These rents not associated with any special service are an additional cost for the economy and the population.

3 The restrictions on competition weaken the innovation efforts of transport enterprises and lead to rationalization potentials not being exploited and productivity improvements being delayed. The sharp increase in own-account transport on the roads is an indication of the weakness of competition in the transport industry.

4 Market regulation has been one of the reasons for the concentration in freight transport since the 1970s. Market entry for new suppliers has been restricted and the takeover of businesses together with the corresponding concessions has been possible only for the bigger transport firms.

5 In practical competition on the freight transport markets there are constant breaches of the regulations. This 'underground competition' is a thoroughly desirable expression of market forces from the standpoint of the economy as a whole, but it involves unnecessary transaction costs and favours large enterprises which can offer full service packages with the corresponding cross-subsidizing possibilities.

6 Market regulation has not been able to achieve one of its essential goals – protection of the railways. Competition-neutralizing tariff co-ordination has meant that the railways have lost traffic to the roads and could not defend themselves aggressively against the waterways. Public service obligations have forced the railways to retain unprofitable traffics. Railway tariffs have been politically manipulated so that it has not been possible to cover cost increases through price adjustments.

7 The result of limited possibilities for competition and the lack of competitive pressure has been increased subsidies, above all for the railways but also for monopoly-protected urban public transport undertakings. This has absorbed public financing resources that would have been much better used in expanding and enhancing the service capacity. The regulation of transport

markets must be held partly responsible for the capacity bottlenecks now existing in the transport system.

Critique of deregulation operations

Critics of state intervention in transport markets on theoretical or practical grounds all support their arguments by reference to the positive experience of conrete deregulation programmes in both European and non-European countries.[9] The fact is, however, that the overall balance of deregulation measures is not quite so convincing as is frequently claimed. The findings are more in the nature of negative tests – they show that deregulation has not brought the market turmoil and breakdowns often feared. But it is not so easy to prove that deregulation has brought clear and significant advantages compared with the former market regulation. The impact analyses of the US Motor Carrier Act, the deregulation of air transport and the deregulation and privatization of urban public transport in the UK have shown in any event that the opening of markets has by no means run smoothly or been free of undesirable effects. Alongside the expected positive effects, including price reductions, fiercer competition, cost reductions, enhanced productivity and the reduction of subsidies, there have been in some cases wild swings on the market, increased numbers of bankruptcies, concentration phenomena, service reductions and safety problems. Empirical analysis turns out to be extremely difficult and demonstrates no rigorously proven causalities. This is partly due to the fact that the deregulation measures were introduced in a period of unfavourable general economic conditions. Deregulation was introduced in the USA at the beginning of the 1980s, precisely when the American economy was entering the worst recession since the world economic crisis.

However, the problems of market liberalization are also partly due to the fact that in political practice deregulation was sometimes introduced without adequate supportive monitoring and cushioning instruments. What is more, the competition policy now responsible for market developments was not sufficiently prepared for the new task. Lastly, in parallel with deregulation, public sector demand for the provision of transport services was reduced because of the lack of money to pay for it. Deregulation, which meant only a freeing from state shackles, was thus built up into the withdrawal of the state from the provision of public services, causing corresponding deficiencies of supply in, for example, urban public transport.

These lessons have unfortunately not yet found their way into political practice. Even groups of experts still give the impression, through their adoption of positions allowing no room for doubt, that total deregulation would in itself solve all the problems.[10] The preconditions for competition, potential conflicts, transition problems and the necessary transport policy adjustments are scarcely considered at all. Transport policy makers can only be recommended to interpret correctly the experience to date and to take care to introduce a support programme for their deregulation measures.

7.5 TRANSPORT MARKET DEREGULATION

Deregulation programmes in Europe

In virtually all European countries, as well as within the wider framework of the European Community, there are deregulation programmes for the different transport markets. Of particular importance are those for road haulage, air transport and urban public transport.

As from 1993, because of European Community decisions, there will no longer be any market entry restrictions in frontier-crossing road haulage. The compulsory forked tariff system was replaced from 1989 by free prices, after a transitional period with reference tariffs. Tariff liberalization has been introduced on the national markets. In some countries, including Germany, there are still certain reservations with respect to the complete freeing of market entry. It is unclear to what extent the European Community decisions on frontier-crossing traffic are binding for national market organization. The European Court did not clarify this question in its judgement of 1992, but merely allowed member states a period for adjustment. Another open question is that of the development of cabotage. In 1990, concessions were granted for limited regular cabotage, but initially only half of these were used. A further extension of cabotage going as far as unrestricted regular cabotage is being made dependent upon progress on the harmonization question by some member states.

European air transport is being liberalized in stages. In the first stage, starting in 1988, the tariff system was eased, automatic authorization was given for capacity increases in bilateral scheduled flights and market entry was made easier. Since 1990, the second liberalization phase has allowed further tariff flexibility and has further opened access to the market. The third phase, as from 1993, should bring tariff freedom and the abolition of all market entry restrictions (freedom of establishment and unrestricted cabotage). However, because of harmonizations still to be introduced, complete deregulation is not to be expected until 1997.

In local passenger transport on regional and urban markets there are deregulation and privatization tendencies in various countries. Since 1985 local bus services have been placed on a private enterprise basis in the UK. A need for action on a Europe-wide level could lead to the introduction of a European

Community guideline on the granting of concessions. 'Competition for the field' is being considered as a deregulation option, with lines or networks in profitable market segments being put up for auction.

Deregulation risk scenarios

Traffic induction through deregulation

An argument against deregulation raised by the environmentalists is that the expected price reductions will run counter to a desirable reduction of traffic. They see transport services as being too cheap anyway, compared with the costs they entail, so that there is no incentive to be sparing with the transport resource (Umweltbundesamt, 1991). The delocation of residential areas and work places, dispersed production units, transport-intensive production and distribution systems, including low production intensity, just-in-time concepts and centralization of warehousing, are all favoured by deregulation.

This kind of argument inadmissibly mixes two aspects, however. Deregulation serves to place economic calculation and allocation both between the transport sector and other branches of the economy and between the different transport modes on a competitive basis, and thus to improve them. Independent of this is the question of a necessary imputation of the external costs, which would improve allocation from the ecological standpoint. In view of the impacts, failing to deregulate can by no means be seen as a substitute for the imputation of external costs.

Little change in modal split

There will be no explosive increase in road freight traffic or sudden fall in the railway share as a result of deregulation (PLANCO, 1988). Estimates of the price elasticity of transport demand lead to the conclusion that the main effect will be the substitution of own-account transport by commercial road haulage. Shippers will increasingly switch to the specialized and then also cheaper services of the transport industry. The railways have real possibilities for defending themselves aggressively against their competitors and maintaining their market share through appropriate price and service policies. Deregulation will bring no dramatic changes in modal split.

Cut-throat competition

Excess capacities and ruinous competition processes are feared as a result of exaggeratedly numerous market entries and delayed exits. In the short term, there may well be an inelastic supply reaction to falling prices, but with increasing experience such a tendency to 'self-exploitation' will not be durable.

Regional policy goals

As a result of deregulation – or so it is claimed – economically weak areas poorly served by transport will be further disadvantaged. Since the costs per transport operation in these regions are relatively high owing to the low volume of transport and the lack of return freights, they must expect transport price increases in the case of deregulation. Tariff regulation and the principle of tariff equality throughout the territory have hitherto prevented this type of discrimination.

With the opening of the market, however, the higher transport prices will be accompanied by a more abundant and qualitatively better transport supply. Here there will be a shift in the supply structure – the railways will cease to serve the area and road haulage will move in to fill the gap. Shippers in economically weak regions today complain above all about the excessively long transport times and the difficulty of respecting delivery dates. Since the tendency is for relatively high-value goods to be produced in the peripheral regions, the quality of the transport supply is more important for the competitiveness of enterprises than the transport price.

Loss of efficiency in transport operations

One of the arguments used against deregulation is that because of the market exit problem the level of efficiency in the transport sector will decline, with above all an increase in the proportion of empty hauls. A counter-argument to this hypothesis is that competition and cost pressure on a deregulated market will promote rationalization efforts by both transport enterprises and shippers. There are many areas with rationalization potential (Baum et al., 1992):

1 increased vehicle capacity utilization in freight transport;
2 co-operation between transport enterprises;
3 use of freight traffic centres;
4 optimization of the vehicle fleet structure;
5 better dispatching and fleet management within the enterprise;
6 reduction of idle time and more intensive consignment formation by shippers;
7 packaging material savings.

The freight transport sector still offers many opportunities for increasing the degree of efficiency of transport operations. Thus in the Federal Republic of Germany capacity utilization is about 60 per cent in commercial road haulage and significantly less, about 45 per cent, in own-account traffic. The present restrictions on competition imposed by administrative market regulations give rise to 'regulatory inefficiencies' through, for example, the ban on return consignments for reward in the case of own-account transport, limited cabotage possibilities over domestic links and distortions in the size structure of the truck fleet. The rationalization effects of deregulation will mean that for a given growth in transport output (tonne-kilometres), vehicle use (vehicle-kilometres), which is what counts for road traffic pollution, will increase less than proportionally.

Transport safety and environmental protection

It is often feared that deregulation might bring about a deterioration in road safety (Bundesverband des Deutschen Güterfernverkehrs, 1986).

The changes to be expected in transport volumes and vehicle numbers in road haulage due to deregulation are relatively small, and so no increase in accident rates is to be expected on these grounds. It cannot be ruled out, however, that as a result of replacing own-account transport by commercial haulage the accident risk may be increased. Deregulation alters the economic conditions on the transport market and it cannot be excluded that the increased cost competition may result in behaviour that impairs safety, e.g. breaches of the rules or technically unsound vehicles.

These possible safety problems are nevertheless no reason to shy away from deregulation. Competition and road safety are entirely compatible provided that compliance with safety standards is guaranteed. Any attempt to enhance road safety by protecting transport enterprises from competition would be very imprecise in its effects. It is by no means certain that the rents received by transport enterprises thanks to administrative competition restrictions are used for safety measures. Instead, it should be possible on a deregulated market to reduce potential offences against safety by intensifying controls and sanctions.

The accusation that deregulation would lead to growing environmental pollution is not very convincing either. It will bring no serious shift of modal split in favour of road haulage. Greater competitive pressure will lead to better capacity utilization, so that the same transport output can be achieved with less vehicle use. If total transport output increases significantly, then this will be due to the economic growth brought about by integration and not to deregulation. Under certain circumstances there could be negative environmental effects due to the lower rates of return resulting from deregulation. Vehicle replacement investment would be delayed, bringing a deterioration in the age structure of the vehicle stock. Since emission limits are defined for new vehicles, the diffusion of new, more environmentally friendly technologies will be made more difficult. The fact is, however, that it is uncertain whether excess profits resulting from regulation are used for investment in environmentally friendly vehicles. Environmental protection will be promoted through competition if the environmental costs are internalized through prices.

Market policy enforcement of deregulation

Market observation and crisis management

In order to be able to identify any undesirable developments in the transition phase to a free market, a systematic statistical analysis of market events is required. In 1979 the European Community introduced a market monitoring system for freight transport, which needs to be continued and expanded. In addition to trends in transport output, prices and costs, data concerning capacities and their utilization, indicators of the financial situation and productivity changes can be obtained.

There is some dispute over the necessity for and possible form of a 'crisis mechanism'. There is an umbrella clause in the European Community provisions to the effect that, in the case of fundamental market distortions with a serious mismatch between transport supply and demand, any member state can apply to the Commission of the European Communities for crisis measures. The measures envisaged are minimum prices in a compulsory cartel of transport enterprises, market entry quotas and financial incentives for market exit in the form of allowances for taking vehicles out of service.

The critics of such rules fear that this paves the way for any latent interventionist potential to materialize and that there could thus be an over-hasty return to regulation. This risk should be countered by restricting the field of application to really serious emergency situations.

Harmonization of competition conditions

A transport market organized on market economy lines presupposes the harmonization of national and international competition conditions.

At the national level there is a great need for harmonization in the imputation of infrastructure costs, and external costs, to the different transport modes. The imputation of external costs is also necessary because the market regulations existing up to now were virtually a substitute for the internalization of external effects. If the regulatory system is replaced by a competitive system, then the internal imputation of the costs of transport to the economy as a whole is necessary to constitute a framework for proper operation.

The imputation of infrastructure costs puts the modal split on a rational basis. There will be a relative rise in road haulage prices and a relative fall in railway and inland waterway prices. This will mean a shift of transport volume from the roads to the railways and waterways, but the modal split effect should not be over-estimated, because the relative disadvantage of road haulage as regards external costs is partly compensated by the relatively low infrastructure cost coverage of the railways and waterway transport.

In international competition there are harmonization problems in the artificial competition conditions, including taxes and charges, labour and social security conditions and technical standards. Another important task is to ensure that the rules are complied with. There are serious problems in the field of subsidies, e.g. coverage of operating losses and investment aid. Without harmonization the competitive position would be arbitrarily distorted, and some shifting of enterprises out of the disadvantaged countries is to be expected.

As far as taxation is concerned – with fuel taxes to a large extent harmonized – the main problem is the (annual) motor vehicle tax. Certainly the best solution would be equalization at a medium level while maintaining the nationality principle, i.e. each country fixes the tax for its own nationals. If this does not come about, the territoriality principle can be used, i.e. nationals and foreigners pay the same charges for the use of the country's infrastructures. The territoriality principle runs counter to integration because it reactivates the national frontiers as tax frontiers and may trigger retaliatory moves on the part of other countries (Aberle, 1989). After the rejection by the European Court of the German plans to equalize the tax burden between nationals and foreigners through a differentiated charge in road haulage, member states again have to face the task of finding a workable compromise in the harmonization.

Qualitative conditions for market entry

Qualitative market entry restrictions are intended to ensure that on a liberalized transport market there is not an influx of unqualified transport entrepreneurs with the corresponding risk for the economic stability of the market. In the European Community, to make up for the abolition of the quantitative restrictions on market entry, the qualitative conditions (personal reliability, financial soundness, professional capacity, minimum proportion of own-capital) will be made more stringent.

Qualitative market entry restrictions ensure certain minimum conditions for competition. These entry conditions do not guarantee the functional stabilization of competition, however. Policy makers could attempt to minimize the risks of competition through making the requirements even higher, but then there is a limit at which these conditions turn into barriers to entry.

Stringent entry conditions are often called for in the name of transport safety, e.g. special concessions for the carriage of dangerous goods. The fact is, however, that the safety aspect is best handled through strict regulations with appropriate monitoring and sanctions. Market entry conditions are too unspecific with respect to the safety goal. In view of the present undoubtedly high level of non-compliance with labour and social regulations and technical safety standards, more stringent safety measures on a deregulated market are called for.

Capacity adjustment and control

An important aim of deregulation is to bring about a capacity with producers of transport services that is appropriate to the market. It is questionable whether the resolution of the adjustment problems, i.e. structural excess capacities on certain markets resulting from regulation, should be handed over to deregulation. If the new system had to start off with such a burden, the adjustment pressure would be extremely high precisely in the initial phase, so that there is much in favour of the introduction of a capacity adjustment programme in the meantime.

In inland waterway transport, for example, the 'scrapping action' in the Federal Republic of Germany took about 5000 craft out of the market between 1969 and 1990. The European Community 'structure clearing' in 1990 led to a 10 per cent reduction in inland waterway transport capacity in the Rhine riparian states. The European Community 'old for new' regulation scheme for the period 1989–93 provides that in the case of investment in new waterway craft either old ones have to be scrapped or a penalty equivalent to the scrapping allowance has to be paid. This type of capacity adjustment is sometimes rejected as market-distorting intervention (Monopolkommission, 1990). It is true that in the future, on a deregulated market, there should no longer be a place for this type of adjustment aid. This does not mean, however, that the excess capacities built up in the past, partly through state measures, should not be reduced. That this involves the destruction of economic assets has to be accepted because of their, to some extent, sunk cost nature. The costs to the economy as a whole of such capacity adjustment measures are lower than those of failure of the market reform. In any event the rules would have to be so framed that they do not lead to a contradictory expansion of capacity. In view of the growth perspectives of the transport sector, the excess capacity argument is not of great importance for the immediate future, and so further capacity reduction measures are unnecessary.

In the case of road haulage, flexible capacity management will continue to be required in the future on a deregulated market (Bundesverband des Deutschen Güterfernverkehrs, 1992). This concept implies an examination of the individual capacity requirements of the enterprise, taking account of the following criteria in particular: technical and temporal capacity utilization of the vehicle fleet, costs and earnings of the enterprise, regional importance of the transport supply, reserve capacities in the other modes, pollution balances and reduction targets. This suggestion represents a line of defence against the general opening up of the market. It certainly has the advantage that it removes the objective barriers to market entry, but on the other hand it goes beyond merely setting a framework, which is the case with the subjective market entry conditions, and requires a number of individual, discretionary examinations. It would be a departure from the basis of objective entry decisions, transparent for all, and would end up in a jungle of official regulations for firms. The aim of deregulation is precisely to transfer decisions, which here again would be taken by the administration, to the market and the entrepreneur.

Rationalization and co-operation aid for the transport industry

The fear is often expressed that deregulation would meet an entrepreneurially poorly prepared transport industry and that because of this inefficient methods of operation with undesirable consequences in terms of traffic volumes and environmental pollution would arise. It is therefore important that on a deregulated market the possibilities for the rationalization of transport operations and for co-operation should be fully exploited by transport enterprises. Both approaches would bring advantages for the individual firm and for the economy as a whole.

It is a major aim of deregulation to provide incentives for a rationalization offensive in the transport industry that would extend the reserve capacities of the transport system. The potential users of the rationalization possibilities will partly act spontaneously through their own efforts to operate as efficiently as possible, but certain barriers are to be expected, such as lack of knowledge, the high cost of investment in new information technologies, limits imposed by competition rules, reluctance to co-operate because of competitive relations and inadequate infrastructural conditions.

There is an important task for the trade organizations here: that of supporting enterprises with information and initiatives. The competition authorities have given the green light for more extensive co-operation. The state too, in order to avoid undesirable effects of deregulation, should promote both innovation and the diffusion of rationalization measures through financial aid, technological development, appropriate shaping of the legal framework and complementary public investment.

Competition-neutral transport infrastructural policy

On the free transport market of the future, transport policy will no longer have the possibility of intervening in the market process through price and supply regulations. However, since the desire of policy makers and the administration to exercise control is scarcely likely to diminish, it is to be expected that there will be a danger of this type of intervention simply being replaced by discriminatory transport infrastructure investment policy. Replacing regulation by the economically unjustified advantaging or disadvantaging of the different transport modes would have even more serious consequences than the former market regulation. Infrastructural investments determine the supply potential and hence the competitiveness of the different modes over the longer term. Once a wrong turn has been taken it is very difficult to correct because of the irreversibility and long lead times of infrastructural investments. In any event, there is no possibility of short-term change as in the case of administrative market regulation. There is thus a requirement for a competition-neutral infrastructural policy on the part of the state.

One possibility would be to charge carriers for the use of the transport infrastructure in such a way that the internalization of external costs does not distort competition. Independent institutions, e.g. the competition authorities, would have to monitor the pricing policy of the state as the monopoly supplier of infrastructural services in order to avoid modal discrimination (the problem of pricing of infrastructure services is treated in more detail in chapter 8).

7.6 PRIVATIZATION OF TRANSPORT UNDERTAKINGS

Interdependence of ownership and competition regulation

In addition to the deregulation of transport markets, a second necessary step in the implementation of the market economy organization of the transport sector is the creation of a private ownership system. The fact is that major transport service suppliers, e.g. railways, urban public transport undertakings and airline companies, are either completely or to a large extent state owned. The co-ordination of markets can admittedly be achieved on a non-regulated, decentralized basis – as has been demonstrated in the industrial sector, for example – but it is doubtful whether the co-ordination results in this case still meet the requirement of the best possible division of labour.

1 Economically optimal market behaviour by enterprises is possible only if the market decisions are sanctioned by loss of property. So long as the state is the owner of all or a substantial share of the capital, there is certainly such a *de jure* responsibility, but not *de facto*.
2 Enterprise responsibility and performance are closely linked. State ownership opens the way for many claims and intervention possibilities for politicians and political pressure groups. Responsibilities are thus not clear-cut: inefficiency is in many cases the result of broadly spread property rights. The upshot is that the competitiveness of public transport undertakings suffers and the market share that would be desirable from the standpoint of the economy as a whole is not achieved.
3 Transport undertakings that are state property can impair the market chances

of competing private firms as a result of the financial and political power of the state and thus also distort allocation. Because of the certainty of receiving subsidies, they sometimes participate in market segments that they would leave to private suppliers if they had to bear all the risks of full responsibility. It is also not to be excluded that certain transport policy decisions are taken in such a way that public sector transport undertakings are advantaged.

4 On the other hand, the transport system does have public functions to perform, including opening transport links and ensuring mobility, land use and reduction of environmental pollution. These functions should not be dropped because of privatization.

The transport policy task is therefore to create the preconditions, through a change in the ownership system, for market-oriented entrepreneurial action and, through transferring the risks of responsibility, virtually to force success, but it must also guarantee the fulfilment of the public obligation functions.

Railway privatization

Economic necessity

In view of the unfavourable economic situation of the railways in Europe, it would appear that the demands for privatization are to be met.[11] In the case of the German railways, the Government Commission for the Bundesbahn put forward a privatization proposal (Bericht der Regierungskommission Bundesbahn, 1991) and on 15 July 1992 the government decided on privatization in the form of a company to be known as Deutsche Bahn AG (German Railway Plc), or DB AG.

Privatization is intended to open up the possibility for the railways to adopt a thoroughly commercial approach and perform the public service obligations in return for appropriate remuneration. Apart from the associated taking over of the debt by the state and the abolition of the public service rights, this should greatly improve the economic efficiency of the railways, through such improvements as increased turnover, savings on purchasing prices, enhanced labour productivity, additional income through the sale of routes to third parties and better property management.

This reform, however, does not amount to 'privatization' in the strict sense, since the capital would still at first be almost 100 per cent state owned. The state can therefore influence the railway management, a source of considerable potential conflict. The state continues to have responsibility. A thorough-going privatization would require increasing private ownership of the railways. The generally successful privatizations in Japan and the USA took this path, and the privatization plans for British Rail in the UK are also heading in this direction (Kobayashi, 1988; Moore and Kroszner, 1988; Department of Transport, 1992).

Ownership of networks and services

The core problem in the structural reform of the railways is that of the ownership of networks and of the operations side. The decisions here determine the extent to which the railways can continue to perform public tasks in the future and what opportunities for economic improvements there will be (cf. Rothengatter, 1991).

These problems have different solutions depending on the reform concept adopted. The privatizations in the USA and Japan involved the complete transfer of ownership – on a regional basis – to the private sector. This type of lock, stock and barrel privatization is also envisaged for British Rail in the UK. In Sweden, the reform of 1986 took a different path, with the separation of infrastructure and operation, the former being a concern of the state, the latter of private enterprise (Jansson and Cardebring, 1989; Jansson and Wallin, 1991). The German railway reform involves a separation strategy too, with three legally independent undertakings: passenger transport, freight transport and infrastructures. The separation principle is also part of the reform of the railways in the Netherlands (Wijffels et al., 1992).

A privatization scheme differentiating operations from infrastructures has the following advantages over lock, stock and barrel privatization.

1 The positive economic effects for the railway are significantly greater in the case of separation. There are as yet no reliable calculations as to what expenditure is necessary for the rail network, but there is a suspicion that the main reason for the deficit lies here. If the entire railway undertaking is privatized, this risk to profitability remains for the future private entrepreneur, a factor which might significantly reduce the chances for privatization.
2 Profitability pressure in a privatized total undertaking would mean that the network would be reduced to the profitable stretches (shrunk network). Such a microeconomically optimal network conflicts with the public service and general objectives (including urban and suburban passenger services, the linking of peripheral regions and maintenance of a network potential for a shift of traffic flows). The transport system as a whole could be impaired by such a shrinkage of the network.
3 If it is desired to increase the intensity of competition in rail transport through having more than one operator, network access must remain open for all potential rail transport enterprises. A private railway undertaking responsible for both operations and the network could perhaps discriminate against access for competitors. Competition on the rail network would therefore not come about, or would be very restricted.

A privatization strategy with an institutional separation of operations and network has to decide whether only railway operations or the network too should be privatized. The privatization of railway operations should be relatively problem free. With structural rationalization it should be possible to mobilize private capital for the operating company.

On the other hand privatization of the network remains critical. It is desirable to take the rail infrastructure out of the state budget in order to exploit the incentives to innovation and enhanced performance provided by private ownership. With the network under public ownership there would be too much room for discrimination with respect to certain railway operators. There is thus much to be said in favour of a private economy Network Plc in which the state holds the shares. Since the network company – again because of public service obligations – will at best be able to aim at cost coverage as an entrepreneurial goal, the participation of private investors will be very small. It is not clear in fact whether the network undertaking can work as an independent enterprise at all. It is not impossible – though there are as yet no suitable cost analyses – that cost-covering prices for network use just cannot be charged because the prices for rail services would have to rise so much that the modal split would shift away from the railways on an extent undesirable for the economy as a whole.

The network remains the critical point in the context of railway privatization. The network undertaking has a monopoly position and would have to be regulated by the state, but it is doubtful whether any incentives for improved efficiency could be created in this case. In Sweden, for example, following the structural reform of the railways there was criticism of the efficiency of the state railway office responsible for the infrastructure, which in a number of cases did not comply with the infrastructural wishes of the rail transport undertaking, SJ (Brandborn and Hellsvik, 1990). In any event, the performance incentives will be greater in a private economy solution than in the case of state administration of the rail network.

An important component of competition in the railway system will be the 'multiplicity of operators'. The admission of third parties to the rail network is provided for in the European Community Guideline 91/440 and has had to be translated into national legislation as from 1 January 1993. This will exert competitive pressure on the rail transport operators really to use the new room for manoeuvre. Possible competitors include international groupings of several railway undertakings in frontier-crossing traffic, own trains in combined transport or even forwarding companies.

Competition between the operating companies will be controlled through the auctioning of routes. Here there are many practical organizational problems, such as the integration of the operators in the timetable system, route allocation periods, compensation for disturbance of operations and the organization of market monitoring in order to prevent discrimination with respect to certain operators or any pricing abuse by the network monopolist against transport undertakings. In addition, however, there is the more fundamental problem of ensuring an appropriate public transport supply. A satisfactory solution to this problem is what in the final analysis determines the success of the privatization.

Public interest and a privatized railway system

Privatizing the railways is an attempt to give the railway undertaking commercial independence without compromising an appropriate public transport supply. The greater efficiency of the railways should increase the scope for satisfying public interests. These are seen in demands for efficient passenger services in the conurbations, satisfactory links to all regions, reasonable tariffs and a satisfactory potential for relieving the roads. A good proportion of these demands already today comes into the category of performances in the interest of the community as a whole that cannot be run commercially at a profit. A privatized railway will not provide such services of its own accord, and so the state will have to allocate public service tasks with specific remuneration, with the most appropriate supplier being determined by means of calls for tenders.

This construction has the advantage that no excessive demands are made on the railways from the political side. The instigating institutions would have to examine whether the service requirement is politically justifiable in relation to financial cost, whether the level of the demand can be reduced or whether some other form of provision would be more appropriate (e.g. bus rather than rail transport). Through the regionalization of local rail passenger traffic at regional and municipal levels, the state tasks and responsibility for them should be brought together in the hands of authorities on the spot.

This principle is correct from the standpoints of the distribution of responsibilities, the control mechanisms and the efficiency effects. The big risk, however, lies in the political field. In view of the chronic shortage of funding, it cannot be excluded that the desirable standard of public service will not be implemented and the money will be diverted to serve other political ends. The privatization of the railways would have its function changed to that of the privatization of public tasks in any event – a problem that is not of a transport policy nature, but rather of social policy. A legal framework should ensure that the state fulfils this task, that adequate financial resources are made available and that earmarked resources transferred to the regions and municipalities are effectively used for public transport. Otherwise the privatization could be entry into a purely commercial 'cannibalization' of the transport system, with a substantial deterioration of the service standard. The economic resource benefits of privatization might not be realized because privatization under these auspices would just not be politically feasible.

Urban public transport privatization

The privatization debate concerning rail transport has now been extended to the whole field of urban public transport (Deregulierungskommission, 1991). Privatization here means transfer of the ownership of public transport undertakings to the private sector, deregulation of market access for private passenger transport enterprises and the abandonment of public tariff regulation.

In Europe, growing interest in competitive solutions is to be seen in the field of urban public transport too. Following the Transport Act of 1985, local bus services in the UK were deregulated and privatized. Similar efforts are being made in Portugal. In many countries (e.g. France, Belgium, Spain, Denmark), private enterprises play an important role as subcontractors for the public transport undertakings.

The calls for liberalization are justified by the cost disadvantages of public transport services, the need for large subsidies, inadequate service quality and the low level of innovation in supply.

Examination of deregulation and privatization operations in urban public transport reveals highly ambivalent results. As in the case of the railways, also here a conflict between public goals of road traffic relief and modal shift and the private enterprise and commercial aspects manifests itself.

Impact analyses for the privatization of urban public transport in the UK indicate the following results (Dodgson and Katsoulacos, 1988; Evans, 1990; Beesley, 1991).

1 There has been a rapid structural change in urban transport supplies. The number of transport undertakings has substantially increased. In the conurbations there are in some cases up to 40 entrepreneurs. Market entry by new suppliers is stepping up competition not only on the commercial lines but also through calls for tenders for subsidized stretches.
2 In the big cities there are wide fluctuations, with market entries and exits.
3 The competition behaviour of urban transport operators covers the whole range from collusion to predation. The competition authorities are therefore called upon, but in view of the large number of undertakings and their small size the possibilities for action by the control bodies are limited.
4 It has been possible to reduce operating costs considerably through reducing staff levels, closing down unprofitable lines and pruning administrative costs. Labour costs have been reduced through flexible working hours and lower pay. The private firms have significantly higher productivity. Their costs are between 10 and 30 per cent lower than those of the public undertakings. The subsidy requirement has been cut by at least 10 per cent.
5 Service quality has developed in different ways: the supply improved in some respects, deteriorated in others. There were many changes in timetables,

lines and tariffs. The network structure, i.e. the distribution between commercial and 'social service' traffic, in many cases turned out to be unstable. Integrated transport systems were split up and the uniformity and unity of the public transport supply has been diminished.

6 Tariff competition is relatively limited. The expectation that prices on the stretches competed for would fall has not been fulfilled. After being frozen for years, tariffs have in some cases increased faster than the inflation rate.

7 After privatization ridership fell for many undertakings. Through the use of minibuses vehicle-kilometres have nevertheless increased, with negative environmental consequences.

Deregulation and privatization bring the commercial objectives of urban public transport to the fore. In this respect the liberalization programme has been thoroughly successful. On the other hand, however, deregulation has made the integration and networking of the urban transport system more difficult, thus reducing its attractiveness *vis-à-vis* the private car. Competition within the network is pushing the competitiveness of the system as a whole into the background.

In view of these findings, the transport policy task is that of profiting from the advantages of liberalization without having to accept its disadvantages. This requires a phased and differentiated process in which market monitoring is necessary and from which further steps can be developed.

1 In rural areas the possibility for privatization through call for tender procedures with a new allocation of concessions for lines running at a loss should be exploited. Here the rail passenger traffic can also be switched to bus transport with the participation of private suppliers.

2 Because of their size and inter-modal co-operation advantages (metro, bus, park-and-ride) it does not make sense to privatize the public transport undertakings in the big conurbations. The auctioning off of individual lines would amount to skimming off the cream. Auctioning all lines or the network would have disintegrating effects that would be undesirable from the standpoint of public benefits of urban transport. Complementary services supplied by private enterprises may be considered, however, e.g. in radial and tangential traffic, for links with residential areas and sub-centres. An appropriate solution here is often a combination of already existing municipal transport undertakings, railways and private bus services.

3 Public wheel-on-rail urban transport (metro, tram, railway) is not suitable for deregulation and privatization. The separation of network and operations with a multiplicity of operators comes up against the problem of the necessary timetable co-ordination, very short headways and bottlenecks in densely occupied areas. The auctioning off of route rights would impair the

technical and operational advantages of unity of infrastructure and operation (economies of scope). However, limited joint use (e.g. the railways and local transport undertakings in Stockholm) can certainly be considered.

4 An important element in the private economy operation of urban transport services is the implementation of the 'subscriber principle'. Transport enterprises should be freed from public service obligations, and instead the political authorities desiring such services should conclude contracts with specific remuneration of them.

7.7 REPLACEMENT OF REGULATION BY CONTROL THROUGH COMPETITION

From control of competition to control by competition

Inter-enterprise and inter-modal competition on transport markets must be safeguarded against undesirable development (Baum, 1991). This task is incumbent upon the state competition authorities (for national transport) and the Commission of the European Communities (for frontier-crossing transport). Under the regulation regime that has prevailed up to now, this task has been performed by the regulation authorities, as a rule coming under the Minister of Transport. The quality of market supervision will change under deregulation conditions.

The sole criterion for competition policy is that it should maintain and guarantee fair competition, i.e. the prevention of restriction of competition through agreements, restraint or market power. Competition control requires abstinence from regulation; it leaves no room for dirigistic manipulation. Restrictions to competition for the purposes of achieving transport policy goals, e.g. protection of the railways, relief of the roads, environmental protection and road safety, should not be allowed. Inadmissible re-regulation on the part of the competition authorities is to be prevented through examination by the anti-trust courts.

Is the transport market a contestable market?

The type and extent of the necessary competition policy control to ensure the proper functioning of competition depends on the degree of competition to be expected on the transport markets after deregulation. In the industrial economies a reference standard has recently been developed with the theory of the contestable market (Baumol et al., 1982), from which the need for competition policy action can be derived. If there is contestability, then only relatively minor competition policy precautions are required. The competition process ensures that the economically optimal market results are achieved independently of the market structure.

Contestable markets exist where the following conditions are fulfilled:

1 established undertakings and potential competitors must have access to similar technologies, i.e. there must be no economies of scale or of scope;
2 market exit must not involve costs, i.e. there must be no sunk costs (e.g. liquidation losses on capital goods);
3 there must be no significant information or transaction costs;
4 there must be a reaction-free period of time on the part of the established suppliers, i.e. old suppliers react to the more favourable supply of the newcomer only after a certain delay.

As has already been shown in chapter 3, analysis of contestability on the different transport markets shows a by no means consistent picture. In view of these findings, it cannot be assumed that there will be virtually automatic self-regulation on deregulated transport markets. Instead, it is to be expected that there may be friction and restriction of competition, requiring competition policy controls and counter-measures. The main problems here will be possibly exaggerated competition, concentration tendencies, blocking strategies and demand power.

Main tasks of competition policy

Concentration

In the run-up to the single European market, concentration on the transport markets, through mergers, has significantly increased. This development will temporarily slacken off owing to the market entry of new suppliers as a result of deregulation, but subsequently it is not unlikely that there will be a further impulse to concentration under the pressure of fiercer competition.

This was what happened on the deregulated US air transport market. Substantial restructuring is also to be expected in European air transport, possibly leading to greater concentration (Monopolkommission, 1990). Air transport is characterized by substantial economies of scale resulting from the extension of the network structures – notably hub and spoke networks. Compared with point to point links, hub and spoke systems have the advantage of permitting the bundling of transport volume and hence the use of larger more cost-advantageous aircraft. Since the network structure in Europe has up to now often resulted from bilateral air transport agreements, more economically efficient structures will be built up in the future. An associated increase in concentration would not be harmful from the overall economic standpoint. Compared with the USA, the concentration tendency in Europe is likely to be less extreme because of the national independence of the airline companies and the bigger market niches.

Threats to competition in air transport come essentially from the vertical integration of the established airline companies in the airports as a result of the temporally unlimited concession of scarce slots and the preference given to the big airlines in the computer reservation systems. Both competition factors should be kept open for potential competitors in order to prevent any economically unjustified concentration.

There is a twofold picture in road haulage. In purely transport companies there will be deconcentration through market entries. In the past, 'regulatory' economies of scale have favoured concentration. In the forwarding sector, deregulation will tend to encourage concentration, while market entries by new suppliers will tend to be limited by the lack of branch networks, economies of scale and lack of the necessary know-how.

The external enterprise growth in the transport and forwarding industry should be monitored by the competition authorities. This is to prevent the development of concentration trends which could later provide opportunities for obstructing competition. The competition laws in most European Community member states permit an administrative veto on mergers. However, these laws are for the most part aimed at the problems in the industrial sector and are not so well tailored for the service sector. As a result, the rules – notably if the control authority depends on absolute size criteria – do not always cover the conditions in the transport industry where firms are relatively small. A re-examination of the quantitative intervention criteria may be required.

Market dominating positions in air transport can be avoided if access to the airports and the electronic ticketing systems is kept open. This implies that the slots need to be allocated more in line with market criteria, e.g. through auction. All airline companies should have access in a non-discriminatory fashion to the big computer reservation systems. If the conditions laid down by the Commission of the European Communities in the liberalization regulation do not stand the test of time, consideration should be given to the separation of airlines and ticketing.

Obstacles to competition

A second major aspect of competition policy will be concerned with the obstruction practised against competitiors by transport enterprises with a certain market strength in order to avoid having a greater degree of competition. This involves above all reciprocal business between transport undertakings and shippers (exclusivity clause), price discrimination within transport chains, strategic alliances between certain modes and co-operation of transport undertakings (e.g. load pool) with market exclusion effects *vis-á-vis* third parties. Also qualifying as obstructing strategy is the supply of transport services at below cost price, a variant of 'predatory pricing'. The railways in particular are accused, through internal cross-subsidies and thanks to state subsidies, of offering prices on fiercely competed for markets that do not cover the variable costs and serve only to oust others.

Blocking strategies of this type play an important role in practical competition policy. They are in some cases difficult to pinpoint as restrictions on competition and do not have the same high publicity profile as abusive pricing, for example, so they tend to spread precisely for this reason. Their increasing importance on transport markets is therefore to be expected.

Competition law in the majority of European countries makes it possible to combat this type of competition obstruction and discrimination. Here competition policy enters the basic conflict between freedom of contract and the preservation of competition. In principle, all suppliers have the possibility of shaping their market relations to suit their own interests. The competition authorities will have to demonstrate through an appropriate case study for the transport sector that the legal provisions are adequate and permit the effective maintenance of competition.

Demand power

A final competition problem is demand power. This can appear in the case of shippers with respect to transport undertakings and forwarding agents with respect to carriers.

Both variants of demand power are to be expected on a deregulated market. However, it is also to be assumed that both shippers and forwarders in the longer term are interested in the competitiveness of transport undertakings. This self-interest will prevent both transport demand groupings from exploiting their market strength to the limit. Competition policy action against the abusive use of demand power is also possible, though diagnosis and prevention are more problematical to implement than is the case with supply power.

7.8 CONCLUSIONS

Transport markets – both passenger and freight – were for a long time organized as exceptions to the normal rules of competition, with a high degree of state intervention. Policy makers, political parties and governments thus founded, extended and defended public non-market regulation with protection in favour of the producers, the consumers and the public at large. This policy was not successful, however. It was weighted down by a high potential for conflict, ineffectiveness in some areas and many external goals which restricted the efficiency of the transport system and the growth capacity of the economy.

In the single European market, it is intended that these weaknesses of the transport sector should be remedied through introducing market economy conditions, with deregulation, privatization and competition. This will mean positive development in the direction of an economically rational transport policy.

However, analysis of the conditions and effects shows that transport policy safeguards are required to accompany this transition to a market economy. The favourable prognosis for the effects of a liberalized transport market depends on a number of premises and presupposes the removal of a number of distorting interventionist hangovers from the past. Such transport policy support would also create the possibility of observing the expected desirable or undesirable effects as they turn out in practice, of taking temporary corrective action and of cushioning the shock of entering into free competition. This task concerns both the deregulation of transport markets and the implementation of a private ownership system, and also the combination of these two vital components into a competitive market system.

The future division of roles between market and state will be a field of considerable conflict. On the one hand, transport policy even on a deregulated market will have to ensure that public service obligations are met and that there is a certain standard of service in the interest of the public at large. On the other hand, transport policy will have to impose upon itself abstinence from control if new distortions and disruptions are to be avoided. The key problem here lies in the very close production links between the provision of transport services and the transport infrastructure. This gives rise to market complexes with several layers, which on the transport services side are on a private economy basis while the infrastructures belong to the public sector (see chapters 8 and 9). If transport policy in the shape of deregulation and privatization loses its possibilities for control on the transport service markets, attempts might be made to bring about politically desired market developments through the supply structure of transport infrastructures. There are in fact signs of this type of investment interventionism and they need to be taken seriously. It is therefore necessary to have synchronization of market economy control on both market levels. Control policy must not be restricted to the field of transport service provision, but must also concern the supply and utilization of infrastructures.

NOTES

1 An overview of regulated markets in the economy is given by Müller and Vogelsang (1979).

2 On the different variants of the theory and possibilities of using them see Mueller (1989), Frey (1981) and Mackscheidt (1973).

3 On the delimitation and economic theory of interventionism see von Mises (1929) and Küng (1956).
4 A survey is to be found in Violland et al. (1991).
5 See the theoretical and empirical analyses by Baum (1983), Hamm (1980), Werner (1988) and Laaser (1991).
6 Presentations of empirical cost–benefit analyses of US deregulation are to be found in Friedlaender (1975) and Braeutigam and Noll (1984).
7 Cf. Monopolkommission (1990), Deregulierungskommission (1991), Bernadet (1991), Baum (1983), Seidenfus (1988) and Beesley (1991).
8 PLANCO (1988).
9 Cf. Kobayashi (1988), Lieb (1988), Moore and Kroszner (1988) and Willis (1989).
10 Thus, for example, in the case of the Federal Republic of Germany the Monopolkommission (1990) and the Deregulierungskommission (1991).
11 For more on this subject see European Conference of Ministers of Transport (1993).

REFERENCES

Aberle, G. (1989) Harmonisierung und Lenkung – Facetten der EG-Straβengüterverkehrspolitik in den 90er Jahren. *Zeitschrift für Verkehrswissenschaft*, 117–28.

Baum, H. (1983) *Possibilities and Limits of Regulation in Transport Policy*. Round Table 62. European Conference of Ministers of Transport. Paris: OECD.

——(1991) The role of government in a deregulated transport market (access, competition, safety). In Round Table 83, *The Role of Government in a Deregulated Transport Market*, European Conference of Ministers of Transport, Paris: OECD, 5–43.

Baum, H., Gierse, M. and Maβmann, C. (1990) *Aufbereitung von Preiselastizitäten der Nachfrage im Güterverkehr für Modal Split-Prognosen*. Essen: Verkehrsforum Bahn.

Baum, H., Maβmann, C., Schulz, W.H. and Thiele, P. (1992) *Rationalisierungspotentiale im Straβenverkehr*. Frankfurt-am-Main: Forschungsvereinigung Automobiltechnik.

Baumol, W.J., Panzar, J.C. and Willig, R.D. (1982) *Contestable Markets and the Theory of Industry Structure*. New York: Harcourt Brace Jovanovich.

Beesley, M. (1991) UK experience with freight and passenger regulation. In Round Table 83, *The Role of Government in a Deregulated Transport Market*, European Conference of Ministers of Transport, Paris: OECD, 45–76.

Bericht der Regierungskommission Bundesbahn (1991), 1.

Bernadet, M. (1991) Deregulation of freight transport – France. In Round Table 84, *Deregulation of Freight Transport*, European Conference of Ministers of Transport, Paris: OECD, 5–39.

Brandborn, J. and Hellsvik, L. (1990) Verkehrspolitische Strategien – Die neue Eisenbahnpolitik in Schweden. *Internationales Verkehrswesen*, 342–8.

Braeutigam, R.R. and Noll, R.G. (1984) The regulation of surface freight transportation: the welfare effects revisited. *Review of Economics and Statistics*, 80–7.

Bundesverband des Deutschen Güterfernverkehrs (1986) *Die Folgen der Deregulierung des Straβengüterverkehrs in den USA – USA als Vorbild für eine Liberalisierung*? Frankfurt.

—— (1992) *Flexible Kapazitätssteuerung im Straßengüterverkehr*. Frankfurt.

Department of Transport (1992) *New Opportunities for the Railways. The Privatisation of British Rail*. London: HMSO.

Deregulierungskommission (1991) *Marktöffnung und Wettbewerb*. Berichte 1990 und 1991. Stuttgart.

Dodgson, J.S. and Katsoulacos, Y. (1988) Models of competition and the effect of bus service deregulation. In *Bus Deregulation and Privatisation*, Aldershot: Avebury Gower, 46–67.

European Conference of Ministers of Transport (1993) *Privatisation of Railways: Methods and Obstacles*, Round Table 94, Paris: OECD.

Evans, A. (1990) Competition and the structure of local bus markets. *Journal of Transport Economics and Policy*, 225–82.

Frey, B.S. (1981) *Theorie demokratischer Wirtschaftspolitik*. Munich: Franz Vahlen.

Friedlaender, A.F. (1975) *The Dilemma of Freight Transport Regulation*. Washington DC: Brookings Institution.

Giersch, H. (1960) *Allgemeine Wirtschaftspolitik – Grundlagen*. Wiesbaden: Gabler.

Hamm, W. (1980) Regulated industries: transportation. *Zeitschrift für die gesamte Staatswissenschaft*, 576–92.

Jansson, J.O. and Cardebring, P. (1989) Swedish railway policy 1978–88. *Journal of Transport Economics and Policy*, 329–37.

Jansson, K. and B. Wallin (1991) Deregulation of public transport in Sweden. *Journal of Transport Economics and Policy*, 97–107.

Kobayashi, H. (1988) Deregulierung und Privatisierung in Japan. In O. Vogel (ed.), *Deregulierung und Privatisierung*, Cologne: Deutscher Instituts-Verlag, 70–85.

Küng, E. (1956) Interventionismus. *Handwörterbuch der Sozialwissenschaften*, vol. 5, Stuttgart-Göttingen, 321–9.

Laaser, C.-F. (1991) *Wettbewerb im Verkehrswesen. Chancen für eine Deregulierung in der Bundesrepublik Deutschland*. Tübingen: Verlag Mohr.

Lieb, R.C. (1988) Deregulierung des amerikanischen Güterverkehrs. In Bundesverband der Deutschen Industrie (ed.), *Liberalisierung der Verkehrsmärkte-Erfahrungen des Auslandes*, Cologne, 31–7.

Mackscheidt, K. (1973) *Zur Theorie des optimalen Budgets*. Tübingen-Zürich: Verlag Mohr.

von Mises, L. (1929) *Kritik des Interventionismus, Untersuchung zur Wirtschaftspolitik und Wirtschaftsideologie der Gegenwart*. Jena: Fischer Verlag.

Monopolkommission (1990) *Wettbewerbspolitik vor neuen Herausforderungen*. Hauptgutachten 1988/89. Baden-Baden.

Moore, T.G. and Kroszner, R.S. (1988) Deregulierung, Privatisierung und der freie Markt in den Vereinigten Staaten von Amerika. In O. Vogel (ed.), *Deregulierung und Privatisierung*. Cologne: Deutscher Instituts-Verlag, 49–69.

Mueller, D.C. (1989) *Public Choice II*. Cambridge: Cambridge University Press.

Müller, J. and Vogelsang, I. (1979) *Staatliche Regulierung*. Baden-Baden: Nomos Verlag.

PLANCO (1988) *Ordnungspolitische Szenarien zur Verwirklichung eines gemeinsamen europäischen Verkehrsmarktes, Teil B: Quantitative ökonomische Wirkungsanalysen*. Essen.

Rothengatter, W. (1991) Deregulating the European railway industries, theoretical background and practical consequences. *Transportation Research* A, 181–91.

Seidenfus, H. St. (1988) *Ordnungspolitische Szenarien zur Verwirklichung des gemeinsamen europäischen Verkehrsmarktes, Teil A. Szenarien und ökonomische Wirkungszusammenhänge*. Münster.

Stigler, G.J. (1970/71) The theory of economic regulation. *Bell Journal of Economics and Management Science*, 3–21.

The Japanese Delegation to the OECD, Noulton, J., Violland, M. (1991) Regulatory reform in the transport Sector: experience and implications. In Round Table 83, *The Role of Government in a Deregulated Transport Market*, European Conference of Ministers of Transport, Paris: OECD, 77–123.

Umweltbundesamt (1991) *Verkehrsbedingte Luft- und Lärmbelastungen – Emissionen, Immissionen, Wirkungen*. Berlin.

von Weizsäcker, C.C. (1982) Staatliche Regulierung – positive und normative Theorie. *Schweizerische Zeitschrift für Volkswirtschaft und Statistik*, 325–42.

Werner, M. (1988) Regulierung und Deregulierung des Verkehrssektors in der wirtschaftswissenschaftlichen Diskussion – Die Theorie der Regulierung. *Zeitschrift für Verkehrswissenschaft*, 44–70, 128–62.

Wijffels, H.H.F., Veld, R.J. in 't and Soet, J.F.A. de (1992) *Sporen voor straks. Advies over de toekomstige relatie tussen overheid en Nederlandse Spoorwegen*. s.l.

Willis, D.K. (1989) Erfahrungen mit der Verkehrsmarktderegulierung in den USA. In *Initiative '92 - Vollendung des Europäischen Binnenmarktes im Verkehrssektor* (Schriftenreihe des Verbandes der Automobilindustrie e.V., Nr. 58). Frankfurt, 44–55.

8

Government and Transport Infrastructure – Pricing

Jan Owen Jansson

8.1 SCOPE AND LIMITATIONS

What is the responsibility of governments at different levels for the transport infrastructure? Why do governments interfere at all in the free play of market forces in this area?

Judging from the real situation, the answers are that governments have comprehensive co-ordinating responsibility for almost all transport infrastructure. Market forces are important, too, because the transport infrastructure services, with the notable exception of inland waterways, belong to that minority of publicly provided services which are more or less fully charged for. Governments will be concerned with the questions of how to invest in and make use of the transport infrastructure in the best public interest. For this purpose a goal of net social benefit maximization will be defined. From this follow pricing principles, the main subject matter of section 8.4, and investment criteria, discussed for non-urban and urban transport infrastructure in chapter 9.

Will optimal pricing of the services of transport infrastructure pay for the facilities? This question is raised in section 8.5, where the financial problems are analysed. The discussion of pricing and investment in sections 8.4 and 8.5 and in chapter 9 is based on the general cost analysis in sections 8.2 and 8.3.

Some parts of the transport infrastructure have always been run by public agencies. Others were originally private, but have been transferred to the public sector because of bankruptcy, or to prevent exploitation of users and/or to make co-ordination easier. A few pieces of transport infrastructure remain in private hands.

Is there a tendency for a reversal of this process in the wake of the privatization movement? It is interesting that at the present time two diametrically different schools of thought are advocating radical change. On one hand, encouraged by the triumphal progress of the market economy way of doing things, even well-established dogmas like the necessity of cost–benefit analysis for investment in roads, railway, airports etc. are questioned. The utopia of a self-regulating transport infrastructure system, where no visible hands of planners are needed, is on the *tapis* again. On the other hand, partly as a result of advances in mathematical programming and computer performance, and in spite of the planned economy debacle, there is an urge in another quarter for more sophisticated infrastructure planning methods. The ambition is to integrate the location of industry, housing etc. and transport infrastructure into economy-wide, spatial general equilibrium models for superplanning.

The missing link between these contradictory schools of thought is X-efficiency. More ambitious planning and co-ordination of investments and operations may be negated by the 'human factor', or, conversely, the seemingly suboptimal resource allocation as a consequence of far-reaching decentralization may be compensated by higher motivation of private operators and an innovative spirit that is lacking when brain and hands are too distant. X-efficiency is said to exist when the actual cost of production is equal to minimum obtainable cost. As the name suggests, X-efficiency does not lend itself easily to the kind of quantitative analysis developed for problems of allocative efficiency. It is to be regretted, and the only excuse for carrying on traditional economic analysis of the role of government for transport infrastructure is that the reform potential with respect to pricing principles and investment criteria is, to all appearances, very great indeed.

Definition of transport infrastructure

'Infra' means (in Latin) 'situated below', and the most common understanding of transport infrastructure is in accordance with this meaning: in the first place it is the substructure or foundation for cars, buses, trucks, locomotives etc. which makes it possible for them to move smoothly and rapidly, thereby realizing their potential as transport vehicles (on the definition of infrastructure see also chapter 6, section 6.1).

Natural transport infrastructure is water and air. Inland waterways often require heavy investments in canals and locks; but sea transport, like air transport, also requires man-made supplements – navigational aids, traffic control devices etc. – to make complete fairways and airways.

Freight transport vehicles need special infrastructure as well as elaborate gear for loading and unloading. This is obviously less important in passenger transport. Certain facilities for boarding and alighting are required for different modes of public transport, whereas a private car can take on or let go a passenger almost anywhere at the roadside. Somewhat inadequately these parts of the transport infrastructure are called 'terminals', as if they were ends of journeys. From the point of view of a traveller or shipper, they are places where a change of mode of transport is made.

Idle transport vehicles have to be put somewhere where they are out of the way and/or safe. Again there is no good collective name for this third part of the transport infrastructure. It is really important for just one type of vehicle, the private car, because cars are idle over 90 per cent of the day on average. Therefore 'parking facilities' will do as the general term.

It can be argued that 'transport infrastructure' should not be restricted to tracks, terminals and parking facilities for transport vehicles but should also include pipelines for oil transport, underground pipes for transport of water etc., electric powerlines and telecommunication networks. The following discussion is confined to the items mentioned above, not because such a narrow definition is superior, but because the space of this chapter is limited.

Organizational disintegration of the natural production function

Both in engineering and economics the 'natural' production function includes as a matter of course various capital as well as labour inputs. Similarly, by Coase's (1988) way of thinking it is rational in the interest of keeping transaction costs down that a firm integrates the basic capital and labour required for its output by ownership and/or long-term hire contract, so that the most important inputs can be combined with maximum flexibility by command rather than market transactions.

This administrative order is the exception to the rule in transport production. With the main exception of rail transport producers, apart from Swedish railways, transport firms do not own the fixed capital used in the production process, i.e. the transport infrastructure, but acquire transport infrastructure services on a 'pay as you go' basis. The reason for this apparent oddity is, of course, that sharing the fixed capital with others is normally more economical for an individual transport operator, let alone private car rider in the case of road transport, than acquiring the required pieces of transport infrastructure for one's own exclusive use.

The marginalistic approach versus optimization 'from scratch'

Long distance door-to-door transports cover several track links and terminals, so somebody has to take on the responsibility for connecting links to chains and networks. The existing transport infrastructure has been built up over a very long time. It does not last for ever – in fact maintenance and repair of the existing transport infrastructure are primary tasks for our generation – but some pieces have a physical, if not economic, life that is very long indeed. Transport infrastructure system analysis could be very complicated if system design from scratch were at issue. The transport infrastructure heritage from previous generations, however, is so substantial, and largely irreversible that marginal economic analysis is both feasible and justifiable.

It is commendable to bear all the system dimensions in mind even in a basically marginalistic approach, because 'the whole frequently turns out to be different from the sum of its parts'. However, the system characteristic focused on in what follows is the organizational disintegration of the essential factors of production, because this is what more than anything else distinguishes the economics of transport systems from 'general' microeconomics.

8.2 THE RELATIVE IMPORTANCE OF PRODUCER, USER AND EXTERNAL COSTS

In terms of total cost, transport infrastructure comes third or fourth in importance compared with the other main arguments in the transport production function. Considerably greater are the user time costs in the case of personal transport and the capital and operating costs of the transport vehicles. This means for all kinds of transport infrastructure that in optimization of facility design, maintenance policy etc. the user costs, as seen from the point of view of the transport infrastructure owner, play a decisive role; a narrow limitation to the producer costs could be very misleading.

Mention should also be made of the costs of 'third parties', which do not exactly correspond to any inputs in the transport production function, but which are very important in some cases all the same: the environmental damage that would be made by certain roads, railways or airports is often critical for the possibility of expanding the capacity of the transport system, especially in urban areas.

An illustration from the road transport sector of the total cost structure is given in figure 8.1. As is seen, for the transports produced on the state-owned road network in Sweden, the total user costs of time, vehicles and traffic accidents are some ten times greater than the total road expenditure, of which repair and maintenance make up three-quarters. Road users also pay taxes on motor vehicles and fuel, which together outstrip total road expenditure by a factor of 4.

This structure is roughly representative of other transport systems in one important respect, no matter whether based on rails, air or water, the user costs are dominant. Road transport systems stand out in two other respects.

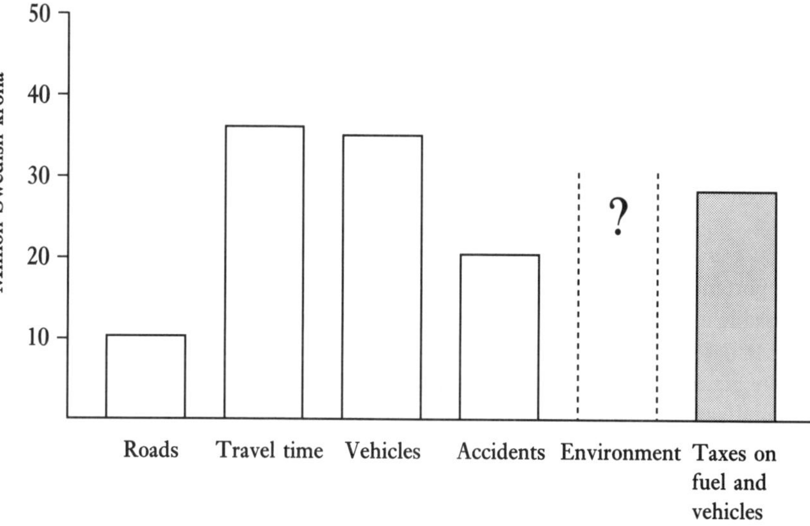

Figure 8.1 Cost components in the total costs of road transport on the Swedish state-owned road network in 1990.

1 The high proportion of accident costs is unique. In view of the fact that the road transport volume constitutes some 80 per cent of total transport – personal and freight – it is apparent that (the lack of) road safety is of utmost concern.
2 The substantial excess of tax revenue over expenditure on roads is almost unheard of for the infrastructure of other modes of transport.

The economic justification for the 'overcharging' of road users is that both the external costs of accidents (for sure) and the costs of noise and air pollution caused by road traffic (probably) are of an order of magnitude well above total road expenditure. The proven low elasticity of demand is probably a contributory explanation of why the strict earmarking of revenue from taxes on motor cars and fuel for road finance has been abandoned in most countries, with the notable exceptions of Japan and the USA.

'The importance of being unimportant'

The fact that the road owners' total costs constitute a relatively small part of the total system costs is not the exception but the rule in the transport sector. The seaport and airport owners' total costs are only a few per cent of the total costs of the terminal services in question, including *inter alia* the cost of ships' laytime and the waiting time costs on the ground of airline passengers. In rail transport systems, the total costs of the transport infrastructure services concerned make up a higher proportion, on an aggregate level, than in any other transport systems; about 20 per cent would be a representative order of magnitude. To beat this, one has to single out the road transport system of the inner areas of large cities, where the costs of the car parking facilities, owing to the high cost of land, will boost the transport infrastructure part of the total system costs.

In a transport chain of a number of links, it can be very important to be unimportant, to pursue the Hicksian pun. In the absence of good substitutes, it is possible to exploit the inelastic demand that follows from one's unimportance, i.e. relative smallness, and the fact that each link in the chain is equally vital.

The generalized cost of different transport services corresponds roughly to the total system cost per unit of output. Given that the absolute values of the generalized cost elasticity for different modes of transport are to be found in the 1–2 band, with railway transport at the upper limit and road transport at the lower limit (compare the recent surveys of transport demand elasticities by Oum et al., 1992, and Goodwin, 1992), it is possible to conclude that, looked at as an aggregate, transport infrastructure services face price elasticities as low as from below 0.1 to 0.5 at most. So financing transport infrastructure systems by user charges should be no great problem!

It must immediately be said that competition can make all the difference between complete inelasticity and almost infinite elasticity of demand. For example, when a new, better road between two points A and B is opened, its demand can have the characteristic 'logit shape', implying that below a certain price almost everybody chooses the better road, and above this price level only a few motorists with high values of time are willing to pay the price. If the old road is shut down, on the other hand, the demand for the new road may become very inelastic. This simple fact is all-important for the financial viability of toll-roads.

8.3 COST AND OUTPUT RELATIONSHIPS

The reflected image of the transport production function approach is the following total cost categorization, where the costs of the transport infrastructure owner, i.e. the producer of transport infrastructure services, constitute just the first term:

$$\begin{aligned} TC &= TC^{prod} + TC^{user} + TC^{ext} \\ &= f(X, Y, Q) + g\left(X, \frac{Q}{K}\right)Q + h(X, Q) \qquad (8.1) \end{aligned}$$

where $TC^{prod} = f(X,Y,Q)$ is the total cost for the producer of transport infrastructure services as a function of facility design, physical conditions for the construction and the traffic volume; $AC^{user} = g(X,Q/K)$ is the average cost of users of transport infrastructure services as a function of facility design and the rate of capacity utilization; $TC^{user} = g(X,Q/K)Q$; $TC^{ext} = h(X,Q)$ is the total cost of the rest of society (apart from actors within the transport production system) as a function of facility design and the traffic volume; $K = k(X)$ is the capacity of the facility as a function of facility design; X is the vector of facility design variables (width, curvature etc.); Y is the vector of physical conditions at the location of the facility (piece of transport infrastructure); Q is the output in terms of traffic volume; and $Q/K = \Phi$ is the rate of capacity utilization.

It is practical to look at each of the main total cost components separately as long as the important interrelationship between the producer and user costs via the capacity K and/or the facility design variables X is borne in mind.

The reason for expressing the total user cost as a product of the average user cost per unit of traffic and the traffic volume is that the former factor is a basic entity for both cost and demand analysis. It is the real part of the generalized cost, perceived as the private marginal cost of an individual user, provided that his perception of his own travel/transport cost is realistic.

The section below looks at the short-run costs, which are dominated by the user costs, and the long-run producer costs in turn.

Short-run user costs

As indicated by writing the average user cost function as $g(X,\Phi)$, there are two fundamental influences on this cost that should be grasped: in the short run, when it can be assumed that facility design including its capacity is given, it is the rate of capacity utilization which is important, and in the long run, or rather in the planning stage of an investment, it is the effect on user costs of the design of the piece of transport infrastructure concerned that should be focused on. The special feature of capacity and quality jointness observed by Walters (1968), so far as roads are concerned, is a general characteristic of transport infrastructure. It is expressed here by making capacity K a function of the design vector X, as well as introducing X as a separate argument in the user cost function. For example, improving the alignment of a rail track increases the capacity and the running speed, given the capacity utilization. As a general rule it can be stated that when

$$\frac{\partial g}{\partial X} < 0 \qquad \frac{\partial K}{\partial X} > 0$$

Needless to say there are many other aspects of the relationship between facility design and transport infrastructure user costs. It is a wide and important area of engineering economy studies, which is well beyond the scope of this chapter.

Economists have been more concerned with the short-run relationship between the rate of capacity utilization Φ and user cost, presumably because it is of direct relevance for optimal pricing of transport infrastructure services. Even in this case engineering operational research, rather than econometric studies, is fundamental for our present knowledge.

The basic notion is that g as a function of Φ is more or less constant for low to moderate rates of capacity utilization, and rises gradually as the capacity limit of a particular facility is approached. In generalizing about the short-run user cost and output relationship a distinction between facilities for common use and departmentalized facilities is helpful. With common facilities like roads the rise in cost with an increasing rate of capacity utilization is caused by congestion. At departmentalized production plants congestion in the production process is avoided by definition. Instead, queuing before entering the production stage may occur. Congestion theory for road transport – roads are the most important common transport infrastructure facilities – and the character of congestion costs are well known and will not be taken up here. The user cost of occasional excess demand for departmentalized facilities like seaports, airports and parking facilities is not as well understood and will be briefly discussed.

In goods manufacturing a high rate of capacity utilization in the production stages is achieved by buffer stocks at both ends (of input material and finished goods, respectively). In the production of services, which cannot be stored, the target as regards the rate of capacity utilization has to be set at a much lower level. Otherwise the queuing time of customers will be intolerable.

Departmentalized facilities – seaport as an example

The general-purpose seaport supplies service to ships, cargo and land transport vehicles arriving more or less at random and making different demands on port resources. The short-term demand for port services will therefore vary – one week all resources may be occupied and the ships will be waiting in the roads, the next week there may be no ships in the port at all. What is the correct trade-off between the two objectives of a high level of utilization of port facilities and a low likelihood of delays for ships?

A useful tool for tackling port optimization problems is provided by the theory of queuing: ships can be regarded as 'customers', while the 'service stations' of conventional queuing models can be represented by the berths of a seaport. In fact, alongside telephone services, seaports constitute a major area for the application of queuing theory.

Total expected laytime of ships can be divided into queuing time and service time. It is the queuing time that depends critically on the rate of capacity utilization. The mean queuing time for customers (ships) arriving more or less randomly at a single-channel facility (a port section with one berth only) will rise quite steeply even at modest levels of utilization. If the customers' capacity requirements differ significantly, i.e. if individual service times for loading and unloading a ship vary substantially, this tendency will be reinforced.

This can be illustrated, using elementary theory, on the basis of the following standard assumptions:

1 customers arrive at random, which means that the distribution of arrivals can be described by the Poisson probability distribution;
2 similarly, the duration of the service time is a random variable, fitting the 'negative exponential' probability distribution;
3 there is no upper limit to the length of the queue, i.e. customers are indefinitely 'patient'.

The expected queuing time in statistical equilibrium will then be

$$q = \frac{As^2}{1 - As} = s\frac{\Phi}{1 - \Phi} \tag{8.2}$$

where q is the expected queuing time per customer (days), A is the expected number of arrivals per day, s is the expected service time per customer (days) and Φ is the occupancy rate ($= As$).

A characteristic of this model, as of many other more complicated queuing models, is that, given the occupancy rate, the mean queuing time q is proportional to the mean service time s. As can be seen, q moves towards infinity as Φ approaches unity. The sharp rise in the mean queuing time as the occupancy rate increases is shown in the middle column of table 8.1, which gives the ratio of q to s for different values of Φ.

The root cause of the queuing that occurs is, of course, the variability of A and s. The laytime of similar ships varies because a great many more or less random factors significantly affect the actual value of the service time. Such factors include the weather and stoppages due to breakdown of handling or other equipment. In addition, the type and size of ships and the type of cargo can vary a lot. What difference does it make if the variability of s can be reduced?

The Pollaczek–Khintchine formula provides a general answer to the question of how the mean queuing time is affected by the distribution of service time. It states that for any arbitrary distribution of s it is possible to express the steady-state mean queuing time q as a function of the arrival rate A, the mean service time s and the variance var(s) of the service time distribution:

$$q = \frac{A[s^2 + \text{var}(s)]}{2(1 - As)} \tag{8.3}$$

Table 8.1 Queuing time in the single-stage single-channel model

Occupancy rate	*Mean queuing time as a proportion of service time*	*Expected additional queuing time caused by another arrival as a proportion of the service time*
0.1	0.11	0.12
0.2	0.25	0.31
0.3	0.43	0.61
0.4	0.67	1.11
0.5	1.00	2.00
0.6	1.50	3.75
0.7	2.33	6.26
0.8	4.00	20.00
0.9	9.00	90.00
1.0	∞	∞

In the case of a negative exponential distribution of s, the variance is s^2. It is easily checked that the previous expression (8.2) for the mean queuing time is obtained by inserting this for var(s) in (8.3). In the case of constant service time, the variance of s is zero and the general formula gives

$$q = \frac{s}{2}\frac{\Phi}{1 - \Phi} \tag{8.4}$$

The elimination of service time variability will, *ceteris paribus*, reduce the mean queuing time by half.

It is clear from expression (8.3) above that, given the occupancy rate, the mean queuing time is proportional to the sum of the service time and its relative variance (s + var(s)/s). Consequently, to reduce the queuing time it is as important to achieve a reduction in the variability of the service time as it is to achieve a reduction in the mean service time itself. In the case of seaport operations this means that the expected queuing time may be reduced either by increasing the handling speed or by making each call by the ships more homogeneous, e.g. by specializing in serving a particular type of ship or cargo.

Long-run producer costs

Cross-section cost studies of transport infrastructure have a special interest because there is ample opportunity to trace out the entire long-run relationship between cost and output. The whole range of the general L-shaped average cost

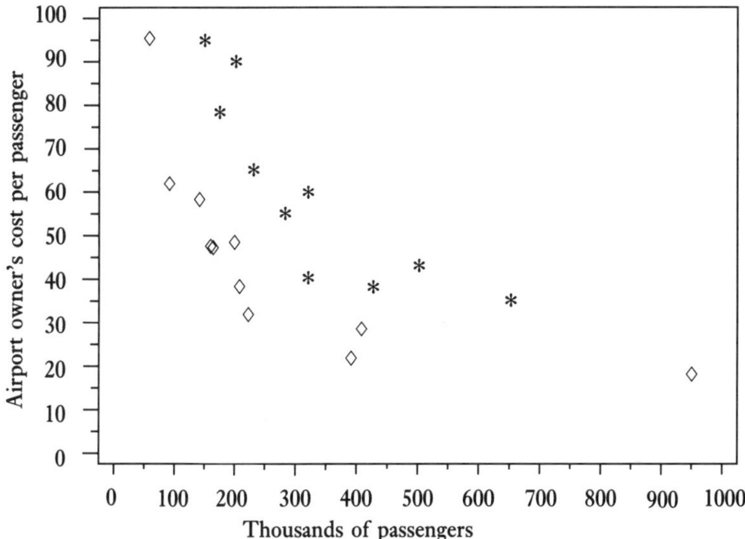

Figure 8.2 Airport cost per passenger against passenger volume.
Source: SOU, 1990

curve will be represented among the observations. In manufacturing industries, the average costs of all plants and/or firms of a particular industry making easily transportable goods should be more or less on the same level; a high-cost plant or firm could not survive where all plants in the industry serve the same national or even global market. Individual roads, on the other hand, are natural local monopolies. The fact that a particular motorway produces road services at a fifth of the cost per vehicle-kilometre of a small road between two villages in a different part of the country is of no consequence for the viability of the latter.

Small-scale diseconomies

The main proposition is simply that very marked small-scale diseconomies are revealed by the empirical evidence, while it is more difficult to say what will happen at the other end of the scale.

The airport owner's total cost per passenger for the 24 primary airports in Sweden illustrates well the magnitude of small-scale diseconomies that is typical. The impression given by figure 8.2 is a little distorted by a systematic cost difference between two categories of airport – partly military and/or municipality owned versus state-owned. By including an appropriate dummy variable in the regression of average airport cost on passenger volume the main message is very

Table 8.2 Road capital and running costs per passenger-car-unit(pcu)-kilometre for different least-cost road designs

Traffic flow per day	*Road costs per pcu-km*
400	55
1,350	21
7,000	6
14,000	5
27,000	5
40,000	5

Source: Jansson, 1984

clear: airports serving passenger volumes in the range 100,000–200,000 per year are some five times more costly than airports serving 1 million passengers.

By international standards 1 million passengers per year is not a large volume. There are three Swedish airports handling traffic volumes exceeding that limit; they did not fit into the diagram of figure 8.2, especially not Arlanda, the biggest, which handles 15 times more passengers than the biggest airport represented in the diagram. Big airports have a more diversified line of products than small airports, which is why it is a little more difficult to calculate a single, comparable unit cost; it seems, however, that all three 'outliers' are at the cost level of the two airports with the lowest cost in the diagram.

A similar cost picture for British airports is given by Doganis and Thompson (1975).

When it comes to roads the highway engineering manuals point in the same direction: very marked diseconomies of small-scale operation prevail, but the scale economies seem to be largely exhausted in the traffic volume range where motorway standards are justified. Since topography and the condition of the soil can differ greatly, the variability in construction costs is quite significant. The figures in table 8.2 are rough averages: within each class of road, capital costs that are twice as high per kilometre or only half the value given are not rare.

There is no empirical evidence of rail track costs taken separately. Sweden so far is the only country in the world with a formal separate rail track administration ('Banverket'). It has not existed long enough to produce reliable figures of the cost of rail track services with respect to traffic volume. There is no reason to doubt that the cost picture is much the same as for roads. The question of economies of scale in rail transport (rail track and train) services was once a hotly debated issue, until it was made clear that one has to distinguish firm size economies and economies of traffic density. Why were twig and branch lines closed down when the Railways Administration tried to improve its financial position? Obviously it was because costs per unit of traffic are typically many times higher there than on trunk lines, in spite of a high sunk cost portion of the capacity costs. Harris (1977) pointed out the irrelevance of the question of firm size economies for the issue of line discontinuation, and showed that significant economies of traffic density exist in the US rail freight industry. The average costs comprise both track costs and freight train costs in that case. It seems, however, that more than half of the sharp cost decline is due to strong small-scale diseconomies in the capital and maintenance costs of the rail track.

When it comes to departmentalized facilities, multichannel queuing theory provides good insight into the root cause of the very marked small-scale diseconomies of this kind of service production plant.

Suppose that the seaport model discussed above consists of n identical berths rather than just a single one. Under the same conditions as in the previous model, the standard multichannel queuing model can be used for predicting how far queuing time depends on the rate of capacity utilization. Since this model is mathematically more involved, it will be helpful to derive the steady-state mean queuing time in two steps.

Let p be the probability that an arrival will find all channels occupied. The mean queuing time can then be written as

$$q = \frac{s}{n(1 - \Phi)} p \qquad (8.5)$$

The occupancy rate Φ is now As/n. The left-hand factor represents the expected queuing time for those customers who actually meet with a delay, while p is the probability that a delay occurs. This probability is a function of n and Φ, but is independent of s. This means that the proportionality between q and s, which applies in the corresponding single-channel model, is retained in this multichannel model.

The influence on the queuing time of the number of service stations originates from both factors in (8.5). Given the occupancy rate, the value of the left-hand factor is inversely proportional to n. This is an interesting relationship. If the occupancy rate remains constant when demand increases, i.e. the number of service stations grows in proportion to the demand for service, the total queuing time will be equal to a constant multiplied by p. And given the occupancy rate, p decreases continuously as n increases. This is a well-established fact of queuing theory (see, for example, Saaty, 1961). From numerical simulations it is clear that the combined effect of these two factors makes the advantages of multichannel service facilities truly remarkable. The total queuing time decreases when demand and capacity increase at the same rate.

Table 8.3 Possible rates of capacity utilization for maintaining a given quality of service

Number of service stations	*Rate of capacity utilization*
1	0.20
2	0.45
3	0.57
4	0.65
5	0.70
6	0.73
7	0.76
8	0.78
9	0.80
10	0.82
11	0.83
12	0.84
13	0.85
14	0.86
15	0.87

Another expression for the same relation is given by the figures in table 8.3. Holding the quality of service constant, i.e. given the expected queuing time per arrival at a level of, say, a fifth of the service time, the rates of capacity utilization possible for facilities of successively more service stations are as shown.

Finally it can be mentioned that the economies of number can be realized either in the form of lower queuing costs, lower capacity costs per customer, or a combination of both. It can be shown that the occupancy rate will increase steadily along the 'expansion path', while the mean queuing time will decrease. This means that both the capacity cost and the queuing cost per unit of throughput will fall as throughput increases, provided that an optimal factor combination is chosen.

Are the plant-size economies boundless?

It is interesting to see that the economies of number of service stations are almost exhausted for n in the range 10–15. This is a feature which reappears in many other cases, also of common facilities. The old idea that there is a limit to everything may apply also to transport infrastructure facility-size economies. Large-scale diseconomies may set in sooner or later to balance and eventually offset the kind of economies which have been focused on here and which, no doubt, initially are very prominent indeed. There is no space to go deeply into the question of whether an L-shape or a U-shape is most characteristic of the long-run average cost of transport infrastructure service production. A modest example is given in figure 8.3 of an empirical result pointing to the possibility that diseconomies of density of demand may in fact exist in the area of transport infrastructure service production.

A cross-section study of the total costs of staff for sale of tickets including seat reservation, information etc. at railway stations in Sweden and the number of tickets sold was made as part of a project concerning railway transport pricing (Jansson et al., 1992). The data can be divided into one large group of small and medium-sized stations and a small group of large stations. In the former group the total cost and output relationship has the expected degressive shape figure 8.3(b). When both groups are considered, the remarkable result is that the textbook cubic relationship appears: increasing returns are succeeded by decreasing returns. It should be pointed out, however, that the uncertainty is much greater in the interval where observations are few.

At the system level, there is at least one important example of decreasing returns in the production of road services. For radial road transport in big cities there is a long-run capacity limit that shows itself in increasing costs of various kinds as more and more of the extremely scarce space is taken up by roads and parking facilities. In mega-cities like Tokyo, New York and London the car share in the market for central city commuter trips does not exceed 10 per cent. The passenger flow capacity of car traffic per metre of track width is relatively low, which means that elevated expressways have to be constructed if the market share of car traffic on radial routes of urban areas is to be substantially increased, and this is obviously an increasingly costly option, if it is an option at all in view of the environmental harm.

8.4 OPTIMAL PRICING

To the man in the street, the rationale for charging for transport infrastructure services is that roads etc. cost a lot to provide and maintain. Since Dupuit (1844), transport economists have had the hardly enviable task of explaining that this is not so: charges for transport infrastructure services should ensure an efficient use of facilities, which means that a great many pieces of transport infrastructure, in addition to Dupuit's bridge, should be free. The man in the street is then likely to follow up his argument by the rhetorical question: who should finance the building and maintenance of the bridge, if the use of it is free?

One reasonable answer is that the total road network contains many links, in particular in urban areas where demand exceeds supply by far, and these links

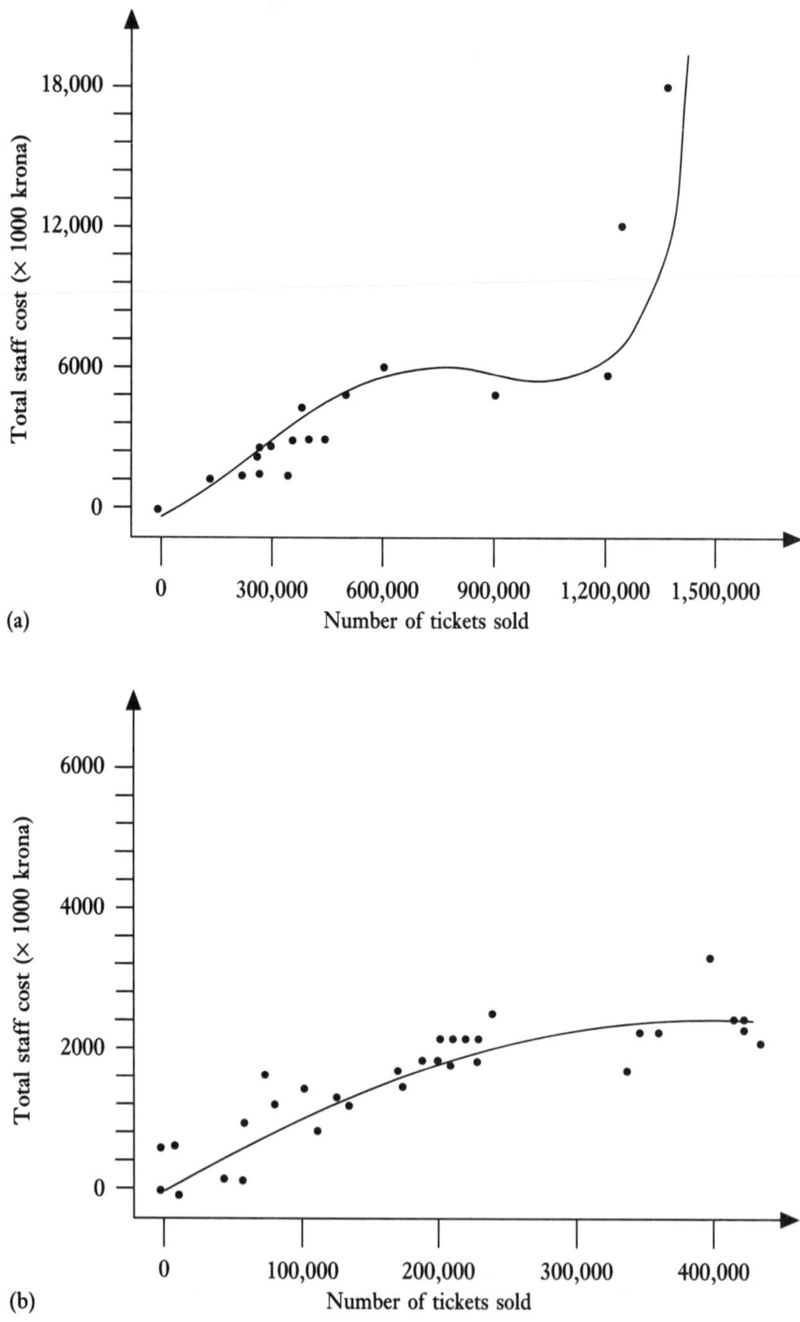

Figure 8.3 Relationship between total staff cost and the number of tickets sold: (a) for all SJ stations; (b) for SJ stations where sales are below 450,000 tickets per year.

should have prices that cover their total costs many times over: spatial 'cross-subsidization' between markets of high and low density of demand should be a typical pattern in transport infrastructure systems if efficiency is a principal objective.

Even a normally very busy road is sometimes almost empty. Peak load pricing is strongly required for many transport infrastructure services, and so cross-subsidization in time is equally characteristic of an efficient price structure in the transport infrastructure sector. This pattern is clearly in sharp contrast to the present uniformity in time and space of prices for transport infrastructure services.

The pricing-relevant cost of transport infrastructure services

For the existing pieces of service-producing transport infrastructure the facility design, including capacity, is fixed for a long time onwards. Now the best use will have to be made of the resources available. For any given piece of transport infrastructure the objective should be for each period of time to maximize the sum of the consumers' surplus and the producer's surplus minus the costs of negative externalities falling on the rest of society. The total costs as written in equation (8.1) represent the cost side in the following net social benefit maximization. The gross benefit to users is represented by the integral of the applicable marginal utility (MU) function.

$$\text{MU} = U(Q) \qquad (8.6)$$

$$\text{consumers' surplus} = \int_0^Q U(Q)\mathrm{d}Q - (P + \text{AC}^{\text{user}})Q$$

The gross benefit is defined not to include the user costs of time and other real efforts to come into possession of the service in question: to arrive at the consumers' surplus, both the price P paid and the user cost AC^{user} have to be deducted from the gross benefit.

$$\text{producer's surplus} = PQ - \text{TC}^{\text{prod}}$$

$$\text{total external cost} = \text{TC}^{\text{ext}}$$

Adding up these three items gives the total to be maximized:

$$\text{net social benefit (NSB)} = \int_0^Q U(Q)\mathrm{d}Q - Q\ \text{AC}^{\text{user}} - \text{TC}^{\text{prod}} - \text{TC}^{\text{ext}}$$

Specifying the cost functions according to equation (8.1), but taking into account that the facility design variables are fixed and therefore can be ignored, yields this final form of the maximand:

$$\text{NSB} = \int_0^Q U(Q)\mathrm{d}Q - g(Q)\,Q - f(Q) - h(Q) \tag{8.7}$$

The sum of price P and the average user cost AC^{user} is customarily called the 'generalized cost' (GC):

$$\text{GC} = P + g(Q) \tag{8.8}$$

An equilibrium condition that has to be observed is that GC equals the marginal utility:

$$P + g(Q) = U(Q) \tag{8.9}$$

Now, taking the derivative of NSB with respect to quantity Q and setting it equal to zero gives the following first-order condition for a maximum:

$$\frac{\partial \text{NSB}}{\partial Q} = U(Q) - Q\frac{\partial g}{\partial Q} - g(Q) - \frac{\partial f}{\partial Q} - \frac{\partial h}{\partial Q} = 0 \tag{8.10}$$

Substituting $P + g(Q)$ for $U(Q)$ from (8.9) gives the final result:

$$P = \frac{\partial f}{\partial Q} + Q\frac{\partial g}{\partial Q} + \frac{\partial h}{\partial Q} = \text{MC}^{\text{prod}} + Q\frac{\partial \text{AC}^{\text{user}}}{\partial Q} + \text{MC}^{\text{ext}} \tag{8.11}$$

Unsurprisingly the above ends up with the well-known postulate that, for maximum net social benefit of the existing pieces of transport infrastructure, a necessary condition is that price is set equal to the sum of the short-run marginal cost of the producer of transport infrastructure services, the cost imposed on fellow users and the cost imposed on outsiders by an additional user of the transport infrastructure facility concerned.

The first item consists mainly of use-dependent wear and tear and is normally rather small. The second item is usually called the 'congestion cost component'. This and the third item, which contains a variety of negative externalities, are the major components in the pricing-relevant cost. Now its content will be looked at more closely for common facilities as well as departmentalized facilities.

Common facilities

With a common facility like a road, the users' interference with each other takes two related forms – a reduction in speed to avoid collisions when traffic density goes up and (multi-)vehicle accidents that occur in spite of speed moderation. Some excellent work on road pricing theory and problems of application exist for which the speed–flow relationship forms the basis. Mention can be made of two pioneering contributions, Walters (1961) and the Smeed report of 1964, and a recent survey by Goodwin and Jones (1989; as well as Jansson et al., 1990). Here another somewhat neglected aspect is taken up. Total accident cost in road transport is approximately half the total cost of travel time, and so potentially the relationship between traffic accidents and the intensity of traffic is very important.

Empirical studies with a view to establishing a functional relationship between traffic accidents and probable determinants such as traffic flow are very difficult because of the fortunate fact that accidents are rare occurrences. In a cross-section study where traffic on different roads constitute the observations, the observation period has to be rather long in order to arrive at a reasonably representative number of accidents in each particular case (road). And during that long observation period, explanatory variables such as weather conditions, the state of the road, the composition of traffic as well as the traffic flow do not stay constant. A lot of averaging is inevitable, which greatly reduces the accuracy of the data.

So far the weight of evidence speaks for a constant risk for accidents per unit of traffic with respect to traffic flow, in a range from rather high traffic density to free flow, all other things remaining equal.

The constancy hypothesis is the somewhat shaky basis for the current treatment of accident costs in calculations of optimal road user charges, which in the briefest possible summary is as follows.

The expected accident cost per car-kilometre is bc, where b is the constant (traffic flow invariate) risk and c is the expected cost per accident. The latter unit cost is divided into three main components: $c = c_1 + c_2 + c_3$ where c_1 is the human 'warm-blooded' costs of death and injury (for principles of valuation of these costs see chapter 5) and c_2 and c_3 represent the external 'cold-blooded' resource costs, of which c_2 is the expected value of the difference between future production and consumption of victims of an accident and c_3 is the cost of hospital treatment etc.

The basic hypothesis is, as mentioned above, that an additional unit of traffic does not increase the accident risk for the existing traffic. Since the idea of optimal road user charges is to make road users aware also of the external costs of road use to the rest of society, the accident cost component in the charge is normally obtained by taking $b(c_2 + c_3)$ minus the possible part of the total traffic insurance premium intended to cover some external costs.

This principle of calculating the pricing-relevant accident cost seems incomplete when it is taken into account that different categories of road users constitute very different threats to each other. The main difference is between unprotected road users, i.e. pedestrians, cyclists and motorcyclists, and those travelling in cars and buses. It must be borne in mind that the accident risk per car-kilometre, b, is the sum of the accident risk of car (and bus) users, b_I, and the accident risk of unprotected road users, b_{II}. Therefore there is also a difference between private and social costs as regards the human cost component; the car user is facing a private human cost equal to $b_I c_1$, but the change for car use should also include the expected human cost of death and injury suffered by unprotected road users, equal to $b_{II} c_1$.

In cost–benefit analyses of road investments in many countries the human costs of traffic accidents play an important role on the benefit side. For efficiency in resource allocation, human costs should play a fully congruous role in the road user charges; lives of unprotected road users will be saved by car traffic reduction. If the human cost values applied by national road administrations for investment appraisals were also applied for the calculation of road user charges, an appreciable rise of these charges in urban areas would be indicated in many cases, even on uncongested roads (for a further discussion see OECD, 1985).

Departmentalized facilities I: patient customers

The queuing model outlined in the previous section gives one simple example of how the pricing-relevant cost could be calculated in a situation where occasional excess demand leads to an actual waiting line. The optimal price should be equal to the expected additional time cost caused by another customer to the rest of the customers. For example, at an occupancy rate of 0.6 this cost is $(3.75 - 1.50)sw = 2.25sw$ in the single-channel case illustrated in table 8.1, where s is expected service time and w is the value of waiting time. As seen, the pricing-relevant cost rises steeply with occupancy rate. For $\Phi = 0.9$ it is as high as $81sw$.

In practice it can be rather difficult to calculate the applicable queuing cost function (cf. Jansson and Shneerson, 1982), but it is even more difficult to estimate accurately the matching demand function. Some trial and error is necessary before the right solution can be found, i.e. before the price is found which equals the pricing-relevant expected cost.

In this case, as in many other cases in transport, there is the problem of perceived versus actual cost. The price theory presumes that each customer knows what to expect both as to queuing time and as to service time. The price is just motivated by the delay caused to others. Suppose customers systematically under- or over-estimate the time requirement, either the mean queuing time or mean service time or both. Should that be reflected in the price? There are arguments both for and against. One can argue that the marginal time cost should be equal to the sum of price and the perceived average time cost rather than the sum of price and the actual average time cost. On the other hand, it is somewhat unsatisfactory to burden customers twice when actual costs are under-estimated, or to fail to include the whole cost of delay caused to others in the price when actual costs are over-estimated.

Departmentalized facilities II: impatient customers

The queuing model case above is the simple case. Much greater difficulty in monetizing the user costs of excess demand arises in cases where these costs assume the shape of frustration of not attaining possession of service at the facility concerned, because queuing would be out of the question.
This case may in turn be divided into

1 the case where customers go to another facility for the same service, and
2 the case where the excess demand cannot be satisfied anywhere but simply drops out (for the time being).

Urban parking can provide good examples of both cases: if a particular downtown parking garage aimed at is fully occupied, one looks for another, or knowing from experience that on, say, Saturday night it is very difficult to find parking space reasonably close to the theatre district, one refrains from going downtown for the theatre altogether.

The latter case and the previous queuing model with completely patient customers are two polar cases. All sorts of in-between cases exist. The common characteristic is that the pricing-relevant cost occurs as a result of excess demand before the proper production starts. In each particular case, a suitable representation of the cost of occasional excess demand seldom comes easy. One should not aim at 'perfection'. In practice peak-load pricing of services provided at departmentalized transport infrastructure facilities, if it exists at all, is rough and ready. The important thing is to understand the nature of user costs of excess demand and, second, to try to get a quantitative idea of its relationship with the mean rate of capacity utilization. It should perhaps also be said that one must not be misled by simplistic deterministic models, where 100 per cent capacity utilization is a natural target. Last but not least, good *Fingerspitzengefühl* (intuitive feeling) is required to devise an efficient price structure by time period.

Pricing of transport infrastructure services versus pricing of 'transport infrastructure goods': parking pricing as an example

An alternative way of looking at the product so far called 'transport infrastructure services' is to view it as very-short-term renting of space of a transport infrastructure facility, where the 'first come, first served' principle is applied. It is then interesting to note that this transaction form is one end-point of a continuum, where the other end-point is to purchase a whole piece of transport infrastructure for one's own exclusive use. The latter option is quite frequently chosen by big users as regards departmentalized facilities. A middle form is the renting of a piece of transport infrastructure on a long-term basis, e.g. a berth with supplementary transit storage facilities in a seaport. Liner shipping companies often choose this transaction form to avoid the risk of queuing time. In the case of what is usually regarded as common facilities, buying or renting a whole piece is more rare, but strictly private roads and private sidings complementing the national rail network exist. From a price-theoretical point of view this difference in transaction form is really fundamental: it changes the object of pricing from non-storable services to goods, and it can change the market form from one extreme of (local) monopoly to the other extreme of almost pure competition.

The parking market

In the parking market the whole continuum of transaction forms is well represented. Since parking is an important transport infrastructure service in its own right, it is worthwhile to look closer at parking in urban areas.

For a car commuter working in the central business district of a million-city the parking cost is the dominant component in the daily travel cost, provided that he has to pay the full market price for a parking space, which is rare for various reasons. Then the daily parking cost can be anything from $6 upwards depending on city size, whereas the private car operating cost of the journey itself is normally below $6. In a city like Stockholm the cost of renting a parking space on a monthly basis is about $6–10 per day in the central business district. In central Tokyo, for instance, or on lower Manhattan it is many times more.

Looking at the parking market from the demand side, a useful distinction is between 'parking at the base' and 'parking away from the base'. Like its owner, every car has a home, or 'base', where the car is kept at night-time etc. The characteristics of the demand for base-parking are (i) that each parking period is fairly long term and (ii) that it occurs frequently and at the same place.

When the car is used for various trips to destinations away from the base – to shops, to visit customers, to do different errands – short-term occasional parking in many different places is needed.

In the base-parking market segment, parkers typically own or long-term hire parking space, and in the other market segment parkers pay per hour of parking space occupation. It is the same market segmentation as in the market for accommodation with owner-user apartments at one end and hotel rooms at the other. The interesting additional fact, however, is that whereas the price of a hotel room per night is many times higher than the rent of a comparable flat, this rational price ratio is often upside down in the parking market.

Occasional short-term parking on-street and base-parking off-street – a natural division of the parking market

Optimal on-street parking pricing is a fairly complex matter when it comes to the detailed structure of the charges by time period. A basic feature, all the same, is that the average level of charges should not deviate too much from the value of the land used. If the average level of on-street parking charges is much higher, more curbstone spaces should be provided, and if it is much lower, better use of some of the existing curbstone parking space could probably be found.

Bearing this in mind, the appropriate relative prices of on-street and off-street parking can be considered: normally, on-street parking should be substantially more expensive than off-street parking because

1 the former is provided on a per hour basis, whereas garage space etc. can be rented on a monthly basis; and
2 the cost of the land taken up can be distributed between several floors in the multi-storey parking garages typical of central cities.

With such a price structure, which in fact is reversed in many cities in the world, a rational division of short-term and long-term parking would arise: long-term parkers could simply not afford to park in the streets, where practically only short-term parkers would be found.

8.5 WILL OPTIMAL TRANSPORT INFRASTRUCTURE CHARGES PAY FOR THE FACILITIES?

The normal procedure in price theory when the question of the financial result of optimal pricing is taken up is to explore whether or not economies of scale apply. When both short-run and long-run efficiency conditions are fulfilled, a well-known implication is that the ratio of optimal price to the average total cost equals the inverse of the scale elasticity of the production function concerned. Economies of scale imply a financial deficit and diseconomies of scale a surplus as a result of optimal pricing.

When it comes to optimal pricing of transport infrastructure services, the scale elasticity of the production function plays a similar critical role for the financial result. However, there is an additional condition which tends to make the financial result of optimal pricing much more sensitive to deviations from constant returns to scale. This will be explained in what follows.

Congestion tolls as a contribution to track costs, or 'quasi-rent'

The discussion will be limited to 'congestion tolls' or the equivalent type of charge for regulating capacity utilization. The pricing-relevant cost also includes an item MC^{ext} to account for the significant negative effects external to the traffic: noise, air pollution and certain consequences of traffic accidents are the most important in this category. These components in the optimal price of transport infrastructure services cannot be viewed as contributing to covering the facility capital costs. If charges with a purpose of internalizing the costs of negative externalities such as exhaust fumes were to be earmarked for something, it should be for compensation to those who suffer from the negative externalities.

Even if transport vehicles eventually become silent, clean and safe, the basic reason for charging for their use of roads etc. will remain where and when various pieces of transport infrastructure are scarce resources. So the basic question is whether optimal congestion tolls would pay for the facility concerned. It turns out that the form of organization of transport has an interesting role to play in this connection. A number of cases can be distinguished. The first case below is imaginary but instructive as a starting-point.

Case (a): Fully integrated road transport system

Imagine a road transport concern where the road owner is also the seller of transport services: the unit of output is a standard truckload-kilometre. It can be assumed either that the road owner also owns all the trucks or that he acts as a forwarding agent and just hires truck inputs on behalf of shippers. The objective is assumed to be net social benefit maximization.

In figure 8.4 the average variable cost (AVC) represents the costs of the truck inputs per truckload-kilometre. The fact that the AVC is gradually rising is due to the given capacity of the road network. Since the road owner controls all truck movements, he calculates the short-run marginal cost (SRMC) by taking the derivative of the total truck transport cost function with respect to total output of truckload-kilometres.

There is no allocative need for a separate road track charge: the congestion costs are internal to the transport concern. The difference between SRMC and AVC constitutes the 'contribution margin', C in the diagram of figure 8.4, in the price P for the transport services, i.e. the financial contribution towards covering the track costs. In microeconomics textbooks this is often called 'quasi-rent'.

It should be assumed that operations take place at the 'expansion path': the least-cost solution, including the track costs, is found for each actual level of

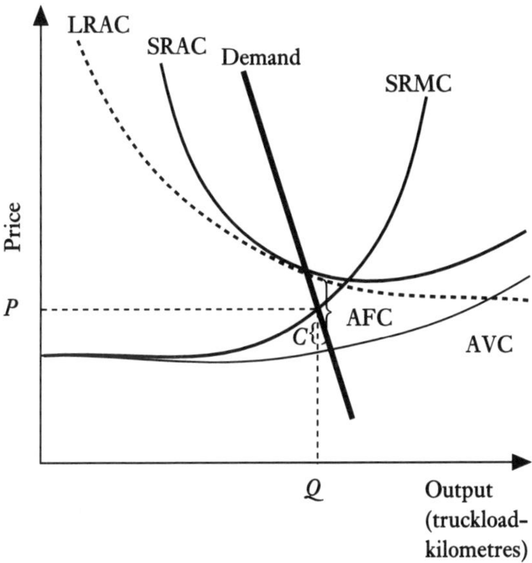

Figure 8.4 Ideal output Q and price P for transport services.

output. It is then helpful to introduce the scale elasticity E of the truck transport production function: $E = 1$ means that constant returns to scale apply, $E < 1$ means decreasing returns to scale apply and $E > 1$ means increasing returns to scale apply. As P is set equal to SRMC the following holds:

$$\frac{1}{E} = \frac{\text{SRMC}}{\text{AVC} + \text{AFC}} \tag{8.12}$$

where AFC stands for the average fixed cost in the short run, which corresponds to the road track cost per truckload-kilometre in the present case. From (8.12) it can be seen that the financial result of the whole concern, measured by the ratio of total revenue to total costs, is equal to the inverse of the scale elasticity E.

This is, of course, elementary and very well know. The question focused on here is how the contribution margin is related to the road track costs under different conditions as to returns to scale. The main point should be intuitively clear, since the contribution margin is a residual by nature: in the first place the short-run variable factors of production are fully remunerated (this cost corresponds to AVC). The contribution to the short-run fixed costs will be what is left of total revenue after that remuneration is paid out.

The ratio of the contribution margin C per unit of output to the track cost is written

$$\frac{C}{\text{AFC}} = \frac{\text{MC} - \text{AVC}}{\text{AFC}} \tag{8.13}$$

Combining equations (8.12) and (8.13) gives the following result:

$$\frac{C}{\text{AFC}} = \frac{[(\text{AVC} - \text{AFC})/E] - \text{AVC}}{\text{AFC}} = \frac{1}{E} + \frac{\text{AVC}}{\text{AFC}}\left(\frac{1}{E} - 1\right) \tag{8.14}$$

When constant returns to scale apply ($E = 1$), the last term on the right-hand side of (8.14) is zero and, as expected, the contribution margin is just sufficient to cover the track costs. When E deviates from unity, the effect on the C/AFC ratio is strengthened by this additional term: when increasing returns apply, the contribution margin falls short of track costs to a larger degree than is indicated by the inverse of E, and conversely when decreasing returns apply the difference between the optimal price and the average truck transport cost will be still higher than is indicated by the inverse value of E.

From the point of view of the whole road transport concern, however, the ratio of the contribution margin to the track cost is just an accounting relationship. The financial result of the concern depends on E, exactly as the textbook has it. In the next, real world, case this will appear to be different.

Case (b): One road owner, many truck transport operators

In reality the road owner has no direct co-ordinating power over truck traffic but has to rely on incentives such as congestion charges. It can still be assumed that AVC of the previous model corresponds to the remuneration per truckload-kilometre to truck owners. The only difference in this case is that what previously could be regarded as a track cost contribution margin in the price of transport services is now an actual road user charge. The financial result for the whole road transport sector will be the same as in the previous case, assuming, of course, that optimal congestion tolls are levied.

In the present case, however, the trucking companies and the road authority make separate financial accounts. The financial result of the road authority corresponds to the accounting ratio of the contribution margin to the track cost in the previous case. The fact that this ratio can take values in a much wider range than follows from 'normal' deviations from unity of E is a matter of some concern.

The cost picture is exactly the same as before except for the following changes in designation:

$$\text{AFC} \Rightarrow \text{AC}^{\text{prod}} = \text{average road service producer cost}$$
$$\text{AVC} \Rightarrow \text{AC}^{\text{user}} = \text{average road user cost}$$

Table 8.4 The financial result for the owner of the transport infrastructure of optimal pricing C/AC^{prod} for different values of the scale elasticity E and the ratio of AC^{user} to AC^{prod}

	Scale elasticity E				
AC^{user}/AC^{prod}	*0.8*	*0.9*	*1*	*1.1*	*1.2*
0	1.25	1.11	1	0.91	0.83
1	1.50	1.22	1	0.83	0.66
2	1.75	1.33	1	0.72	0.49
3	2.00	1.44	1	0.64	0.32
4	2.25	1.55	1	0.55	0.15
5	2.50	1.66	1	0.46	0.00

Expression (8.14) for the ratio of the contribution margin to the fixed capital cost is renamed 'the ratio of the congestion toll to the track cost' and consequently is rewritten as

$$\frac{C}{AC^{prod}} = \frac{1}{E} + \frac{AC^{user}}{AC^{prod}}\left(\frac{1}{E} - 1\right) \tag{8.15}$$

Bad news about the financial result of optimal congestion charges

The first observation is that the ratio AC^{user}/AC^{prod} normally takes relatively high values. In the total costs of a transport system – be it road transport, air transport or sea transport – the transport infrastructure costs are a relatively minor part. In personal transport in particular, AC^{user} is typically many times greater than AC^{prod} because the time and effort of persons are dominant items. This gives the above formula a markedly high-geared character: as soon as E is different from unity, the last term becomes operative, and when AC^{user}/AC^{prod} has a high value the financial result, C/AC^{prod}, will deviate widely from the value of $1/E$. In table 8.4 this is illustrated by some examples where the scale elasticity is varied around unity and where the ratio of user cost to producer cost of transport infrastructure services is increased from 0 to 5.

It is interesting to note, for example, that in interurban and rural road transport the AC^{user}/AC^{prod} ratio is at least 5. The scale elasticity is not constant with respect to traffic volume; in the range 400–40,000 vehicles per day it is about 1.2, on average, according to highway engineering cost studies (Jansson, 1984). This is consistent with practically zero charges in the whole range.

By pointing out the jointness of road capacity and quality (see section 8.3), Walters (1968) argued that roads approximate public goods in a wide initial range of traffic volume. A simpler and more general explanation is apparently to hand, which also expounds the dramatic change in optimal charges from zero to a level of twice the track costs or more. It does not contradict Walters' original idea. However, labour-saving capital investment is not special for road transport. In many industries the larger plants often have a markedly labour-saving potential. The special feature about road transport is that the capital services are disintegrated from the labour and charged for separately.

The problem is that zero charges for public goods, for which excludability is technically possible, are not acceptable for reasons other than allocative efficiency. At the other end of the scale it is easily imagined that road pricing for central-city-bound traffic that brings in revenue that covers radial road investment costs many times over is quite consistent with efficiency conditions. However, now that the technique for charging urban traffic exists, the lasting difficulties of getting acceptance for urban road pricing bear witness to the opposition to the idea that the motorists of a particular city should pay two or three times more than is spent on the roads of the city in the form of congestion tolls on top of the fuel tax.

A similar impasse exists as far as the congestion problems of big city airports (and airways) are concerned: efficient congestion tolls would most probably cover airport costs many times over, but no one seems to have the determination and/or voter support to introduce them.

In previous literature exploring the relationship between short-run and long-run costs of road transport (notably Mohring and Harwitz, 1962; Mohring 1976; Small et al., 1989), the point that has been emphasized is that optimal congestion tolls just cover the total road investment costs in the case of constant returns to scale. This was presented as good news, and it is no doubt a soothing possibility for the conflict averse, but it is representative neither of rural and interurban roads nor of urban roads.

Other modes of transport should also be considered in this connection.

Rail track charges, airport and seaport pricing

Case (c): Fully integrated rail transport system

The railways have until recently been the only mode of transport where the fully integrated form of organization of case (a) exists. It is true that this situation is gradually changing, as has already happened in Sweden and will happen in countries such as Britain and the Netherlands. Leaving these more recent developments out of the discussion for the moment, the ratio of the contribution margin in the fares to the rail track cost obeys the same formula

(8.14) as was deduced earlier. The interpretation of E and AVC respectively, however, is different when a public transport undertaking is the track user. The 'Mohring effect', i.e. that additional passengers lead to positive 'external effects' on the original passengers via a rise in the frequency of service, makes a substantial difference compared with the hypothetical case (a) where full-load transport for hire makes up the system output. It is necessary either to take this effect into account or to extend the system definition to comprise complete door-to-door transport chains. In the latter case the relevant scale elasticity E should be calculated on the basis of a production function in which the trips to and from railway stations and the 'frequency delays' (cf. Panzar, 1979) of train passengers are treated as inputs on a par with rail track and trains. This system extension will tend to make economies of scale (or, better, economies of density of demand) more pronounced. Even more important is that the ratio AVC/AFC will rise very considerably when passenger access and waiting time and effort are included together with the costs of the train operator.

While not going deeper into this matter it is worth discussing some organizational variants of the main case of a fully integrated railway transport system.

Case (d): The Swedish model of one rail track owner and a separate main line train operator

In the present Swedish case where only one train operator (SJ) uses the main rail network, the separate track owner (Banverket) should not charge any congestion tolls because the congestion costs are already internalized in SJ's accounts. SJ can and should keep the quasi-rent for itself. To require SJ to pass it on to Banverket would lead to a misallocation of resources. It would mean that SJ pays for congestion twice, both in the form of delays, which it is entirely aware of, and in the form of rail track charges. This would result in too little congestion in the rail network, so to speak, i.e. too low a rate of capacity utilization.

From the point of view of Banverket, the financial situation looks rather odd. No matter whether constant, decreasing or increasing returns to scale prevail in the railway transport system, SJ should make no contribution to the track costs of Banverket; only traffic-dependent rail track wear and tear should make up the rail track charges. Banverket is and should be a subsidized enterprise. The total corresponding financial burden on the central government would not, of course, become lighter by a merger of Banverket and SJ, i.e. a return to the old form of organization.

Looking at SJ, the corollary may seem to be that the government should require that a substantial profit is made even when the goal is net social benefit maximization, since all the quasi-rent stays with SJ. This is not necessarily the right conclusion in reality, however, *inter alia* because of the Mohring effect.

An additional point is that the financial requirements on SJ should be differentiated. On some lines, where rail track services are next to public goods, a deficit for SJ is consistent with net social benefit maximization. On other lines, the opposite should apply.

Case (e): One transport infrastructure owner and a few transport infrastructure users/transport operators

A basic idea of the Swedish separation of track and trains is that, eventually, competition on the rails should be possible. The road transport system and rail transport system would then be organizationally more or less equal. Congestion charges on trains could be justified provided that there are a fairly large number of independent train operators (on the same line, which seems rather unlikely). The latter will probably argue that they can co-ordinate timetables etc. by negotiation without the stimulus of rail track congestion charges.

That hypothetical situation resembles the present state of affairs of congested airports, where peak-load pricing is long overdue. Airlines naturally view this as just another unwanted cost increase. It may well be true that the allocation of slots between airlines can be managed without resort to the price mechanism. The main economic problem, however, is that airlines individually and/or collectively fail to establish the peak/off-peak differentials in the fare structure which would be forced upon them, as it were, by airport congestion tolls.

In seaports a similar case can be made for congestion or queuing surcharges on cargo and ships. Generally speaking, however, the cost consciousness is not very prominent, either in port pricing or in the elaborate rate-making of liner shipping. The ancient principle of 'charging what the traffic can bear' is still very dominant (see Jansson and Shneerson, 1982, 1987).

8.6 SUMMARY AND CONCLUSIONS

The main economic characteristics of transport systems described at the outset (section 8.1) are that, with the exception of nearly all railways, transport firms do not own the fixed capital used in the production process ('organizational disintegration of the natural production function'). This observation was followed up in sections 8.2 and 8.3 by a definition according to which the total costs to be considered are the cost to the producer of infrastructure services, the cost to users and external costs.

Next, the nature of the user costs and the producer cost were considered in the light of empirical findings. The salient features of the user costs are (i) its strong dependence on the rate of capacity utilization and (ii) the fact that the facility design vector of variables is both a determinant of capacity and a separate argument with marked influence on qualities of service such as free-flow speed, comfort and the risk of accidents.

With common facilities like roads, access is not regulated and congestion may therefore occur. In departmentalized facilities, such as parking facilities, congestion is avoided by definition.

Pronounced small-scale diseconomies in the producer costs are characteristics of all sorts of transport infrastructure – common facilities as well as departmentalized facilities. At the other extreme of density of demand where, in addition, space can be very limited, as in central cities, plant-size economies cease very definitely, with dramatic consequences for optimal pricing.

Each of the three cost items above plays a role in the determination of the optimal price. In the case of road infrastructure the external cost should, generally speaking, be the main item, because the cost of accidents and environmental costs are important both in congested and uncongested conditions.

When asking the question whether optimal road pricing will pay for the roads, however, the focus is on the congestion cost. In section 8.5 the point was made that what is a congestion toll for a seller of road services maximizing net social benefit, is a financial contribution towards the covering of the fixed infrastructure costs for a seller of transport services in a concern where track and transport vehicles have the same owner. In both cases the ratio of the contribution margin to the track cost depends on the economies of scale of transport service production, but not in the same simple fashion as the ratio of price to total average cost does.

Since the ratio of the average cost of transport vehicles (including passenger or freight time costs) to average track cost is normally quite high, deviations from constant returns to scale will have a strongly aggravated effect on the financial result of optimal pricing for the track owner.

REFERENCES

Coase, R.H. (1988) *The Firm, the Market and the Law*. Chicago.

Doganis, R. and Thompson, G.F. (1975) The economics of regional airports. *International Journal of Transport Economics*, 167–78.

Dupuit, J. (1844) On the measurement of the utility of public works. In D. Munby (ed.) (1968), *Transport*, London: Penguin.

Goodwin, P. (1992) A review of new demand elasticities with special reference to short and long run effects of price changes. *Journal of Transport Economics and Policy*, 155–69.

Goodwin, P. and Jones, P. (1989) Road pricing: The political and strategic possibilities. In Round Table 80, *Systems of Road Infrastructure Coverage*, European Conference of Ministers of Transport, Paris: OECD.

Harris, R.G. (1977) Economies of traffic density in the rail freight industry. *Bell Journal of Economics*, 556–64.

Jansson, J.O. (1984) *Transport System Optimization and Pricing*. New York: Wiley.

Jansson, J.O. and Shneerson, D. (1982) *Port Economics*. Cambridge, MA: MIT Press.

—— and —— (1987) *Liner Shipping Economics*. London: Chapman and Hall.

Jansson, J.O., Nemoto, T. and Pettersson, H. (1990) *Road Pricing from Theory to Practice – A Digest of Economic Technical, and Political Considerations of three Decades*. VTI Notat T97.

Jansson, J.O., Andersson, P., Cardebring, P. and Sonesson, T. (1992) *Prissättning och finansiering av järnvägens persontransporttjänster*. TFB and VTI forskning/research 5.

Ministry of Transport (1964) *Road Pricing: The Economic and Technical Possibilities* (Smeed report). London: HMSO.

Mohring, H. (1976) *Transportation Economics*. Cambridge, MA: Ballinger.

Mohring, H. and Harwitz, M. (1962) *Highway Benefits: an Analytical Framework*. Evanston, IL: Transportation Center at the Northwestern University.

OECD (1985) *Co-ordinated Urban Transport Pricing*. Paris: OECD, Road Transport Research.

Oum, T.H., Waters II W.G. and Yong, J.S. (1992) Concepts of price elasticities of transport demand and recent empirical estimates. *Journal of Transport Economics and Policy*, 139–54.

Panzar, J.C. (1979) Equilibrium and welfare in unregulated airline markets. *American Economic Review, Papers and Proceedings*, 92–5.

Saaty, T.L. (1961) *Elements of Queuing Theory*. New York: McGraw-Hill.

Small, K.A., Winston, C. and Evans, C.A. (1989) *Road Work*. Washington, DC: The Brookings Institution.

SOU (1990) *De svenska flygplatserna i framtiden*, Statens Offentliga Utredningar 55. Stockholm: Allmänna Förlaget.

Walters, A.A. (1961) The theory of measurement of marginal private and social costs of highway congestion. *Econometrica*, 676–99.

—— (1968) *The Economics of Road User Charges*. World Bank Staff Occasional Papers No. 5. Washington, DC: International Bank for Reconstruction and Development.

9

Government and Transport Infrastructure – Investment

Jan Owen Jansson

9.1 NON-URBAN TRANSPORT INFRASTRUCTURE INVESTMENT: QUALITY IMPROVEMENT

Introduction

A difference exists in the nature of the problem of investment in transport infrastructure between when a non-urban context is considered and when an urban context is considered. Of particular importance in an urban context is the integration of transport planning and general land-use planning. The difference between the two situations is such as to warrant separate treatment. First, in this section the problems of investment in non-urban – i.e. interurban and rural – infrastructure will be discussed. The next section, section 9.2, will deal with investment in urban infrastructure.

The need for investment in a non-urban transport infrastructure system, which in a static sense is complete, arises in reality for three main reasons:

1 demand is autonomously growing;
2 technical change, e.g. with regard to transport vehicles, takes place;
3 relative values of time, the risk for accidents etc. change.

Figure 9.1 illustrates the principal cause of road investments during the period of motorization, i.e. the steady growth in car traffic (which has largely paralleled the growth in car ownership), which in Europe started about 1950. At the beginning of that period a particular road associated with short-run total average cost $SRAC_1$ was built to accommodate a traffic volume of about Q_1. The

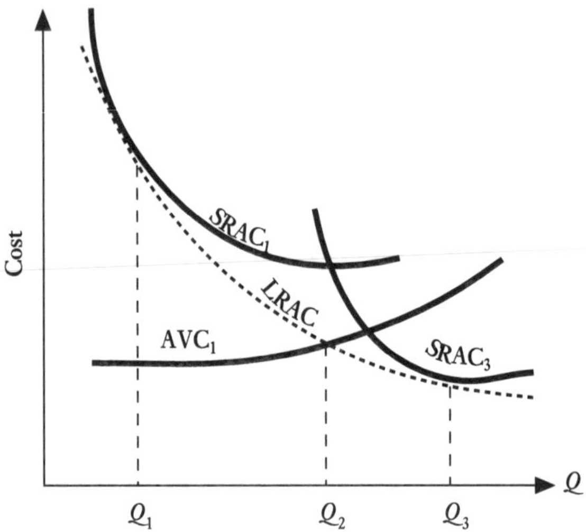

Figure 9.1 Long-run and short-run average costs of road transport.

traffic has been steadily growing and when it reaches the level Q_2 the existing road is no longer the least-cost solution.

The capital invested in the past is a sunk cost, which is why the average variable cost AVC_1 is the relevant cost of the incumbent to be compared with the long-run total average cost LRAC of the least-cost challenger. At Q_2 LRAC equals AVC_1. However, bearing in mind that the traffic volume is likely to continue to grow, a road of a somewhat higher standard, e.g. one associated with $SRAC_3$, will turn out to be a better alternative, seen over the whole economic life of the new investment considered.

In the post-war period non-urban road investments can to a very large extent be characterized as replacements, not necessitated by incumbents being worn out but justified as socially profitable upgradings. Despite the fact that the post-war period has been an unprecedented road building era, the total length of the main road network in a country like Sweden increased by only about 10 per cent in the first 20 years, and since then has not increased at all. It should be remembered, of course, that the replaced roads do not disappear physically, but are classified as no longer belonging to the main road network from when the challengers take over their tasks.

Benefit components

A simplifying assumption widely made in practice is that all traffic growth is autonomous: no new traffic generation on account of new investments is assumed

Table 9.1 Shares of the main benefit components of the planned road investments in the state-owned Swedish road network, period 1991–2000

Time saving	42%
Accident reduction	26%
Vehicle operating cost saving	12%
All other savings	20%
Total	100%

to occur. Looking back at the whole radical improvement of the road network of 1950 which was to a considerable extent unpaved, it is obviously unreasonable to think that this has not induced car traffic. Some of the total traffic growth assumed as exogenous is probably induced traffic. How much it is difficult to say, and it is therefore also difficult to say whether or not this simplifying assumption has caused an appreciable over-estimation of the benefits of road investments.

However this may be, on this assumption the total benefit-side of road investments has a quite similar composition in many countries of the world. Table 9.1 gives the percentages of the main benefit components in the aggregate benefits of all Swedish (non-urban) road investment planned for the 1990s. Road user time savings is the unchallenged, most important component. This is a general feature (see the Leitch report (Department of Transport, 1978) for a retrospective view). A close second is accident cost reduction. The relative importance of this component and the vehicle operating cost savings differs somewhat between countries depending on circumstances such as the value put on risk reduction. In the residual the two biggest items are increased 'comfort' and decreases of 'severance effects'.

For typical railway (track) and airport investments, time savings of passengers are even more dominant on the benefit side. For seaport investments 'vehicle cost savings', i.e. laytime reduction for ships, but also savings due to new possibilities to use bigger ships or ships with special requirements, which could not be accommodated before, are naturally the most important benefits, since freight time cost, although appreciable, is still only a fraction of passenger time cost.

Traffic safety and road building

It is thought provoking that accident reduction is very important for road investments – it is much less so for other modes of transport – in view of the fact that road transport now and in the foreseeable future is very dominant and

Table 9.2 Cost of accidents on different types of non-urban road in France (FFr per car-kilometre)

Two lanes, 6–7 m	0.13
Three lanes, 9 m	0.15
Three lanes, 10.5 m	0.11
Four lanes, 14 m	0.12
2 × 2 lanes, level intersection	0.08
2 × 2 lanes, grade separated intersection	0.04
Motorway	0.03

Source: Méthodes d'évaluation des investissements routiers en rase campagne, *Direction des Routes*, Paris, 1986

has steadily increased its market share in the post-war period. Total road accident costs have not, generally speaking, tended to decrease in recent times. The death toll is also frighteningly large despite the huge sums spent every year on road investments justified to a considerable degree by increased road safety. The total accident costs are likely to increase markedly in the future owing to successive appreciation of values of life and limb; or, put in another way, by an apter philosophy, the benefit of road safety promoting measures is likely to increase because the value attached to accident risk reduction is likely to be raised (Jones-Lee, 1989; Persson and Cedervall, 1991). This tendency will have a strong positive effect on the comparative advantage of road investment, which is somewhat paradoxical: road transport is by far the most dangerous mode of transport, and as this negative side of road transport carries greater and greater weight the road transport system will be built into society even more irreversibly. The basic reason for the apparent paradox is, of course, that the greatest advantage of motorways is the relatively low accident risk associated with them compared with roads of inferior standard (table 9.2).

Modification of single-mode cost–benefit analysis in the case of intermodal competition

Interurban and rural road transport have been almost unchallenged up to now. The rapidly growing air traffic has affected only a relatively small segment of long-distance travel. Railway transport has been stagnant, but with high-speed trains a different development may be ahead of us. In this situation cost–benefit analysis of rather short road links, for which it seems justified to ignore induced traffic benefits, may seem unsatisfactory. For interurban transport, the main issue for the future is the modal split, and total railway investment may be raised to a level comparable with that of road investments; certainly, if rail transport is not going to take substantial portions of the road and air market shares, few of the planned, large railway investments will turn out to be profitable. The principal necessary modifications of traditional road investment cost–benefit analysis are illustrated in figures 9.2 and 9.3.

The example used here refers to a long-distance route between two big cities, Here and There. In the initial situation the total volume of passenger transport is fairly evenly divided between train, car and airline travel. It should be observed first that, since it is just the market for travel between Here and There that is considered, only the total air traffic on the route coincides with the volume of travel illustrated in figures 9.2 and 9.3. Total rail-passenger-kilometres on the route may be twice as high as the volume of rail travel just between Here and There, and total car-kilometres on the route would typically be many times higher than the total car-kilometres of the trips going the whole way. It should be noted that this is one of the great advantages of roads, i.e. their flexibility in being able to serve everything from very short-distance to very long-distance travel demands.

Now consider a railway investment, the effects of which are illustrated in figure 9.2. The investment, undertaken to accommodate the expected increase in rail transport demand, is assumed to include both an upgrading of the rail track and a concomitant improvement in train speed as well as frequency.

It is appropriate to make the traffic benefits calculation in two steps. For the first step, from position 1 to position 2, the generalized costs (GCs) of the alternative modes to the improved mode are assumed to stay constant. A second step is required if this assumption does not hold good, which it does not as a rule when a public transport mode is among the alternatives. The left-hand shift in the airline demand curve is likely, sooner or later, to lead to an increase in GC_{air}. The second step in the traffic benefit calculation takes us from position 2 to position 3, where the repercussions of that increase are accommodated in a final equilibrium.

Step 1 The consumers' surplus A for the train passengers between Here and There is enhanced by the area B when the train fare P_{train} exceeds the pricing-relevant cost P^*_{train}. On the markets for car travel and air travel the respective demand curves shift to the left because of the decrease in GC_{train}. This results in an additional benefit on the former market equal to C, if it can be assumed that the road user charge for cars, P_{car}, is below the pricing-relevant cost P^*_{car}. On the air travel market, on the other hand, it is possible that a disbenefit will have arisen already after the first step, provided that the airline's fare P_{air} exceeds the pricing-relevant cost P^*_{air}.

Step 2 The decrease in demand for air transport leads to fewer flights, which raises GC_{air}. This in turn gives rise to a right-hand shift of the train demand curve. This does not increase the consumers' surplus of train passengers; on the

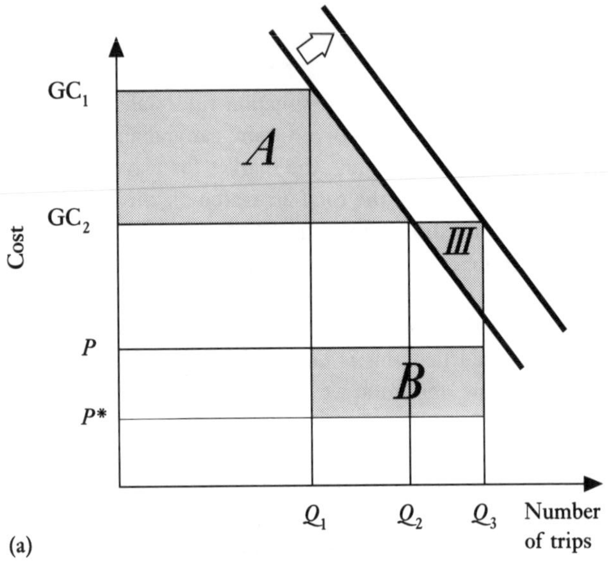
GC1
GC2
Cost
A
III
P
B
P*
Q1
Q2
Q3
Number
of trips
(a)

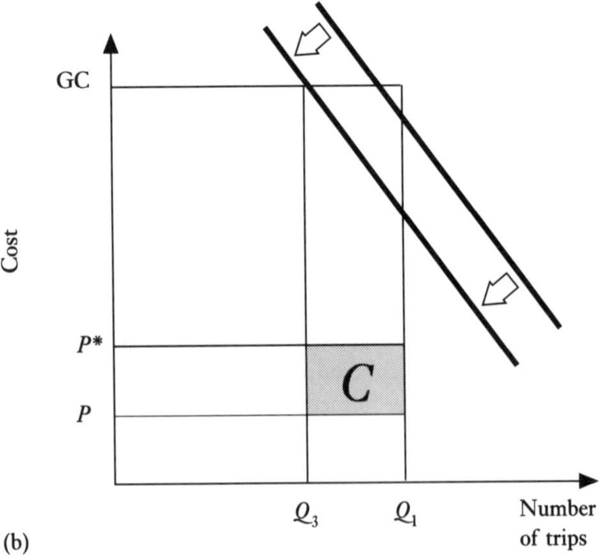
GC
Cost
P*
C
P
Q3
Q1
Number
of trips
(b)

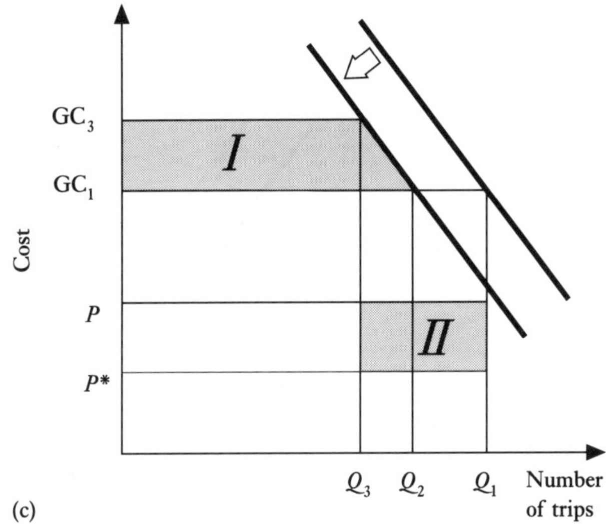

Figure 9.2 Total traffic effects of a railway investment: (a) train; (b) car; (c) airline.

contrary, train travellers gained from the competing airline are worse off in position 3 compared with position 2 by the triangle area III in figure 9.2. With regard to car travel in figure 9.2, the demand shift illustrated represents the sum of the two steps; since it can be assumed that GC_{car} stays constant all the time, a separation of the first and second steps is not necessary. The total benefit for travellers between Here and There of the railway investment considered thus amounts to A+B+C–I–II–III.

When, as shown in figure 9.3, a road investment is considered in the same relation, it is seen that, against the consumers' surplus A' on the market for car travel between Here and There, possibly six disbenefit items arise under the same assumptions as in the previous case. The total sum of benefits for travellers between Here and There is A'–I′–II′–III′–IV′–V′–VI′.

It is now that one should remember that the major part of total road user benefits will fall on car travellers not going the whole way. To get a complete picture of total benefits for all travellers on the route, similar sets of diagrams should be prepared for all the markets for successively shorter travel distances. The air alternative will be absent, as explained before, and the benefits for car trips will be counter-balanced to a successively smaller extent by disbenefit for train travellers, as the market share of road transport is increasing.

The main point, however, is that when private (individual) transport and public (collective) transport are competing, a road investment creates indirect disbenefit because public transport is a pronounced decreasing-cost activity; the

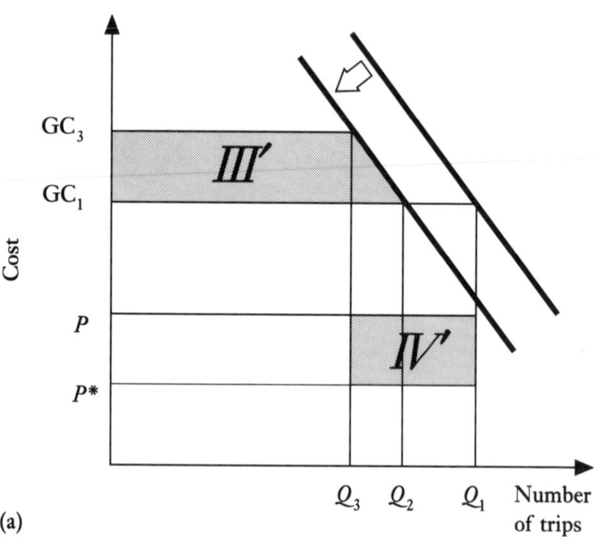

GC$_3$
III′
GC$_1$
Cost
P
IV′
P*
Q$_3$
Q$_2$
Q$_1$
Number of trips

(a)

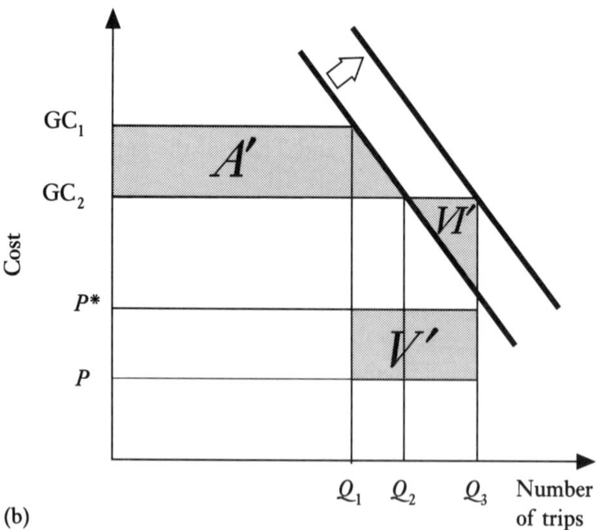

GC$_1$
A′
GC$_2$
VI′
Cost
P*
V′
P
Q$_1$
Q$_2$
Q$_3$
Number of trips

(b)

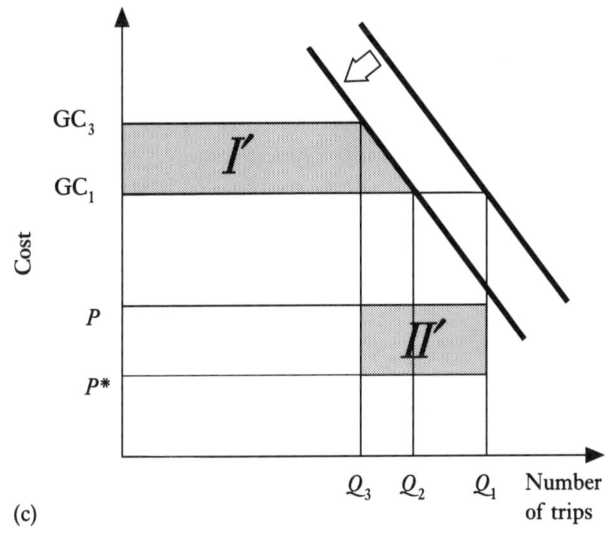

Figure 9.3 Total traffic effects of a road investment: (a) train; (b) car; (c) airline.

most important modification of traditional road investment cost–benefit analysis takes this into account. A secondary point is that the road traffic may include long-distance scheduled coach traffic, for which a 'Mohring effect' (see chapter 8, section 8.5, case (c)) is operative, too.

A final reflection is that to give priority to the fulfilment of a national or international motorway network as a main strategy seems more grand than wise. Interurban, long-distance transport is the natural niche for both the railways and airlines. Therefore, road investments for short- and middle-distance transport, in particular where the density of demand is too low to support good public transport, often show a higher benefit–cost ratio than investing large sums of money in the upgrading of long thoroughfares to motorway standard. But, alas, to an 'empire builder' a lot of smaller road improvements here and there is less appealing than an interregional, let alone international, motorway system.

9.2 URBAN TRANSPORT INVESTMENT: CAPACITY EXPANSION

One problem is to sort out the various benefit and disbenefit items as was done in figures 9.2 and 9.3. Another more demanding task is to make the required calculations. Needless to say, it is the relative magnitude of the items concerned that determines the overall outcome of the cost–benefit analysis of an investment project. The relative size of individual items as drawn in figures 9.2 and 9.3 is, of course, only illustrative. For example, the positions of P and P^* can even be reversed in some cases, which would change benefits to disbenefits. As regards non-urban transport infrastructure investment, it can be argued that in many cases the indirect traffic effects are of secondary importance compared with the direct benefits as calculated by traditional cost–benefit analysis, restricted to a single mode of transport.

This is not true for urban transport infrastructure investment appraisal. The indirect urban traffic effects are all-important in major travel markets. The same kind of diagrams are, in principle, applicable in urban transport systems, too. The situation is complicated by congestion in the system, i.e. by the fact that operations regularly take place at a much higher rate of capacity utilization than in non-urban road networks, which makes cost and output relationships non-linear in the relevant range.

A more fundamental difference concerns the very nature of the investment problem in urban versus non-urban transport infrastructure facilities.

The nature of the problem

While movement of people in rural areas and between urban areas is largely a pure transport problem, urban road building, public transport supply, traffic management, parking regulation etc. is – or should be – an integral part of the superior aim of creating good living and working conditions for people in built-up areas. An urban railway or a road is a 'plant for production of motorized transport of people and goods' just as an airport is a plant for production of aircraft take-offs and touch-downs, and although the land requirement, temporary noise level and hazardous conflicts are apparent in the latter case, the same basic facts hold true: the location, design and degree of capacity utilization of a plant of either kind cannot be determined just on pure transport grounds, i.e. by balancing the capital cost of the piece of transport infrastructure under consideration and the corresponding user costs and benefits in the same way as for non-urban road investments. To be strictly true, the distinction between the urban transport problem and the non-urban transport problem is a matter of degree rather than kind, especially in densely populated countries. The environmental problems of 'motorized transport plants' conflicting with other human pursuits will hardly anywhere completely disappear. It is just that second-order considerations get first-order importance when population density is such that one speaks of a built-up area.

Most city governments seem now to be well aware of the need to integrate transport planning and general land-use planning in a way that takes the strong interdependence between transport and the location of various activities into account, as well as making them co-operate towards the overall goal of improving the quality of life of the citizens. Looking back, however, a fairly general value judgement by transport experts about the urban transport development during the period of motorization in Western Europe is that too much road and parking capacity were offered to motorists in urban areas and that in this process cuts were made in the old city structure which were too deep (see, for example, OECD, 1975).

What could have been done instead? Many critics of our reshaped cities find it difficult to give a consistent answer to this question. It is important to pay due attention to the 'historical' question in view of the fact that the developing countries are now at the beginning of motorization. The situation in many of the rapidly growing great cities in the developing world is alarming. Even though car ownership is many times less than in the developed countries, cities like Mexico City, Caracas, São Paulo, Rio de Janeiro, Buenos Aires, Teheran, Bangkok, Manila etc. are literally coming near to being choked by motor traffic. Also in very poor cities like Calcutta, Bombay, Jakarta, Cairo and Lagos, where car ownership is still only a small fraction of that in Western Europe, chronic traffic congestion rules the streets (see World Bank, 1975, 1986). The general advice that they should not make our mistakes is not very helpful. We must seek to specify more exactly what our mistakes were.

One major unsettled issue of urban transport investment policy which should be a main focus of transport economics is simply: 'can urban road capacity expansion really relieve congested cities, or is that a basically futile pursuit?' There are two variations of this question. In one case, one or more existing roads are the main alternative to the new road considered, and in the other case, public transport is the alternative (see Downs, 1962; Thomson, 1978; Mogridge et al., 1987; Holden, 1989).

The classic two-roads parable

To start with, let us consider the classic two-road case discussed already by Pigou (1924). One road is very wide but lengthy, and the other road, connecting the same two places, is narrow but straight. A car travelling on its own will make the journey in t_0 minutes on the lengthy road and in t_1 minutes on the straight road. However, the total traffic will be divided between the two roads such that the journey time is t_0 on both; congestion will build up on the straight and narrow road to a degree that makes travellers indifferent between the two alternatives. The question now is whether a capacity-expanding investment is called for.

For the sake of argument it will be assumed that the capacity of the lengthy and wide road is very great, and, despite the fact that the traffic flow on the wide road at present is many times greater than the traffic flow on the narrow road, traffic conditions that can be characterized as free flow are ruling on the wide road.

A doubling or trebling of the capacity of the narrow road would still leave a substantial traffic flow on the lengthy road, because the expanded road would be as congested as before, and the travel time would still be t_0 on both roads. Obviously, it would be madness to undertake such an investment. The whole investment cost would be wasted because no benefit whatsoever would come out of it.

This paradoxical result can be further clarified by observing that the generalized cost of one road constitutes the demand curve for the other road. Under the present assumption that the generalized cost of the lengthy road is independent of the traffic volume in the relevant range, the demand for the straight road appears nearly infinitely elastic.

It may be intuitively more acceptable to put the point in this way: capacity expansion to relieve congestion is useless when the demand is very elastic. No relief will be obtained in the end. In the two parts of figure 9.4 this case (b) is contrasted with the opposite extreme case (a) of completely inelastic demand, which is the standard assumption for rural road investments. In case (a) the benefit of a road investment equals the cost savings to the existing traffic, $Q_1(GC_1 - GC_2)$, and in case (b) the benefit is zero.

A final point is that if the straight road was optimally priced, implying that the generalized cost of using it consisted of a time cost and a monetary charge, the situation would be completely different. In that case a capacity-expanding investment might well be worthwhile: the charge would be raised and the time cost reduced as a result of the new investment. The same generalized cost would remain on both roads before and after the investment, but the time costs of those choosing the straight road would be reduced.

Modal-split models for evaluating urban road investments

When the demand for car travel is elastic because of a good public transport alternative, cost–benefit analysis of a road investment is still trickier in the absence of efficient road pricing. This problem is addressed here by a sort of cautionary tale, which has its roots in early work by Mishan (1967) and Thomson (1978). Their contributions seem close to fading into oblivion. This would be unfortunate because, although both Mishan's model and Thomson's model are exceedingly simple, they make some relevant points, and to quote the methodological justification of the classic 'urban transport parables' by Strotz:

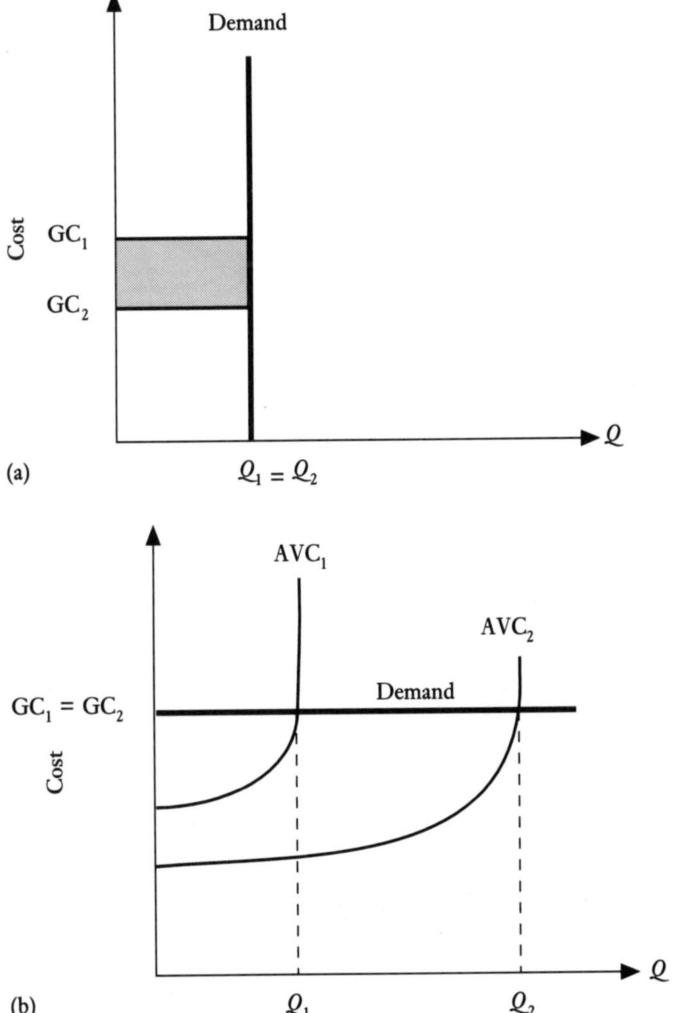

Figure 9.4 Non-urban and urban transport demand and road investment, extreme cases.

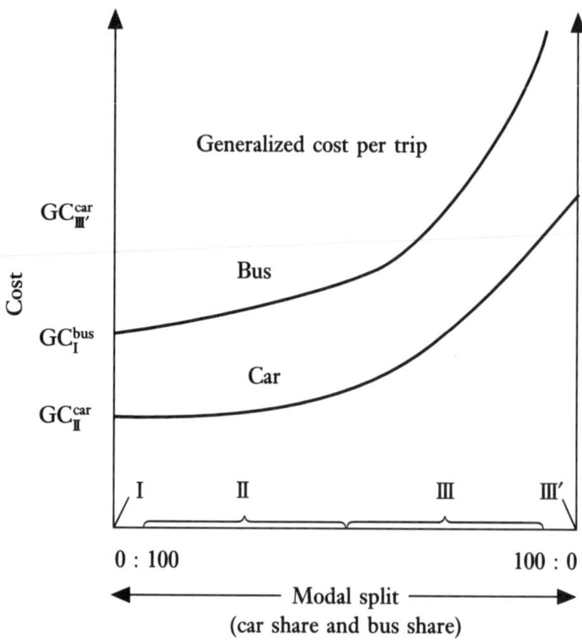

Figure 9.5 Diagrammatic account of Mishan's parable.

> due to the immense complexities of the problem a prescientific approach has to be adopted . . . telling simple little stories, each of which highlights a particular though ubiquitous problem. From each of these we wish to draw a moral, a principle that ought not to be overlooked when a more complex situation is to be faced.
>
> (Strotz, 1965, p. 128)

Mishan's parable: a 'corner equilibrium' model of the travel market

Mishan's parable is an attempt to put the car era in a nutshell as far as urban areas are concerned. A diagrammatic summary of it is as follows (figure 9.5). A given total number of commuters are all travelling by bus to begin with. The generalized cost of bus transport as a function of patronage should be read from right to left. Since it is a decreasing-cost activity in the whole range, the average generalized cost, GC^{bus}_{I}, is at a minimum when all are travelling by bus, i.e. when the story begins. However, anyone who can get hold of a car can improve on this. So in the transitional phase II the first car travellers are incurring the lower generalized cost GC_{II}^{car}. However, the more motorists there are, the higher the generalized cost of car travel will be because of congestion. In the intermediate phase III, car trips are already costlier than the bus trips in phase I. Still, car traffic is on the increase because going by bus is at present a worse alternative. This is the heart of the matter: bus travel will always be at a disadvantage from an individual's point of view because the congestion will have the same adverse effect on buses as on cars. In phase III, the ultimate, logical consequence is that the bus services close down, since everybody is travelling by car. The mean generalized cost, GC_{III}^{car}, is at its highest ever, according to Mishan's basic presumption.

The modal-split equilibrium is continually a corner solution determined by current car availability. This makes Mishan's parable inapplicable to the central city-bound travel market. It applies *inter alia* to suburb-to-suburb routes. On these routes there is no general law saying that the total generalized cost of everybody travelling by private car has to be higher than the total generalized cost of everybody travelling by bus. That depends on a number of circumstances, in the first place on the existing road capacity relative to total travel demand. Mishan's parable, however, was intended 'to reveal some of the circumstances under which consumers' surplus, when used as an index of the benefits to be derived from private automobile travel, may give perverse results . . . leading to over-investment in road construction . . .' (Mishan, 1967, p. 184), rather than to make an empirically based social cost comparison of different modal splits on particular routes. We shall return to Mishan's methodological point after the presentation of Thomson's model, where GC^{car} and GC^{bus} intersect owing to the sharply rising shape of the former in the face of a long-run capacity limit.

Thomson's parable: an 'interior equilibrium' model of the travel market

In his seminal study *Great Cities and Their Traffic* Thomson (1978, p. 279) argued that an increase in road capacity, when existing capacity is less than the potential demand for it, may well lead to a final equilibrium which is worse both for road users and for public transport passengers.

In the illustrative example of figure 9.6 an interior equilibrium is assumed. Two capacity levels for car traffic are considered and the question is: what are the costs and benefits of expanding the car transport capacity from level I to level II?

The basic proposition is that the modal-split equilibrium occurs where the average GC^{bus} and the average GC^{car} intersect. In towns and cities without urban railways it is unlikely that such an equilibrium could ever occur, unless

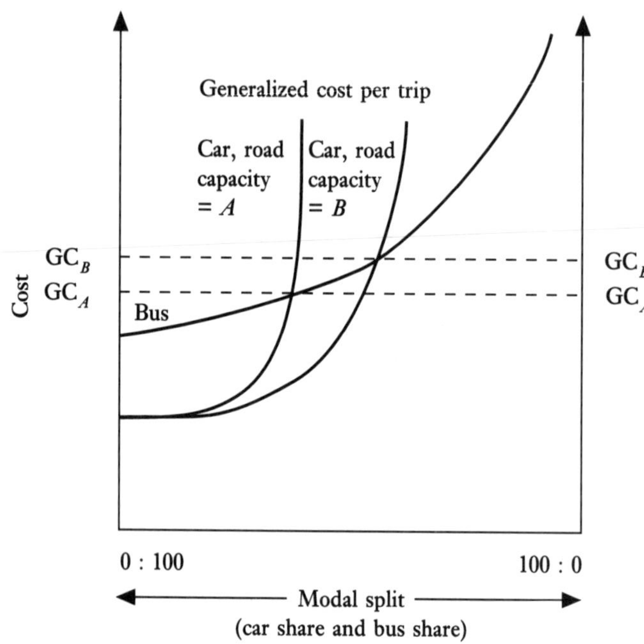

Figure 9.6 Illustrative picture of the effects of radial urban road capacity expansion.

separate bus lanes or busways existed. By the capacity expansion considered, the equilibrium point will move upwards to the right. The result is that, contrary to the intention, the average generalized cost for all trip-makers increases from GC_A to GC_B! This constitutes an equivalent social cost increase, assuming that the fare component of GC^{bus} equals the operator's average cost.

The cost side of the road capacity investment consists of the highly tangible capital costs of the new roads and the less tangible environmental costs. But where are the benefits? The usual case of road investments is that the capital costs are compensated for by savings in road users' running costs. In this case such savings are non-existent or, rather, have turned into additional costs at least in the peak period. Only in off-peak periods is it conceivable that some benefits have been obtained.

The moral of Thomson's cautionary tale is very provocative: no matter how large the pressure of demand for extended radial road capacity is, the right policy is to reduce road capacity and increase public transport capacity.

It is obviously very important to examine whether this basic conclusion is true in a less simplistic model.

Additions for greater realism to Thomson's model

The main limitations of Thomson's parable are its insufficient recognition of (i) the fact that two rather different categories make up total car traffic, i.e. commercial vehicles and private cars, and that commercial and private car drivers have substantially different time values, and (ii) the fact that car trips and public transport trips along a particular route towards the centre have systematically different origins as well as destinations. Therefore it is too strong an assumption to postulate that, in equilibrium, the GCs are typically the same for all. This point has been elaborated in a model presented by Jansson (1987).

Here a brief summary of the model result will be given. For continuity, the basic format of Thomson's parable will be adhered to, i.e. it is assumed that a given number of commuters are choosing between private car and public transport. The commercial traffic is separated and not included in the modal-split determination. The resulting travel time will, of course, also apply to the commercial traffic, but since that traffic demand is assumed to be completely inelastic, the commercial traffic volume will not be affected by changes in travel time.

In figure 9.6, the downward-sloping (from right to left) generalized cost of public transport as a function of market share plays the role of the long-run demand for private car commuting. In Thomson's version this demand curve is 'perverse' because, the higher the generalized cost of car commuting is, the larger the car share will be. By taking into account the fact that a trip between home and work has three main links – one main haul link and two access transport links required to complete the door-to-door transport chain – the demand curve will obtain a more familiar shape. It can still have a rising portion, as the public transport share dwindles down.

A second set of diagrams, given in figure 9.3, can be used to sort out the applicable benefits and disbenefits. Only one mode of public transport is assumed to exist in the market in question, and so figure 9.3(c) is left out of consideration. The total benefits for commuters of a road investment are consequently confined to A'–III′–IV′–V′–VI′. It is quite possible that the four negative items together exceed the only positive item (A'). Mishan's main methodological point is that the consumers' surplus on the market for road services can grossly overestimate the true benefits in the case when a decreasing-cost substitute exists, without the offsetting disbenefits being necessarily greater than the direct benefit. Thomson's extreme case of car commuting time going up as the result of a road investment is especially interesting because, taking commercial traffic into account too, it is obvious that the effects for this road user category, which otherwise would be an appreciable benefit, would be an additional disbenefit in this case.

Table 9.3 Examples of the ratio of true benefits to cost savings for existing traffic of four successive 50 per cent additions to road capacity for city–bound car commuters from a suburb of 1 km^2 at a distance of 10 km from the CBD

Total peak-hour trips by car and public transport	*Car availability rate*		
	0.1	*0.5*	*0.9*
500	−0.27	−0.33	−0.40
	−0.22	−0.30	−0.43
	−0.13	−0.28	−0.55
	−0.01	−0.26	−1.28
1,000	−0.10	−0.14	−0.18
	−0.03	−0.08	−0.15
	0.08	0.00	−0.12
	0.21	0.10	−0.14
5,000	0.14	0.14	0.13
	0.24	0.23	0.22
	0.36	0.35	0.33
	0.50	0.48	0.45
20,000	0.21	0.21	0.21
	0.31	0.31	0.30
	0.43	0.43	0.33
	0.57	0.56	0.56

The results of extensive simulations with a numerical model (Jansson, 1987) indicate that the offsetting indirect traffic disbenefits of urban road investments are very considerable. An example of this is shown in table 9.3, where commuter (dis)benefits are related to the 'cost savings to existing traffic'. As mentioned in the preceding section, the latter is a common proxy for non-urban traffic benefits of road investments (cf. figure 9.4(a)). In non-urban conditions this is supposed to represent a slight under-estimation of the true benefits. The hypothesis here is rather that this is a considerable over-estimation of the true benefits in urban conditions.

The numerical examples presented in table 9.3 take as a starting-point a situation where the road capacity in a particular radial corridor is a fifth of the maximum potential peak-hour car flow. Then successive additions to capacity of 50 per cent are assumed, and the result, expressed as the ratio of the true benefits to the 'cost savings of the original traffic', is calculated in 12 different cases with regard to the number of total peak-hour commuter trips and the car availability rate in the suburb concerned. Negative values of the ratio mean that the true benefits are negative, i.e. are disbenefits in total.

The reason why the ratio of the true benefits to the cost savings of existing traffic is relatively high for populous suburbs generating 5000 or more peak-hour commuter trips is that the level of service of public transport is high, even when only carless persons use it. When the highway capacity is comparatively low compared with the potential demand – just a fifth in the initial situation of the present example – a 50 per cent addition to capacity will not relieve traffic congestion very much: true benefits are in the range of 10–20 per cent of the cost savings to the original traffic. This percentage range will steadily increase as further capacity additions are made. Ultimately it will approach 100 per cent. This may give a false impression of increasing profitability. When the capacity is more than sufficient for the potential demand, the cost savings of the existing traffic due to additional capacity are small.

In conclusion, the 'addition for greater realism' to Thomson's parable has modified, but not basically changed, its moral: when public transport is the main alternative mode of transport, large investments in road capacity can be very unprofitable and bad for both car travellers and public transport users. The right policy direction is likely to be just the opposite, i.e. to expand the capacity of separate track public transport.

This cautionary tale cannot replace a full-fledged cost–benefit system analysis based on extensive origin and destination matrices. However, when working with large and complex urban transport models, there is a risk that one gets lost, or 'does not see the forest for the trees', if a basic strategy is lacking.

Which urban development do you want?

Radial road capacity expansion above ground is out of the question in European cities. If this generalization can be ventured, the next question is: what about ring roads through more or less built-up areas and/or parts of a green belt, with a view to diverting central city through-traffic?

This may seem to be a very worthy purpose also to environmentalists. Two problems which exist are that the ring roads do a lot of harm by their sheer existence both in built-up areas and in recreational areas, and that the through-traffic that can be diverted onto them is rarely large enough to justify their huge investment costs, caused to a considerable degree by an expensive design necessary to minimize the visual intrusion and environmental damage. If they could be combined with central city road pricing, the latter problem would be much less. Such a rational combination remains to be seen in practice. What is more likely to appear, unfortunately, is toll-financed ring roads, in the worst case with free central city entrance.

To be financially viable, and to show a reasonable traffic benefit–road cost ratio, it is often necessary to add substantial newly generated traffic to the diverted traffic. There is typically an appreciable potential for traffic generation

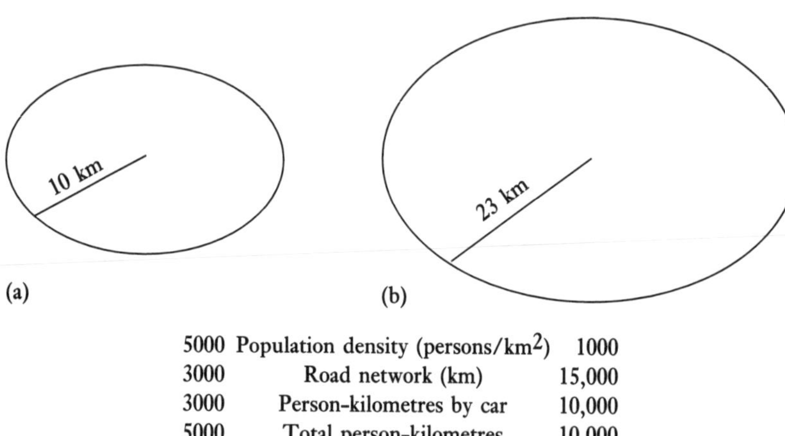

5000	Population density (persons/km^2)	1000
3000	Road network (km)	15,000
3000	Person-kilometres by car	10,000
5000	Total person-kilometres	10,000

Figure 9.7 Salient features of big cities in Europe and the USA, 1980: (a) European 1.5-million city (Copenhagen, Munich, Vienna); (b) American 1.5-million city (Denver, Phoenix).
Source: Newman and Kenworthy, 1989

by ring roads. In the absence of such roads relatively little travel is made between suburbs in different outskirts. After some time of adjustment such travel can grow very substantially, if the generalized cost is radically reduced.

The big question is thus: should we in the name of higher car mobility start to connect distant suburbs of a big city by urban expressways – justified on the political scene by their capability to divert central city through-traffic – which will open up new land where sprawling new developments can find a new outlet? Or should we continue to concentrate new settlements along radial, separate-track public transport lines? Let us make this big issue more concrete with some data from typical large cities in the old and new world, respectively.

West of Mississippi, with the outstanding exception of San Francisco, American cities are rather similar in basic layout and are almost completely car-dependent. If the population is about 1.5 million, as in Denver and Phoenix, the figures in figure 9.7 are typical: the built-up area is about 1500 km^2 and the population density is consequently 1000 persons per square kilometre. The total length of the roads in the urban area is 15,000 km. People travel some 10,000 km annually per person almost exclusively by car (this figure seems to have gone up by at least 25 per cent from 1980 to 1990 according to the *Nationwide Personal Transportation Study* (NPTS) of 1990).

Traditional European cities of the same size in terms of population have quite a different layout. The population density in Copenhagen, Munich and Vienna, which represent the data to the left in figure 9.7, is five times higher than in Denver and Phoenix. Total road-kilometres, on the other hand, are only a fifth. The average mobility in the big European cities is, as seen, about half of that in the wholly car-dependent cities of the American West.

Characteristic of the car-cities in the new world is that, apart from a few skyscrapers constituting the central business district, a central city of European type is difficult to identify. Car mobility is almost the same in every direction, wherever you are. A main advantage of this could be that all the jobs in the city are accessible to everybody who has a car at his or her disposal. The conditions for matching supply and demand on the labour market should be very good.

Taking a long view, however, a note of caution is required: the car-city tends to grow much faster by area than by population, which tends to make the general mobility somewhat illusory. In the American cities west of Mississippi one travels twice as many kilometres per day as in typical European cities of comparable population. The question is whether Americans reach a greater number of important destinations than Europeans.

It should be added that, although the approximation to zero of the public transport share in the above-mentioned typical cities of the American West is not too far from the truth, New York and a number of other cities in the north-east have well-developed public transport systems. In the aggregate, however, the role of public transport appears minor compared with Europe. According to NPTS 1990 the share of bus and railways in total personal travel is only 2.3 per cent in the USA.

9.3 CONCLUDING REMARKS

Cost–benefit analysis has proven its potential for investment appraisal so far as rural and interurban transport infrastructure is concerned. There are still problems to be solved concerning values of time (and frequency of public transport services), accident costs, noise and visual intrusion, but the systematic structure for the relevant information provided and the discipline of thought required by cost–benefit analysis are indispensable for rational decision making.

It is then a little hard to concede that in urban transport cost–benefit analysis is insufficient as the basis for strategic choices. Transport system design and city shape are too mutually dependent. It must be through the political process that citizens decide in which type of city they would like to live and work – e.g. a dense city where public transport can meet a lot of the medium- to long-distance travel demand, and where it is safe, convenient and pleasant to carry out short-distance travel by foot or bicycle, or a sprawling urban area which is increasingly losing its traditional city character but where gardens of suburban single-family houses are relatively large and the private car has an unbeatable comparative advantage.

Economic analysis has an important role in furthering the understanding of the dynamics of city evolution in general, and, in particular, to settle the issue of whether it makes sense or is nonsense to 'build roads to get rid of traffic'. In particular instances it can be correct to claim that, by building a certain bypass, traffic in the town or village passed by will decrease, but it is too opportune and intellectually unacceptable to hold up traffic diversion, if not outright total traffic reduction, as the guiding-star for road investment policy as is often done nowadays, just because 'environment' is the password of the day, and carry on more or less as before.

Looking back at the post-war history of cities, there are some clear-cut cases where every major road investment was meant to divert traffic from densely populated built-up areas. The ring roads have been located successively further away from the city centre, and the end result is that there is today as much or typically more traffic in practically every place in the city.

A reinforcing factor in this process was parking policy, which also aimed at getting rid of cars in the street. Town and traffic planners thought that it was necessary to provide low-priced or free off-street parking facilities and/or force developers and property owners to do the same at their premises.

A great challenge for the future is still to demonstrate, first in theory and then in practice, how the fine slogan 'better towns with less traffic' (OECD, 1975) can be realized.

REFERENCES

Department of Transport (1978) *Report of the Advisory Committee on Trunk Road Assessment* (Leitch report). London: HMSO.

Downs, A. (1962) The law of peak-hour expressway congestion. *Traffic Quarterly*, 393–409.

Holden, D. (1989) Wardrop's third principle, urban traffic congestion and traffic policy. *Journal of Transport Economics and Policy*, 239–62.

Jansson, J.O. (1987) *Investment Policy in Highways for Central-city-bound Travel.* VTI working paper, Linköping.

Jones-Lee, M.W. (1989) *The Economics of Safety and Physical Risk*. Oxford: Blackwell.

Mishan, E. (1967) Interpretation of the benefits of private transport. *Journal of Transport Economics and Policy*, 184–9.

Mogridge, M.J.H., Holden, D., Bird, J. and Terzis, G.C. (1987) The Downs/Thomson paradox and the transportation planning process. *International Journal of Transport Economics*, 284–311.

Newman, P. and Kenworthy, J. (1989) *Cities and Automobile Dependence. An International Sourcebook*. Aldershot: Avebury Gower.

OECD (1975) *Better Towns with Less Traffic*. Conference Proceedings, 14th–16th April, Paris.

Persson, U. and Cedervall, M. (1991) *The Value of Risk Reduction: Results of a Swedish Sample Survey*. The Swedish Institute for Health Economics.

Pigou, A.C. (1924) *The Economics of Welfare*. 2nd edn. London: Macmillan.
Strotz, R.H. (1965) Urban transportation parables. In J. Margolis (ed.), *The Public Economy of Urban Communities Resources for the Future*. Washington, DC.
Thomson, J.M. (1978) *Great Cities and their Traffic*. Harmondsworth: Penguin.
US Department of Transportation; Federal Highway Administration (1991) *Nationwide Personal Transportation Study: Early Results*. Washington, DC.
World Bank (1975) *Urban Transport*. Sector Policy Paper, Washington, DC.
——(1986) *Urban Transport*. A World Bank Policy Study.

10

Transport Policy in an International Setting

K.M. Gwilliam

10.1 INTRODUCTION

The previous three chapters have presented an analysis of the role of government with regard to the transport sector. In this, more or less implicitly, mostly a national background has been assumed. In the present chapter a further dimension will be added to the discussion of transport policy, namely that transport policy is often developed also in an international setting.

In this section some general notions that are instrumental for treating the problem of transport policy in an international setting will be introduced. Section 10.2 examines which elements make a transport policy issue one of international concern. The following step is an analysis of the areas of specific interest in international transport policy (section 10.3). From this analysis a number of conclusions are drawn concerning the feasibility of an international transport regime (section 10.4). Section 10.5, finally, summarizes the main ideas developed in this chapter.

Transport policy issues may be classified in a number of ways according to

1 jurisdiction
2 agency
3 objective
4 instrument

The dimensions are not independent. The nature of the jurisdiction certainly will determine the objectives. The objectives affect the choice of agency and instrument and so on.

Jurisdiction

Transport policy may be formulated and pursued at different levels, namely:

1 local
2 regional
3 national
4 supranational
5 multinational

In principle at least, policy at the various levels should be conceptually and practically consistent. In the construction of such an interdependent system the crucial issue is then where sovereignty is vested. Historically, in the nation-state this has been at the national level, with regional and local authority delegated from the nation-state and international or multinational policy-making being subject to ratification at the national level. Within federal systems sovereignty may be divided between spatial levels according to some pre-ordained, written, constitution. Amongst the problems which are currently facing the international community in Europe is the extent to which federalism – involving some formal abrogation of the traditional powers of the national governments – is to be accepted.

Objectives

As has been mentioned in chapter 7 the objectives of transport sector policy may be very diverse. They include the following.

1 *Transport sector efficiency* may be seen as consisting of a combination of the efficient operation of each individual mode and the most efficient combination of modes.
2 *Environmental protection* is a more recent and more contingent objective. In this respect the objective is to limit the damage caused by transport to the environment. This can be done by technical regulation of the individual modes, by fiscal inducements to the adoption of clean technology or by administrative measures to control the choice of mode.
3 *Safety and security of employees, passengers and third parties* is of concern in most countries. In the international field the question of security against acts of terrorism is an increasing problem for governments and operators alike.
4 *National development* may be seen in a number of ways. The instruments of national transport policy may be used to give advantage to national over foreign transport firms in home or foreign markets; to give advantage to

national suppliers of transport equipment; to advantage national consumers of goods or transport services; or to give advantage to suppliers of national over foreign goods in home or international markets. Efficiency of the transport sector will obviously contribute to national development, but there is also a fairly common belief, without obvious economic foundation, that low-price transport (irrespective of cost) is a stimulus to development.

5 *Regional structuring and development* may be sought through policies on infrastructure investment and on service pricing. For example, traditionally rail freight price structures in Italy were designed to support the industrial development of the Mezzogiorno.

6 *Distribution of welfare* also has a number of dimensions. Traditionally, transport policy has been openly used to redistribute income in the direction of the poorer groups (e.g. through public transport subsidies), of particular locations (through regional discrimination in service or subsidy provision) or of particular disadvantaged sub-groups (i.e. the handicapped or the aged). In a more discreet way it has been used to redistribute income in the direction of groups with political power (e.g. public transport labour unions).

These objectives fall into two groups. The first three are concerned more directly with the working of the transport sector itself. The latter three see transport policy as an instrument for the achievement of objectives outside the transport sector. That distinction coincides closely with what we later term the distinction between the 'compatible' and 'competing' objectives.

Instruments

The major instruments of a transport policy for a government are as follows.

1 *Direct execution by government.* In most countries government has taken responsibility for the provision of the major transport infrastructure. In some countries certain aspects of transport operations are also retained as direct activities of government or its chosen agencies (see below).

2 *Regulation of commercial organizations.* This is in order to secure those aspects of public policy which will not automatically be assured by a free market pursued through a specific set of regulatory institutions. Entry and prices in the public road passenger transport sector have traditionally been handled in this way.

3 *Fiscal measures.* These have been commonly used by governments for both efficiency and equity reasons. They might take the form of subsidy for public transport or fuel and other forms of specific taxation on users of publicly provided infrastructure.

4 *Industrial self-regulation.* This may include codes of conduct and financial guarantees of security of contract which are implemented by trade associations in the travel agency and tourism business in many countries, with government approval. Similarly, slot allocation at airports (i.e. the distribution among airlines of times of arrival and of departure of their airplanes) is in a number of countries left in the hands of a committee of air transport operators. The danger that self-regulation turns into protection of the existing operators against new entrants makes this a very suspect form of policy instrument.

Agency

The necessary actions to implement a transport policy may be taken by different agencies. The main possibilities appear to be as follows.

1 Government departments normally administer fiscal policies and in some cases infrastructure provision is also maintained as a direct executive action.
2 Quasi independent agencies may be created for indirect execution of government policy. In many countries licensing is undertaken by a commission which must operate within guidelines given by government, but with considerable discretion to interpret generally set objectives. The merit of this kind of agency is that it has at least an apparent independence from short-term political pressure. Within the limits set by regulation the private sector is then able to make its initiatives.
3 Government-owned companies may be established with some degree of freedom of commercial operation, but with politically determined objectives and financial constraints. National ownership has been the rule for railway systems in most countries, and also applies in some cases to air transport and bus transport companies.
4 Trade associations may be involved in self-regulation with government approval.

Packages

These jurisdictions, objectives, instruments and agencies can be combined into a wide range of packages. There would seem, however, to be two major categories into which they fall, namely (i) 'plan'-oriented arrangements and (ii) 'market'-oriented packages.

The essence of the 'planning' approach is that targets are predetermined for some major outputs, and the instruments are put together in ways which are designed to secure those objectives. That does not necessarily imply the existence of a command economy. For example, Dutch transport policy is set out in a national transport plan which sets explicit priorities (e.g. for freight over passenger movement on the roads) and targets (e.g. maximum delays in traffic congestion). The difficulty of the planning approach within a democratic system is that the plans may only be achievable by actions which do not secure approval when subjected piecemeal to the democratic process. The contrary difficulty within the command economy is the lack of inducements within the system and the lack of flexibility when the targets are not being achieved.

The essence of the 'market' approach is that it does not define, *ex ante*, the outcomes, but concentrates instead on determining the context in which the market is to be allowed to produce an outcome. That does not necessarily imply a complete lack of regulation or of social (i.e. non-commercial) objectives. What it does do, however, is concentrate on obtaining a 'level playing field' within which market operators can perform. The market approach may be consistent with the existence of statutory monopolies and direct subsidy of socially desirable services.

The categories are thus not clearly separated. Countries such as the Netherlands, which defines its transport sector objectives in terms of specific performance targets of a national transport plan, are in some sub-sectors very liberal (e.g. in the road freight sector). The most market-oriented economies, such as the USA, intervene extensively where this seems appropriate (e.g. in protecting its national maritime fleet).

The consequence of the differences that have been described in the objectives of national policy and the basic philosophies in which those policies are founded means that individual countries will adopt different agencies and different balances between policy instruments. For example, the more planning-oriented a country is, the more likely it is to use direct executive action in the implementation of its transport policies. Moreover, the same type of instrument may be used in quite different ways. For example, within 'planning-based' approaches fiscal instruments are more likely to be used primarily to generate income to finance transport activities rather than to act as instruments of market harmonization.

The corollary of this is that harmonization across nations of one element of the package (e.g. access to markets) may imbalance the whole package. For example, recent German transport policy has combined tight entry and price control in the long-distance road haulage industry with heavy subsidy in rail transport. Free entry into the road haulage industry, without adjustment of the other instruments in the package, would clearly instigate modal shifts contrary to (at least the traditional) policy objectives. Replacement of a nationally oriented policy regime by an internationally oriented transport policy regime is thus fraught with difficulty, and cannot be achieved simply by approximation of the individual instruments unless they have a similar function within each national package. It is to the international dimension of policy that we now turn.

10.2 THE INTERNATIONAL DIMENSION

In the context of current policy discussions within the European Community it is of considerable importance to identify first what the elements are which make a transport policy issue one of international concern. As one might expect, any of the national objectives of transport policy discussed above which is affected by international transport movements, or any other international effect transmission mechanism, is of international policy interest. This thus includes

1 efficient international movement
2 safety and security
3 the international environment
4 indirect effects on national industry

The combination of independent national policies, impacting only on transport within the boundaries of the state, will be sub-optimal for a number of reasons.

Ignorance

In some cases the problem is merely that of ignorance. For example, while the local environmental impacts of transport are very apparent and are bringing forth local solutions, there still remains very sketchy appreciation of the full nature of the continental and global environmental impacts of transport, with the result that they tend to be ignored in the formulation of policy with regard to international transport.

Lack of jurisdiction or leverage

The obvious problem here concerns behaviour in international waters or air space over which no individual nation has control. But it may also be the case that some aspects of international vehicle movements within a state are very difficult or expensive to control. For example, it would be enormously expensive and damaging to subject all vehicles crossing international boundaries to the checks on condition of operation which are enforced on a periodic basis on nationally operating vehicles. An internationally enforced control is obviously more efficient in this respect.

Beggar my neighbour policies and the prisoners' dilemma

The global environment problem is now widely recognized as a case of the prisoners' dilemma. If all nations pollute all suffer. If none pollute none suffer. If most do not pollute then those who continue to do so reap the benefits without any cost. If that is seen to be so, and no one nation is a dominant source of pollution, then all see the advantages of being a 'free rider' on the altruism of others and everyone pollutes. Moving from that recognition to some effective form of international compact does remain difficult, however. The same may also be argued in respect of trading policies. If one country can have free movement outside its boundaries but can control the ability of foreigners to move within its boundaries, it can secure differential advantage at the expense of its neighbours. This is exemplified by the pricing policies in some nation-states.

Lack of international compensation trade-offs

A rather special form of 'beggar my neighbour' problem relates to transit countries such as Austria, Switzerland or the states of the former Yugoslavia. In these cases transit traffic was imposing both economic and financial costs through the use of the road infrastructure of the country. Where that infrastructure is tax rather than toll financed, and particularly where there is no attempt to internalize the external costs of environmental damage, the only recourse that the transit country has is to restrict traffic, as in the case of Switzerland. This diverts traffic to neighbouring routes (Austria and France) and encourages the development of countervailing policies there also. In this way bad policies may drive out good. At the heart of this problem is the absence of any mechanism to ensure international compensation. The solution, territoriality of charging systems for infrastructure use (see chapter 7, section 7.5), is of even wider significance, however, as it allows a degree of freedom for countries to make their own evaluations of costs, without recourse to such discriminatory instruments as to invite retaliation.

Institutions and instruments of international policy

The range of instruments of international transport policy is rather different from that of national transport policy.

Industrial self-regulation agreements

In many cases, where there is a common interest in standardization of technology or operational procedures between countries, those agreements are reached through single-mode multinational negotiations. On technological matters, and even in some cases on commercial matters, the supplying organizations are directly involved, and agreements are subsequently ratified by governments. The International Air Transport Association (IATA) in respect of air fare agreements and the International Railway Union or Union Internationale des

Chemins de Fer (UIC) in respect of railway operational agreements are examples of international industrial self-regulation. This approach works best when there is either a statutory monopoly or restricted entry into the industry so that there is little internal conflict of interest within the industry. It tends to break down (e.g. IATA) when a more liberal commercial regime prevails.

Government Bilateralism

Where there is mutual interest between states and only two are concerned, issues may be determined by bilateral agreements enforced through the relevant national procedures in each state. It is particularly relevant for sectors which are fragmented in supply, or where there are perceived to be national interests at stake which go wider than those of the national transport industry interests. This has traditionally been the way of resolving issues of landing rights in civil aviation and of international road freight movements. It becomes a very time consuming and complicated basis for international movements when, as in the case of European road freight, there are many countries of transit, for each of which an authorization is required.

Non-sovereign multilateralism

An extension of government bilateralism is multilateral intergovernment agreement in which all of the governments concerned undertake to ratify the agreements reached. The presumption is that each government involved in such negotiations is ensuring that it only makes agreements which are in its national interest. These would include such United Nations sponsored organizations as the International Maritime Organization (IMO), the United Nations Conference on Trade and Development (UNCTAD) etc. That self-interest can of course be tinged with some altruism, as in the case of the liner conference agreement of UNCTAD V.

Partial abrogation of sovereignty

Occasionally there arise areas of international policy concern in which nations voluntarily abrogate their separate national sovereignty by treaty. One of the longest lasting of such abrogations has been the acceptance of a free market on the Rhine navigation, established by the Treaty of Mannheim (1868) and overseen by the Central Council for Navigation on the Rhine. One of the interesting features of such abrogation is that it tends to be based on, and incorporates, a central principle (such as free access). In that sense it tends to be associated with 'market' rather than 'planning' philosophy. The consequences of such a partial application of free market principles may be seriously distorting, however, if the free access is not associated with any appropriate rules or institutions for the imposition of efficient charges.

The international transport regime

The difficulty with all of the forms of international transport policy-making which we have discussed so far is that they are limited either in spatial or industrial coverage and can only include specific measures which are consistent in each detail with the separate national interests of the parties.

The ultimate step in multilateralism is the transfer of powers from the governments to an international organization, such as the European Community. In this case the community itself has powers to make legislation which will, in the specified areas, be binding as law in all of the member states of the organization. *Prima facie*, the adoption of this approach totally changes the nature of international transport policy-making from being a set of *ad hoc* agreements to being, at least in principle, a complete and consistent policy package.

10.3 THE INTERNATIONAL POLICY ISSUES

In the establishment of such an international (or supranational) regime there appear to be a number of critical questions which need to be addressed.

First there is the question of the location of responsibility. Within federal regimes the allocation of tasks and functions between the federal and the state level is an important constitutional issue. The outcome will be determined by a range of considerations such as the historic relationships between the parties, the extent to which there are generally conflicting interests involved etc. Increasingly, however, the principle of 'subsidiarity' is adopted. This principle says that a function should be performed at the lowest level within a hierarchy of governmental organizations at which it can be effectively undertaken. A converse statement, which is logically consistent but has a quite different spirit, is that functions which cannot be performed effectively at lower levels in the organizational hierarchy should be performed at the federal level.

Second, implementation responsibility is of great importance. The most elegant logical policy construct is useless if there is no effective way of implementing it. This can be difficult in the context of an international transport policy regime if all of the administrative instruments are national or local. It is particularly difficult if the local administrative agencies have no real commitment to the international objectives. For example, the adoption by the European Community of a regime of price control on international road haulage was almost totally ineffective because of the absence of any effective means of implementing it. That lack of leverage arose both because there were too many points at which it had to be administered for it to be effective in such a fragmented sector as road haulage and because some countries had little interest in administering the regulation.

Third, it follows from our observations on implementation that some instruments are more appropriate for international policy than others. The criteria for appropriateness would seem to be as follows:

1 the number of points of application must be limited;
2 the administrative requirements must be simple;
3 the national administrations must be committed to effective implementation;
4 there must be some pressure for self-enforcement.

The implication of this set of criteria seems to be that the greater the extent to which the policy impacts on governments, and requires actions of them, and the less it requires detailed administrative intervention in operations, the more successful it is likely to be.

Finally there is the question of the policy philosophy. We distinguished earlier between what we called 'planning-oriented' and 'market-oriented' approaches. To some extent the choice will depend on the prevalent political philosophy of the federation. For example, it is not surprising that the transport policies adopted within COMECON were essentially of the planning school, with administrative direction of traffic to the rail and waterway modes. The control of international trade by state trading organizations also made it possible to discriminate in favour of home fleets in international trade. But there was also another important contributor to that outcome, namely the dominance of a single power within the federation. In cases where the balance of power is much more even, or diffused, it seems more difficult to reach agreement on the predetermined outcomes necessary for the planning approach as the basis for international policy. Hence we would argue that the selection of an international transport policy philosophy is not simply a reflection of the prevailing general political philosophy, but does have some internal dynamics of its own.

'Compatible' and 'competing' objectives

From an international policy perspective the national policy objectives appear to fall into two main categories.

First, there are those dimensions where all nations would appear *prima facie* to have a common interest, and where the nature of the international transport regime will be more positively directed to finding arrangements which are in the common interests. We call these the 'compatible' objectives.

Second, there are those dimensions where the separate national interests are competitive with each other. National economic development (and particularly the protection of domestic industry), spatial restructuring of activity patterns and to a lesser extent welfare distribution between income groups are all areas in which the interests of different countries do not naturally coincide. The nature of an agreed international transport policy in these areas is thus likely to be of a negative kind, seeking to ensure that individual nations do not manipulate the international transport arrangements to their partial, rather than to the global, benefit. We call these the 'competing' objectives.

The categories are not, of course, wholly independent. Standardization of certain technical aspects of vehicles engaged in international traffic may be a common interest while the selection of the particular standard to be adopted might well be motivated by the desire to advantage, or at least not to disadvantage, national equipment suppliers in the international market.

In what follows the policy objectives as distinguished in section 10.1 will be looked at from the angle of the making of international transport policy.

Transport sector efficiency

The primary requirement is of course an efficient system of international movement, in so far as there are substantial economies of scale of scope that may imply operations organized and managed on an international scale. In the past that has tended to be limited by the desire of national governments to control their own international transport capacity for military and economic strategy reasons. In shipping, the flagging out of vessels undermined this to such an extent that some countries have taken steps to maintain the fleet under the national flag (e.g. the protection of US coastal shipping for the national flag). In air transport, control over landing rights has enabled governments to protect a share of the market for national carriers, and has therefore preserved a strong sense of nationality in the structure of the industry. However, increasing liberalization both on the North Atlantic and in Europe is now leading to the formation of genuinely international companies (e.g. the move of both European and US airlines to find transatlantic partners). In rail transport the use of railways as instruments of national economic policy, and the relatively small proportion of international traffic for most national rail companies even in Europe, has kept the business essentially national, with international arrangements being predominantly in rather loose intercompany agreements. Many commentators have argued that the development of an efficient international rail service in Europe is seriously handicapped by that structure.

Efficient international movement also implies that there should be no greater or different impediments to movement on an international scale than would exist in respect of national transport. That implies the elimination of costs or delays associated with national borders. It does not, however, imply that there should never exist any congestion – as suggested to the European Community by the Group Transport 2000 Plus (1990). Whether a completely uncongested system is economically efficient depends on the balance between the benefits of cost reduction and the costs of the investment necessary to achieve it. In some circumstances, e.g. in major urban areas, it is almost certainly the case that the total elimination of congestion would be economically very inefficient. The same may be true of other pinchpoints in transport networks (e.g. major water crossings), where the costs of expansion of capacity to eliminate any delay are particularly high.

For air and sea transport the possession of an efficient infrastructure for international movement has usually appeared to be in the national interest. No special international concern therefore arises in securing it. In road and rail infrastructure the situation appears to be somewhat different. Because the majority of traffic on road and rail networks is national the emphasis in investment tends to reflect the essentially national traffic flows. Countries only concentrate on their international links when they consider it to be in their immediate self-interest to do so (e.g. the priority given to links to the ports in UK road programmes of the 1970s). In the European Community context this has given rise to considerable concern about the quality of land transport infrastructure on the main international links.

The current moves to increase the efficiency of the international transport system are thus heavily concentrated on a market-oriented approach. The same is not always true of the other objectives, as we shall now show.

Environment

The impact of transport on the environment is a matter of increasing national and international concern. Chapter 5 (section 5.3) has already given data on the effects of transport on the environment. For the purpose of analysing international transport policy those impacts can be classified as falling into a number of categories.

1 Global atmospheric change is caused by the greenhouse gases (CO_2, tropospheric NO_x etc.) and by those which deplete stratospheric oxone (CFCs).
2 Air pollution is caused by those emissions which have obvious impacts on the quality of life in the short or medium term. It includes some very local human irritants (CO, particulates etc.) and some which are more widely and less immediately felt (ecological effects of acidification due to NO_x, SO_2 etc.).
3 Noise is also a very immediate and local effect.
4 Urban life quality may be adversely affected by other, less measurable impacts of traffic and transport, such as fear for personal safety, visual intrusion, severance of activity patterns etc.

Transport is recognized as a significant contributor to environmental degradation. It appears to be responsible for about 25 per cent of the greenhouse gas emissions and over half of the acidifying NO_x emissions and is the primary source of noise nuisance in urban areas.

Such impacts are of more than national concern because they are transferred internationally in two distinct ways:

1 by international movement of transport vehicles, the impacts of road vehicles, ships and aircraft all being significant;
2 by the international flows of pollutants in the atmosphere; this particularly relates to the transport contribution to acidification which impacts on a continental scale and to climatic change and ozone depletion which operate on a global scale.

In principle, therefore, there should be common interests in environmental objectives.

In the air transport industry the possibility of enforcement of high standards by one country, together with the high degree of collaboration that exists from mutual self-interest in the safety and security field, has facilitated the rapid introduction of best practice technology. Rail transport is less polluting, and the environmental impacts do not appear to have been an issue at the international level. Shipping is a particular problem because of the lack of effective leverage in international waters. But port state controls are increasingly being used as in air transport to force standards of internationally active vessels towards those required by the more environmentally progressive countries. The main polluting mode, however, is road transport. Within the European Community the development of supranational standards for fuel composition, vehicle gas emission and noise levels is now progressing rapidly. Transport policy with respect to environmental objectives may now be characterized as in Table 10.1.

Safety and security

By safety we mean immunity to hazard emerging from unintended accident, whilst by security we mean immunity from conscious aggressive acts. There is an almost global consensus that both of these forms of protection can only be achieved by public actions. In so far as some of the hazards arise outside national jurisdictions (e.g. piracy or pollution in international waters) or arise in states who do not directly control the agents causing them (vehicle condition regulation), it is also generally agreed that they are a matter for international as well as national policy.

Security measures at national boundaries slow down international movements

Table 10.1 Environment and policy level

Dimension	*Instrument*	*Agency*	*Philosophy*
Local air pollution	Vehicle emission standards	National Supranational	Planning
Global air pollution	Emission standards	National Supranational	Planning
	Fiscal	National	Market
Noise	Vehicle emission standards Infrastructure design	International National government	Planning Planning
Urban quality of life	Traffic management	Regional or local	Planning

Objective, environment; Nature, compatible.

and to some extent impose a cost on international movement which does not fall on national movement, and hence distort trade. In some cases, e.g. air transport, the problem is not specific to international movements but appears so simply because (at least within Europe) such a large proportion of air transport is international. In principle, however, there should be no special case for enforcing any more stringent checks on security on international than on national movements. In so far as the protection of the safety of one's nationals is concerned the same might be expected to hold also for safety regulation and control.

In practice there appear to be two reasons why this is not so. First, where enforcement is only periodic, as in the case of road vehicle inspections, countries may suspect that foreign vehices from countries believed to operate with lower safety standards will be a hazard to its own nationals. Hence there will be particular emphasis at borders to ensure the maintenance of the national standards for all vehicles operating within its frontiers. Maritime port state controls arise very much for this reason. The greater the degree to which the national standards can be harmonized, the less will be the need for any such checking at borders.

The second reason for attempting to impose national standards on incoming foreign vehicles is not to protect the safety of nationals but to affect the terms of competition. For example, 'flagging out' of nationally owned shipping into a foreign registry is partly done to avoid the more rigorous controls on the conditions of employment and higher wages of labour in the developed countries. Attempts to prevent this, or to minimize the advantage that it confers, are partly to ensure the maintenance of a strategic merchant shipping capacity in

Table 10.2 Safety and security and policy level

Dimension	*Instrument*	*Agency*	*Philosophy*
Vehicle safety	Technical standards Use regulation Speed controls	International, national or industrial	Planning
Passenger security	Administrative	Industry	Planning

Objective, safety and security; Nature, compatible.

the national flag, but largely to protect the employment of seafarers of higher income countries. That is no different in principle, of course, from the imposition of tariffs on imported products to equalize labour costs. As such it conflicts with the precepts of comparative advantage and is difficult to justify in an ostensibly liberal international trading regime.

There is clearly a common interest in both safety and security regulation, so that it should be relatively easy to reach international agreement. Moreover, in many cases the interests of suppliers of services, consumers and governments seem to coincide closely so that industrial self-regulation can be relied on (as, for example, in air safety). The limitations to this appear particularly to concern sectors with a large number of operators, where a combination of competitive pressure and imperfect information to customers may lead the commercially optimal level of safety for the operators to be less than that considered to be socially optimal by governments. Where that is the case implementation will need to be at least at national government level, to standards agreed internationally.

Although there may be a common international interest in safety, the same standards may not be adopted by all countries. Put crudely, if low levels of income make life cheap in other respects (i.e. through low levels of medical service) it will not appear rational to a country to be willing to pay high prices for improved safety in transport. Thus, for example, there is nothing necessarily inconsistent in having standards of safety for mariners which differ according to the nationality of the mariners.

There is one other paradox which should be mentioned in this context. There appear to be quite different implicit valuations given to safety, even within a country, between public and private transport modes. In almost all countries it appears to be the case that a shift of resources from safety protection in public transport modes to safety of private transport modes would yield a net reduction of accident loss for a given economic cost. Transport policy with respect to safety and security may be summarized as in Table 10.2.

National economic development

Transport policies may have two different kinds of important effect on non-transport industries in nation-states.

1 Technical regulations on vehicle weights and dimensions may have differential effects on the suppliers of transport equipment. It is clearly advantageous if the standards to which the equipment producer is conforming in his home market also become the international norm. This has been an important consideration in slowing down the development of international standards within the European Community.
2 Both economic and technical instruments may have influence on the relative advantage of producers of goods in different locations. Nation-states will try to avoid international agreements which have the effect of reducing the export market size for their companies or improving accessibility of the home market to foreign suppliers.

Both of these interests are essentially competitive. They will be pursued by nations typically by the use of administrative, i.e. planning philosophy, instruments designed to distort the conditions of international competition to their own national advantage. This has the consequence that sovereign nation-states will not easily delegate powers affecting these issues either to a lower body or to a higher (supranational) body. In order to be persuaded to do so they will need to be convinced that the benefits to total welfare of such a delegation or abrogation will be such that the sovereign unit will actually gain by giving up some sovereignty. That, of course, is the driving force behind the creation of customs unions, of general free trade agreements and of the voluntary creation of federal government systems (as opposed to those imposed by force by a dominant member).

Spatial structuring

At the national level it is common for governments to have spatial restructuring objectives. In particular they may aim to shift employment possibilities to areas where levels of employment are high, or to shift more highly remunerative activities to regions where incomes are abnormally low. A whole range of fiscal and regulatory policies can be used to these ends. In the transport sector the main instruments are discrimination in transport pricing and the control of infrastructure investment.

The objective of 'levelling up' employment or incomes may also be adopted at the international level. Thus, within the European Community, one of the few bases on which transport aids have been acceptable has been in support of identified target development areas. Similarly in infrastructure policy the problems of 'peripherality' have been given special consideration, particularly in the application of European Regional Development Fund monies. There are three kinds of problem which arise in this context.

First, there is the question of how 'special status' will be established. In the international community at large there is a certain willingness to grant favourable treatment to less developed countries (LDCs). In the transport sector this is particularly exemplified by recognition of a special case for cargo reservation for the fleets of LDCs in the United Nations Liner Code promoted by UNCTAD V at Manila.

Second, there is the question of policy effectiveness. Many would argue, for example, that protection of national shipping is often not in the interests of the developing countries as it drives up costs of imported materials and of products in competition. Within the developed countries there is also some scepticism about the effectiveness of transport policy instruments in spatially structuring activities. For example, infrastructure investment tends to have the same effect as the reductions of tariffs, giving greater market advantage to those locations which have the lowest production costs. Given some immobility and inflexibility of labour this is not necessarily to the advantage of the less developed.

Third, there is the question of implementation leverage. For most countries international transport is a relatively small part of total transport in the national network. Discrimination in directions which are internationally acceptable may run counter to immediate national interests and hence need implementation at an international level. In infrastructure this implies a supranational investment budget accompanied by either a political process or an administrative process for its allocation to secure restructuring objectives. The sad history of the European Community transport investment budget is testimony to the inherent difficulty of achieving this. Similarly price discrimination may be extremely difficult to structure and control in transport sectors where there is very fragmented supply or where there is commercial freedom of contract.

Welfare distribution

The distribution of welfare is not merely, or even primarily, viewed at the national level as a matter of spatial redistribution. Rather it is a matter of the interests of income or social groups. The two particular interests which it has been common to attempt to protect in the transport sector are those of low income households and transport employees.

The use of transport policy to assist the poor has usually taken the form of the provision and subsidy of public transport, viewed in some cases as essential for the maintenance of employment possibilities for those without access to a private car.

The protection of transport employees is sometimes justified on the same

Table 10.3 Welfare distribution and policy level

Dimension	*Instrument*	*Agency*	*Philosophy*
Maintain employment opportunities	Public transport subsidy	Local or central government	Planning
Low income support	Public transport subsidy	Local or central government	Planning
Employee benefit	Employment law	National government	Planning
	Entry controls	National government	Planning

Objective, welfare distribution; Nature, competing.

grounds that they represent a low income group of the population. This is a policy of doubtful validity on many grounds. Transport employees are frequently not the lowest income group and intervention in product markets is a particularly distorting way to pursue such objectives in any case. In reality the protection of public transport employees occurs frequently as a consequence of the market power that monopoly state operation of public transport gives to organized labour and to the capture of the local political process by municipal labour organizations. Transport policy with respect to welfare distribution may now be characterized as in Table 10.3.

10.4 TOWARDS AN INTERNATIONAL REGIME

Our analysis of the areas of interest in international transport policy yields some interesting conclusions concerning the relationships between objectives, instruments and institutions.

Efficiency and distributional policy areas

We have distinguished between those objectives which appear to be held in common between partners in the international economy and those where the interests of the partners are to a large degree competing or mutually incompatible. The tables show that the greater the extent to which the objectives are common the greater the likelihood and usefulness of a planning approach, using international standards of behaviour or performance as instruments and depending on the suppliers themselves as the agents of implementation. The apparent exception of welfare distributional objectives to this generalization can be explained by the fact that most of the aspects of welfare distribution policy are essentially national rather than international.

This is not to say that planning approaches dominate. In those transport sectors where there are no substantial economies of scale the national markets are in many countries competitive. In these circumstances it is likely that the countries will also prefer a market philosophy to prevail. The issues which then arise concern the conditions of that international competition.

For the competitive policy areas it is much more difficult to agree desired outcomes – which are essentially matters of political negotiation. There may, nevertheless, be some overbridging interest which does form the basis for an international regime. Usually this is derived either from a sense of equity or from a belief in the productive capabilities of market mechanisms. Either reason directs policy towards the concept of 'fair competition', and hence again to the establishment of what are the conditions in which competition in transport is fair.

The future of supranationalism

In a curious way recent political developments in Europe may make the development of a supranational transport policy easier to achieve. The smaller are the national states the greater the proportion of their trade that is likely to be international. The greater that proportion the greater the extent to which they are dependent on a stable well-organized international transport regime. The smaller are the states the less likely they are to be able to practise explicit discrimination within their international transport policies in support of their trading ends. In the desire for 'fair' trading relationships they are more likely to accept a supranational transport regime.

A 'market' philosophy for that supranational regime has several advantages in these circumstances. First, given the *de facto* association between national fragmentation and political liberalization, there may be a predisposition also to liberal transport regimes. The market process may appear to be 'neutral', in the sense of not patently favouring any of the participants in the international trading regime. It may also appear to be inherently more efficient than managed regimes.

The 'level playing field'

In international as in national markets the necessary basis for a market solution to yield an optimum outcome include the following:

1 all competitors have equivalent financial objectives;
2 all operators have equivalent commercial freedom;
3 operators are required to cover all of the costs they impose on society.

Structurally this will typically mean that a market solution cannot apply in fields where there is substantial state intervention or state ownership. International air market liberalization is hampered by the continued commitment of many nations to retain a national flag carrier. For rail transport the existence of national undertakings which are subject to social service impositions and associated compensation arrangements are very difficult to incorporate in an essentially market solution. This may create substantial difficulties in an international multimodal regime, as we shall discuss later.

On the cost front an efficient market solution requires that (i) infrastructure (track) costs are paid for by the users and (ii) any significant externalities are internalized. These requirements are not simple to satisfy. The establishment of the total infrastructure costs imposed by transport in a given country is not always simple given the fragmentation of responsibilities among several layers in the hierarchy of government. The allocation of those costs between vehicle categories is both theoretically and practically difficult and has not been attempted in more than a few countries. Environmental costs are similarly difficult to estimate and allocate. All these difficulties point to the importance of international agreement over the fiscal structure for the transport sector as being an important component of the development of a truly international transport regime.

Another aspect of the management of a free transport sector creating particular difficulties in the international context concerns market structure. If the market is neither inherently perfectly competitive (because of economies of scale) nor perfectly contestable (because of sunk costs or reaction lags), the possibility of cartelization and restrictive practice or monopolization and predatory practice arises. Liner conferences are time honoured examples of the former, while the current trend to concentration in the international airline industry is an incipient example of the latter.

Even within national markets in countries with strong monopoly and restrictive practice legislation the transport service sector has been notoriously difficult to control. Predation in particular is difficult to define and identify when, because of the temporal variability of demand and the separation of the unit of production from the unit of consumption, fixed costs are high and average utilization levels relatively low. The danger that international free trade in transport services converts into monopoly power for a small number of multinational (and increasingly multimodal) operators is a nightmare scenario.

Finding means of reconciliation of freedom in international transport markets with a workably competitive industrial structure is a critical problem for the coming decade.

10.5 SUMMARY

All national governments have multiple objectives in transport policy. The policy 'packages' which seek to secure these ends may be categorized as either 'planning'- or 'market'-oriented, the first concentrating on target setting and administrative regulation to secure the target outcomes and the latter concentrating on the creation of the appropriate conditions for the working of markets to achieve the objectives. The distinction, however, is not rigid, with some specific regulatory devices being used within the market-oriented packages and vice versa.

In the international context some of these national objectives turn out to be internationally compatible (e.g. environment, safety and security), while others are not (e.g. national economic advantage, spatial relocation). The greater the extent to which the objectives are compatible, the greater seems to be the chance that an international transport regime can be founded on common regulations within an essentially planning type philosophy. For the competing objectives, however, agreement on common regulations is less likely, and a multilateral international regime will only emerge in so far as countries can see the advantage of abdicating some degree of their sovereignty in the short term to achieve the benefits of a stable international regime in the long term.

National fragmentation and political liberalization are seen as twin forces leading to the increasing acceptance of a free-market-oriented international transport regime. For that to mature a 'level international playing field' must be created. The immediate tasks – already being confronted – are the treatment of the environmental impacts of transport, whether through regulation or through internalization of external costs. In the longer term the establishment of structural conditions for effective competition to survive in the face of the pressures to international cartelization and restrictive practice or international monopolization and predatory practice may turn out to be the real testing points of a truly international transport policy regime.

REFERENCES

Beesley, M.E. (1990) Collusion, predation and merger in the British bus industry. *Journal of Transport Economics and Policy*, 295–310.

Beesley, M.E. and Gwilliam, K.M. (1979) Transport policy in the United Kingdom. *Journal of Transport Economics and Policy*, 209–23.

COWIconsult (1991) *Monetary Valuation of Transport Environmental Impact – The case of air pollution – Methodology assessment*. Copenhagen: Danish Ministry of Energy.

European Conference of Ministers of Transport (1986) *International Traffic and Infrastructural Needs*. Paris: OECD.

European Round Table of Industrialists (1988) *Needs for Renewing Infrastructure in Europe*. Brussels: European Round Table of Industrialists.

Group Transport 2000 Plus (1990) *Transport in a Fast Changing Europe. Vers un réseau européen des systèmes de transports*. Brussels.

Gwilliam, K.M. (1980) Realism and the common transport policy of the EEC. In J.B. Polak and J.B. van der Kamp (eds), *Changes in the Field of Transport Studies*, Amsterdam: Martinus Nijhoff.

—— (1984) *Aims and Effects of Public Financial Support for Passenger Transport*. Round Table 67. European Conference of Ministers of Transport, Paris: OECD.

—— (1985) The future of the common transport policy. In A. El Agraa (ed.), *British Within the European Community – The Way Forward*, London: Macmillan, 168–86.

—— (1990) The common transport policy. In A. El Agraa (ed.), *Economics of the European Community*, London: Philip Allan, 230–42.

—— (1991) Transport policy and the environment in the European Economic Community. *Investigaciones Economicas*, 309–35.

Mackie, P.J. and Preston, J. (1992) *Regulating the Deregulated Bus Market*. Paper presented to the World Conference on Transport Research, Lyon.

Moses, L.N. and Savage, I. (1989) *Transportation Safety in an Age of Deregulation*. Oxford: Oxford University Press.

Netherlands Ministry of Transport (1989) *Second structure plan for transport and traffic. Part a*. The Hague: SDU Uitgeverij.

OECD (1988) *Transport and the Environment*. Paris: OECD.

Rietveld, P. (1989) Infrastructure and regional development – a survey of multiregional economic models. *The Annals of Regional Science*, 225–74.

11

Industry, Industrial Location and the Role of Transport in a Single European Market

Brian Bayliss

11.1 INTRODUCTION

This chapter examines the relationship between industry and the role of transport in a single European market (SEM). By embracing both industry and the creation of an SEM the chapter impinges upon many aspects of transport economics and so builds on much of the material presented in the previous chapters.

The creation of an SEM, encompassing the 12 European Community (EC) countries and the seven European Free Trade Association countries, has a direct influence upon the functioning and structure of both industry and freight transport.

Industry, and manufacturing in particular, is rapidly changing its form of operations, which is influencing both its location policies and its demands on the freight transport sector.

Freight transport for its part is changing its practices, which is having a direct effect upon industry. It is also the case that industrial and transport practices are influencing the form that an SEM is taking, but in this chapter causality is only looked at one way, namely the influence of the SEM on transport and industry. Chapters 7 and 10 approach causality from the other direction.

Figure 11.1 sets out the relationships to be investigated. These interrelationships are extremely complex and yet transport economists have in the past made little attempt to analyse them. Attention has been too focused on the transport sector, and a too superficial and theoretical view of industrial practices has been taken. For example, the assumption has been made that industry

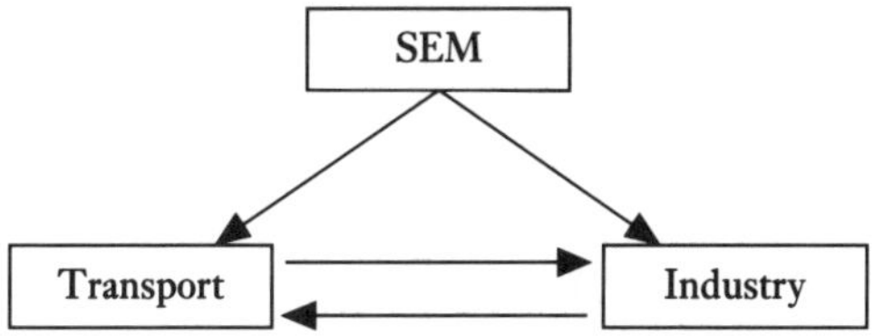

Figure 11.1 Relationships relevant in this chapter.

makes its decisions on the basis of operating costs, including transport costs, within the EC common market. However, much of industrial strategy with respect to location within the EC is determined by the existence of non-tariff barriers, and unless this is understood attempts to forecast transport demand and the impact that new infrastructure, for example, will have on land use will be unsuccessful.

An important reason for the marked failure of so many of the freight forecasts, and particularly those in relation to infrastructure investment, has been the failure of transport economists to understand fully industrial practices and, with respect to the EC, to understand fully what has been happening in the EC outside the transport sector.

In this penultimate chapter an attempt is made to bring together these complex interrelationships and to see how they bear upon the transport sector. By so doing it is hoped that insights will be gained into how methodologies for forecasting and analysis in the transport sector might need to be developed to take account of them.

The chapter falls into four sections: industry in an SEM (section 11.2), transport in an SEM (section 11.3), transport and industry (section 11.4) and a concluding section (section 11.5).

11.2 INDUSTRY IN A SINGLE EUROPEAN MARKET

The aim of this section is to consider industrial strategy within the EC, and particularly the role of transport costs in such a strategy. This should *inter alia* provide insights into industrial location strategies and help clarify, for example, the relationship between land use and transport infrastructure.

Broadly speaking, customs union theory suggests that the positive benefits of such a union stem from the static effect of an improved allocation of resources and the dynamic effect of economies of scale and increased competition. Increased specialization, based on comparative advantage, leads to an improved allocation of resources; increased market size leads to economies of scale; increased competition leads to greater economic efficiency.

An important stimulus to the attempt to achieve these benefits has been the threat to EC industry in a range of high-technology sectors from US and Japanese multinationals (Servan-Schreiber, 1967; Pelkmans, 1985; Mytelka and Delapierre, 1987; Pierre, 1987) and the increasing competitive pressure from Japan and the newly industrializing countries (NICs) in a number of mature industries (EC Commission, 1986a; Millington, 1988).

This external competition has given impetus to the opening of the fragmented national markets of the EC to intra-EC competition in order to create a single market within which enterprises of a European scale could develop and compete in global markets (EC Commission, 1970, 1973, 1985).

This emphasis on specialization and economies of scale in an enlarged market suggests that the importance of production and transport costs in determining the location of economic activity would increase with the creation of a customs union.

Following the removal of barriers firms enjoying a comparative advantage should grow and serve larger markets in both volume and geographical terms. Additionally firms should relocate activities, all or in part, in order to benefit from minimum operating costs within the expanded market.

Many of the studies on EC integration and investment flows have focused on US foreign direct investment (FDI) in the EC using demand pull models (Scaperlanda and Mauer, 1969; Schmitz and Biari, 1972; Lunn, 1980; Scaperlanda and Balough, 1983). The results have emphasized the importance of market size and growth in determining FDI. Later studies (Cantwell, 1987; Dunning and Robson, 1987) have shown the importance of production costs in the location decisions of multinational companies (MNCs) pursuing global strategies, i.e. MNCs invest in order to minimize costs within an integrated production system serving EC and global markets.

A recent study (Culem, 1988) has supported the importance of market size and growth in determining FDI both within the EC and from the USA to the EC. However, in this case it was argued that the factors determining the choice between domestic or foreign production were different from the factors that determine any subsequent choice between foreign locations.

In the case of domestic versus foreign location, Culem argues, 'intra-EC FDIs are not motivated by the search for lower unit costs than at home'; but in the case of a subsequent choice between foreign locations he concludes, 'the lowest cost foreign location was preferred' (Culem, 1988, p. 900).

Although Culem was only able to speculate about the reasons for his findings, it has subsequently been established (Millington and Bayliss, 1991) that the persistence of non-tariff barriers (NTBs), and particularly barriers of an institutional and of a legal nature, in the EC obliges firms to locate activities abroad.

In order to penetrate these foreign markets firms can be obliged to locate part of their activity in them; location choice exists, therefore, only within the foreign country and not between the foreign country and the domestic one.

These institutional and legal NTBs are very extensive. The EC Commission has estimated (EC Commission, 1988a) that such barriers increase costs to industry by some 70 billion ECU or about $2^1/_2$ per cent of total EC gross domestic product (GDP). If dynamic effects are included the cost is estimated at between $4^1/_2$ per cent and $6^1/_2$ per cent of GDP.

The Millington and Bayliss study suggested that UK FDI in the EC was principally motivated by barriers to the sale and distribution of goods within national markets. In contrast to the predictions of customs union theory factor and transport costs did not provide a general explanation of UK investment in the EC. Factor costs were of importance for less than one in ten of UK companies, and transport costs were clearly sector specific – they were a dominant factor in just under two-fifths of firms engaged in mineral products and basic chemicals, but in less than one in five firms overall.

In a subsequent study (Millington and Bayliss, 1992) on cross-frontier joint ventures (JVs) in the EC, the same authors found that firms with a turnover of less than £100 million (140 million ECU) undertook vertical ventures, i.e. between producer and supplier or producer and distributor, in order to penetrate specific individual EC markets, whilst larger firms formed horizontal linkages, i.e. same product, in order to reap economies of scale.

A detailed analysis of the location of these JVs showed that in the case of horizontal JVs, involving the largest firms, only about half of the JV sales were in the country of location compared with four-fifths for all JVs.

It was concluded that firms may perceive the EC either as a single market or as a set of discrete national markets. In the first case it is a question of very large firms using JVs to reap economies of scale, rationalize production and take advantage of technological complementarities as part of an EC or global strategy. In the second case it is a question of smaller firms acquiring access to marketing expertise and distribution networks to circumvent NTBs and penetrate other EC markets.

The evidence from all these studies is therefore that on balance the largest multinationals view the EC as a single market, whilst less large firms concern themselves with individual markets and frequently locate in a foreign country in order to circumvent NTBs. Operating costs do, however, play the predominant role for these firms in choosing the actual location in the foreign country.

It can be concluded that although customs union theory predicts that operating costs, including transport costs, will play a critical role in firms' behaviour within a common market, the existence of NTBs within the EC has meant that the creation of the common market has not of itself led generally to this outcome; an exception is found in relation to the largest multinationals.

The establishment of an SEM after 1992 will assist in the removal of many of the legal and institutional NTBs, but it is probable that major barriers such as those involving public procurement will remain for a considerable period, not least by reason of a lack of enforcement.

Public works contracts, for example, have been covered by a procurement directive since 1971 and public supply contracts since 1978,[1] yet in 1986 the EC Commission reported (EC Commission, 1986b): 'Project splitting and abuse of procedures continues as in the past, and the directives do not provide any means whereby such abuses can be controlled.' Again, five years later the Commission (1991) noted that 'it had established that the rules of Community law were not being observed in many cases . . .'. Also, a recent study (Butt Philip, 1988) based on research for the EC Commission on the social regulations for road haulage concluded: 'It is all too easy for Member States to adopt such legislation and then deliberately to give it a low enforcement profile with minimum sanctions for non-observance.'

The move of the largest multinationals towards EC and global operating strategies is very much based on relative operating costs; but at the same time the sheer size of such firms does mean that they have continually to take account of the possible responses of governments to their actions. Thus, for example, an MNC may decide as part of its global strategy that it wishes to locate a plant within the EC, but in deciding the choice of country it will amongst other things take into account its own corporate balance of payments in particular countries; where global production and sourcing is concerned the 'invisible hand' can be that of a government.

Nevertheless it is the very large MNCs that are increasingly pursuing global strategies and increasingly dominating EC and world trade. A recent World Bank study (World Bank, 1992) has shown that international trade inside the world's largest 350 MNCs accounts for almost two-fifths of world trade in goods. This integration of the largest MNCs has resulted in substantial increases in FDI. According to the World Bank study, after 'unremarkable' growth up to 1982 FDI grew fivefold to average over US$125 billion a year between 1985 and 1989. Almost one-half (47 per cent) of this investment was in the EC.

Changes in the process of internationalization have greatly speeded up the time taken to establish production facilities abroad. Research in the late 1970s and early part of the 1980s pointed 'generally to a process of evolutionary, sequential build-up of foreign commitments over time' (see Millington and Bayliss (1990) for a review), but the latest research supports 'a life cycle model which is based on the international development of the firm rather than the market or product . . . international experience may be transferred across markets and between products, thereby enabling firms to leap-frog the incremental process within markets' (Millington and Bayliss, 1990).

Although the establishment of an EC common market has not as yet led to a prominent role for transport costs in firms' strategies, the progressive removal of NTBs after 1992 and the rapid globalization of world trade underpinned by rapidly increasing FDI will ensure that such costs will play an increasing role in corporate competitive strategy.

11.3 TRANSPORT IN A SINGLE EUROPEAN MARKET

The advantages of trade and customs unions derive from an extension of the theory of competitive markets to the theory of trade. Basically the larger the competitive market, the greater the benefits.

If markets fail resource allocation is not optimized and the full advantages or benefits which are seen to stem from a market system are not realized. Because major parts of economies are interdependent and competing for scarce resources, market distortion in one sector can lead to distortion in others, and this is particularly the case in the transport sector.

In Chapter 7 the extensive intervention of government in both domestic and international transport markets was analysed. Such intervention has led to market distortions, but with the *raison d'être* of a common market based on competitive markets, the EC Commission has battled over more than three decades to establish market forces in the transport sector. Until 1985 the Commission enjoyed very little success but on 22 May of that year the European Court ruled in favour of a complaint from the European Parliament against the Commission in relation to the failure of the latter to have created a common market in transport. The Court ruled that such a market should be introduced by 1992. In line with the general legislation requiring the creation of an SEM by the beginning of 1993 the Commission has attempted to create a common market in transport as part of the total package of proposals aimed at creating one EC internal market.

Under a 1988 Council Regulation all bilateral quotas regulating the international movement of road haulers within the EC have been abolished from the beginning of 1993 and access to the international road haulage profession will be determined solely by qualitative criteria. These relate to good repute, financial standing and professional competence. These rights of access also include rights of cabotage but, although certain progress has been made in this area and limited cabotage has been permitted, since July 1990, through a quota of cabotage permits for each member state, regulations have not yet (1993) been finalized.

The inevitable movement towards the liberalization of international freight markets since the European Court's decision has also impacted upon domestic freight markets. In France, a country which alongside Germany had the most dirigist regime, the 1986 Transport Act has led to a substantial liberalizing of the road haulage industry. Between the end of 1986 and the end of 1989 the number of licences for operators in the *zone longue* (long distance transport) increased by some 50 per cent. This liberalization has led to a sharp fall in the economic rent attaching to such licences. In 1984–5, for example, the market value of a class A licence was FFr200,000, but by 1990 its value had fallen to FFr50,000–FFr70,000.

It is EC policy, therefore, that is leading to an end of market power exploitation in both international and domestic freight markets. Also the qualitative criteria relating to good repute, financial standing and professional competence which are required to obtain an operating licence will reduce the degree of asymmetric information in the market.

Harmonization of operating conditions is an essential conjunct of competition if market distortion is not to occur. The three main areas in this respect are social, technical and fiscal.

The EC has introduced measures relating to drivers' hours and the weight and dimensions of vehicles in international traffic, but measures for fiscal harmonization are not yet agreed. With regard to the latter the Commission has proposed a first phase whereby the vehicle tax structure is harmonized on the basis of the nationality principle (i.e. taxes are only payable in the country of registration) and a second phase whereby vehicle tax rates are harmonized on the basis of common methods for calculating, allocating and paying infrastructure costs.

Again, in relating vehicle tax rates to infrastructure costs and internalizing certain externalities as a result the EC is acting to remove market distortion.

Finally, reference should be made to infrastructure investment. As already indicated, such investment has not necessarily followed economic criteria but has been determined by the attitudes of governments to such factors as economic management and regional and social policies. Even where economic criteria have been used they will have reflected distorted transport markets; for example, investment in a rail project may have indicated a higher rate of return than in a competing road project but if the transport market had not been distorted the reverse could have been the case.

Individual countries evaluate the impact of infrastructure changes with respect to their own territories. The impact on other countries is not generally part of the remit. As the EC countries move towards a single market, however, the logic of ending analysis at national borders becomes more tenuous and, certainly where financing is supranational in nature, i.e. by the EC, untenable.

In 1986, in its medium-term programme for transport infrastructure, the Commission detailed a network for road, rail and inland shipping which was of Community interest, and identified projects of Community interest in relation to that network with a total investment of over 20 billion ECU for the 10–15 year period under consideration. Among the priority projects identified were

1 the removal of bottlenecks on sections of axes with high transit traffics, e.g. the axis route to the Mont Blanc tunnel, the axis Benelux–France–Italy and

the Aachen–Cologne section on the axis Benelux–Germany–Switzerland–Austria;

2 the strengthening of rail axes for relieving bottlenecks or for combined transport on overloaded road corridors, e.g. the Alps, the axes Amsterdam–Brussels, Luxemburg–Metz–Strasbourg–Basel–Milan–Rome;
3 road and rail axes to a fixed Channel link or the completion of high-speed passenger networks between capitals and major urban areas.

In 1988 the Commission formulated an action programme in the field of transport infrastructure with a view to the completion of the integrated transport market in 1992. Among its priority points were

1 construction of a combined transport network;
2 development of new telecommunication and information technologies to improve the management of road traffic and information to car and commercial vehicle drivers;
3 construction of a high-speed rail link between Paris, London, Brussels, Amsterdam and Cologne.

Here again, the EC has been active in ensuring that externalities in the form of environmental costs are taken into account in assessing transport infrastructure. Under a 1985 Council Directive all major transport infrastructure projects are made subject to an environmental assessment.

The opening-up of international and domestic freight markets, investment in infrastructure on a Community basis and appropriate infrastructure charging policies will have very important implications for industry.

In an industry increasingly functioning in greater geographic areas and increasingly adopting operating and production methods that are transport dependent (see section 11.4 below), transport costs will take on greater importance in corporate strategy. It is therefore important that these costs are not distorted by market failure.

With industry more dependent upon physical distribution systems, flexibility in the choice of transport mode takes on an increased importance, and the opening-up of transport markets will greatly facilitate the operation of such systems.

Also, investment in infrastructure on the basis of Community benefits will assist firms in pursuing EC and global strategies.

11.4 TRANSPORT AND INDUSTRY

In the previous sections attention has been drawn to the role of transport costs in customs union theory and in industry strategy in an SEM, and the distortion of such costs through government intervention. It has also been argued that,

Table 11.1 Knowledge of operating costs by firms operating their own vehicle fleets (1953)

	Percentage of firms with fewer than 200 employees	*Percentage of firms with more than 200 employees*
No accurate information on actual costs	46	14
Knowledge of overall costs from accounts	52	28
Knowledge of overall ton-mile costs	–	30
Knowledge of particular ton-mile costs or certain services	2	13
Operating costs of each vehicle related to traffic carried	–	15
Total	100	100

Source: Walters and Sharp, 1953

although transport costs have not played a leading role in industrial strategy within the EC before now, they are likely to grow in importance with the establishment of an SEM and the deregulating of transport markets.

In this section two important aspects of industry and transport are considered: first, industry's knowledge of transport costs, and second, changes in industrial operations independent of the SEM that are currently taking place and which are resulting in a much greater emphasis on transport.

Much of the work on transport forecasting and policy analysis in the transport sector has assumed both that transport costs are important in industry decision-making and that transport markets are transparent, i.e. firms have a full knowledge of costs and charges.

The evidence of the 1950s, 1960s and 1970s, however, is of both a lack of market transparency and a low order of priority for transport costs in corporate decision-making.

A 1953 UK study which included an analysis of firms' knowledge of the costs of operating their own vehicles showed that, even in the case of firms employing more than 200 people, all but a small minority had no detailed knowledge of operating costs (table 11.1). An analogous study in the late 1960s showed similar results (table 11.2).

An analysis (Bayliss and Edwards, 1968) in the UK of about 2500 consignments sent by manufacturing industry in 1968 showed that only in the case of about one-quarter of them was the shipper able to indicate, either accurately or

Table 11.2 Knowledge of operating costs by firms operating their own vehicle fleets (1969)

	Percentage of firms
No more than general knowledge of total costs of fleet	49
Some broad estimates available of average cost per ton	13
Detailed costing of certain vehicles or groups of vehicles or selected traffic flows	20
Detailed and up-to-date information of fleet operating costs	18
Total	100

Source: Sharp, 1970

Table 11.3 Knowledge of charges by alternative modes (number of consignments)

Mode used	*Cost of alternative mode known*	*Cost of alternative mode not known*	*Total consignments*	*Column 2 as percentage of column 4*
Own vehicle	207	734	941	22
Customer's vehicle	17	83	100	17
Road hauler	233	597	830	28
Rail	118	156	274	43
Post Office	73	251	324	23
Other	1	13	14	7
Total	649	1834	2483	26

Source: Bayliss and Edwards, 1968

inaccurately, what the charge would have been by an alternative mode (table 11.3).

A 1965 study in Germany (EMNID, 1965) gave similar results. Here it was found that in the case of industrial companies 50 per cent, and in the case of trading 75 per cent, made no systematic charges comparisons.

Studies of industrial location during the same period, not surprisingly in view of the above findings, indicated that transport costs were of little or no importance in locational decision-making.

A 1970 study by Townroe of 59 firms showed that only 13 costed transport as an important variable. Hamilton (1975) attributed the accelerated industrial mobility during the 1950s and 1960s to the 'continuing decline in the already limited relative importance of transport costs'. And Luttrell, in a 1962 study of 90 firms establishing new branches, found little evidence of the influence of transport costs in the choice of location.

These findings should not be taken to mean that the pre-war theories of location (Weber, 1909; Robinson, 1937; Hoover, 1948) were necessarily wrong; changes in the structure of industry, and particularly the move from basic industries to manufacturing, together with vastly improved transport systems would most certainly have changed the relative importance of transport costs in corporate decision-making.

What these findings do suggest, however, is that during these three decades any government intervention or economic system, e.g. a common market, that relied upon market transparency and an important role for transport costs in corporate strategy was unlikely to be successful. These conclusions, therefore, fit alongside the findings on FDI in the EC (see section 11.3), namely that such investment has in many instances not been driven by the factors foreseen in the theory of customs unions.

The end of the 1970s, however, heralded the beginning of major changes in industrial operations which have had major implications for the role of transport in corporate strategy.

Reference has already been made to the impetus given to the creation of a European common market by the threat to European industry in both high-technology and mature industries from Japanese competition. Japanese competitive advantage had in part been based upon new approaches to production and operations management, and particularly the application of a just-in-time (JIT) manufacturing strategy, and EC industry has found itself needing to respond in kind.

JIT, originally known as the 'Toyota Manufacturing System', stemmed from a series of new approaches to the management of the manufacturing process that were developed at Toyota in the 1960s. By the mid-1970s other Japanese companies had begun to adopt these approaches, and by the late 1970s the Toyota Manufacturing System was being seriously considered in US and European industry. By 1990, according to a World Bank estimate,[2] some 28 per cent of all shipments in the USA and EC were on a JIT basis, and the proportion projected for 1995 is over one-third.

The name 'just-in-time' perhaps conveys to the non-specialist the impression of a particular technique rather than the more accurate impression of a total manufacturing system.

> Just-in-time . . . is a disciplined approach to improving overall productivity and eliminating waste. It provides for the cost-effective production and delivery of only the necessary quantity of parts at the right quality, at the right time and place, while using a minimum amount of facilities, equipment, materials and human resources. JIT is dependent on the balance between the supplier's flexibility and the user's flexibility. It is accomplished through the application of elements

> which require total employee involvement and teamwork. A key philosophy of JIT is simplification. (Voss, 1987)

Three key words are apparent in this description of JIT: quality, timing, minimum resourcing. These fundamentals of JIT have very important implications for certain aspects of manufacturing operations that impinge on physical distribution. The more important of these aspects and the way they relate to transport are considered below, under the headings *quality and timing*.

Quality Firms are increasingly restricting their corporate activities to their core business. The corporate value added of all the major automotive manufacturers, for example, is less than 50 per cent, and for a number it is less than one-third. The essence of this practice is that the firm can concentrate on a specialist activity, and outsourcing is likewise with specialist firms able to offer quality and frequently benefiting from scale economies. Physical distribution is typical of this strategy. For example, in the UK road haulage market, which has been deregulated since 1970, traffic was equally shared between own-account and hire or reward operators in 1980 but by 1989 hire or reward operators had a 60 per cent share of the market.

In order to ensure quality there is an increasing trend to both single and global sourcing, i.e. firms have long-term contracts with a single supplier and suppliers are selected on a global basis, so that both the level and the geographic spread of outsourcing is placing increased demands on the physical distribution system.

Timing An essential part of JIT strategy is the full utilization of all resources – manpower, buildings, equipment, materials. Resources should be available at the exact point in time that they are required in the business process, and only at this time.

Outsourcing is thus a means by which a firm only pays for a particular service or good at the point of utilization. Ideally firms take delivery of materials and products at the exact point in time when they are required in the manufacturing process; thereby stockholding and its associated costs are avoided. The rejection rate must be zero, hence the need for quality suppliers. Within the firm, processing times are reduced so that work-in-progress stock costs are not incurred. Goods are despatched to customers just as soon as they are completed so that no costs relate to the holding of finished goods.

Purchasing, production and despatch must be absolutely synchronized and therefore they make substantial demands on the logistics system.

Although an ideal situation has been described, industry during the last decade has been moving towards this goal.

Before considering the implications of such quality and timing practices for physical distribution it is important to consider the extent to which such practices have been adopted by industry.

Changes in purchasing practices are resulting in substantial reductions in stock levels. It has been calculated (Coyle et al., 1992) that in 1974 the manufacturing and trade inventory in the USA was equivalent to 20 per cent of gross national product, whereas by 1990 the percentage had fallen to under 15 per cent. A World Bank survey[2] of 625 North American and 225 European firms showed that between 1987 and 1990 the frequency of inventory turnover increased by almost one-quarter, and it was estimated that by 1995 it will have increased by almost three-fifths. The same survey showed that the order cycle time had fallen by almost one-quarter over the three-year period.

The role of transport in such a system is crucial. Lot sizes are smaller, deliveries more frequent and distribution networks much greater, yet delivery schedules allow for no deviations. On top of adherence to schedules transport is expected to make its own contribution through increased speed, and particularly where high-value goods are concerned. In the electrical and electronics sector, for example, total processing time has been reduced from 23 weeks in 1979 to five weeks in 1990, and figure 11.2 shows the direct contribution of physical distribution.

With EC and global sourcing the cost of inventory 'on the move' is of particular concern to industry. The point is well illustrated in relation to traffics between the UK and continental Europe.[3]

Some one-half of all UK trade is with the EC. Excluding trade in fuel about one-half of all seaborne trade in tonnage terms is by bulk and general cargo, and the remaining one-half is carried in containers, unaccompanied trailers and powered vehicles (table 11.4). Two important features should be noted from table 11.4: first, unaccompanied trailers and accompanied powered vehicles are of equal importance in tonnage terms as a means of transport; and, second, the value of goods carried varies substantially between the modes. In value per tonne terms goods carried on powered vehicles are twice as valuable as goods carried on unaccompanied trailers, and almost ten times as valuable as goods carried as bulk and general cargo.

This pattern of traffic is explained by two factors – control and speed. Control and speed are both greatest with accompanied powered vehicles and both least with bulk and general cargo, with unaccompanied trailers in between. Costs of operation for the three modes follow a similar pattern, with the powered vehicle being the most expensive.

Shippers demand a higher quality of service in terms of both speed and security for higher value goods, and they balance out transport costs against inventory costs in making modal choice.

The cost–speed relationship and its bearing on choice between unaccompanied trailers and powered vehicles is well illustrated in port choice.

The vast majority of powered vehicles going from Great Britain to the Continent take the shortest crossing, namely via the Dover Strait to France,

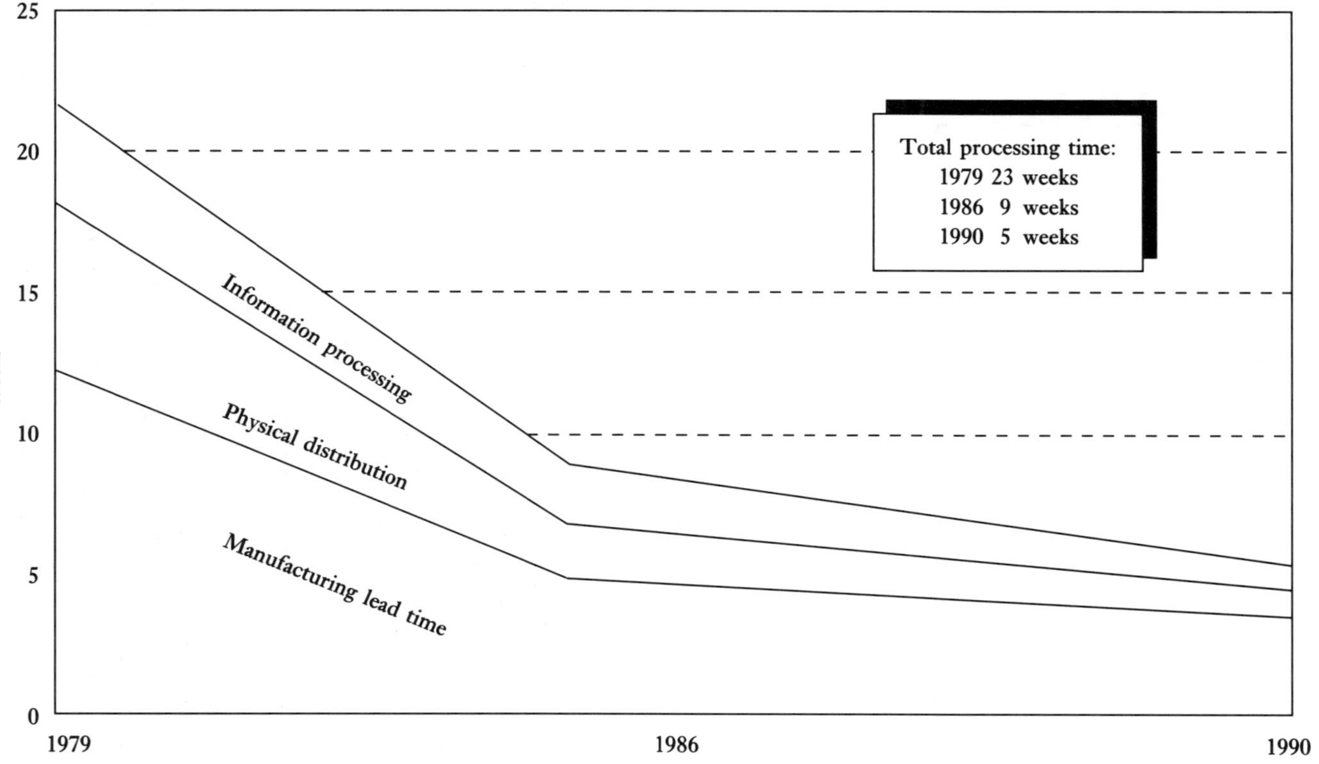

Figure 11.2 Order cycle time development (electrical/electronics industries).
Source: Philips International BV

Table 11.4 UK trade with European Community countries (excluding air trade), 1990

	Million tonnes (net)		*Average price per tonne (£)*	
	Exports	*Imports*	*Exports*	*Imports*
Irish land boundary	3.1	2.3	671	756
Seaborne trade	77.1	63.1	596	940
of which:				
non-fuel trade	29.3	46.0	1404	1257
of which carried by:				
bulk and general cargo	16.0	22.9	341	434
LO–LO containers	2.9	5.7	1820	1107
unaccompanied trailers	5.2	8.8	1619	1701
RO–RO powered vehicles	5.2	8.6	4219	3096
of which:				
containers on PVs	0.2	0.1	6359	7980

Source: HM Customs & Excise

whilst the vast majority of unaccompanied trailers take the longer North Sea crossing (figure 11.3). It is cheaper in terms of transport costs to send the trailer on a sea-leg rather than on a road-leg; therefore in terms of transport costs alone the advantages of the trailer over the powered vehicle are greatest where the sea-leg is long and the land-leg short. The longer the land-leg the less the relative advantage.

The lower transport costs of sea-legs relative to land-legs have to be balanced against longer journey times. As already noted, the tendency is for lower value goods to be sent by unaccompanied trailers so that inventory costs are less significant. Although all types of commodity are carried by trailer, the value of goods in each individual commodity group is below that for the corresponding group carried by powered vehicles, the average value per tonne of the highest value group (manufactured goods) carried by trailer being below the average for all commodity groups carried by powered vehicles – the relative figures for exports being £1939 per tonne and £4331 per tonne, and for imports £2601 per tonne and £3188 per tonne (table 11.5).

This example serves to demonstrate how sophisticated the approach of industry to physical distribution has become. The vital position of transport in modern industry is also well illustrated in relation to industries' current attitudes to location.

Nissan, for example, in seeking a European location in the 1980s, stipulated

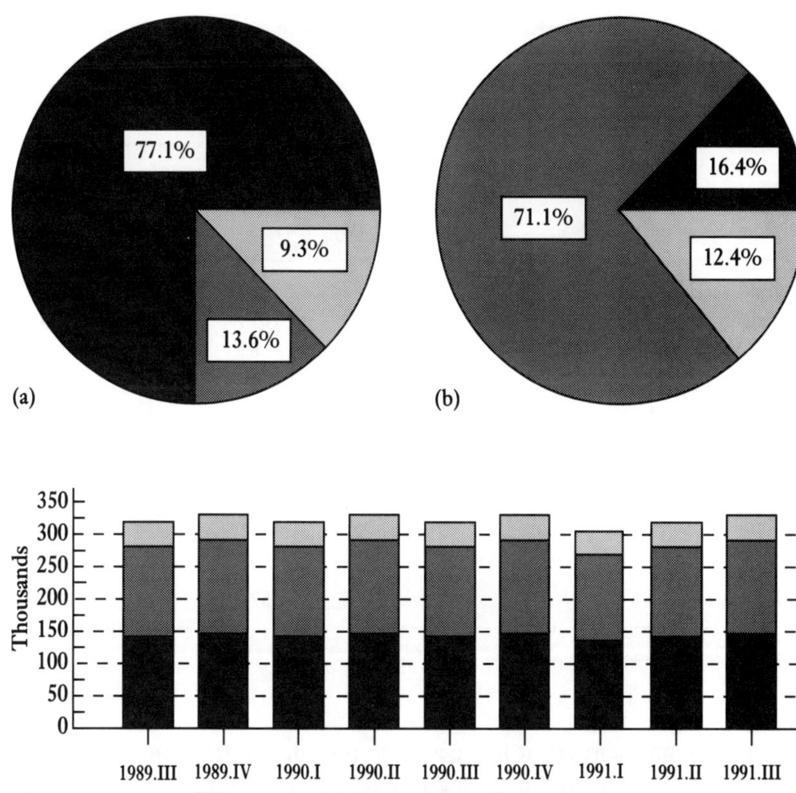

Figure 11.3 All vehicles by port group, 1991.III: (a) unaccompanied trailers; (b) powered vehicles; (c) all vehicles, historical record.
Source: Department of Transport

14 points which had to be met by any prospective location. Alongside the necessity of a suitable site for development, the transport requirements were of prime importance. These were as follows: container and roll-on–roll-off (Ro-Ro) facilities within 25 km; the national motorway network within 15 km; rail within 15 km; an airport within 25 km.

Likewise when Hewlett Packard looked for a suitable location for a major activity in Europe in the 1980s, it stipulated three principal conditions: a greenfield site, good transport facilities and a suitable workforce. The prioritizing of the modes of transport was road, air, rail, sea.

In the last decade the pressure of competition faced by EC industry has forced it to modify its operating practices. Modern industry makes very substantial

Table 11.5 Non-containerized commodities on unaccompanied trailers, seaborne trade (excluding ships), 1990

	Exports		*Imports*	
	Net tonnes (1000)	*Average value per tonne*	*Net tonnes (1000)*	*Average value per tonne*
Agricultural products	183	1039	918	622
Foodstuffs	310	1028	1105	1365
Solid fuels	21	63	114	79
Petroleum products	36	410	25	550
Metal ore and waste	76	1119	41	691
Metal products	1594	580	662	1087
Building materials	241	342	382	388
Fertilizers	8	367	34	155
Chemicals	969	1463	1678	1403
Manufactured goods and miscellaneous	1745	2939	3155	2601
Total	5183	1575	8114	1673

Source: The Overseas Trade database

demands upon transport: it is expected to provide fast deliveries on frequent and tight schedules over increasingly larger distribution networks. Industry's approach to transport is now very sophisticated, with the balance between cost and quality of service finely assessed. The extension of modern manufacturing techniques and the high quality of transport service demanded, combined with the development of Europe as a single and geographically large market, will further encourage both outsourcing of physical distribution and the development of large operators able to operate large and sophisticated networks.

11.5 CONCLUSIONS

Customs union theory places emphasis on industrial specialization. Such regional specialization within a large geographical market such as the EC suggests that transport costs will play an important role in industrial decisions. Much of transport forecasting and policy analysis has been based upon this assumption.

The evidence, however, is that the distortion of EC industrial markets through NTBs and transport markets through government intervention has meant that transport costs have not in reality been of major importance in industrial decision making. Moreover, until recently market transparency with respect to transport costs was very limited.

In the light of this evidence, therefore, much of transport forecasting and policy has been based upon incorrect assumptions.

However, recent changes in industrial operations have led to a central position for physical distribution in corporate strategy, and industry now approaches this activity with considerable sophistication. The liberalizing of both domestic and international freight transport markets is greatly assisting the development of the high quality physical distribution service now demanded by industry. It will therefore become increasingly realistic to base transport policy on costs.

The greater demands made on transport and the increasing perception of the EC as a single market will mean greater demands upon an EC approach to infrastructure development and the necessity of correctly accounting for externalities.

The EC Commission has played a vital role in opening up international freight markets and many domestic ones, and it is important that it ensures the proper functioning of those markets and a proper approach to infrastructure investment. The ability of EC industry to meet external competition could well depend upon its success.

NOTES

1 Certain sectors including transport were originally excluded; they have recently been included.

2 Study by H. Peters of the World Bank, to whom the author is grateful for supplying the data and also providing figure 11.2 and the previous information on the extent of JIT activities in the EC and North America.

3 This illustration is taken from Bayliss (1992) where a detailed analysis can be found.

REFERENCES

Bayliss, B.T. (1965) *European Transport.* London: Mason.

—— (1978) *The role of transport in counter-cyclical policy.* In Round Table 41. European Conference of Ministers of Transport, Paris: OECD, 5–48.

—— (1981) *Planning and Control in the Transport Sector.* Aldershot: Avebury Gower.

—— (1992) *Physical Distribution Across Borders: A UK–EC Case Study.* Washington, DC: EDI World Bank.

Bayliss, B.T. and Edwards, S.L. (1968) *Transport for Industry.* London: HMSO.

Booz Allen and Hamilton (1990) *The Competitiveness of the EC Rail Equipment Industry.* Report to the EC Commission, Brussels.

Butt Philip, A. (1988) *Implementing the European Internal Market: Problems and Prospects.* London: Royal Institute of International Affairs.

Cantwell, J. (1987) The reorganisation of European industries after integration: selected evidence on the role of multinational enterprise activities. *Journal of Common Market Studies*, 127–52.

Coyle, J.J., Bardi, E.J. and Langley, C.J. (1992) *The Management of Business Logistics*. New York: West Publishing.

Culem, C. (1988) The locational determinants of direct investments among industrialized countries. *European Economic Review*, 885–904.

Dunning, J. and Robson, P. (1987) Multinational corporate integration and regional economic integration. *Journal of Common Market Studies*, 103–26.

EC Commission (1970) Principles and general guidelines of an industrial policy for the Community. *Bulletin of the European Communities*, Supplement 4/70, Luxemburg.

—— (1973) Towards the establishment of a European industrial base. *Bulletin of the European Communities*, Supplement 7/73, Luxemburg.

—— (1985) *Completing the Internal Market*. White Paper from EC Commission to the European Council, COM(85)310 Final, Luxemburg.

—— (1986a) *Improving Competitiveness and Industrial Structures in the Community*. COM(86)40, Luxemburg.

—— (1986b) *Background Report on Public Procurement*. Luxemburg: EC Commission.

—— (1988a) *1992 The European Challenge*. Aldershot: Avebury Gower.

—— (1988b) *Research on the Cost of Non-Europe, Basic Findings, Vol. 5: The Cost of Non-Europe in Public Sector Procurement*. Luxemburg: Office for Official Publications of the European Communities.

—— (1991) *Public Procurement and Community Funding*. Luxemburg: Office for Official Publications of the European Communities.

EMNID (1965) *Qualitativer Verkehrsbedarf der Industrie*. Hamburg: Institut für industrielle Markt-Werbeforschung.

Hamilton, F.E.I. (1975) Aspects of mobility in the British economy. *Regional Studies*, 153–65.

Hoover, E.M. (1948) *The Location of Economic Activity*. New York: McGraw-Hill.

Lunn, J. (1980) Determinants of US direct investment in the EEC: further evidence. *European Economic Review*, 93–101.

Luttrell, W.F. (1962) *Factory Location and Industrial Movement – A Study of Recent Experience in the UK*, vol. 1. London: NIESR, 174–9, 319–22.

Millington, A.I. (1988) *The Penetration of EC Markets by UK Manufacturing Industry*. Aldershot: Avebury Gower.

Millington, A.I. and Bayliss, B.T. (1990) The process of internationalisation: UK companies in the EC. *Management International Review*, 151–61.

—— and —— (1991) Non-tariff barriers and UK investment in the European Community. *Journal of International Business* Studies, 695–710.

—— and —— (1992) *Transnational Joint Ventures Between UK and EC Manufacturing Companies and the Structure of Competition*. CEIS Discussion Paper, University of Bath.

Mytelka, L.K. and Delapierre, M. (1987) The alliance strategies of European firms in the information technology industry and the role of ESPRIT. *Journal of Common Market Studies*, 231–54.

Pelkmans, J. (1985) De interne EG-markt voor industriele produkten. *WRR Voorstudies en Achtergronden*, V47. The Hague: Staatsuitgeverij.

Pierre, A.J. (ed.) (1987) A high technology gap? Europe, America and Japan. *Europe America Series*, 6, Council on Foreign Relations. New York: New York University Press.

Robinson, E.A.G. (1937) *The Structure of Competitive Industry*. London: James Nisbet, Cambridge: Cambridge University Press.

Scaperlanda, A. and Balough, R. (1983) The determinants of US direct investment in the EEC: revisited. *European Economic Review*, 381–90.

Scaperlanda, A. and Mauer, L. (1969) The determinants of UK direct investment in the EEC. *American Economic Review*, 558–68.

Schmitz, A. and Biari, J. (1972) EEC tariffs and US direct investment. *European Economic Review*, 259–70.

Servan-Schreiber, J.J. (1967) *Le Défi Américain*. Paris: Denoel.

Sharp, C.S. (1970) *The Allocation of Freight Traffic: A Survey*. London: Ministry of Transport.

Townroe, P.M. (1970) How Managers Pick Plants. *Management Today*, October, 54.

Voss, C.A. (ed.) (1987) *Just-in-time Manufacture*. London: IFS.

Walters, A.A. and Sharp, C.S. (1953) *Report on Traffic Cost and Charges of Freight Transport in Great Britain*. Birmingham: Birmingham University Press.

Weber, A. (ed.) (1909) *Reine Theorie des Standorts*. Part I of *Über den Standort der Industrien*. Tübingen: Mohr.

World Bank (1992) *Global Economic Prospects and the Developing Countries*. Washington, DC: World Bank.

12

Epilogue

A. De Waele

12.1 THE FACTS

Instead of trying to summarize the issues dealt with in the foregoing chapters it seems preferable to draw attention to a number of key points and to show how they relate to the main matters of concern to policy makers.

First, it is clear that personal mobility is under increasing threat and has become a highly controversial subject. Road and air traffic have expanded to such an extent in recent years that they are now pushing up against both physical and financial barriers and are therefore meeting with resistance of a political nature too. It is in the literal sense of the term that transport is increasingly becoming the vehicle of our personal well-being, although it is also taking up more and more space and more and more of the environment, a process that is progressively stirring up public feeling. Transport is one of those human activities which attracts most attention since it is a source of movement, by definition, and also the embodiment of freedom.

There is a price to pay for such freedom, however, and it has its limits. We can have freedom of movement only if we respect that of others. A car's freedom of movement, for instance, ends at the next car's bumper!

The degree of congestion now occurring is more or less severe according to the particular location and the time of day, week or year. Nevertheless, as congestion is tending to become more common in certain locations, it is increasingly a matter of concern to individuals.

The subject is therefore readily taken up by the media and lends itself to dramatization. The debate on transport is characterized by an impressive number of personal views, and so it is important that research should counter-balance this fairly chaotic state of affairs with objective thought and analysis. It is first essential to rid this debate of all passion if a consensus is to be reached. That is the minimum requirement for determining solutions that are economically and ecologically satisfactory and, moreover, achievable from the policy maker's standpoint.

By and large it can be said that a balance has to be struck between four fundamental elements: development, movement, land-use planning and environment. As each of these elements is in a constant state of flux, we have to strive incessantly to establish new equilibria.

The researcher has to advance by what are often complex processes in order to answer questions that are in many cases stated quite simply: 'is the just-in-time system really indispensable?'; 'do we have to have all this transport to lead a happy life?'; 'is it essential to eat strawberries at Christmas?'. Some people talk about 'irrational' transport and therefore seem to ignore the fact that a transport operation is always rational for someone, otherwise it would not exist. What we have to do, therefore, is adjust the economic framework so that resources can be used more efficiently.

A little more light can perhaps be thrown on the problem by means of a few figures based on the data compiled by the European Conference of Ministers of Transport (ECMT): Is personal mobility now becoming excessive? What is the average number of kilometres travelled each day by a citizen of an ECMT member country by car, motor coach and train? If put to a group of people, even including transport specialists, the answer to this question can vary between 5 and 60 km. The Western European in fact travels an average of 25 km per day: 21 by car, 2 by coach and 2 by train.

This average would seem to be quite modest and is likely to increase quite considerably in the future, in view of the financial and leisure resources that people may be expected to have. As these people cannot be expected to limit their mobility voluntarily, any curb or reduction will only result from other factors. At the same time it should also be mentioned that the mobility in question is that of only a relatively small proportion of the world's population. In the longer term, an ever-increasing proportion of that population will want to enjoy the prosperity and, accordingly, the mobility it confers. One hardly dares imagine the potential problems of capacity inherent in such prospects.

The above figures indicate that roads handle nearly 12 times the passenger-kilometres of the railways, while lorries have four times the tonne-kilometre output of trains. The traffic volumes and proportions involved here show that there is no immediate possibility of a mass transfer from road to rail to relieve the road network, since a switch to rail of only 10 per cent of road freight would amount to an increase of some 40 per cent in the freight carried by rail, a volume that not all railways would be able to handle. Some rail links are already operating at full capacity, whereas the shift of 10 per cent from the roads would have no more than an ephemeral effect on road freight.

The fundamental problem is somewhat paradoxical since it involves the use of economic incentives and technical improvements to move an ever-increasing volume of traffic on an infrastructure that remains virtually unchanged.

The capacity of the infrastructure could be raised by some 30 to 40 per cent if guidance systems were used for both road and rail vehicles. However, the capacity of a rail link depends less on the throughput on the open track than it does on flows at particular points such as the forking or crossing of lines, junctions and systems of routing trains in and out of stations. Extremely costly work is in many cases called for in order to provide crossings at different levels and thereby step up line throughput.

Passenger and freight transport by road has almost doubled since 1970, whereas the overall volume of rail and inland waterways traffic has remained virtually unchanged. Passenger traffic by rail increased by about 20 per cent. These global figures do of course cover very different patterns of development for particular routes and types of transport.

An analysis of the figures reveals a number of interesting points. First, annual growth has been far from uniform over time in that it was quite slow in the early 1980s, then the additional traffic suddenly tripled each year from 1985 to 1988, and there has since been an appreciable slowdown. The level of traffic forecast in 1985 for the year 2000 was in fact reached by 1990. One might also query the relevance of forecasting a further sharp increase in 1993 when all barriers are to be raised at frontiers. The fact is that road traffic is no longer really expanding to any great extent as we now approach that deadline. Shippers and carriers have already clearly anticipated the events of 1993 and would certainly have been lacking in foresight if they had not. So far as they are concerned, 1993 occurred from 1985 to 1988. In all likelihood the opening of frontiers is simply a relative matter and is in fact the conclusion of a process that began some decades ago. If haulage deliveries were late in the past, it was seldom attributable to regulatory or customs barriers, but more often the result of natural disasters or social unrest.

There was of course particularly strong growth of road traffic on motorways and on international routes. Lorry traffic on motorways increased by a third from 1985 to 1988.

Two patterns of development are to be found within the growth: first, the increase in the number of journeys and then, more particularly, the greater length of these journeys, the latter factor being the reason why congestion occurred quite suddenly and is spreading rapidly. A new geography of transport operations is now to be found on an infrastructure that was not always designed to meet the relevant requirements.

12.2 THE PROBLEMS

The attribution of so many pernicious effects to the heavy goods vehicle is the result of a misunderstanding of its real function. The lorry will be with us for a long time to come and may be regarded in many cases as irreplaceable. Even if a substitute were to be offered, it would be of interest for only one segment of the present road haulage market. That substitute would, moreover, have to be found acceptable by shippers.

For some decades now, heavy bulk traffic has remained at about the same level or is in a process of conversion. New needs have arisen rapidly and concern smaller volumes in a greater number of individual consignments dispatched from many different points of origin to many destinations. Road haulage is unquestionably the mode that can cater most effectively for this demand from both the technical and economic standpoints.

The substantial growth of this type of traffic has resulted in major flows along trunk routes on which there is to some extent a confluence of traffic originating in different areas. The scale of this confluence gives rise to the question whether some of this traffic might not be switched to an alternative mode with a view to relieving the trunk routes in question, these being motorways in many cases. The alternative mode should offer a new and decisive benefit to the community and/or user. However, such a benefit would not seem to be provided by existing combined transport techniques, at any rate not on a sufficiently broad scale. What this means is that, if the combined transport systems of the future are to be really attractive, they must be designed to ensure minimum costs, rapid – and probably simultaneous – transshipment of loads and sufficiently frequent services. In addition, such combined transport would have to be standardized on a Europe-wide basis.

Over the past few years we have seen what might be called the rediscovery of the railways, but anyone who discovers something that has never ceased to exist and has been ignored for a long time may very well be subject to error, illusions and disappointments. The partial eclipse of the railways for a few decades has perhaps made us forget some of the lessons of the past which might reduce the risk of error.

A specific example can highlight the problems that would be encountered if rail transport were to be substantially developed. Some major motorways at present carry as much or even more than 12,000 lorries per day, i.e. five lorries per minute in each direction. At a speed of 90 km/h, these lorries follow one another with 300 metres between them. If, in order to relieve the motorway, half of these lorries were switched to rail – on the basis of 20 lorries or equivalent loads per train – the trains would be following each other at eight minute intervals. It could be done but only if all the trains on the line travel at the same speed, which is in fact the system adopted on metro lines and some high-speed lines. It is also adopted less systematically on some links where the existence of two more or less parallel routes allows for full or partial specialization of passenger or goods trains, since such specialization provides for a substantial increase in throughput on a rail link.

On the other hand, the regular operation of railways with trains running at quite different speeds is not really conducive to optimal throughput. The output is neither continuous nor uniform and cannot be regarded as industrial in the modern sense but remains that of a small operation. Perhaps that would explain the financial results of this type of operation.

In some parts of Europe where networks are still quite dense, the relatively systematic specialization of lines is possible. In other cases, new high-speed lines have released considerable capacity on what are now called old lines which no longer handle fast passenger trains. However, doubling up in this way would be far too costly on routes crossing mountainous areas and on short sea crossings where all the trains have to go through a single long tunnel at the same speed, a fact that might make certain high-speed links less attractive.

Given the prospects for a substantial increase in rail transport, considerable care has to be shown with respect to the closure of a line on which there is too little traffic to warrant maintenance of services. Such infrastructure might be needed in the longer term if, for example, parallel routes were to become saturated. It is therefore inadvisable to abandon old rail routes whenever there remains a possibility of bringing them back into service, even in the much longer term. This elementary precaution can help to avoid expenditure in the future which may in some cases be on an enormous scale. Foresight is central to planning and development. This is particularly true for a number of central European regions that will soon become important crossroads but whose networks will initially need to be improved.

Any significant switch of traffic to the railways will not only require suitable tracks but also rolling stock and personnel. The size and quality of access to terminals might also give rise to new kinds of problems if they are used by very heavy traffic. Congestion might then be shifted from the motorways to the points of access to terminals.

12.3 SOLUTIONS

Time and money is needed in order to build high-performance networks. It might also be said that the enthusiasm of the new converts to rail has to some extent eclipsed the possibilities offered by waterways/sea transport. While much of western Europe consists of peninsulas and islands which provide an impressive coastline, the East–West rapprochement has meant that Europe as a whole has regained its deeper and more continental dimension, thus laying new stress on two aspects of transport: on the one hand transit traffic and on the other the increased need for intermodal co-operation so that genuine transport chains can serve this area with the required fluidity. It is difficult not to think of water when fluidity is mentioned.

Aerial photographs of our regions, taken at different times of the day during the week and during other periods, enable us to pinpoint road congestion in both time and space. In the mornings and evenings it is on the access roads to our towns and cities; the commuter traffic produced by a high degree of suburban development is the main culprit where traffic jams are concerned. Leisure-time traffic ranks second and is found at the beginning and end of weekends and especially at holiday-time peaks. The longest tailback (160 km) was observed on 1 November 1991 on the Berlin–Nuremberg motorway and, as that day was a holiday, there were probably very few lorries involved. One should not, therefore, automatically blame the lorry for road blockages.

Cars have enabled us to work in the city and live in the country. The motorway has gradually led to the establishment of zones for new or relocated activities.

While the car has made it possible for suburban areas to extend further and further from city centres, the motorway has been diverted from its initial function which was of an interurban and not suburban character. Access points to motorways should perhaps never have been constructed too close to large towns, but the divorce between regional development and transport planning is a *fait accompli* which cannot be remedied by trying to arrange some kind of rapprochement or even integration.

Our transport systems lack a rapid and comfortable form of public transport that can cater for this suburban development by picking up its passengers before the point at which the congestion starts. Neither metros nor buses are suitable, and only a regional express railway can offer the speed and throughput required. It is notable in this respect that some cities are connected up by rail to many destinations but only suburban-type trains are used and services are far too infrequent. More frequent services might be an incentive for motorists to leave their cars at the many stations which have no parking problem. Investment would of course be called for but would be far below the price per kilometre for a metro. Subsidies would also have to be provided, but would this not be a new type of public service? Here is the infrastructure needed – it already exists and can be used more efficiently.

It is frequently said that transport does not cover its costs, including external costs. A substantial increase in taxes and charges would curb any unduly rapid growth of the various types of traffic. A dual distinction has to be made in this respect in order to throw more light on a debate that sometimes seems to be somewhat confusing. One has to differentiate, first, between the amount to be obtained to cover the costs and the way in which it is to be obtained and, second, between the immediate and longer-term effects.

Transport consumes scarce or non-renewable resources such as space, energy and the environment, and so a very sharp increase in prices cannot be ruled out in the longer term, an increase that would not be uniform for all modes and all routes, however. It would probably be higher for lorries on motorways and for cars in towns. Some people advocate a certain priority for commercial traffic which is seen as more vital.

In any event, any increase in the price of transport must occur gradually in accordance with a predetermined programme since abrupt measures may lead to crises or shift the problem to other sectors. Both economic decision makers and individuals must be given the time to look ahead and make the necessary adjustments. The regulatory impact of policies relating to fares and freight rates can only take effect over the longer term because it involves decisions to change, e.g. from one mode of transport to another or from one location to another.

Lastly, if such regulation is to be effective, it must be in the form of pricing, i.e. the user pays according to what is consumed. Our systems of paying for use have remained very mixed and still include a substantial proportion of fixed taxes or charges which are in no way related to the degree of use. The taxes on vehicles for their purchase, maintenance, insurance etc. are all incentives to use the vehicle as much as possible rather than optimize its use. While a secure source of tax revenues, they have no regulatory effect on transport since they do not provide a response to two basic questions: will the transport operation take place and by what means?

Payment for use which warrants being qualified as pricing may assume three forms: taxes or duties on fuel, a charge for parking and tolls. A further advantage with tolls is that they can be scaled according to the real cost on the route and according to the volume of traffic.

At the present time, the capacity of infrastructures has become the main concern for transport policy; it most probably will remain so during the years ahead. The use of this capacity can still be improved both by technological measures and by more appropriate pricing systems for the use of these infrastructures.

As far as new infrastructures are concerned, the optimal allocation of resources can be better obtained by private funding because private investment will give priority to the highest volumes of demand, whereas in public funding the relationship between supply of infrastructure and demand is sometimes less clear. The financing intervention of public authorities in this area should be restricted to relations where other reasons than transport demand could become predominant, e.g. regional development or environment. Finally, the planning of a consistent European infrastructure network should be revised substantially with a view to multimodal and multifunctional systems, so that account is taken of a large range of possible future developments.

Select Bibliography

Bauchet, P. (1991) *Le Transport International dans l'Economie Mondiale*. Paris: Economica.

Baum, H., Maβmann, C., Schulz, W.H. and Thiele, P. (1992) *Rationalisierungspotentiale im Straβenverkehr*. Frankfurt a.M.

Bayliss, B.T. (1981) *Planning and Control in the Transport Sector*. Aldershot: Avebury Gower.

Ben-Akiva, M. and Lerman, S.R. (1985) *Discrete Choice Analysis: Theory and Application to Travel Demand*. Cambridge, MA: MIT Press.

Benefits of Different Transport Modes (1992) Round Table 92, European Conference of Ministers of Transport, Paris: OECD.

Bos, D. (1986) *Public Enterprise Economics*. Amsterdam: North-Holland.

Bovy, P.H.L. and Stern, E. (1990) *Route Choice: Wayfinding in Transport Networks*. Dordrecht: Kluwer Academic.

Bruinsma, F. (1990) *Infrastructuur en werkgelegenheid*. The Hague: OSA.

Culem, C. (1988) The locational determinants of direct investments among industrialized countries. *European Economic Review*, 885–904.

Department of Transport (1978) *Report of the Advisory Committee on Trunk Road Assessment* (Leitch report). London: HMSO.

Domencich, T.A. and McFadden, D. (1975) *Urban Travel Demand: A Behavioral Analysis*. Amsterdam: North-Holland.

Dunning, J. and Robson, P. (1987) Multinational corporate integration and regional economic integration. *Journal of Common Market Studies*, 103–26.

EC Commission (1988) *1992 The European Challenge*. Aldershot: Avebury Gower.

Evers, G.H.M., Meer, P.H. van der, Oosterhaven, J. and Polak, J.B. (1987) Regional impacts of new transport infrastructure: a multisectoral potentials approach. *Transportation*, 113–26.

Ewers, H.-J. (1986) Kosten der Umweltverschmutzung – Probleme ihrer Erfassung, Quantifizierung und Bewertung. In Umweltbundesamt (ed.), *Kosten der Umweltverschmutzung*. Berlin, 9–20.

Fischer, M.M., Nijkamp, P. and Papageorgiou, Y.Y. (eds) (1990) *Spatial Choices and Processes*. Amsterdam: North-Holland.

Giannopoulos, G.A. (1989) The influence of telecommunications on transport operations. *Transport Reviews*, 19–43.

Goodwin, P. and Jones, P. (1989) Road pricing: The political and strategic possibilities. In Round Table 80, *Systems of Road Infrastructure Coverage*. European Conference of Ministers of Transport, Paris: OECD.

Gwilliam, K.M. (1984) *Aims and Effects of Public Finance Support for Passenger Transport*. Round Table 67. European Conference of Ministers of Transport, Paris: OECD.

Harris, R.G. (1977) Economies of traffic density in the rail freight industry. *Bell Journal of Economics*, 556–64.

Jansson, J.O. (1984) *Transport System Optimization and Pricing*. New York: Wiley.

Jones, P. (ed.) (1990) *Developments in Dynamic and Activity-Based Approaches to Travel Analysis*. Aldershot: Avebury Gower.

Jones-Lee, M.W. (1989) *The Economics of Safety and Physical Risk*. Oxford: Blackwell.

Kearney, A.T. (1989) *Etude Prospective d'un Réseau Européen des Transports Combinés*. EUROMODAL Conference, Brussels.

Laaser, C.-F. (1991) *Wettbewerb im Verkehrswesen. Chancen für eine Deregulierung in der Bundesrepublik Deutschland*. Tübingen: Mohr.

Lakshmanan, T.R. (1989) Infrastructure and economic transformation. In A.E. Andersson, D. Batten, B. Johansson and P. Nijkamp (eds), *Advances in Spatial Theory and Dynamics*. Amsterdam: North-Holland, 241–61.

Liew, C.K. and Liew, C.J. (1985) Measuring the development impact of a transportation system: a simplified approach. *Journal of Regional Science*, 241–57.

Millington, A.I. and Bayliss, B.T. (1991) Non-Tariff Barriers and UK Investment in the European Community. *Journal of International Business Studies*, 695–710.

Nijkamp, P. (1986) Infrastructure and regional development; a multidimensional policy analysis. *Empirical Economics*, 1–21.

Nijkamp, P., Reichman, S. and Wegener, M. (eds) (1990) *Euromobile: Transport, Communications and Mobility in Europe. A Cross-National Comparative Overview*. Aldershot: Avebury Gower in association with the European Science Foundation.

OECD (1988) *Transport and the Environment*. Paris: OECD.

—— (1992) *Advanced Logistics and Communications in Road Freight Operations*. Final report DSTI/RTR/TA1 (91) 121 REV.1.

PLANCO (1988) *Ordnungspolitische Szenarien zur Verwirklichung eines gemeinsamen europäischen Verkehrsmarktes*, Teil B: Quantitative ökonomische Wirkungsanalysen. Essen: PLANCO.

—— (1990) *Externe Kosten des Verkehrs: Schiene, Straße, Binnenschiffahrt*. Report for the Deutsche Bundesbahn. Essen: PLANCO.

Pommerehne, W. (1986) Der monetäre Wert einer Flug- und Straßenlärmreduktion: Eine empirische Analyse auf der Grundlage individueller Präferenzen. In Umweltbundesamt (ed.), *Kosten der Umweltverschmutzung*, Berlin, 199–224.

Quinet, E. (1990) *Analyse Economique des Transports*. Paris: Presses Universitaires de France.

Rietveld, P. (1990) Employment effects of changes in transport infrastructure: methodological aspects of the gravity model. *Papers of the Regional Science Association*, 19–30.

Rothengatter, W. (1991) Deregulating the European railway industries, theoretical background and practical consequences. *Transportation Research* A, 181–91.

Seidenfus, H. St. (1988) *Ordnungspolitische Szenarien zur Verwirklichung des Gemeinsamen Europäischen Verkehrsmarktes*, Teil A: Szenarien und ökonomische Wirkungszusammenhänge. Münster.

Stiglitz, J.E. (1990) On the economic role of the state. In A. Heertje (ed.), *The Economic Role of the State*. Oxford: Blackwell.

Telematics in Goods Transport (1989) Round Table 78, European Conference of Ministers of Transport, Paris: OECD.

The Role of Government in a Deregulated Transport Market (1991) Round Table 83, European Conference of Ministers of Transport, Paris: OECD.

Thomson, M. (1978) *Great Cities and Their Traffic*. Harmondsworth: Penguin.

Vickerman, R.W. (1991) *Infrastructure and Regional Development*. London: Pion.

Voss, C.A. (ed.) (1987) *Just-in-time Manufacture*. London: IFS.

Walters, A.A. (1968) *The Economics of Road User Charges*. World Bank Staff Occasional Papers No. 5. Washington, DC.

Werner, M. (1988) Regulierung und Deregulierung des Verkehrssektors in der wirtschaftswissenschaftlichen Diskussion – Die Theorie der Regulierung. *Zeitschrift für Verkehrswissenschaft*, 44–70, 128–62.

Author Biographies

H. BAUM

Herbert Baum, born in 1944 in Mönchengladbach in Germany, studied economics at the universities of Berlin and Cologne. He took up his present appointment as Professor of Economics and as Director of the Institute für Verkehrswissenschaft (Institute for Transport Economics) at the University of Cologne in 1990. He has held previous posts as a professor in Hamburg, Bochum and Essen. He is a member of the Scientific Advisory Council of the Ministry of Transport in Bonn and is the author of numerous publications on transport and the environment, road transport, railways, European transport policy and related subjects.

B. BAYLISS

Brian Bayliss, born in 1939 in Hagley, Worcestershire, England, studied at the universities of London, Birmingham and Frankfurt/Main. He took up his current appointment as Professor of Business Economics and Director of the Centre for European Industrial Studies at the University of Bath in 1974. He has also held senior appointments in the Government Statistical Service (London) and at the universities of Sussex, Münster and Aix-Marseille II.

A. DE WAELE

Arthur Elmar Léon De Waele, born 1931 in Ghent, Belgium, is Head of the Economic Research Division of the ECMT. He studied law at the University of Louvain in Belgium and economics, specializing in transport economics, at the University of Cologne in Germany.

In 1958 he became a consultant in transport economics with several public and private institutes and in 1964 became director of a transport studies unit for the Flemish Employers' Federation. In 1966 Dr De Waele became Lecturer at the Saint Louis Faculty in Brussels and in 1967 he was appointed by the ECMT to organize a series of research activities to support political decision-making. These activities developed and gave rise – under his direction – to the creation of the Division of Economic Research and Documentation of the ECMT.

He has written numerous publications and papers in five different languages and was conferred the degree of Doctor honoris causa of Lyons University in July 1992.

M.M. FISCHER

Manfred Fischer is Professor of Geography and Head of the Department of Economic and Social Geography at the Vienna University of Economics and Business Administration. He was born in Nuremberg, Germany, in 1947 and studied mathematics and geography at the university of Erlangen-Nürnberg. Since earning his doctorate in 1975, Professor Fischer has visited many European and American universities as visiting professor, scholar or external examiner. He has published widely in the leading journals in the field. He serves on the editorial board of many distinguished international geography and regional science journals and has acted as Chairman of the IGU-Commission on Mathematical Models since 1988.

G.A. GIANNOPOULOS

G.A. Giannopoulos, born 1946 in Megara, Greece, is Professor of Transportation Engineering at the Civil Engineering Department of the Faculty of Technology of the University of Thessaloniki. He is currently Head of the Civil Engineering Department of the University of Thessaloniki (until the end of 1993) and Director of the Transport Engineering Laboratory. He has written several books and a large number of articles for international journals.

Between the years 1975 and 1981, Dr Giannopoulos was counsellor to the Greek Minister of Transport and his Deputy at the ECMT. He has participated in several committees and working groups at the OECD, ECE in Geneva and the ECMT and was Chairman for 1981–2 of the Economic Research Committee of the ECMT.

He is currently a member of the EC's DRIVE and TELEMATICS Programmes Management Committees and is responsible for the research group EUROPE 2020 of the European Science Foundation.

K.M. GWILLIAM

K.M. Gwilliam is Principal Transport Economist with the World Bank.

Born in 1937 in Wigan, England, he was educated at Oxford University. After a short period in the chemical industry he returned to academic life, becoming Professor of Transport Economics and Director of the Institute for Transport Studies at Leeds in 1967.

He was for six years a director of the British National Bus Company and has acted as advisor to the Transport Committee of the British Parliament and to the Director General of Transport for the European Economic Community. He moved to Rotterdam in 1989 to become Professor of Transport Economics and Director of the Rotterdam Transport Centre of the Erasmus University.

J.O. JANSSON

Jan Owen Jansson, born in 1939, studied at the Stockholm School of Economics and at the University of Stockholm, where he obtained his doctorate in 1980. Dr Jansson is research leader at the Swedish Road and Traffic Research Institute in Linköping and visiting Professor of Transport Economics at the University of Linköping.

P. NIJKAMP

Peter Nijkamp has been Professor in Regional, Urban and Environmental Economics and Economic Geography at the Faculty of Economics of the Free University of Amsterdam since 1975. He obtained his doctorate in economics in 1972.

Since then Peter Nijkamp has visited many universities around the world (including China) as visiting professor and is a member of the editorial board of many distinguished journals. His publication list covers many issues.

Besides advisorships to the Dutch Government, the Commission of the European Community, the OECD, the World Bank and Academia Sinica, his current position includes among other things the Fellowship of the Royal Dutch Academy of Sciences, the Presidency of the Regional Science Association and the Chairmanship of the European Science Foundation Network on Transport, Communication and Mobility (NECTAR).

E. QUINET

Emile Quinet was born in Paris in 1935. He is a graduate from the Ecole Polytechnique and the Ecole Nationale des Ponts et Chaussées in Paris. After obtaining his doctorate in economics, he worked as a civil servant at the Ministry of Transport.

His present position includes his work as Professor at the Ecole Nationale des Ponts et Chaussées and his work for international organizations. Emile Quinet has written several books and many articles on general economics, transport and the environment.

P. RIETVELD

Piet Rietveld was born in Berkel, The Netherlands, in 1952. He studied econometrics at the Erasmus University in Rotterdam during 1970–5. During the years 1975–83 he was Assistant Professor and from 1986 until 1990 Associate Professor in Regional Economics at the Faculty of Economics of the Free University of Amsterdam, where he obtained his doctorate in 1980. Since 1990 he has been Professor of Transport Economics at the Free University of Amsterdam.

W. ROTHENGATTER

Werner Rothengatter was born in Hamminkeln, Germany, in 1943. He studied Management and Civil Engineering at the University of Karlsruhe and became Professor of Economics at the University of Kiel in 1979 and later at the University of Ulm.

During 1986–9 Dr Rothengatter was Head of the Transport Division of the German Institute for Economic Research, Berlin.

Since 1990 he has been Professor of Economics at the University of Karlsruhe and Head of the Institute for Economic Policy Research and the Division of Transport and Communication.

Dr Rothengatter has written numerous publications on transport economics, macroeconomics and regional science. He is a member of the Scientific Advisory Council of the Ministry of Transport, Bonn, a member of the Board of the German Scientific Society on Transport Research and a member of the Scientific Committee of the WCTR in Yokohama and Lyon.

EDITOR BIOGRAPHIES

J.B. POLAK

Jacob B. Polak (1933) studied economics at the University of Amsterdam, The Netherlands. He began his career at the Netherlands Railways. Since 1964 he has been a Lecturer in Transport Economics at the University of Amsterdam. In 1967 he was also appointed Reader and in 1975 Professor in this field at the University of Groningen. Besides other publications he is the main co-editor of books on general transport economics, transport policy and transport for elderly and handicapped persons. He has been chairman of the Benelux Interuniversity Association of Transport Economists.

He is at present chairman of the Transport Committee of the Social and Economic Council in The Netherlands.

A. HEERTJE

Arnold Heertje, born in 1934 in Breda, The Netherlands, began his study of economics at the University of Amsterdam in 1951, where he became Professor of Economics in 1964. He has written books and articles on the economics of technical change, oligopoly, welfare economics, Schumpeterian economics and the history of economic thought. He is the editor of several books which deal with international economic problems and are written by scholars of international repute.

Dr Heertje was President of the J.A. Schumpeter Society during 1986–8. In 1989 he was appointed Honorary Member of the Dutch Royal Society of Political Economy.

Index